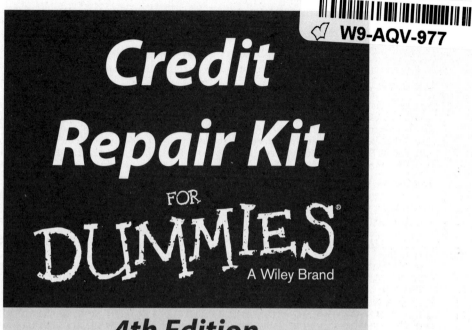

Credit Repair Kit

FOR DUMMIES®

A Wiley Brand

4th Edition

by Steve Bucci, BA, MA

FOR DUMMIES®
A Wiley Brand

Credit Repair Kit For Dummies, 4th Edition

Published by: **John Wiley & Sons, Inc.,** 111 River Street, Hoboken, NJ 07030-5774, www.wiley.com

For general information on our other products and services, please contact our Customer Care Department within the U.S. at 877-762-2974, outside the U.S. at 317-572-3993, or fax 317-572-4002. For technical support, please visit www.wiley.com/techsupport.

Wiley publishes in a variety of print and electronic formats and by print-on-demand. Some material included with standard print versions of this book may not be included in e-books or in print-on-demand. If this book refers to media such as a CD or DVD that is not included in the version you purchased, you may download this material at http://booksupport.wiley.com. For more information about Wiley products, visit www.wiley.com.

Library of Congress Control Number: 2013954101

ISBN 978-1-118-82151-0 (pbk); ISBN 978-1-118-82150-3 (ebk); ISBN 978-1-118-82157-2 (ebk)

Manufactured in the United States of America

10 9 8 7 6 5 4 3 2

Contents at a Glance

Table of Contents

Introduction

· ·

*T*he credit "crisis" has been replaced by the credit "chronic." Now more than ever, your ability to participate in any recovery depends on your credit. We're at the end of what I call a *credit winter*. You've heard of the meteor that killed off the dinosaurs by causing a prolonged winter environment around the globe, and of the consequences of an atomic war called a nuclear winter? Well, you have lived through a financial explosion that caused a "credit winter" that has given way to a fragile and uneven credit spring thaw.

Credit access may have thawed over the last few years, but only for those people who have a solid credit report and credit score. Loan interest rates may be low, but criteria for obtaining credit are high. Jobs may be more readily available, but failing a credit review can keep you unemployed. Foreclosure rates may have slowed down, but student loan problems are growing. Your need for great credit never ends. This book is meant to help you successfully rebuild and manage your credit. Rather than taking an academic approach to the subject of credit, it helps you succeed at integrating credit into your *real* life. It enables you to make great credit an outcome of the decisions you make every day as you pursue life and happiness. I call it your *credit-life connection*.

Tight credit standards mean that you need better credit and higher credit scores to access today's credit products, which are an essential part of leading a rewarding life in today's society. Not only are the criteria for the best access to credit very selective, but the penalties for ignorance and failure have multiplied.

You hear every day that the number of foreclosures is falling. You don't hear about the penalties foreclosed-upon families are facing for years afterward. A resulting credit score drop of 100 to 150 points means years of more-expensive credit, reduced employment opportunities, and more — and rebuilding that score can take up to seven years. Plus, for the uninformed, the loss of a home can be a taxable event, putting the homeowner deep in debt to the IRS. Tens of thousands of people walked away from mortgages without realizing that they'd be shut out of the conventional mortgage market for the next seven years under Fannie Mae rules.

And if all this isn't enough, credit reporting is growing more invasive by the day. Updates to this book tell you about new consumer databases that collect information about your medical history, prescription drug use, rental history, and more. Employers, insurance companies, and lenders use this information to decide whether to hire or promote you, what insurance rates to give you, and whether to offer you new banking products. You need to know what's in these files, and that's one of many things I tell you how to do in this book.

Credit Repair Kit For Dummies comes at a critical time. Credit continues to play an ever-changing and increasingly important role in your life, whether or not you use a credit card. Insurance, employment, home buying or renting, and getting an education with student loans are more dependent than ever on you having good credit. Plus, while the rewards for good credit have never been higher, the penalties for failure — foreclosure, eviction, job problems, mounting debts, collections — have never been greater. For these reasons and more, millions of people are looking for up-to-date, useful, and proven answers from a trusted and knowledgeable resource. I know that if you know the rules of the credit game, you'll get a winning score. That's why I wrote this book, which contains the best of my two-plus decades of experience and research.

About This Book

I'm pleased to be able to help you with your credit, determine what works and what doesn't, and figure out what you can do to help yourself when things don't go as planned. Since 1991, I've advised thousands of people just like you on how credit works and what simple steps everyone can take to have great credit. I've helped people through the advice in my popular online column that also appears in newspapers all over the country, and I've helped many others through one-on-one coaching and counseling. *Credit Repair Kit For Dummies* gives you the best of what I've learned so that you can avoid the pitfalls of a complex and powerful credit industry.

The *For Dummies* approach is different because it's low-cost and simple and drives right to the heart of the matter. With this book, you can manage your credit by applying just a few key concepts. Unlike the talk show approach of making one philosophy fit all after a 15-second question-and-answer period, this book takes the time to give you the concepts and tools you need so that you can apply them to your specific situation and come up with an answer that's custom-tailored to you.

So why this book?

- ✔ Because although credit problems can seem incredibly complex and unfair, you can have good credit with a few simple actions that anyone can master. I give you all the tools and insight you need to rebuild your credit (or build it up for the first time).

- ✔ Because you may need the advice of an experienced advisor to guide you through a mortgage problem. This book tells you how to find a good agency for credit, HUD, or bankruptcy counseling.

- ✔ Because your credit may be in detention due to crushing student loans. This book can help you find the right solution and then rebuild your credit score as quickly as possible.

- ✔ Because you want to get a job or promotion; buy a reliable car to get to your job; start a business; insure your home, apartment, or car; or further your education; so you need a good credit record.

- ✔ Because you may be one of the millions of people who become victims of personal data theft each year. This book provides valuable information to salvage and protect your identity.

- ✔ Because you may be on the brink or even over the cliff of credit trouble. This book gives you budgeting and spending advice that can pull you back from the edge.

- ✔ Because the time is right for you to regain control of your credit and your financial peace of mind, and this book helps you do just that.

Foolish Assumptions

I assume that you're reading this book because you know that repairing your credit is important, but you may not know all the ins and outs of making credit work for you. Whether your credit is not so great and you want to know how to improve it or is just plain nonexistent and you want to establish it on your own terms, you'll benefit from this book. An understanding of your credit and how the credit system works may be especially important during life's transitions. I assume that this book can be of value to you if you're

- ✔ Concerned about your credit report and who may be looking at it
- ✔ Concerned about the credit status of a loved one
- ✔ Considering what to do about overwhelming debt
- ✔ Wondering how to deal with medical bills

✔ Unsure about the credit impact of remaining in your home or walking away

✔ Starting over again after filing for bankruptcy

✔ Taking on or paying back a student loan

✔ Concerned that your personal information may have been compromised or stolen

✔ Already in or soon to be in a marriage or partnership

✔ Recently divorced or in the process of divorcing

✔ Reestablishing credit after the loss of a spouse or partner

✔ Hunting for a job or hoping for a promotion

✔ Establishing credit for the first time

✔ Wanting to know how to maintain good credit after you get back on track

I assume that you don't have a formal education in credit or personal finance. Even if you do, however, I believe that you can still find practical insights in this book based on my experience and that of others whom I've helped.

Icons Used in This Book

Icons are those little pictures you see sprinkled in the margins throughout this book. Here's what they mean:

At www.dummies.com/extras/creditrepair, you'll find all kinds of useful information that I reference throughout the chapters ahead. Whenever I mention a useful form or resource available online, I use this icon.

This icon denotes critical information. Considering the state of my own overcrowded memory, I wouldn't ask you to remember anything unless it was really important.

This image of a credit professional — okay, fine, of Dummies Man — shows up whenever I go into more detail on a concept or rule. If you don't care about the details of how something works or where it came from, feel free to skip these gems.

This bull's-eye lets you know that you're reading on-target advice — often little-known insights or recommendations that I've picked up over the years.

This icon serves as a warning, telling you to avoid something that's potentially harmful. Take heed!

Beyond the Book

Even though these pages are packed with helpful tips and advice for repairing your credit, I've provided even more tools and resources beyond what's in the book. Go to www.dummies.com/extras/creditrepair to find useful forms, worksheets, sample letters, and credit-related legislation and laws. The online material also includes a glossary of commonly used credit-industry terms.

Also, be sure to check out the Cheat Sheet at www.dummies.com/cheatsheet/creditrepair. There you can find contact information for the three big credit bureaus, credit score breakdowns, tips for improving your credit score, and advice on handling an overdue mortgage.

Where to Go from Here

You get to choose what happens next. This book is packed with information to help you repair your credit. You can use the table of contents and index to jump directly to the topics of most interest to you, or you can start at the beginning of the book and take it from there. With the information in *Credit Repair Kit For Dummies,* I'm confident you can get great credit and keep it great for the long haul. I wish you all the best in achieving your dreams, which increasingly require good credit to realize. You and your family deserve it.

Part I

Getting Started with Credit Repair

In this part . . .

- ✔ Understand the basic workings of credit.

- ✔ Find out how to rebuild your credit after a crisis.

- ✔ Discover your consumer protections under new legislation.

- ✔ Fix inaccuracies in your credit reports and boost your credit score.

- ✔ Field calls from debt collectors with confidence.

- ✔ Get the scoop on credit counselors and other kinds of help available to you.

Chapter 1

Introducing Credit Repair, Credit Scores, and Your Life on Credit

* *

In This Chapter

▶ Handling credit problems

▶ Rebuilding your credit after a crisis such as a foreclosure or bankruptcy

▶ Safeguarding your credit and your identity

▶ Discovering how to manage your credit

▶ Keeping your credit solid in every stage of life

* *

Credit plays a larger role in life than ever, and it looks like its influence will only expand in the years to come. The good life, happiness, and credit are inextricably linked. It's not that more material things make you happier, but bad credit exacts a price from your life and your relationships with others. Think of it as your credit/life connection. You must successfully manage your credit and, by extension, your personal finances if you are to lead a successful and satisfying life in these United States.

Financial products, credit foremost among them, have become much more complex and powerful, while the price for having a bad credit report has never been steeper. Your *credit report* is a financial snapshot of your life. When you use credit, the information usually gets reported to a data storehouse known as a *credit bureau*. This information ends up on your credit report for at least the next seven years. The good, the bad, and the ugly are all there for anyone you do business with to see and for FICO and VantageScore to summarize in a three-digit number known as your *credit score*.

Bad credit can keep you from finding a job, getting the promotions you deserve at work, getting insurance (or paying the lowest price for it), securing an apartment or house, and more.

This chapter is all about getting you started in repairing your credit so you can get that job, promotion, home, and insurance to protect it. I start with the basics. If you don't understand credit, you can't fix it, so I discuss how credit works, how to apply that knowledge to get what you want, how to deal with the effects of life's inevitable setbacks on your credit, and how to recover from those setbacks as quickly as possible. Other chapters build on this information, helping to make your credit the best it can be and keep it that way. Why? Because life isn't always fair, but you still need to repair the damage and carry on without being taken advantage of by unscrupulous financial companies or wasting precious years recovering from credit problems that you can avoid or minimize by using the advice in this book.

Repairing Bad Credit

After you've had a rough patch and fallen behind on your payments, you may think that you can never recover. Between the cost of interest and maybe even collection actions, the situation can be overwhelming. But I assure you that you can reverse the cycle. You can not only reestablish good credit but also keep good credit forever. Forever is a long time, but if you follow my advice, you can banish the credit blues permanently! It's not magic, and it won't cost you another dime. By realistically assessing your situation, using free help if you need it, setting goals, planning your spending and savings, and using credit as part of your overall plan, you can quickly rebuild your credit.

Settling debts

You hear the ads all the time: "Settle your debt for pennies on the dollar!" "You have a right to pay less than you owe!" Debt settlement is an often misunderstood option that may work for you, but only if you handle it properly. Many companies that offer debt settlement services help themselves a lot more than they help you. You can avoid huge fees and potential credit damage if you reach a settlement agreement with your lender on your own or if you use your own attorney.

You are personally responsible for the actions of the debt settlement company you hire, and your credit will be ruined in a protracted and adversarial settlement process. Chapter 6 gives you the information you need to decide whether debt settlement is for you and outlines your best options.

Resetting your goals

Just as you did when you first started establishing credit, I want you to revisit your goals from time to time. When your life changes, your goals should reflect that new reality. Goals that once seemed within easy reach may move from short term to long term. Others may change as you mature. Buying that red sports car may not be as important to you now as it was in your 20s. Take the time to reset your sights, as I explain in Chapter 2.

Begin by envisioning your life as you'd like it to be over the short, medium, and long term. Next, create a spending plan (or update your plan if you already have one) so that you know your current financial resources. Then begin to see how long it will take to fund your goals and determine when using credit may be appropriate. Chapter 18 goes into detail about how to create and maintain a spending plan and how to use credit wisely as a part of that plan.

To ensure that your credit is up to the task of supporting your goals for the future, check your credit reports and dispute any inaccuracies or out-of-date information. To rebuild your credit reports, you need to start with an accurate credit history, not one riddled with errors that may hold you back. After you check your reports, look for opportunities to review them for free as often as you can. Part IV tells you everything you need to know about credit reporting.

Rebuilding your credit by using it

The best way to rebuild your credit is to exercise it! Using your goals and spending plan as a guide, start making those payments as agreed, on time and for the correct amounts. Every month you do so, you build better credit while your older, bad credit either counts for less or drops off your credit reports altogether.

Consider opening a *secured credit card* (backed by a bank account deposit) or a *passbook loan* to add a revolving and installment account to fatten your credit history and boost your score. You can find the details in Chapter 9.

Using a cosigner or becoming an authorized user

I normally don't recommend that you cosign for a loan, but in this case, someone else is doing the cosigning! Enlisting a cosigner is a way to get access to credit so that you can begin to rebuild your credit history with the credit bureaus. But you need to keep in mind a few important rules:

- ✔ You have to make all the payments on time.

- ✔ If you can't make a payment when it's due, you have to tell the cosigner in advance so that the cosigner can make the payment and protect his or her credit. You can pay your pal back later.

- ✔ You can't get mad at the cosigner for not being understanding or more helpful while you owe him or her money. Your cosigner is doing you a huge favor at great personal credit risk!

Another way to rebuild your credit is to become an authorized user on someone else's credit card. After you're added to the other person's account, his or her good credit history flows onto your credit record as a positive account and payment stream, beefing up your record and credit score. The person needs to have good credit, though, or his or her bad credit will negatively affect yours. I suggest that you decline getting your own card for the account so that only the other person's charges appear on the account. That way, if he or she has a bad memory (like I do), you're spared monthly calls asking whether this or that charge is yours. Although you won't have access to new credit, your credit score gets a boost.

Finding sources of free help

You can do a lot of things on your own, but sometimes having a pro on your side to give you tips. You can find that help in three main places, and it ranges from inexpensive to free. Nonprofit credit counselors, pro bono lawyers, and HUD-approved counseling agencies offer priceless insight, assistance, and advice. The trick is to know to ask for it.

Nonprofit credit counselors work with you to set goals, develop a spending plan, and assess your ability to repay your debts. They can set up a repayment plan in concert with your lenders to lower your payments and interest rates and get positive information back on your credit reports faster than you could on your own. They're funded by creditors but work for you, and I recommend the good ones highly. Discover where to find the good ones in Chapter 4.

Lawyers sometime offer free or pro bono help if you can't afford to pay. Chapter 4 includes a list of resources to help you find one in your area.

A mortgage is a different and sometimes dangerous type of loan. The rules for handling a delinquent mortgage are different from those for regular consumer debts, and the penalty for a mistake can be the loss of your home. So I strongly recommend that if you have a mortgage problem, you get professional, HUD-certified help. You can find an agency at the HUD website (www.hud.gov).

Watch out for bad help. In a nutshell, if someone approaches you and offers to help for a fee, don't do it. The free resources work well. The costly ones too often are just ways to separate you from your money while you're under stress.

Dealing with collectors

Sometimes, you have to take the call. You know it's a debt collector, but you don't know what to say, do, or offer. Chapter 5 spells out how to take control of the collection process. Collectors must follow certain rules, and if you know the rules, you'll feel more confident in dealing with a stressful situation.

The Fair Debt Collection Practices Act (FDCPA) regulates what collectors can and can't do. In general, this law protects you from abuse and threats. For example, a collector can't threaten an action that it can't or doesn't intend to take, can't make harassing calls, and can't use abusive language. When you know your rights and insist on being treated fairly, you can negotiate a payment schedule that fits your budget. If you need help coming up with a workable plan, you can always ask a credit counselor for assistance.

Chapter 5 offers solutions that work. From how to handle calls and threatening letters to how to craft a repayment proposal, I walk you through how to keep a small collection annoyance from becoming a major and upsetting life event.

Weathering a Mortgage Crisis

Some credit problems are worse than others. In my experience, a mortgage crisis is among the most upsetting, expensive, and damaging to your credit and relationships. Your home is your castle. When you are at risk of losing it, you likely feel as though your very existence is under attack. Thinking matters through and coming up with the best solution for you and your family may be difficult. In this section, I preview the major options to help guide you along the best path. Check out Chapter 7 for more mortgage information.

Mortgages are different from other types of debts and credit because of a number of factors, including the size of the debt, the importance the lender attaches to a debt secured by a home, and the fact that the debt is probably packaged in a security that's been resold many times and is subject to inflexible collection rules. Mortgage delinquency can have a significant and long-lasting negative effect on your credit score. For example, being just 30 days late on a mortgage payment can cost you 100+ points on your credit score and take three years to recover from. The upshot is that if you're in danger of falling behind on your mortgage payments or you're already behind, you're better off seeking professional help.

Opting for help

In a mortgage crisis, the sooner you get help, the better. The reason is simple: The stakes are high and the help is free.

Most people who have a mortgage payment due on the first of the month know that they have until the 15th to pay it. Do you? If you miss that payment on the 15th, you're 45 days late. Mortgages are paid in arrears, so the bill is already 30 days old when you get it. Miss the due date and the 15-day grace period goes away until you catch up. By the 15th of the next month, you're 15 days away from a foreclosure action. Fast, isn't it? So I suggest that you don't delay in contacting a HUD-approved counseling agency. These agencies are often housed in credit counseling agencies, so they can address all your debt issues at once.

Doing it on your own

You may insist on working out your mortgage problems on your own. The process is tricky and long, but it can be done. Chapter 7 goes into details on the steps and time frames for action. In addition to acting quickly, you need to keep excellent notes about who you speak with, when you talk, and what is said. You're dealing with a bureaucracy, and bureaucracies love to forget that they ever heard from you and send you all over the place to avoid responsibility for helping. So good notes are essential. Chapter 7 lists key terms and things to ask for so you can sound like you know what you're talking about.

Just because a bank doesn't want to take your home doesn't mean that it won't.

As in any debt resolution process, you need to do your homework before you call your mortgage servicer. Know what you really need in terms of help to take care of your missed payments, and know what you can offer. You may be able to make additional payments over a six-month period to catch up. Or you may need to ask for a reduced payment amount for a certain amount of time. Whatever you need, you have to be specific. Chapter 7 helps you understand the major options, but they change frequently, so you may have to rely on your mortgage servicer (the bureaucrat) to advise you.

If you can't work out a compromise, there are ways to leave your home that result in less credit damage. Among them are

- **Deed-in-lieu of foreclosure:** You give the house back, saving the bank foreclosure expenses.
- **Short sale:** You get the bank to agree to let you try to sell the house for less than the mortgage value.
- **Friendly foreclosure:** You cooperate with the bank and leave the house in good shape on a timely basis.

Chapter 7 goes into more detail about these options.

Strategic mortgage default

Strategic mortgage default isn't an option that anyone likes. However, a number of people consider walking away from their homes as an alternative to trying to work matters out. Based on how much you owe, you may be very, very unlikely to get back the money you're putting into monthly mortgage payments. According to the Federal Reserve, strategic default is a particularly popular remedy for people who have lost 50 percent or more of their property values and owe large mortgages. Say that you owe $200,000 on your mortgage but your home is worth only $100,000. Why waste $100,000 in overpayments? Following that reasoning, some people are mailing the keys to the bank and walking away from their homes.

Credit damage from a strategic default is significant and lasts a long time. You can expect to have really bad credit for seven years and to see a credit score drop of 140 to 160 points. (See Chapter 14 for more on credit scoring.) Plus, Fannie Mae, the government agency that guarantees most mortgages, won't guarantee a new loan for you for the next seven years, which means that to buy another home in the next seven years, you'll pay more for a new mortgage and you'll need expensive mortgage insurance.

Filing Bankruptcy

There are times in life when you just can't cope. For some people, this is also true in credit matters. If you're unable to come to terms with the aftermath of being overextended, bankruptcy may enable you to hit the reset button and start over again. But there is no free lunch.

While you pay a price in terms of future credit, bankruptcy for the right reasons and in the right circumstances may be your best bet. This section gives you a quick look at an often misunderstood and misused tool so that you can decide whether the cure for your debts is worth the damage to your credit. Chapter 8 has more information on the updated bankruptcy process, what it means to you, and what your alternatives are.

If you do opt for bankruptcy, you need to pass a means test to see which type you can file for. Chapter 7 bankruptcy gets rid of some of your debts but not others. If you don't qualify for a Chapter 7, Chapter 13 bankruptcy requires you to pay what you can afford to your creditors over a five-year period. In a nutshell, if you earn too much money, you have to pay your bills in a Chapter 13.

Even worse, from my point of view, is that filing for bankruptcy may not solve your problem. If you're in debt trouble because you spend more than you make — or, to put it another way, because your expenses exceed your income — then bankruptcy won't change the situation. Before long, you may be back in debt, but without the option of refiling. After filing for bankruptcy, you face a waiting period before you can file again. This period can range from two to eight years, depending on the type of bankruptcy you file and the type you want to file next.

In today's tight credit market, expect a long recovery time from a bankruptcy. Recent FICO research indicates that a Chapter 7 filing can lower a good credit score by up to 240 points and that it takes seven to ten years for the score to recover to its original level. Ouch! That's a long stay in the bad credit hotel. Be sure it's worth it!

Protecting Your Credit and Your Identity

Your credit history is increasingly used for more than just determining the interest rate on your credit card. It affects your ability to compete for a job or a promotion; get affordable insurance; qualify for professional licenses, military service, and security clearances; and even find a decent place to live. At the same time, data breaches have exposed the personal information of millions of people to identity thieves. These thieves can use stolen identities to establish credit in your name without your knowledge and then overuse and default on that credit.

Getting familiar with credit laws

Over the last several years, Congress has passed new laws to give consumers more protections. Knowing about and taking advantage of these safeguards can help you keep your credit safe. If your identity is stolen, knowing your rights is essential to a quick resolution. Among the laws I discuss in Chapter 19 are the

- ✔ **Dodd-Frank Wall Street Reform and Consumer Protection Act,** which created a single consumer watchdog agency and allows consumers free access to their credit scores under certain conditions.
- ✔ **CARD Act,** which restricts lenders from raising rates on existing balances and more.
- ✔ **FACT Act,** which gives you access to free credit reports and identity theft protection and remedies.
- ✔ **Fair Debt Collection Practices Act (FDCPA),** which spells out your rights and the rules that debt collectors must follow.

Receiving free reports and filing disputes

As Chapter 13 explains in more detail, the FACT Act entitles you to a free copy of your credit report annually from each of the three major credit bureaus: Equifax, Experian, and TransUnion. I strongly recommend that you get these reports every chance you can and check them for errors. In addition to the one annual free report, your state may require the bureaus to give you more copies — sometimes many more! In addition, you're entitled to extra free reports, and sometimes free credit scores, if you've been turned down for credit, didn't get the top rate offered, or had an adverse action (like a reduction in credit limit) on a credit card. All these situations are opportunities to check and clean up your credit reports for free.

Signing up for credit monitoring

Every time I turn around, someone is offering to monitor my credit for me. Do you need this service, and are you willing to pay for it? Chapter 15 gets into the details of credit monitoring. With a few exceptions, I find that it's an unnecessary expense. With all the opportunities you have for free reports, paying for more may be overkill. As for credit score monitoring, expect your score to change frequently as new data comes into and leaves your credit report. Unless you're planning a big purchase in the near future that requires new credit, like a house, knowing your score every day is like knowing the value of your home when you don't intend to sell it — relatively interesting but ultimately useless information.

If you have a credit card, you may already have good fraud-monitoring in place. Most cards monitor spending patterns to sniff out fraud and identity theft before they cost the cardholder a fortune. One less reason to pay to have your credit monitored.

Setting alarms, alerts, and freezes

If you're still worried about others accessing your credit data, you have the right to limit access to only those you approve. Chapter 15 covers how to limit access, along with the pluses and minuses of doing so. Among your options, you can

- ✔ Set up alerts with your creditors to spot new activity on your account.
- ✔ Place an alert on your credit file so that lenders use more caution before approving any changes.
- ✔ Place an active-duty alert on your files if you're a member of the military.
- ✔ Freeze access to your account so that no new creditors can access your information without your express permission (except if you owe the government money).

Identifying identity theft

Still the number one reported crime at the Federal Trade Commission, identity theft isn't going away. The number of cases reported is small in relation to the huge amount of identity information that hackers collect every time you hear of a database compromise. Your identity may be in jeopardy for years to come as thieves warehouse your data for a future time.

Simple vigilance can help you stop identity theft in its early stages before serious damage is done. Follow these tips from Chapter 20:

- ✔ Protect your information at home. Most identity theft is low-tech and committed by people whom you invite into your home.

- ✔ Shred financial documents that contain account and Social Security numbers.

- ✔ Use electronic bill paying to avoid bill theft from your mailbox.

- ✔ Check your credit report at least once a year to look for unfamiliar credit lines. If you see accounts you don't recognize, take the actions I suggest in Chapter 20.

If the unthinkable happens and you become an identity theft victim, you need to take fast, effective steps as soon as you find out you've been victimized. Chapter 9 walks you through what you need to do and whom you need to contact. It also helps you reestablish your credit afterward.

Maintaining Good Credit Throughout Life

Your credit report presents a financial snapshot of your life . . . so far. As your life changes, your credit report changes, too. If your life is filled with positives like a steady job, a good income, controlled expenses, and maybe even a partner, then your credit report should reflect that stability. If, however, you have a reversal of fortune with a job loss, income interruption, illness, or divorce, expect your credit to reflect the stress of your life.

Establishing credit for the first time

Getting credit doesn't need to be scary. You have easy ways to establish credit for the first time — or the second time around as a newly single person. Knowing what to do and what to avoid makes this process simple and foolproof. Chapter 10 covers the essentials of getting your credit up and running. Using simple techniques like borrowing your own money and using retail store cards and authorized user accounts, you can establish good credit in no time. Your credit score can be figured on a history of just a month or two, and then you're on your way.

Here are a few ways to build credit for the first time:

✔ Open a savings account at a bank that reports to all three credit bureaus. Then take out a loan using the account as security and make monthly payments on time.

✔ Have a relative add you as an authorized user on his or her credit card. Your relative's history will flow onto your credit report.

✔ Apply for a secured credit card with a bank that reports monthly to all three bureaus.

Making credit changes at life's stages

As you move through life, you find new needs for credit and encounter new challenges in keeping your credit strong when life gets bumpy. Chapters 11 and 12 help you negotiate life's often turbulent credit waters without capsizing your boat. Credit plays a strong role in every aspect of life, including getting a job, buying a home or renting an apartment, purchasing a car, insuring your home and car, getting married or divorced, paying medical bills, planning for retirement and end-of-life expenses, and more!

Many people know that because a prospective employer may check your credit in the hiring process, having good credit while job hunting is important. But how can you keep your credit in good shape when you've been laid off and don't have enough income to handle all your bills? Chapter 12 tells you how. It also gives you practical tips for safeguarding your credit before, during, and after a divorce.

Avoiding pitfalls

Whether you're new to credit or you're a credit veteran, you need to be careful of counterproductive actions. Some examples of things I advise you to avoid if at all possible are payday lenders, refund-anticipation loans, check cashers, and credit repair companies.

You won't go blind from using a *payday lender* once for an emergency, but the very concept of this type of high-interest loan is flawed. If you have no savings, you're living paycheck to paycheck, and an emergency expense comes up, does getting a payday loan make sense? You have to pay back a short-term (two weeks or so) loan on your next payday. But all that money is already committed, so how can you pay it back? Chances are you'll need more than one loan and end up owing lots of money in interest charges.

Refund-anticipation loans are another potentially counterproductive borrowing product. These loans accelerate an e-filed tax refund by a very short period for a very large fee when calculated as an annual percentage rate (APR). Plus, if your refund is held up or reduced, you owe more money on the loan than you expected.

Check cashers perform a valid but expensive function for people with no bank accounts who need to cash checks. I suggest that you get a bank account so you have a place to begin saving and stop paying for unnecessary check cashing.

Credit repair companies have a horrid reputation. Legislation called the Credit Repair Organizations Act has tried to limit the damage caused by fraudulent actions that some companies advise to rig the credit-reporting system. If you're thinking of credit repair companies, think again.

Debt settlers can put you into an adversarial process in which you can get caught in the middle of a financial and legal tug-of-war with potentially devastating consequences. I cover them in Chapter 4.

Managing Credit in Today's Unforgiving Economy

The concept of credit is easy to understand: You receive something *now* in return for your believable promise to pay for it *later*. Mortgages, credit cards, auto loans, and other types of credit all fit this definition.

Some people think that credit is a way to increase their income. It's not, although credit can help you *manage* your income. Others see credit as a way to enhance status — I have a platinum card and you don't! These distinctions are just ways to wrap additional products, features, and profits into the same credit instrument.

Credit enables you to conveniently spend money that you've already earned or saved or to spend money today that you'll earn tomorrow. But spending tomorrow's money today gets people in more trouble than they ever dreamed of — trouble that can cost them huge interest payments and fees and shut them out of future opportunities. For those with a combination of poor credit management and bad luck, the trouble can take the form of collections and lawsuits. But not for you! Managing your finances is easy if you know the rules of the game, do some basic and painless planning, and know where you stand.

Planning for success

Behind every successful person or venture is a plan. Whether it's detailed or general, a plan for your money and your credit is one of the basic criteria for success. Why? Because others have a plan for your money, and if you don't have one, their plan will win.

Your financial plan begins with envisioning your future as you'd like it to be. Do you desire a home, an education, vacations, a family? The basis of your plan consists of your personal dreams and vision expressed as goals. Long- and short-term goals form a firm base on which to build a plan, and they give you the incentive to fund your plan with savings and targeted spending. Counting up all your income and making decisions on how much to spend and how much to put toward your goals comes next. Called a *budget* or *spending plan,* this tool becomes your road map to financial success. Chapter 18 provides step-by-step instructions for setting up your goals and plan.

After deciding on your goals and setting up your spending plan, you want to consider how credit can help. Using credit cards for convenience and auto and home loans for big-ticket items helps accomplish your goals. Each has different criteria to access to the best, lowest-priced products. The criteria you bring to the table are found in your credit report and credit score.

Reviewing your credit report

Your credit is increasingly used to predict your future value as a customer, employee, and insurance risk. Why? Because if you have bad credit, you're more likely to file insurance claims and perform less well in your job. Research shows that employees with credit problems are less productive and have more absences than those with good credit. So employers use credit reports during the hiring process to complete their assessments of candidates. In a competitive job market, a bad credit report can make the difference between getting an offer and seeing the employer move on to the next candidate.

Lending decisions used to be based on who you were. A local banker typically would know you personally and could approve or deny your application based on your reputation and his prior experience with you. Today, few borrowers have personal relationships with their lenders. Even if they do, most loans go before a committee that requires more than a personal reference to approve a loan. Using the information in your credit report enables a group of strangers to objectively assess your payback record. Lenders still like to see evidence of character, capacity, and collateral, known as the three Cs of lending. Your credit reports show your *character* (whether you keep your promises) and help measure your *capacity* (how much credit you've handled before). These two factors can impact the amount of *collateral* you need to secure a loan at a given rate.

The information in your credit report is essential to your financial life, but what if your file contains mistakes? Credit-reporting errors are more common than you may think. Research has shown that 25 percent of all credit reports have errors and that about half of those errors are significant enough to affect your credit score!

Your credit report contains personal information, account information, and public legal records about you. After you know what is in your report, you can take simple steps to delete out-of-date or erroneous information and add positive data that polishes your credit image to get you what you want and need.

Knowing your credit score

Your *credit score* is a numerical analysis of the years of credit data contained in your credit report. The organizations that calculate your credit score use a proven algorithm (formula) that can predict the likelihood of you defaulting on your next loan over the next two years. Your score doesn't take into account characteristics like gender, race, nationality, or marital status. The result is a discrimination- and prejudice-free assessment of you as a credit risk. Boiling down the decision-making process to a three-digit score also gives you the convenience of a quick approval or denial of your credit application.

Two main scoring models are in use today: FICO and VantageScore. Both scores range from 300 to 850. Several weighted factors make up your score. By understanding these factors, you can avoid surprises when you apply for that mortgage or other loan.

Chapter 13 gives you detailed definitions of each of these scoring factors and tells you how to boost your score with simple credit management techniques, like keeping your card balances below 50 percent of your limit and using your savings account to secure a low-interest-rate loan. The differences in interest payments over a number of years can run from hundreds of dollars on a credit card to tens of thousands for a mortgage.

 All the information used to determine your credit score is contained in one place: your credit report. Well, three places. You have at least three credit reports, from the credit bureaus Equifax, and Experian, and TransUnion. The result is that you probably have at least three different credit scores! How can you be sure that the information in each of your credit reports is accurate and as positive as possible, leading to the highest possible credit scores? Great credit begins by knowing what's in your report and what's not. Part IV provides more information about monitoring your credit reports and scores.

Considering credit a renewable resource

Some people have a block when it comes to math. That block can carry over into credit, which is based on seemingly endless and confusing numbers. I've helped clients understand credit by relating it to something everyone understands: the environment. Everyone knows that pollution is bad for the environment. Everyone knows that environmental resources can either be overused and diminished or be managed well and renewed. And everyone knows that a balance among all the environment's parts is necessary for the environment to be healthy and sustainable. The same principles apply to credit; I call this credit environment your *credit ecosystem*.

You may find understanding your credit easier if you view it as its own ecosystem. Each credit-scoring component affects the others, and pollution in the form of negative reported behavior hurts your ecosystem. Like the real-world ecosystem, damage from credit pollution takes time to clean up. If the damage is bad enough, it causes severe systemic damage for years before your credit environment can recover.

You manage your credit environment by limiting your use of credit and monitoring your credit's health by being aware of your credit score and the information flowing into your reports. Doing so keeps everything in harmony, and the resulting balance strengthens your credit ecosystem. Overspending and overusing credit deplete your resources faster than you can replace them, much like overfishing or excessive logging. An ever-increasing accumulation of debt from using more credit than you have income to support strains your credit ecosystem, perhaps to the point of collapse.

Defaulting on payments introduces pollution into your credit report. Like an oil spill, this pollution can't be covered up and hidden; you have to clean it up properly and put safeguards in place to prevent it from happening again. Credit pollution, like its environmental counterpart, has effects beyond your credit report. A polluted credit report can hurt your job prospects, place a strain on your finances in the form of larger payments for insurance and loans, and more.

I call credit used wisely, in accordance with your plan to build a positive credit history and score, *green credit.* Chapter 17 gives you more insight into this way of understanding your credit and managing it like a renewable resource. Green credit is part of a balanced spending and income system that's reflected in your spending plan. By using credit judiciously, as you would organic fertilizer, you increase the buying power of your present income in a responsible way and replenish the resources you're using before they run out.

Chapter 2

Turning Your Credit Around

- -

In This Chapter

▶ Knowing what hurts and helps your credit score the most

▶ Deciding whether to use a cosigner

▶ Cleaning up your credit with some credit tools

▶ Improving your credit with both small and big purchases

▶ Using debt to build good credit

- -

*E*verybody makes a wrong turn or gets lost from time to time. Sometimes you misunderstand a road sign, other times you get bad directions, and then there are times when you just don't know how to get where you're going but decide to try anyway and figure it out along the journey. Credit works the same way. The big difference is that a lot of people watch and keep score of how you find your way. If your credit isn't in great shape, you want to get back on track as quickly as possible.

Like a road trip that takes you where you want to go, building and improving your credit helps you attain your life goals. You're more likely to enjoy your journey if you have specific, self-serving, and enjoyable goals in mind when you begin your trip to get into better credit shape. Identifying those goals is your first step. You don't have to lay out your whole future in financial terms, but thinking at least five years ahead is an excellent way to start, and it's easy and fun to boot! Credit, like a car, is a means to an end — a tool and nothing more. Building up your credit for no purpose is dull. Credit with a destination is exciting!

This chapter is dedicated to helping you improve your credit and boost your credit score. Consider it your travel insurance plan designed to help you prevent those credit negatives from adding up. Allow me to serve as your navigator. Time to gas up the car and hit the road!

Understanding How Your Actions Impact Your Credit Score

Every time you use or abuse your credit, it has an effect on your credit score. The impact varies with the type of action. Positive actions, like paying bills on time, raise your score and lower your risk in the eyes of a lender, insurer, or landlord. Negative actions do the opposite and, depending on what the damaging action was, could be a big deal or a minor and temporary inconvenience. For example, items in the "small drop" category in Figure 2-1 are minimal and can be offset quickly with other positive actions or even the passage of time. Think of them as small meteors that harmlessly burn up in the Earth's atmosphere. The major and maximum impact items in Figure 2-1 are more like dinosaur-killer meteors!

IMPACT OF VARIOUS ACTIONS ON CREDIT SCORES

ACTION	LENDER INTERPRETATION	SCORE IMPACT
Pays bill on time	Wisely handling debt	Improvement
Uses small portion of credit limits	Sufficient access to credit, unlikely to need additional funds	Improvement
Mature accounts	Experienced credit user	Improvement
Uses diverse range of loan products	Experience with different types of repayment requirements	Improvement
Inquiry about new loan	Why the need for credit-exposure or normal expansion?	Small drop
Opens a new loan	Why the need for credit-exposure or normal expansion?	Small drop
New accounts foreclosure	Will consumer effectively manage new credit?	Small drop
Maxes out credit card (At/near credit limits)	Tipping Point: potential for significant exposure	Drop
Pays late-first time	Tipping Point: potential for significant exposure	Drop
Pays multiple loans late	All credit at risk	Larger drop
Misses multiple payments on a loan (3 or more)	All credit at risk	Larger drop
Charge-off	Default	Major score drop
Foreclosure	Default	Major score drop
Bankruptcy	Default	Maximum score drop, extended time impact

LOW RISK

Courtesy of VantageScore

Figure 2-1: The actions and impacts chart shows the relative impact of positive and negative actions on your credit score.

Figure 2-2 helps illustrate the recovery time for five different impacts to your credit score.

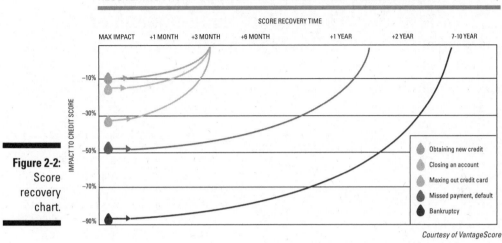

RECOVERING FROM AN ACTION THAT CAUSED YOUR SCORE TO DROP

Figure 2-2:
Score
recovery
chart.

Courtesy of VantageScore

Using a Cosigner to Raise Your Score

Getting a loan by having someone cosign for you is a triple-edged sword. *Cosigning* means that another party (usually a person with better credit) signs alongside you to guarantee future payments if you default, drop dead, or are abducted by aliens. As long as your lender reports to the bureaus, each time you make a payment on time and for the right amount, you and your cosigner both accumulate more positive items. As time goes by, this helps offset earlier negative items on your report. Like falling snow, the good stuff covers all the muck underneath.

Although a cosigned loan can help get positive info onto your credit report, I call it a triple-edged sword because

- **You may be borrowing when you shouldn't.** If a professional lender is reluctant to give you a loan, the lender has a good reason. So now the cosigner, who's not a professional and who likely has emotional ties clouding her judgment, decides that guaranteeing your loan is okay.

- **The cosigner is at risk if you default.** The cosigner is fully responsible for the payment. If it takes 60 days for the cosigner to be informed that you haven't paid on time, his or her credit gets dinged, as does yours.

- **A default could destroy a relationship.** If your ability to pay off the loan is compromised and you incur late fees or penalties or default on the loan, your cosigner is fully liable, and her credit score may be damaged. This scenario just may mean the end of your relationship, but it does not end the loan obligation.

Steve Bucci's theory of good-enough credit

I often advocate the concept of *good-enough credit* as opposed to *perfect credit*. Your credit standing, which is represented by your credit score, is a reflection of your life in financial terms. Lose your job, get a divorce, suffer an illness — the fallout from these life events shows up on your credit report and affects your credit score in one way or another. Late payments and too much borrowing activity are symptoms that may appear in your credit data. Although these events may lower your score to a degree, you shouldn't be driven to aspire to a perfect credit score of 850. Your life isn't perfect (just ask your mother-in-law), so don't

expect your credit history to be perfect, either. Again, credit is only a means to an end. As long as your credit score remains good enough to get you what you need and want, you're in good shape to achieve your financial goals. No use staying up nights worrying if your credit score has dropped from 775 to 774.

A bad credit score can cost a lot in extra payments. For example, say you buy a house for $360,000 at a 30-year fixed rate with a down payment of $60,000. If your credit score is 639 instead of 760, you have to pay about $104,415 more in interest over the life of your loan!

My advice: If you ask a friend or relative to cosign a loan, make sure that the loan is for as short a period as possible. The longer the loan is outstanding, the greater the chance a problem will arise or the relationship will become strained. Also, put your agreement in writing to make it official and to ensure that you both understand what you're agreeing to.

Turning Small Purchases into Big Credit

Because a lot of your credit score is based on using credit and making payments on time (see Chapter 13), I recommend using small purchases to get back into good standing quickly. Why does making small purchases work so well? Because each item costs less, so more purchases are reported to the credit bureaus faster. My rule is that if it costs more than $10, charge it (and pay it off each month).

Major bank cards certainly report your activity to the credit bureaus. Some store cards may report to only one bureau, or they may not report at all. To find out whether your credit card purchases are being reported and scored, call your card's customer service number and ask.

Pick up some extra points on your credit score by following a simple plan when you pay down balances. Scoring models look at how much of your limit you use. The more you use, the higher risk they believe you to be. To maximize your credit score, spread purchases over more than one card to keep your balance on each card as small a percentage of your maximum limit as possible. Say you have two cards, one with a $10,000 limit and one with a $20,000 limit. Simply charge twice as much on the higher-limit card to maximize your score. When your balance exceeds 50 percent of your limit, you begin to lose points.

Are you less concerned about your score than about paying down your balances? Some experts suggest that you pay down balances based on the interest rate (that is, pay them in descending order starting with the highest interest rate) to save money on overall payments. Others say that paying off smaller accounts first gives you a feeling of accomplishment, and therefore, you're more likely to achieve your overall goal. My suggestion is that you choose the approach you find more satisfying. Just be sure that *you* make the choice; don't let the first bill that shows up get the extra payment by chance.

Make a list of each credit card, its balance, and its credit limit. Then allocate your payments to reduce your percentage of credit used to 45 percent or less of the limit on as many accounts as possible. Doing so creates some great positive data in your credit report. This approach not only enables you to regain control of your accounts but also helps you maximize your credit score, because accounts that exceed 50 percent of the limit count more heavily against you. When all your cards are at 45 percent of your limit or below, you may want to allocate more money to the highest-interest-rate cards.

If you don't have a major bank credit card, you may want to try a secured card. You can get one without a fee if you shop around. A secured card differs from a regular Visa or MasterCard in that you maintain a balance in a savings account equal to your credit limit (some cards may allow you more credit than you have on deposit) to guarantee your payment. Secured-card activity is reported just as any other credit card activity is reported, and it affects your credit score in the same way, so it can be a great option if you're trying to build credit.

You can find great card comparisons at www.bankrate.com or www.creditcards.com. The latter has two sections to help you find the right card depending on your circumstance. One section (www.creditcards.com/bad-credit.php) is helpful for those with bad or damaged credit. The other section (www.creditcards.com/no-credit-history.php) is for those who have little or no experience with credit or who need to start a U.S. credit history (credit from overseas doesn't follow you).

Generally, if you make all your payments on time for a year, you should have enough of a positive payment history to get an unsecured credit card.

Creditors that don't report to the credit-reporting agencies

Why doesn't every creditor report your history to all three credit bureaus? Because every time your creditors send data on you to a bureau, they have to pay a fee. Some lenders don't think that this step is worth the expense. Others don't see themselves as lenders. They may order a credit report before approving your loan or credit card application, but they want to save as much profit as they can. Typically, these nonreporters include

- ✔ **Credit unions:** They look to save money where they can, so some may report to only one bureau and not all three.

- ✔ **Utilities:** They don't see themselves as lenders, so they don't use credit reports to hook you up. They also usually don't report unless you pay very late.

- ✔ **Tradespeople:** They aren't lenders, but liens or suits for old bills show on your credit reports because they can be found in public records.

- ✔ **Doctors and hospitals:** They don't see themselves as lenders, so they usually don't pay to report unless they send a bill to an outside collector (collectors report you to the bureaus).

- ✔ **Local finance companies:** They may not report to a bureau, but they may come visit you if you're late.

- ✔ **Landlords:** They don't report to credit bureaus but may report to a rent bureau (see Chapter 14). Experian reports some rental history on its credit reports.

- ✔ **Insurance companies:** They don't report to the bureaus but may report to specialized bureaus like the Medical Information Bureau or C.L.U.E.

Maximizing Your Credit Score with Major Expenditures

Big-ticket creditors — those that specialize in expensive products or services — typically report to the credit bureaus. The reason is simple: They have a lot more to lose if they lend based on inaccurate information, so they want to see as complete and accurate a file as possible.

Examples of big-ticket items that may enhance credit activity are home mortgages, cars, boats, student loans, furniture, and appliances. Major credit purchases may give your credit score a boost for two reasons:

- ✔ **A major purchase is more likely to be in the form of a secured installment loan.** *Secured* means that you pledge collateral on the item you purchase as security for the loan. If you default on the loan, the lender repossesses the security you pledged — in other words, you don't get to keep the item you purchased. Adding secured credit to the other types of credit you use, such as revolving credit (cards), helps raise your credit score.

✔ **You make the same payment each month.** When it comes to credit scoring, making set monthly payments enables the people who figure your score to discover more about your creditworthiness. Making a set monthly payment is a measure of your stability. This is different from paying on a credit card, where you can vary your payments depending on your cash flow. Adhering to a regular payment schedule also indicates that you can handle a higher limit than you may have on a store, gas, or credit card account.

Leveraging your mortgage

Owning a home and paying your mortgage can help build your credit in a few different ways. Credit grantors look at your credit report and credit score in order to rate your lendability, but they ultimately rely on you to be responsible for making the payments. Here's where the three Cs of credit really show up: Character, collateral, and capacity are what credit scoring and lending are all about.

A mortgage on your report tells the reader and the scorer that you have all three of the Cs and that at least one lender was so sure about you that it was willing to lend you a huge amount of money. The report indicates a large installment loan with fixed payments for a long period. All these factors favorably affect your credit score. The opposite is also true: Because of the huge amount of money involved and the seriousness of a long-term commitment, a mortgage default counts for a large negative on your credit history. A foreclosure is an even bigger negative.

A mortgage is secured by the house, so if you default, the lender forecloses and takes the house back to pay off the loan. A foreclosure ends up costing the lender an average of tens of thousands of dollars when all is said and done. But don't feel too bad for the lender: *You're* held responsible in one way or another for any loss on the loan.

Home-equity lines of credit and home-equity loans are a popular subset of traditional mortgages. They're good ways to access money at a low interest rate. They also represent new and additional borrowing on your credit report. For example, you can take out a big mortgage and have only one lender report one loan to the bureaus. If you use a home-equity loan or line of credit in addition to your mortgage, you use the same collateral (your home) and borrow the same amount as you would with a bigger mortgage, but you do so with more than one loan. Thus, more than one item gets reported to the credit bureau each month, building more positive information in the same period. (See the "Lines versus loans" sidebar for more.)

This scenario has a hitch, however: As you stack more debt on your home or your home decreases in value, you may reach the point where you and your castle are *upside-down* — that is, you owe more on your home than it's worth. I've seen some homes so far upside-down that their owners think they'll never get their money back and question whether continuing to pay good money into a bad investment makes sense. You may think that because you have a 30-year mortgage, you can just wait until prices rise to clear up your debt-to-value problem. But what if your boss offers you the general manager's job in a city too far away to commute to? Or what if the company lays you off and you either have to move to find work or downsize to reduce your mortgage commitment? Or what if your adjustable rate mortgage resets and you can't afford the payment anymore? You'd then be in the position of needing to sell the house, but not at a price that would satisfy the loans attached to your home. If you don't have the money to make up the difference, you could face a potential foreclosure or lost opportunity. (See Chapter 7 for more information about how to avoid a foreclosure.)

Lines versus loans

What's the difference between a home-equity loan and a home-equity line of credit? Here's the scoop: A *home-equity loan* is for a specified lump sum or single cash payment — say, $10,000. When you get the home-equity loan, you get the ten big ones to put down on that car (or whatever else you want to buy), and you have an installment payment due every month, usually at a set interest rate for a set amount of time. In the old days, these loans were called *second mortgages,* and they were a sure sign that you were on the path to ruin. Today, they're called *equity products,* and too many of us seem to have more than one. And yes, they're still a sign that you could be on the road to ruin!

With a *home-equity line of credit,* you get a line of credit, maybe for $10,000 or $20,000, depending on how much you want to have available in case you need it. You don't have to take any money out of the line unless you have a use for it. The money just sits there like a wallflower at a dance, waiting for you to ask it to tango.

Generally, you have a set period (called a *draw period*) during which you can access the credit and a set period before which you have to pay it back. So until you use it all, the money is available and just sits there through the remainder of the draw period for free (or sometimes for a small annual fee).

When you do draw money from the line, you generally have the option of paying it off anytime without a prepayment penalty. The loan terms often allow you to pay only the interest and not the principal (an interest-only loan); the principal is due at the end of a period set in the loan agreement. Or you can choose to pay both interest and principal until the debt is paid off. Some loans allow you to decide what you're going to pay on a month-by-month basis, such as paying the principal and interest one month but only the interest the next. Lines of credit are subject to review, and unused portions may be reduced or eliminated if conditions warrant.

Financing your car

Because of the very large price tags on most cars, most of us require some financing in order to purchase one. Such financing typically comes in the form of a two- to five+-year installment loan. Anyone lending you money to buy a car receives and reports credit bureau data. When lenders go on the hook for that much money, they want to be sure that you'll make your payments, even if you get in a cash squeeze. Most car loans are secured by the car.

 If you're debating using equity in your home to purchase a car, be careful. Using a home-equity loan to buy a car may offer a tax advantage (with tax-deductible interest), but it may increase the risk of a home default and subsequent foreclosure if you can't make the extra payment. If you default on that home-equity loan, your car won't be repossessed; instead, and much worse, your home may be foreclosed on. Plus, any mortgage debt forgiven in a short sale or foreclosure may be subject to income taxes. Although the Mortgage Forgiveness Debt Relief Act eliminates taxes due on forgiven mortgage debts, it excludes non–house-related debt. (See Chapter 6.)

Be sure to pay off the loan you used to buy your old car before you buy your next new one! Some people keep old car loans on their home-equity lines long after the cars are gone and keep adding new balances without paying off the old ones. Doing so can lead to an unpleasant surprise when interest rates go up or you need to sell your home.

Weighing the pluses and minuses of leases

Leasing is a popular way to get a car. Please note, I didn't say *buy* a car, because you don't own the car in a lease arrangement. Consider a lease a long-term rental. Leases are popular because they generally require only a small down payment or perhaps none at all. Plus, they're a tax write-off if you're a businessperson. Signing the lease commits you to a stream of payments for an extended period, so this activity is normally reported to the credit bureaus.

 Leases are difficult and costly to terminate. Unlike with a car loan, you can't sell the car and pay off the loan. With a lease, you owe all the payments, and you can't terminate the lease without making all the payments first.

An active-duty serviceperson who is called away for military service can break a car lease. Chapter 5 covers this provision in more detail. For a copy of the Servicemembers Civil Relief Act (SCRA) itself, check out www.dummies.com/extras/creditrepair.

Steering clear of upside-down loans

The term sounds as uncomfortable as it is. Basically, in an *upside-down loan,* you owe more than the value of the item securing the loan. Avoid being upside-down in a car loan, or any secured loan (upside-down home mortgages work similarly), if you can help it. A repossession or default is a negative on your credit report and causes your score to fall — hard!

An upside-down loan can hurt you when you want or need to sell the car and stop making payments. Say you owe $10,000 on a car loan, and the value of the car is $7,000. You have to come up with the $3,000 difference or you can't sell the car. If you're in an accident and the car is totaled, the insurance company pays only what the car is worth; you have to pay the upside-down part.

This situation gets worse if your financial situation changes, you can't make the payments on the car, and the creditor repossesses the car. The car is worth $7,000, but that's the retail value. The lender is likely to sell the car at auction, where the creditor gets only $5,000. Among the towing guy, the attorney, and the sales commission to the auctioneer, the fees on the repossession are $2,000. So you are credited with $3,000 against the $10,000 you owe. Now you owe $7,000 in a lump sum to settle your account, you have no car, and you have bad credit.

Paying back student loans

Because of the increasingly unaffordable price tag on higher education, many people have student loans. Student loans make a lot of sense to lenders: Although the person responsible for repayment may have no income at the time of the loan, the lender expects that good income is just around the corner, and the person will soon pay the loan back. But what really makes these loans attractive to lenders is that they can't lose. Almost no student loans are dischargeable in bankruptcy, except in extreme situations, meaning that you have to pay them back sooner or later.

If you have a student loan, chances are that it appears on your credit report. It may be reported more than once. Why? A loan is usually for a semester's or a year's worth of school expenses. Each loan is reported as a separate loan for each enrollment period. So four years' worth of student loans add either four or eight loans to your credit report. Making payments and/or filing for benefits on time reflects a positive history on your credit report and adds to your credit score. This can be a lot of good news for your credit report!

Conversely, if you end up in default on your student loans, you'll see a lot of negative marks on your credit report from all those individual loan entries, and your credit score will fall. Any missed payments are reported to the bureaus, and you're subject to the full range of collection activity, just like you would be with any other loan.

If you consolidate your loans after graduation, they show up on your report as one loan. *Consolidating* is the process of refinancing all your individual loans into a single loan. The original loans are marked paid in full, and the interest rate for the consolidated loan is often lower and the repayment term typically longer than for the individual loans. The net result is the convenience of a single, lower monthly payment. With a consolidated loan, you typically have a number of different repayment options, including paying the same amount each month, paying less now and more later, and basing your payments on your income.

Student loans aren't secured with collateral in the normal sense of the word. When you default on a student loan, you can't defer payment of the loan. In fact, you may have to pay it all at once unless you can come up with an acceptable repayment scheme. Additionally, you're not eligible for further student aid, your school may withhold your transcripts, state and federal income tax refunds may be used to offset the loan amounts, and your wages (when you get that job) may be garnished. Finally, if you don't pay long enough, your Social Security benefits may be garnished.

Understanding How Good Debt Builds Good Credit

No doubt about it: Getting into debt *can* get you into trouble. And if you're reading this book, chances are you've had some experience with debt trouble or you're being proactive and hoping to avert potential credit problems. Although debt certainly has a downside, borrowing money can also do a great deal of good for your credit record. In the following sections, I tell you how.

Achieving goals with the help of credit

Debt enables you to take advantage of those opportunities and experiences that enhance your life and create joy and fulfillment: that dream home with the white picket fence, the around-the-world cruise, the Ivy League education, and more. When you can train your sights on your life goals and develop a spending plan that allows you to get there in the time frame you set, you've found the secret to the true value of credit.

Sending a message to potential lenders

If you had no debt — ever — then you'd never have used credit, and you wouldn't likely have a credit report or credit score. But let's face it: In today's world, living without credit is hard. Most people need credit to buy those big-ticket items — vehicles, homes, higher education — and they rely on credit for life's emergencies. Creating a positive credit history — a credit reputation, of sorts — says to prospective lenders that you're a good credit risk. Showing that you can handle debt puts you in a position to receive the best rates and terms.

Using credit wisely not only is good for your lifestyle but also gives prospective creditors the opportunity to show you the respect you deserve based on your past performance. Lenders prefer to loan money to individuals who've borrowed before, who can show that they understand the commitment of credit, and who have a history of prompt payment and reliable follow-through. In fact, given the choice between lending to someone who's *never* borrowed before and someone with a history of debt — even with a couple of blips on the report — my guess is that most creditors would favor the credit veteran over the rookie.

Think of it this way: Say your two 20-year-old nephews ask to borrow your car. One has never driven before, and the other has a four-year driving history, but got a parking ticket last year. Who would you give the keys to?

Giving nonlenders a sense of how you handle responsibility

If you've had no debt and therefore have no credit history, you may find yourself disadvantaged in other ways. Many prospective employers check your credit record as part of the hiring process. If you have no record, they can't confirm their good opinion of you. Plus, they can't use your credit history as a positive factor when deciding whether to hire you. Without that credit record, they lack an additional tool when comparing your application to those of other applicants.

The same holds true when it comes to renting an apartment, applying for insurance, and so on. If you have no track record, you're an untested risk.

Selecting the Best Tools for Building Your Credit

I've learned over time that using the right tools makes any job go faster and gives me better results. The tools for mending your credit are readily available, and I show you how to find and use them in this section. I begin with essential preparation by walking you through a spending plan, and then I discuss how to tweak your credit report. Finally, I tell you how to determine when the job is done by using your credit score.

Spending your way to better credit with a spending plan

Unless you have a trust fund or you make a huge amount of money and just can't seem to spend it all, you need a spending plan. A spending plan, which helps you take care of today's responsibilities and tomorrow's goals, has four components:

- **Household income:** This includes all the money coming in from salaries, tips, overtime pay, bonuses, royalties, and so on. Be sure to consider your payroll deductions (such as money you put into a retirement plan) as income.

- **Living expenses:** Your present outlay — from groceries and lunch money to rent or mortgage — makes up your expenses. Also consider those nonessential frivolities that crop up, like your daily dose of designer coffee or the occasional trip to the movies.

- **Savings for financial goals:** In this category you account for vacations, college education, retirement, and other important goals.

- **Emergency fund:** Without an emergency fund to cover unexpected (and usually unpleasant) life events, such as a medical expense or a job loss, you won't succeed. Saving for that unexpected emergency is critical. You need between 6 and 12 months of living expenses; otherwise, when the emergency comes along, you have to get the money from one of two sources: the future (as in spending tomorrow's money today) or your savings for your goals (as in the money you were setting aside for that Ferrari).

Adding up your income

Here's how a spending plan works: You start by identifying all your household income — that's your regular salary or wage, plus overtime pay, bonuses, and predictable windfalls like an IRS refund if you're pretty sure you'll get one. If you're self-employed, I'm talking about your net income from your business or practice here.

Saving in your company retirement account makes sense, especially if your employer matches your contributions. Plus, saving for retirement probably ties into one of your goals (unless you plan to die at your desk).

Adding up all your expenses

After you have the income part down on paper or in your computer, do the same with your expenses. Make sure to include savings as an expense for each of the financial goals you list. The best way to manage this goal-based savings is to estimate how far in the future the goal is, what the goal costs, and what you have to put aside each month to cover the expense in time.

For example, say you want to take a cruise on your wedding anniversary three years from now. The cost is $3,600 for the two of you. That's 36 months at $100 a month. If you can't afford the $100 a month, postpone the cruise for a year and save $75 a month instead, or take a cheaper cruise and still go in three years. The next time you find yourself standing before the flat-screen TV at the mall, your picture of the future will be in clear focus: the cruise or the TV, but not both.

Paying your existing debts

Don't forget to set aside money to pay your existing debts, such as credit card balances and car loans. You may need to tweak your plan now and then to reconcile the numbers and the time frames for your goals. But you're now more firmly in control of your financial future. From here on, *you* make the decisions about what money goes to which categories — not the marketing guys.

You can find forms that can help you set up a spending plan at www.dummies.com/extras/creditrepair. Chapter 18 goes into more detail on budgeting for your future.

Tracking your progress: Paying attention to your credit report and score

Knowing where you and your credit stand is important so that you can gauge your progress and make adjustments if necessary. You don't need to check your credit every day, but you should take advantage of all the opportunities you have for free peeks that come your way. You get a free copy of your credit report annually, another free copy if you apply for credit and don't get the top rate, another when a credit report is used to set your insurance cost, and yet another if you're out of work.

The Fair and Accurate Credit Transactions Act (also known as the FACT Act or FACTA) requires all three major credit-reporting bureaus to provide you with a free copy of your credit report once a year. Some states require that you be given two reports annually. Stagger getting a copy of your report from *each* of the three bureaus, because they often contain different information. (See Chapter 14 for information on how to get your reports.)

When you get your credit reports, read them over and make sure that the information is accurate, complete, and up-to-date. Chapter 14 explains how to scrutinize your credit reports and fix any errors you find.

Generally, negative items stay on your credit report for seven years. The main exceptions are:

- ✔ Overdue tax debts, which stay until they are resolved
- ✔ Child support defaults, which stay posted until they're cleared up
- ✔ Bankruptcy, which remains on your report for up to ten years

Positive account information stays on your credit report for much longer. Some positive trade lines continue to be reported for 10, 20, or even 30 years.

Chapter 3

Cleaning Up Your Credit Reports

*F*acebook, YouTube, Internet cookies, traffic cameras, credit reporting . . . all are different ways that you expose yourself to others. People, including employers, lenders, insurers, and landlords, form impressions of you, and their perceptions aren't always correct. This is particularly worrisome where credit and financial matters are concerned, because in these cases, much of your appearance is influenced by others. Yes, you have a say in how you run your financial life and pay your bills, and such data should be reported accurately. But with billions of pieces of data floating around, errors do happen. Mistakes, misinformation, and other people's negative behaviors can all affect your credit reports from time to time.

Despite a natural desire to restrict access to the more intimate details of your personal financial history, your credit reports and score are accessible to much of the world. More and more decisions are being made from long distances by people who know you only from your credit file. In this environment where your credit reports can make all the difference in whether you get a job, an apartment, or a loan, the best you can hope for is that your credit profile is as accurate as possible.

That's why knowing what's in your credit report and polishing it to its highest luster are vitally important. The tools are yours to use; you just need to know what and where they are. That's what this chapter is all about: helping you look your very best by burnishing your credit reports.

Cleaning up your credit reports is not as difficult as you may have heard. The following sections give you what you need to make your reports look their best, as quickly as possible. Can you erase the past? No. But you can make sure that all the good stuff that may have been missed is added to your reports, that the old bad stuff is removed, and that no one else's information is on your report.

Understanding the True Value of Good Credit

You may think that banks are the main entities that review your credit profile and that they use the information largely to decide whether to approve you for a loan or to determine what interest rate to charge you. Though that's certainly the case, banks, employers, landlords, insurance companies, and others are increasingly using the data in your credit reports to make all kinds of decisions, including whether to

- Extend credit to you and on what terms
- Rent you an apartment
- Grant you insurance coverage
- Hire you for a new job
- Give you a promotion at work
- Award you a professional license in your line of work
- Qualify you for security clearance for your job or in the military

The people who make such decisions know that they're part of an increasingly litigious society. Discrimination on any basis other than hard fact can cost them massive court awards. Consequently, they look for independent data — devoid of discrimination, favoritism, or prejudice — to support and validate their decisions. What does this mean to you? If you have negative items on your credit report, you may pay more for an apartment, an insurance policy, or a loan, or you may not be able to access them at any price. That's why having a solid credit report is important.

The information in your credit report is a good predictor of future financial and nonfinancial behavior in your life. So if you're borrowing, looking for work or a place to live, seeking career advancement, renewing insurance, or getting licensed, you want to make sure that your credit information is accurate, current, and, yes, about you and not someone else.

WARNING!

Steering clear of credit repair companies

If you're desperate to speed up the recovery process, you may be looking at credit repair companies as your best hope (even though you can repair your credit on your own). You may be asking yourself, "Why not?" Well, the answer is this:

✔ **Credit repair companies can get you into a lot of trouble.** Most credit repair companies use one of two strategies. The first is to challenge everything on your credit report, or such a large portion of it that the credit bureau and creditors will not be able to respond to their disputes within the legal time frame. As a result, the items not verified will come off your credit report in 30 days. Sounds good, right? Not really. Although the credit bureaus may be slow, they're tireless machines. At some point in the near future, the information that was removed will be verified, and it will reappear on your credit report. If you're thinking, "Yeah, but I can get a loan while the information is deleted," consider this: When the information comes back on your report, you can be considered to have committed fraud. Ouch!

The other strategy is to establish a new identity for you using an employer identification number (EIN). The idea is that, with your new identification, you'll begin to develop a good credit report and leave all the bad stuff behind. But savvy creditors usually see through this ploy when a credit report shows very limited or no activity. Some credit repair agencies suggest that you use the EIN as a Social Security number. If you pull this off, you'll get into trouble and find yourself facing all sorts of legal unpleasantness. Why? Because you've essentially established a false identity and gotten credit under false pretenses. Nice.

Remember: If you do what a credit repair company tells you to do and any of it turns out to be against the law, you — yes, you, your mother's favorite child — can be prosecuted!

✔ **Credit repair companies have a terrible track record when it comes to delivering what they promise.** Compared to credit counseling, which also has come under fire for having disreputable elements, credit repair is a much more recent phenomenon, and the industry has not yet adopted independent standards of conduct. In fact, the industry has such a poor reputation that it has a very restrictive federal law named after it. One of the two objectives of the Credit Repair Organizations Act is "to protect the public from unfair or deceptive advertising and business practices by credit repair organizations." Need I say more?

✔ **Credit repair services are expensive.** If you are like me, famous for frugality, this is not a small objection. Typically, the cost is at least $400. Chances are, if you need help repairing your credit report, that money would serve you better if you used it to pay off some debt. If you're short on time but long on money, why not hire someone to improve your credit for you? You could ask an attorney or accountant to help you through the process, but it would not be cheap, and unless you have other business with these professionals, I would question why anyone with their credentials would apply their considerable talents and egos to such a mundane task. If you asked your lawyer to wash your car, chances are you'd get a big "no thanks," even if you were willing to pay the attorney her hourly rate. The same should be true of your request to repair your credit. But the hidden answer to this question is that it's difficult to know with whom you're sharing all the information in your financial history. When you consider the damage that information-sharing may cause you, I'm sure you can see that it's not worth the price — in any sense of the word.

Reviewing Your Reports for Problems

The task of knowing what's in your credit reports is a lot easier than some people may lead you to believe. But it does take a little time, some patience, and occasionally persistence. You don't need to pay anyone to monitor your credit or send you hourly updates on what's happening in your credit universe. You can do so on your own, and for free in most cases. You want to keep a close eye on your credit reports for potential problems, because with the large number of items reported daily, errors are not unusual. (The U.S. Government Accountability Office has found that about 25 percent of reports contain errors, and about half of those errors are serious enough to lower your credit score.) In addition, your credit history is used to make an increasingly large number of decisions about your future, financial and otherwise, from lending to insurance to employment.

To begin, arm yourself with the information in your credit reports (one from each of the three major credit bureaus), as well as your credit score from FICO, VantageScore, or a bureau. (Chapter 14 shows you how to get these reports and your score.) If you have to pick one, the FICO score is still the most widely used by lenders. If you plan to apply for a loan in the near future, ask your lender which report and score it uses, and then get that one. Although you probably won't be able to get the same exact score because of multiple versions the lender may have, you can get a snapshot of your credit that is very close to the commercial version actually used. If you can't find out which score is used, any score will do to establish a benchmark of where your credit report ranks and then to track improvement.

As you study your credit reports, you may be surprised by how many accounts you find. Because your report lists negative information for seven years (longer exceptions, such as government debts and bankruptcy, also exist) and positive information for much longer, you're likely to see accounts, referred to as *trade lines,* that you've forgotten about, and perhaps even some that you didn't realize you still had. Some creditors, like retail stores, don't close accounts, even if you haven't used them in years. Your task is to play credit archeologist and sift through the trade lines — current and ancient — and identify errors and inaccuracies. (For a rundown on all the different sections of your credit reports, turn to Chapter 14.)

Here's what you should look for in particular:

> ✓ **Verify that your name, address, birthdate, and Social Security number are correct.** Variations on your name are okay (for example, my report shows both Stephen and Steve). With all the data moving through the financial reporting system, however, a Jr. or Sr. can easily be missed, or confusion over a II or III designation may occur.

✔ **Look to see whether account activity is being reported correctly.** If you see accounts that are familiar but activity that isn't — such as a late-payment notation when you don't recall having been late — report that error to the credit bureau. An account you don't recognize may be a simple misposting of data from someone else's report, or it may be a sign of something more serious, like identity theft. Contact the bureau and find out.

✔ **Look out for accounts from banks or stores with which you've never done business.** Someone else's account information may have been added to your credit report because of a misspelled name, a wrong address, or an incorrect Social Security number. Sometimes a merger or account purchase results in a new trade line showing up on your report. Dispute the account using the instructions on your credit report if you have aren't sure about it.

✔ **Identify and verify any accounts that show negative activity.** *Negative activity* can include anything from a missed or late payment to a charge-off (see Chapter 7 for more on delinquencies) or bankruptcy notation. Make sure that this negative information is really yours and is accurate. Remember, 25 percent of reports contain errors. Also, some negatives are much more serious than others. For example, a 90-day delinquency is more serious than a 30-day delinquency, even though both are negative. Recent negative items are more serious than older ones.

✔ **Be sure that an account that moved from one source to another is listed as open only once.** Bank and store mergers can result in multiple entries for the same account. Multiple entries can make it look like you have excessive amounts of credit available.

✔ **Look for overdraft protection lines of credit.** These lines of credit may be reported to the bureaus even after you close the accounts that the lines were meant to support. Reporting these lines of credit as closed reduces your outstanding credit and can be helpful if you are trying to add new credit.

If you make a correction to your file, the change may not be reflected in your credit report right away if the creditor doesn't generally report to that credit bureau every month. If you're in the process of applying for a loan, ask whether your lender offers a rapid rescore product for sale. Developed by the three major credit bureaus, *rapid rescore* is essentially an unscheduled update to the information on your credit report. If a recent action (such as paying down a balance or closing a card) helps your credit score, then it can be expedited to the bureau as soon as it's made. The credit bureau can then update your file so that you can get an updated score in days, not weeks.

Using the Law to Get Your Credit Record Clean and Keep It That Way

Nowadays, you have expanded rights regarding access to your credit report, granting you more empowerment than perhaps at any other time in the modern history of credit. The Fair and Accurate Credit Transactions Act (FACT Act or FACTA) helps you get the facts about yourself straight. This legislation can help you with new tools to fight the growing crime of identity theft. Additionally, the Dodd-Frank Wall Street Reform and the Consumer Protection Act offer new safeguards to consumers.

In addition to requiring lenders and credit bureaus to play a greater role in protecting you, these laws promote consumer rights by enabling you to

✔ **Receive your credit report for little or nothing.** You're entitled to a free copy of each of your credit reports once a year (see Chapter 14 for information on how to get copies of your reports). You can get additional free reports if you believe that your identity has been stolen or if you've been on the receiving end of bad news caused by information in your credit file. The credit business refers to this as an *adverse action*. Some actions by lenders and some state laws entitle you to multiple free reports each year. Check with your state's attorney general's office to find out the laws in your state. You can also check out this credit bureau site for free or discounted reports: `aa.econsumer.equifax.com/aad/landing.ehtml`.

✔ **Limit access to your credit report.** Only people and institutions with a need recognized by the FACT Act — usually generated by an application with a creditor, insurer, employer, landlord, or other business — may access your credit report.

✔ **Require your consent before anyone is provided with your credit reports or specialty reports that contain medical information.** Your employer, prospective employer, creditors, insurers — anyone — needs your permission or an existing business relationship with you before being able to access your private information.

✔ **Have access to all the information in your file.** Ask and you shall receive. You must be given the information in your file, as well as a list of everyone who has recently requested access to it. Creditors are required to give you an early-warning notice and a free credit report or score if they place any negative information on your credit report.

✔ **Be informed if your report has been used against you.** People who use information in your credit file as a basis for taking action against you — such as denying you credit or a job or making an unfavorable rate decision for insurance — must reveal that they used the information in your credit report to make the decision. They must also reveal

- The name, date, and numerical credit score used in the adverse decision

- The range of possible scores under the model used

- All key factors that adversely affected the credit score

✔ **Dispute and have removed any inaccurate or outdated information.** After you file a dispute saying that your report contains inaccurate information, the credit bureau must remove the information and investigate the items — usually within 30 days — and give you a written report of the investigation and a free copy of your credit report with the revisions made if the investigation results in any changes. If the reported information is later found to be valid, it can be reinserted into your report, in which case you must be given written notice of the reinsertion. The notice must include the name, address, and phone number of the information source. As for outdated info, information that is more than seven years old — ten years for some bankruptcies — should be deleted from your credit report. If it isn't, you may demand that it be dropped.

✔ **Place a statement on your report.** You may include a 100-word statement to explain extenuating circumstances or to note your disagreement with items on your report. For more about this statement, see the section "Adding a 100-word statement" at the end of this chapter.

✔ **Exclude your name from lists for unsolicited credit and insurance offers.** Although creditors and insurers may use credit report information as the basis for sending you unsolicited offers of credit or insurance, they must include a toll-free phone number for you to call if you want your name and address removed from those lists.

The opt-out toll-free number for all the national credit-reporting agencies is 888-567-8688.

✔ **Initiate a fraud alert by calling one of the three major credit bureaus.** If you believe that your identity may have been stolen, you just have to make one phone call or visit one credit bureau website (as opposed to contacting each of the three bureaus individually) to initiate an alert. A *fraud alert* requires the creditor to exercise enhanced levels of protection, such as taking additional steps to verify that you are who you claim to be.

✔ **Freeze access to your credit report.** Freezing your credit report enables you to lock the door on any review or use of your credit information unless you specifically authorize it. The only exception is if Uncle Sam wants to see your credit record. Generally, you can freeze, and then unfreeze or thaw, your information as your needs warrant, for any reason. You may be charged a small fee, but the process is effective.

✔ **Receive damages from violators.** If anyone violates the law, you can sue that person in state or federal court. Some people have, and they've collected millions of dollars!

✔ **Place an active-duty alert to protect your credit as a member of the military.** A business that sees an active-duty alert on your credit report must verify your identity before issuing credit in your name. The business may try to contact you directly, but if you're deployed, doing so may be impossible. Therefore, the law allows you to use a personal representative to place or remove an alert. Active-duty alerts are effective for one year and may be renewed. The alert also cuts down on your junk mail. Your name is removed from the nationwide consumer-reporting companies' marketing lists for prescreened offers of credit and insurance for two years. Sweet!

Identifying and Disputing Inaccurate Information

You can't legally remove accurate and timely info from your credit report, whether it's good or bad. But the law does allow you to request an investigation of any information in your file that you believe is outdated, inaccurate, or incomplete. You're not charged for this investigation, and you can do it yourself at little or no cost.

Inaccurate data serves no purpose for anyone in the credit chain. The credit bureaus and lenders want the information in your reports to be accurate, just as you do.

In the following sections, I show you how to file a dispute with the credit bureaus as well as with a particular creditor.

Understanding the dispute process

The process for disputing and correcting inaccurate information is simple. Your role is to check your credit reports at least once a year. If you see information that looks unfamiliar or wrong, you file a dispute with the credit bureau in question. Dispute procedures come with your credit report.

After you notify a bureau of a disputed item, the bureau contacts the source that placed the data in your report. That source has 30 days to respond. If the source can't verify the data within the time allowed — because the information never existed, the info can't be found, or Helen (the data retriever) is on vacation — the bureau must remove the information from your report. If, on the other hand, the information is verified, it stays on your report. In either case, you're notified in writing of any actions or nonactions that occur as a result of your dispute.

If you disagree with the findings, you can contact the company that placed the erroneous information yourself and try to get it changed. Be sure to ask how the investigation was conducted and who was contacted. You also have the right to add a statement to your report or to a specific trade line saying why you disagree. See the section "Adding a 100-word statement" later in this chapter for details on how to write and submit a clear and concise statement.

If you place a statement on your report, be sure to keep track of the time it's on the report so that it doesn't outlast the negative data it explains and cause you further problems.

Correcting all your credit reports

Not all the bureaus have the same information in their files. So, for example, if you look at your Experian credit report, see an inaccuracy, follow the dispute process, and have it corrected, you may not be out of the woods. TransUnion or Equifax may have *different* inaccurate information. Therefore, you need to get all three reports to see which reports contain *which* false data.

If the same error appears on two or all three reports, you need to dispute it only once; the first credit bureau reports this finding to the other two on your behalf. But, being a cautious person by nature, I suggest that you double-check anyway.

Contacting the bureaus

Correcting all three reports is important, because some lenders and businesses purchase the three-in-one report that includes a credit score and credit history information from each of the three bureaus. Each bureau has slightly different procedures for filing disputes, but all three allow you to dispute inaccurate or out-of-date information by phone, by mail, or online:

- ✔ **Equifax:** Call the phone number provided for disputes on your credit report, and be sure to have your ten-digit credit report confirmation number (on your report) available. You can also dispute by mail at Equifax Information Services LLC, P.O. Box 740256, Atlanta, GA 30374 (no confirmation number is required on written correspondence); or online at www.equifax.com.

- ✔ **Experian:** You can dispute by phone by using the toll-free number on your credit report; by mail at Experian, P.O. Box 9701, Allen, TX 75013; or online at www.experian.com.

- ✔ **TransUnion:** You can dispute information by phone at 800-916-8800; by mail at TransUnion Consumer Solutions, P.O. Box 2000, Chester, PA 19022-2000 (be sure to include the completed request for investigation form found on the website); or online at www.transunion.com.

Though initiating a dispute by phone or online may be easier, most experts suggest that you keep written records of everything you do (names, times, dates, and so on) to create a trail of documentation that you can point to if things go wrong or get lost.

Avoiding a frivolous dispute

A credit bureau must investigate any disputed items in question — usually within 30 days — unless it considers your dispute frivolous, in which case it's required to notify you within five business days. The bureau must tell you why it considers your dispute frivolous and explain what you must do to convert the dispute to one that will launch the dispute process.

So what is frivolous? If you send a long list of disputes — for example, you list all the negative information on your credit report — you may appear as though you're trying to overwhelm the agency with requests just to get items taken off your report while you apply for a loan. In this situation, the bureau may refuse to honor your request. You're better off sending only a few disputes in a single letter.

If you choose to dispute items on your credit report via mail, write a letter stating which item(s) you're disputing. Include any facts that explain your case, and include copies (not originals) of documents that support your position. Enclose a copy of your credit report with the items in question circled or highlighted. Be sure to provide your complete name and address and tell the company what your desired action is (correction or deletion). Send your dispute letter by certified mail, return-receipt requested, so you can document the fact that the letter was mailed and received. Keep copies of your dispute letter and enclosures.

You can find a sample letter to a credit bureau that disputes information on a credit report at www.dummies.com/extras/creditrepair.

Following through with creditors and the bureaus

The credit bureau must forward all relevant data you provide to the company that originally reported the information. When the company receives the request for verification from the credit bureau, it must investigate, review all relevant information, and report the results to the bureau.

- ✓ **If the information is found to be inaccurate,** all three nationwide bureaus are notified so that they can correct your file.

- ✓ **If the company can't verify the accuracy of the information you're disputing,** the information must be deleted from your file.

- ✓ **If the disputed information is incomplete,** the credit bureau must update it. For example, if you were once late in making payments but your file doesn't show that you've since caught up, the bureau must amend your report to show that you're now current on your payments.

- ✓ **If the disputed information includes an account that belongs to another person,** the bureau must delete it.

When the investigation is complete, the credit bureau must give you the written results and a free copy of your updated credit report if the dispute results in a change of information. (The bureau may refer to your request for an investigation as a *reinvestigation;* they're the same thing.) If an item is changed or removed, the bureau can't put the disputed information back in your report unless the company providing that information subsequently verifies its accuracy and completeness. Then the credit bureau must give you written notice that includes the name, address, and phone number of the company that provided the verification.

You can request that the bureau send notices of corrections to anyone who received your report in the past six months. If you've applied for a job, you can have a corrected copy of your report sent to anyone who received a copy during the past *two years* for employment purposes.

If you aren't satisfied with the results of your dispute, you can dispute the item directly with the creditor (see the section "Contacting the creditor" later in the chapter). Be sure to include copies of all the information you have. You also have the right to include a 100-word statement of the dispute in your report and in future reports (see the section "Adding a 100-word statement" later in the chapter). Depending on the bureau's rules, this statement can stay on your report indefinitely, so don't forget about it! When it's no longer relevant, send a letter requesting that it be removed.

Knowing the rules on negative information

When negative information in your report is accurate, only the passage of time can assure its removal. Most accurate information stays on your report for seven years, but certain exceptions to the seven-year rule exist:

- Criminal convictions may be reported without time limitation. They are not reported on a lender's copy of your credit report, but they are reported on credit reports ordered for employment purposes.

- Chapter 7 bankruptcy information may be reported for ten years.

- IRS liens remain indefinitely, until removed by the IRS.

- Student loan delinquencies that are brought current (up-to-date) are reported for seven years and then reported as current thereafter. If the loan is not brought current for seven years, the entire account is dropped from the credit report, and any subsequent positive information is not reported.

- An inquiry due to an application for more than $150,000 worth of credit or life insurance or a job paying a salary of more than $75,000 has no time limit.

- A lawsuit or an unpaid judgment against you can be reported for seven years or until the statute of limitations runs out, whichever is longer.

What to do if you're not sure about your data

The law protects the dispute process from abuse, so you don't want to dispute information that you know is accurate or claim that an account listing is the result of identity theft when you know that's not the case. However, you can dispute any listing in good faith if you're uncertain of its validity — in other words, if you can't find records that confirm the item, you don't recall the status, or you're simply uncertain that the information has been reported correctly.

Follow the dispute process outlined in this chapter and explain why you believe the item is questionable. Just as you may challenge a word that you aren't familiar with in a game of Scrabble, disputing information that you aren't completely sure about is okay. Disputing information that you know is correct, however, is *not* okay.

If you're unhappy with the results of your dispute or think that you've been treated unfairly, contact the Federal Trade Commission (FTC). The FTC works to prevent fraudulent, deceptive, and unfair business practices and provides information to help consumers spot, stop, and avoid these practices. To file a complaint or to get free information on consumer issues, visit www.ftc.gov or call 877-382-4357 (TTY 866-653-4261).

Contacting the creditor

Any financial institution that submits negative information about you to a major credit bureau has to tell you so. This heads-up enables you to jump on errors earlier than you could under the old laws.

You have a right to contact the furnisher of the disputed information directly. The contact process varies; it can be as simple as walking into the credit department and explaining the problem, calling the company's toll-free number, or visiting its website (many companies' websites have information on reporting fraud).

After you contact the creditor, it must investigate the dispute and report the results back to you following the same guidelines that the credit bureaus follow (see the preceding section), including responding within the same time frame as the bureaus.

Best of all, the creditor can't continue to report the negative information without noting that the info is in dispute. And if the information that's been disputed was reported as the result of a possible identity theft, then it can't be reported at all while the investigation is pending.

Again, as with the credit bureaus, the creditor must respond to your request within 30 days. If the creditor doesn't respond, the item in dispute is removed or corrected. If the creditor finds the information to be inaccurate, it must be corrected. If the information is outdated or belongs to someone else, it must be removed. The result must be submitted to each credit bureau with which the creditor has shared the incorrect information. If your dispute isn't found to be valid, you can add a 100-word statement to your report explaining why you dispute the item.

Be sure to keep good records, including names, dates of contact, and copies of letters and e-mails. Any company can experience what I call *bureaucratic memory loss.* So if you get a response like, "We've never heard of this before; who were you speaking to?" you'll have the answer handy. Good record-keeping keeps delays and irritations to a minimum.

Adding Positive Information to Your Credit Report

Insufficient information on your credit report can also cause trouble. The best way to get positive information inserted into your credit report is to pay your creditors on time and in full every month. Do so for a year or more and you'll make great strides in improving your credit history and your credit score.

Called a *thin file* in the industry, a file that contains very little information may not be able to be scored. To get around this problem, you can request that an expansion score be used. An *expansion score* uses information from alternative databases (such as cellphone records) to get enough data to form a valid score. Expect to pay for this service. The major supplier of this type of data is a company named MicroBilt; see `www.microbilt.com/fico-expansion-score.aspx` for more information.

Opening new credit accounts

Another way to get positive information into your data file is to open new credit accounts. Opening types of accounts that aren't already on your credit report is particularly helpful. For example, you may have several credit cards, so you could add an installment account, which can enhance your "type of credit used" profile (see Chapter 14 for more information).

Be careful when using this tactic to improve your credit score. You may do more harm than good if you open an account with a large amount of available credit, which is likely to push your available credit over the limit of what lenders find acceptable. Also, do so well in advance of applying for a loan, because opening a new account may have a short-term negative effect on your score.

Adding a 100-word statement

Don't like what others are saying about you? You can add a 100-word statement to explain certain items on your credit report. Although a statement doesn't change your credit score, it may help answer questions that are raised when a lender or employer reviews your report. Yes, the score is important, but so is the analysis by the person looking at your record. Your statement can accomplish several things:

- ✔ **Explain your side of the story for a series of late payments, collections, or charge-offs.** These may be due to a life event such as a job loss, divorce, or illness.

- ✔ **Document your dispute of information that you believe is incorrect but that the credit-reporting agency won't remove from your report.**

- ✔ **Tell your side of a dispute.** For example, you may have ordered a product that wasn't delivered on time or was unsatisfactory and refused to pay for it. Although the situation wasn't resolved in your favor, you may be able to explain it more clearly in your 100-word note.

You may be able to add more than one statement. Each bureau has its own policy. Experian lets you add several statements: a general statement giving an overview of your credit report woes, as well as individual statements for up to ten items. You may add more, but only after calling Experian. TransUnion lets you file 100 words in dispute and another 100 for a general statement. Equifax allows one 100-word statement.

You can find a sample 100-word statement at www.dummies.com/extras/creditrepair. Just plug in your info!

Do these 100-word statements really help? It depends on who reviews your credit report and what you say. The statement stays on your report for at least as long as the disputed item does, so take time to make your statement clear and concise. You can contact the bureau's customer service department for assistance with your writing if you need it. Send your written statement with your credit file number and the last four digits of your Social Security number using the "Contacting the bureaus" information listed earlier in this chapter.

If you decide to put a statement on your report, don't forget about it. In a year or two, negative information becomes less of a factor in your score, and eventually it drops off your report. Statements don't affect your score but can highlight past payment problems, especially if the credit report shows no recent delinquencies. Your outdated statement could call attention to situations that no longer apply and thus could hurt more than it helps.

To remove an outdated statement from your credit report, send a request to the three major credit bureaus at the addresses listed in the "Contacting the bureaus" section earlier in the chapter.

Chapter 4

Getting the Best Help for Bad Credit for Free

*W*here does bad credit come from? The credit fairy? Bad credit karma? No, it comes from overextending your finances and falling behind on your debt payments. Yes, other factors make up a credit score, such as the length of your credit history and whether you've shown that you can handle a variety of types of credit. But nothing whacks your credit score and report like being delinquent on payments or having to file for bankruptcy because your credit is hopelessly overextended.

FICO and VantageScore, the two main producers of credit scores, count late or missed payments as the most damaging factors to your score. And bankruptcy, the logical result of credit or debt gone wild, is the negative on your credit report from which it takes the longest to recover. Once you've fallen behind, lenders are very hesitant to lend money or change loan terms to help you catch up. So the only legitimate way to get rid of bad credit is to get your spending and income in sync and then make all your debt payments on time, as agreed.

Doing so can be easier said than done, so you may need some help. Getting help from someone with lots of experience is a smart thing to do. Getting it for free is even better. Yet many people avoid seeking help for money or credit problems. Why? Because getting the wrong help can just make matters worse. After all, haven't you been taught that when an offer is too good to be true, it usually is?

In this chapter, I help you sort through the conflicting and overblown claims for help that you find in the media. I also include valuable insights to help you decide which problems you can handle on your own, when to turn to others for assistance, and where to get the help you need.

Knowing Whether You Need Help

If you're asking yourself whether you need to get some outside advice or help, you're no doubt feeling some pressure, even if it's only a squeeze. This is a very personal decision with one or two exceptions, which I cover in the following sections.

Gauging your need for outside assistance

To help decide whether outside assistance is right for you, ask yourself — and include your partner if you're not in this alone — a few simple questions:

- **Are you stressed out?** You know you need to get some help when

  - You screen your calls to avoid creditors (see Chapter 6).

  - You argue with your partner about money or credit.

  - Your sleep is interrupted because of financial worries, and you don't look forward to greeting the day in the morning.

- **Are you (or you and your partner) being pulled in multiple directions regarding possible solutions?** You may be unsure about which approach to use:

  - Increasing income to support your current bills and future goals (see Chapter 18).

  - Decreasing expenses to bring your lifestyle in line with your present income (check out Chapter 16).

  - Getting a loan to pay off debt or reduce payments.

  - Filing for bankruptcy (see Chapter 8).

- **Are you dealing with multiple creditors or multiple problems?** You probably can use outside help if

  - More than two or three collectors or creditors have you on speed dial (check out Chapter 5).

  - You have many problems (financial, employment, medical, and/or marital) creating stress in your life at the same time.

- **Are you more than one month late on your mortgage payment?** No matter what else is going on, you need to see a counselor now! A delay or the runaround from your servicer can cost you

  - Thousands of dollars.

  - Your credit.

  - Your home (see Chapter 7 to avoid a foreclosure).

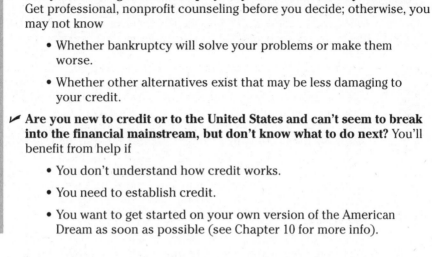

✔ **Are you thinking that bankruptcy may not be so bad for your credit?** Get professional, nonprofit counseling before you decide; otherwise, you may not know

- Whether bankruptcy will solve your problems or make them worse.

- Whether other alternatives exist that may be less damaging to your credit.

✔ **Are you new to credit or to the United States and can't seem to break into the financial mainstream, but don't know what to do next?** You'll benefit from help if

- You don't understand how credit works.

- You need to establish credit.

- You want to get started on your own version of the American Dream as soon as possible (see Chapter 10 for more info).

Handling situations on your own

In this section, I outline three credit situations that you can probably resolve without much help.

To solve any credit/debt problem, you need to

✔ Identify the cause of the problem and resolve to fix it.

✔ Know how much money you have to work with.

✔ Act quickly.

Credit cards

If you can't make this month's credit card payment, or if you've missed a payment already, you need to take action. As long as you know what you can afford and you don't mind explaining your situation over the phone, you can get quick results. Here's what to do: Call the toll-free customer service number and explain who you are, what happened, and how you'd like to handle the situation. If you need a break from making payments, say so. If you can make up the missed payments over the next month or two, make an offer. Just make sure that you can make good on your offer. Be sure to ask the customer service representative not to report your account as late to the bureaus. This decision is up to the credit card company; often, the company is willing to go along with the request as long as you keep your end of the bargain.

If you're polite and proactive and you contact the credit card company before the company contacts you, this approach establishes you as a good customer who needs and deserves special consideration — much better than a customer who is behind in payments, doesn't call, and may be a collection risk.

Be careful about asking that a payment be stretched out for more than a month or two. If you need three months to catch up, you may get it — or even qualify for a longer hardship program — but the creditor may close your account, which hurts your credit. Also, don't be surprised if the company asks you to pay more than you think you can. The company doesn't know the details of your situation. Do *not* agree to anything you don't think you can deliver. Saying that something isn't possible and explaining why is much better than caving in but not being able to follow through. Ask to talk to a supervisor — he or she may have more authority to bend the rules.

Mortgages

If you're behind on your mortgage payment, but you're within the grace period allowed in your mortgage loan documents (typically 10 to 15 days from your contractual due date) and you have the money to make up the shortfall, send it in. If you're past the grace period, what you need to do to catch up depends on the state in which you live. Say you haven't yet made your payment of $1,000 from last month. This month you can send in only $500 extra with your $1,000 payment. So you're short $500, right? Wrong. You may be behind the full $2,000 if the bank doesn't accept either payment because you didn't catch up in full. Or the bank may apply the extra $500 to this month's principal payment rather than to last month's deficit. The gist is, if you aren't far behind and you can catch up in one shot, do it. Otherwise, don't delay — see the section "Considering credit counseling" later in this chapter and get help.

Mortgage lenders count delinquency occurrences differently than credit card issuers. As soon as you're one day beyond the grace period, mortgage lenders consider you late, back to the original, contractual, non-grace due date. After you're 90 days late from the contractual due date (not the grace period), all the rules change, and you're in serious danger of a foreclosure! (Check out Chapter 7 to find out what a foreclosure can do to your credit and how to avoid it.) Also, be mindful that some banks have shorter grace periods for mortgage holders who don't have bank accounts with them.

Student loans

Getting some breathing room on a student loan isn't difficult if you have a qualifying reason for being unable to pay. Unemployment, a low-paying job, illness, a return to school — any of these reasons may qualify you for a short-term waiver, but only if you give the lender a call before you get into a default situation. Student loan people usually cooperate as long as they think you're playing it straight with them.

If you don't think that you have enough money to catch up on your payments, you may have an alternative: The money may be hidden in your financial budget clutter. The first step in addressing a financial problem is to maximize your income and minimize your expenses. A spending plan (or budget) helps you with that. Only a real spending plan that accounts for at least 90 percent of your income and expenses will help; rough guesses don't yield the results you need. Turn to Chapter 18 for more on budgeting.

Identifying Help You Can Get for Free

Many sources of financial advice and help, including debt settlement firms, debt reduction companies, debt-erasing lawyers, for-profit credit counselors, credit-monitoring services, and credit repair companies, charge one way or another. And despite the ads that seem to promise better credit and relief from debts, collectors, and even the IRS, only three sources provide truly helpful, truly free assistance for those with credit or debt problems:

- ✔ **HUD-certified mortgage counselors:** Mortgage counselors can obviously help you with mortgage issues. They're experts at helping people decide whether to stay in their homes and then making the decision work in the best way possible. See the next section for help finding a mortgage counselor.

- ✔ **Nonprofit credit counseling agencies:** I'm a big fan of good credit counselors for a number of reasons: They're free, they take the time to tailor solutions to your situation, they're well trained, and their mission in life is to help, pure and simple. The main things they deal with are goal setting, identifying the sources of problems and solutions, and budgeting (the foundation of everything financial). For tips on locating a good credit counselor, see the section "Finding a great credit counseling agency" later in this chapter.

- ✔ **Pro bono lawyers:** Because credit and collections are governed by laws, and because life isn't always fair, the time may come when you need an attorney. But if you're broke or quickly getting there, paying for an attorney may not be possible. Pro bono lawyers work for little or nothing. See the section "Working with an attorney" later in this chapter for advice on how to find a pro bono lawyer.

Celebrity financial gurus may be entertaining and sometimes motivational, but they can't take the time to understand your situation. Plus, you can't get important follow-up advice to fine-tune your options and actions. Magazines offer still more generic help that may give you ideas but rarely solutions.

Getting help with your mortgage

Home mortgage debt is different from all other types of debt and can be very complicated. I strongly urge you to use a professional to make sure that you don't make costly and damaging credit mistakes. Here are a few places to look for professionals:

- ✓ **HOPE NOW:** This organization is an alliance among counselors, mortgage companies, investors, and other players. It helps distressed homeowners work out mortgage problems so that they can stay in their homes. The folks at HOPE NOW know the ropes, have access to decision makers, and can help you with the necessary paperwork for free. They support the Making Home Affordable Program (www. makinghomeaffordable.gov) by helping you understand your options, prepare your application, and work with your mortgage company. The U.S. Department of the Treasury and the U.S. Department of Housing and Urban Development back this alliance. For help, call 888-995-4673 or go to www.hopenow.com.

- ✓ **State housing authorities:** Every state has a housing authority. These organizations offer help to first-time homebuyers and homeowners in crisis, referrals to counseling, and sometimes funds to cure a delinquency. You can find the housing authority in your state or community at www.ncsha.org/housing-help.

- ✓ **Legal/document review:** One of your last resorts is to have an attorney review your loan documents. Some documents may have been drawn or executed incorrectly and may be challenged in court. A pro bono attorney may be able to help you for free. See the section "Working with an attorney" later in this chapter.

Considering credit counseling

A legitimate, certified credit counselor may offer just the help you need to get a handle on your financial problems. A nonprofit credit counseling agency serves as an objective party to help you see your financial situation without emotion and fear clouding your vision. In addition, a trained and certified counselor may be able to offer you some credit education, personalized budgeting advice, and a custom-tailored plan to get you out of debt — all for nothing or next to nothing.

Recognizing debts credit counseling can help with

Although credit counseling can help in a variety of circumstances, I believe that it's essential in five situations. So if you find yourself dealing with any of the following scenarios, I suggest that you get some outside advice pronto, before matters get further out of hand.

- **Mortgage default:** The rules are complex, the dates are often inflexible, and the servicers are often paper pushers who waste your time until a foreclosure is imminent. Many credit counselors, but not all, are certified mortgage counselors who can get to the right people faster than you and can lead you through a complex process based on a lot of experience and special access to decision makers.

- **Multiple bill collectors:** You can handle one or two collectors, but when you get to five, ten, or even more, conflicting demands can be impossible to balance.

- **Joint credit problems:** Credit problems are exacerbated when you share them with someone who doesn't see things the way you do. An outside, dispassionate point of view can make all the difference.

- **Debts that are backed by assets:** Loans for cars, houses, and boats are all secured by assets. If you don't or can't pay, the lender can repossess and sell your car, home, or boat. If you don't pay your credit card bill, the lender doesn't have any collateral that it can take, because it has no security beyond your word and your willingness to pay as agreed. As a general rule, the more security lenders have, the less willing they are to work with you to solve what they see as your problem.

- **Bankruptcy:** You must get credit counseling before you can file for bankruptcy. Be sure to pick a good agency that does a lot of this stuff. The agency should be fast, efficient, and cost-effective, or you may run into problems and delays later on. See Chapter 8 for more info.

In all these situations, you stand to benefit from talking to a professional who can help you with experience, resources, and a clear and unbiased outside view of your situation that you can't get when you're stuck in the middle.

Knowing what a credit counseling agency can offer you

Although no magic wand exists to make all your financial problems disappear, a good, certified credit counselor can offer thoughtful and useful solutions. Expect more than one option for resolving things, including some options you won't like. Your counselor can give you a balanced perspective of what you need to do, how long it will take, and what resources are available to help you along the way. Your counselor will probably discuss bankruptcy as well as other solutions.

Goals for the future

A good credit counselor offers solutions with your future goals in focus. A solution that works for you not only deals with current issues but also takes into account how you see your future. For example, if you're planning to buy a house, get a security clearance at work, or send your triplets to college in five years, that future goal affects which courses of action best fit your needs.

Improved communication with your family

For about 70 percent of the more than 2 million people who bare their souls to credit counselors each year, advice and direction are all they need. One unexpected by-product of credit counseling is improved financial and other communication. For many couples and families, the credit counseling session is the first time they openly communicate about goals, spending priorities, and even secrets such as hidden debts.

A plan that works for you

Expect to have a customized action plan when you're finished with credit counseling. An action plan has to fit the way you live, or you won't follow it. A comfortable budget designed with your spending and saving style in mind is more likely to be effective.

An often overlooked aspect of using nonprofit credit counseling agencies is that they know a lot about other community resources that may be able to help. Doing due diligence before making referrals to community, legal, and other resources is part of a good agency's service.

The credit counseling process isn't something you can breeze through in 15 minutes, because the plan you walk away with is tailor-made for you and your financial situation. Fully online credit counseling is still the exception in the U.S. Great Britain has had good success with an Internet-only version, so we may see it here at some point.

Periodic checkups

Expect some fine-tuning to adjust to changes down the road. Although your counselor anticipates bumps in the road as much as possible when developing your plan, the counselor can't foresee the future. Murphy's Law applies to financial and credit problems in spades. Not only can things go wrong, but with limited financial resources, every bump in the road feels much worse. Ongoing involvement with your credit counseling agency as you navigate this credit repair journey helps you stay the course. Expect the agency to make it easier for you by giving you the names, e-mail addresses, and phone numbers of people to contact beyond the agency for more help. You should be able to ask your counselor for additional suggestions and referrals as you go along, although most people, when they have a workable plan in hand, are off on their own.

Finding a great credit counseling agency

Here are some things to look for in a quality credit counseling organization:

- ✔ 501(c)(3) tax-exempt status
- ✔ Accreditation by a national independent third-party accrediting organization, especially the Council on Accreditation

✔ A willingness to spend at least 45 to 60 minutes with you, and more if needed — and for free

✔ A willingness to offer help the way you're most comfortable receiving it — in person, by phone, or via the Internet

Here are a couple of organizations that can help you with your credit counseling needs:

✔ **The National Foundation for Credit Counseling:** www.nfcc.org; phone 800-388-2227

✔ **The Association of Independent Consumer Credit Counseling Agencies:** www.aiccca.com; phone 866-703-8787

Deciding on debt management plans

For about 25 percent of those who turn to credit counselors, more than advice is prescribed. In these cases, in addition to an action plan, a debt management plan is recommended. A *debt management plan* (sometimes called a *debt repayment plan*) requires that the agency act as an intermediary, handling both communications and payments on your behalf for a small monthly fee. This plan includes revised payments that

✔ Are acceptable to all your creditors

✔ Leave you enough money to handle your living expenses

✔ Generally get you out of debt in two to five years

The value of an intermediary

You may wonder why a credit counseling agency has to serve as an intermediary as part of a debt management plan. Why can't the agency just set up the plan and leave you to follow it on your own, without paying the agency a monthly fee? The answer is twofold:

✔ **Most people hit a bump or two in the repayment road.** Through its ongoing involvement, your credit counseling agency can explain your situation to the creditor dispassionately and professionally. Many plans would blow up at the first misstep without a trusted intermediary to smooth strained communications.

✔ **Creditors want the credit counseling agencies involved.** Creditors can easily reach agencies for questions, the agencies' checks don't bounce, and the agencies don't get excited and yell over the phone the way consumers and creditors have been known to do, thereby calming down the whole repayment process.

Debt management plans are an alternative to bankruptcy and often go by other names, such as a *workout plan, debt consolidation,* or an *interest-rate-reduction plan.* A debt management plan offers all these benefits and perhaps a lot more. Here's how it works: When creditors realize that you can't meet the original terms of your credit card or other loan agreements, they also realize that they're better off working with you through your credit counselor. Under a debt management plan, your creditors are likely to be open to a number of solutions that are to your advantage, including

✔ Stretching out your payments so that the combination of *principal* (the amount you originally borrowed) and interest pays off your balance in 60 months or less

✔ Changing your monthly payment to an amount you can afford to pay

✔ Reducing your interest rate and/or any fees associated with your loan

✔ Refraining from hounding you day and night

Why would creditors be willing to do these things for you? Because if they don't, and you really can't make the payments, they'll spend a lot more money on collections than they'd give you in concessions. Plus, if you file for bankruptcy, your creditors may *never* get their money.

The critical point here is that the creditor has to believe you can't make the payments as agreed. But how does the creditor believe that without staking out your home? The creditor generally takes the word of the nonprofit credit counseling agency you go to for help. Still, being lenders, creditors check your credit report from time to time while you're on a debt management plan to make sure that you haven't opened new lines of credit.

Sounds like a good deal: lower interest rates and smaller payments. Well, a debt management plan isn't a free lunch. The minuses may include

✔ A negative impact on your credit report, depending on how your creditors report your credit counseling account (although just being in a debt management plan doesn't affect your credit score)

✔ Restricted access to credit during the term of the plan

✔ Difficulty changing credit counseling agencies after you begin a debt management plan

The bottom line is this: If you're in debt crisis or you're concerned that you may be getting close to it, a debt management plan from a good credit counseling agency may be a solution. If you're just shopping for an interest-rate reduction or a consolidation-loan alternative, a debt management plan may *not* be in your best interest.

Steering clear of debt settlement plans

Debt settlement isn't the same as credit counseling or a debt management plan. It's sometimes advertised as a way to save money, but it can be one of the most expensive methods of all! In a debt settlement plan, you pay money to a company that holds your money without making any payments until the creditor stops hounding you and supposedly is ready to take less than the face value of the debt.

This course of action *severely* damages your credit for years to come. If that's not enough to scare you off, consider this: Often, if you

actually get to a settlement, the amount the creditor forgives actually becomes taxable income to you! You guessed it: The IRS wants you to pay taxes on the forgiven amount, which can add up to thousands of dollars due on April 15 to Uncle Sam. And those agents at the IRS don't go away! Even if you later decide to go the bankruptcy route, the IRS still gets its money.

Debt settlement is an unsavory, confrontational business. My advice: Don't do it! If you must, use a qualified attorney whom you know to negotiate settlements on your behalf.

Working with an attorney

You may be asking yourself if an attorney can possibly be free or low-cost. The answer is yes, if that's what you need. I said *need,* not *want.* If you can't afford an attorney, free or very-low-cost services are available if you know where to find them, and that's what this section is all about.

The phrase *pro bono* comes from the Latin and means "for the public good." Pro bono lawyers exist in most firms; they can be the very same lawyers who charge well-heeled clients hundreds of dollars an hour but will help you for little to nothing. The trick is to find one.

Here are some suggestions for finding free legal help:

✔ **Legal Services Corporation (LSC):** LSC is the largest provider of civil legal aid for those who can't afford it. LSC is a nonprofit corporation that supports 136 legal aid programs through more than 900 offices throughout the United States. It offers a variety of help, including cases involving family law, housing and foreclosure issues, and consumer issues such as protection from lenders, debt management, and bankruptcy. LSC serves consumers who are at or below 125 percent of the poverty level — in 2013, $14,363 for an individual or $29,438 for a family of four. Visit www.lsc.gov or call 202-295-1500.

- ✔ **Local bar association:** Your local bar association can help you find the help you need for what you can afford to pay. The American Bar Association has a consumers' guide to legal help on its website to help you find such resources in your state; see `apps.americanbar.org/legalservices/findlegalhelp/home.cfm`.

- ✔ **LawHelp:** LawHelp (`www.lawhelp.org`) helps low- and moderate-income consumers find free legal aid programs in their communities and provides links to other social service agencies.

- ✔ **Pro Bono Lawyers:** This website (`probonolawyers.org`) has nearly 200 links covering all 50 states, with info about lawyers who may be willing to work for free or for a reduced rate depending on your circumstances.

- ✔ **Armed Forces Legal Assistance (AFLA):** All branches of the military can find legal assistance at a central routing site: `legalassistance.law.af.mil/content/locator.php`.

A qualified attorney can handle anything a mortgage counselor or credit counselor can. The big difference is that most attorneys don't deal with credit situations every day. As a result, they'll probably take longer to get to the same place than someone who deals with hundreds or thousands of these cases every month. So although you can make a versatile tool fit most situations, sometimes you're better off with one designed specifically for the job at hand — especially when it comes to mortgage issues.

Chapter 5

Coping with Debt Collection

. . . .

In This Chapter

▶ Knowing the collection rules

▶ Opening a dialogue with your creditors

▶ Being proactive with creditors and collectors

▶ Finding someone who can help you when a collector can't (or won't)

▶ Controlling your spending and paying your bills

. . . .

Chances are that you opened to this chapter because you're feeling anxious about debts. You may be behind on your bills and wondering what to do. You may be getting calls from collectors and wondering how you can possibly meet their demands for payment. Well, you've come to the right place to relieve your anxiety. Relax, take a calming breath, and read on.

When it comes to coping with bad debt, you have an important ally in the Fair Debt Collection Practices Act (FDCPA). This federal law prohibits abusive practices by debt collectors. That's right, laws exist to protect you from overzealous collectors, who can be prosecuted if they threaten you, harass you, or lie to you. I bet you feel a little bit better already just knowing that specific rules govern how far a collector may go and that you have rights — legally enforceable rights! Knowing your rights under the FDCPA gives you some much-needed confidence when you must communicate with those who attempt to collect from you. I cover your rights and protections in detail in this chapter.

You can read the text of the FDCPA at www.dummies.com/extras/creditrepair or on the Federal Trade Commission (FTC) website (business.ftc.gov/documents/fair-debt-collection-practices-act).

I hope that your heart rate has decreased and you're feeling more comfortable about dealing with your debts. Let's get started!

Handling Those Collection Phone Calls

You have some late bills, but you put off dealing with them, and now you're getting calls from collectors. You may find yourself in the middle of a recurring nightmare of insatiable callers who won't go away and who seem to draw strength from your inability to give them what they want.

This scenario doesn't have to be the case. The Fair Debt Collection Practices Act (FDCPA) protects debtors from harassment by collectors, particularly harassment via telephone. Armed with your knowledge of the rules and a plan of action, as I describe in this section, you can handle those calls before they handle you.

Knowing what collectors can do

First, the *must do* rules: If a collector contacts you about a debt by phone, the collector has five working days to send you a written notification of the amount you owe and the name of the creditor that referred the debt to the collector. The notice has to state that this is an attempt to collect a debt and that any information obtained will be used for that purpose. The written notice also must disclose that you have the right to dispute the debt within 30 days of receiving the notice.

A debt collector *may*

- **Contact you directly, unless you tell the collector not to call you again or to contact your attorney instead, and you give the collector the attorney's contact information.** In this case, the file usually goes straight to a collection attorney.

- **Contact you by phone between 8 a.m. and 9 p.m., unless you agree to other times.** The collector may contact you outside those hours only if you give your permission to do so.

- **Call you at work.** However, if you tell the collector that your employer prohibits such contact, the collector must not call you at work.

- **Contact you by mail.** However, the collector can't put information on the outside of the envelope that indicates a collection attempt or send information on a postcard.

- **Contact others to get information about where you live and work.** The collector can request only contact information. The collector can't say that he or she is calling in regard to an owed debt. The sticky part is that if the collector calls your sweetie and *your sweetie* asks who the collector is, the collector can state his or her name and the name of his or her employer.

✔ **Supersize your statement.** Only charges that you agreed to under the original terms of your loan may be added to your bill. You can find a list of them in the account terms, in the fine print. These charges include endless fees, huge interest rate hikes, and the costs of collection.

✔ **Ask for postdated checks.** Depending on the state in which you live, the collector may be entitled to ask for postdated checks. Look into your state's guidelines. Although your state may permit collectors to ask for postdated checks, providing one is not in your best interest (see the nearby sidebar "Postdated checks: Good for the collector, bad for you").

✔ **Tell the credit bureaus that you're behind on your payments.** A delinquency that shows up on your credit report stays there for seven years and lowers your credit score (see Chapter 14).

✔ **Hike your interest rate.** You may be hit with a penalty rate. You can't pay the current bill, so why would the creditor increase your interest rate to 20 or 30 percent? Because you're a higher risk than the creditor thought.

✔ **Repossess your purchase.** Repossession is almost always a bad deal for you because the creditor determines the value of the repossessed item and can charge you for costs incurred in reselling it, too.

✔ **Sue you in court.** The collector may ask a judge for a judgment against you in a court of law. Depending on your state's laws, this judgment can be a prelude to garnishing your wages or placing a lien on your home. A court action further damages your credit report (see Chapter 14).

✔ **Change the terms of your agreement.** Some collectors may allow you to make up what you owe over time by adding an amount to future payments. Some, to their credit, offer hardship programs, but usually only if you ask. Be sure to get any changes to your agreement in writing, particularly if communications are strained at best. You need documentation to ensure that the agreement is honored.

✔ **Accept or offer a debt settlement option for less than the full amount owed.** If a lower amount is agreed on, the collector usually wants the settlement at once and in a single payment. The debt is reported negatively on your credit report as "settled." Depending on the amount of debt forgiven (usually a $600 threshold), you may get a Form 1099C from the creditor in the mail at tax time. The IRS considers the forgiven portion of the debt as income and requires you to pay taxes on it. (Check out Chapter 6 for more on settlements.)

Knowing what collectors can't do

Debt collectors are *not* allowed to

✔ **Threaten you.** In writing or over the phone, collectors must use businesslike language. Threatening, abusive, or obscene language is not allowed.

✔ **Be annoying.** An annoying collector — isn't that redundant? This rule means that collectors aren't allowed to make repetitive or excessively frequent phone calls to annoy or harass you.

✔ **Be deceptive.** No "trick or treat, smell my feet!" Collectors can't pretend to be anything other than what they are in order to get you on the phone.

✔ **Lie about the consequences.** Collectors can't claim that you've committed a crime or that you'll be arrested if you don't send payment. The United States doesn't have debtors' prison.

✔ **Make idle threats.** Collectors can't threaten you with illegal actions or actions that they have no intention of carrying out. If they don't intend to take you to court, they can't threaten to do so.

Deciding whether to answer the phone

You may find yourself reluctant to answer the phone for any number of reasons. You may have had a hard day at work, you may be overtired, or you may not be feeling in control of your emotions at the moment. If you've been contacted by the collector and you've already explained that you're doing your best and that's all you can do, having the same conversation again and again may feel frustrating and unproductive, especially if the collector is on the overbearing side. Don't answer the phone if you know that you won't be able to have an effective conversation.

You don't have to pick up the phone. Keep in mind, however, that although caller ID and voicemail can help you screen calls (and may help save your sanity), they won't help you avoid or solve your debt problems. If collectors can't reach you by phone, they'll try to find another way to contact you.

Preparing to answer collection calls

When you decide that it's time to bite the bullet and talk to the collector, make sure you're prepared. Write down the key points you want to cover in your conversation with the collector. Having a plan in mind helps you stay on track and in control of the call. It also helps you not to over-promise and under-deliver, to avoid losing your temper, and to know when to terminate the call if it gets abusive. If you start to feel overwhelmed or backed into a corner by the collector, get outside professional help. You can find out about getting help in Chapter 4.

Even though you may feel nervous, guilty, or angry, you aren't the first or only person to have gone through debt collections. It happens all the time, and you *will* get through it.

If you're late on some bills, expect that you'll get a call from a collector sooner or later — typically when you're 30 to 90 days late or more. If you decide to pick up the phone, here's what you need to do:

- ✔ **Get the caller's name and contact information.** Use the collector's name during your conversation.

- ✔ **Ask for proof of the debt.** Mistakes happen, and crooks call to try to get money from people all the time. (See the section "Asking for proof that the debt is yours," later in this chapter, for more information.)

- ✔ **Explain what happened.** Provide a very short story of why you're behind and what, if anything, you're able to do about the debt.

- ✔ **Make a payment offer.** See the section "Negotiating a payback arrangement" later in this chapter.

- ✔ **Don't agree to a payment schedule that you can't keep.** Be realistic, or you may find yourself agreeing to a plan you know you can't follow through on. (See the section "Keeping your promise" later in this chapter.)

- ✔ **Get it in writing.** If you come to an agreement, ask the collector to put it in writing so it's clear to both parties. If the collector won't do so, write the letter yourself (keeping a copy for your records) and send it to the collector by certified mail (return receipt) so you have proof that the collector received it.

Knowing what not to say

Saying the wrong thing in a conversation with a collector may be unproductive and can turn the conversation into a hostile confrontation that could end up causing you more harm. No matter how adversarial your caller seems, here are some definite don'ts:

- ✔ Don't let yourself get drawn into a shouting match.

- ✔ Don't make threats.

- ✔ Don't say that you're getting a lawyer if you don't intend to.

- ✔ Don't say that you're going to file bankruptcy if you don't plan to.

- ✔ Don't lie for sympathy (for example, "My mother's in the hospital," when your mother's on a cruise in the South Pacific). If you're caught stretching the truth, even once, people have a hard time believing you again.

Taking Charge of the Collection Process

The best way to deal with the collection process is to face your debts head on and as quickly as possible. Debts don't improve with age, and they certainly don't go away if you ignore them. In fact, as debts age, they get bigger, uglier, and harder to satisfy. Unresolved debts also have an uncanny knack for resurfacing when you're least prepared to deal with them.

Accounts that are 30 to 90 days *delinquent* (overdue) are usually handled by people who work for the company from which you bought your product or service, or *inside* collectors. If you're contacted by an outside or third-party collector early in the process, chances are the company hired the collection agency because of its tact and effectiveness rather than its skill at offending people. Outside collectors are covered by the FDCPA and must abide by those rules (see the section "Keeping Collectors in Check" later in the chapter). The biggest difference between an inside and an outside collector is that an inside collector may want to keep you as a customer in addition to collecting the money due. However, if the company determines that you're unlikely to make your payments, your customer status becomes less and less of a factor in the way the company attempts to work things out with you.

Calling your creditors before they call you is always better because it places you in a much different category than the one you find yourself in if they do the dialing. Good faith is on your side (but even that fades if you don't deliver on your commitments). Plus, you're prepared and ready for business instead of having to respond to an unexpected call.

This section explains what to do to give yourself the greatest chance of success when dealing with collectors.

Asking for proof that the debt is yours

When you get a call or a letter claiming that you have a past-due financial obligation, make sure to verify its accuracy. Even if you're sure that you owe the money, ask for details: which account it pertains to, what the bill was for, how old the debt is, when the statement was mailed to you, and so on. Asking these questions never hurts. Why? Here are two good reasons:

- ✔ **Mistakes happen.** Creditors make mistakes, so asking for a little proof is reasonable. You're not denying that you owe the debt; you're just making sure that you owe this particular debt and that the creditor has the right customer and the right account.

✔ **Scammers are out there.** These people will call, e-mail, or write and say that you owe money. Maybe you do, but not to them. They may even have proprietary information that persuades you that they must be legitimate. Get the facts in writing through the U.S. mail before you act. Having the information mailed to you opens scammers up to mail fraud charges.

FDCPA rules say that you have 30 days to respond to a collection attempt, and you're both smart and well within your rights to dispute a debt. Here's how you do it: Send the collector a letter via certified mail with a return receipt. In the letter, ask the collector to provide proof of the debt. Keep copies of everything you send. When you dispute the debt, the collector must stop all activity and provide you with proof of your obligation before reinitiating contact.

Disputing a bill stops collection activity, but it doesn't stop the clock. Your debt continues aging during the process. So try to resolve matters as quickly as possible when you're sure that the debt is yours and the collector is legit.

Knowing when debts fade away: Statutes of limitations

The United States is the land of the present, the here and now. As a result, people tend to let the past, well, be history. This philosophy applies to old debts, too. Every state has a *statute of limitations (SOL)* that limits how long the courts can be used to collect a debt. After a debt is between 2 and 15 years old (depending on your state of residence) without a payment having been made, it becomes history as far as the law is concerned.

I don't have enough room here to give you every state's SOL rules, so I've included a chart at www.dummies.com/extras/creditrepair to help you find out where you stand. Debts that are too old can't be enforced in a court of law. This turns even the fiercest collector into all bark and no bite.

A debt may be too old to collect under the SOL, but if it is less than seven years old, it will stay on your credit report and detract from your creditworthiness until it drops off.

Here's what to do if you think you may have an old debt that qualifies for SOL treatment:

✔ **Verify the last time you made a payment.** Use your credit report or, if you keep checking account records for seven years like I do, find your old check registers. Depending on your bank, you may be able to access checking-account payments from long ago. You don't want to see any recent payments here. Making a payment resets the clock on the SOL.

Say it has been 6 years and 51 weeks since your last payment, and the SOL is 7 years. If you make a payment, the 7-year period starts all over again. So expect some pressure from the collector to get you to send in any amount as the SOL date approaches.

✔ **Check out www.dummies.com/extras/creditrepair to see what your state's age limit is for SOL status.** The info isn't a legal guarantee, but it is grounds for you to see a lawyer if you believe that your debt may qualify.

✔ **Get a real legal opinion.** Yes, I suggest that you see a lawyer even though it may cost you some cash. Don't trust your friends or cousins. This is a legal matter, and only a lawyer can drive a stake through the heart of a dead debt.

✔ **Have the attorney write a letter.** So you look like a champ, the letter should include documentation of the debt's age, proof that it's over the SOL limit, a statement that you don't intend to pay a penny, and (here's the crusher) a note that all future contact must go through the attorney. No collector I know of will bother to try to collect an uncollectible debt from a lawyer who knows better. And collectors can't go around the attorney after you notify them that you have a lawyer, or they can be sued. Oh, yes indeed, sued by your attorney!

Negotiating a payback arrangement

When you and the collector agree that all the particulars of the debt are legitimate, it's time for you to make an offer to resolve the obligation, whether the cause of the delinquency was an unintended error or unfortunate circumstances. You can make an offer for a period of time. Say you owe $1,000. If you offer to pay $50 per pay period for the next 20 weeks, that plan may be acceptable. Or you can offer to pay $25 per pay period until your next raise in three months, at which time you'll pay $75 per pay period. Offering the amount you're able to pay is always better than waiting for the collector to demand a certain amount.

You want to convey your concern and reassure the collector that you're sincere in your commitment to pay. But that doesn't mean you shouldn't try to negotiate some concessions. For example, you may want the collector to

✔ **Keep the matter between the two of you.** If, for example, you're able to pay off your obligation and you're only 30 to 60 days past due, ask the collector not to report your oversight to the credit bureaus.

✔ **Lighten the late fees.** It doesn't hurt to ask if they'll waive any late fees. Be sure to tell them that, if they do, you'll be happy to get off the phone so you can run to the post office to mail your check. Most — but not all — will agree if they're getting the balance due without delay.

✔ **Reduce your interest rate.** Not the ideal time to try to get a better interest rate? Actually, it is. The collector wants what's called a *promise to pay* from you to resolve your situation. So ask for a break on the interest rate in order to help you pay the debt faster. On a delinquent credit card account, for example, you may be looking at a 30 percent default interest rate. The lender knows that adding this much to a strained budget increases the chance of a longer and more costly default or even a bankruptcy if you feel you have no way out. Lenders are often willing to help if you're sincere.

If you're under extreme financial duress, go a step further and ask if they have a hardship program. You may have to meet some qualifications, but if you do, your interest rate may drop dramatically, perhaps even to zero, and may lower your payments for six months to a year.

If you feel that any repayment plan is unrealistic and may push you over the financial edge, work on a spending plan (see Chapter 18). After you establish your goals, identify your sources of income, and tally up your living expenses, you'll discover what you can actually afford for debt service.

If working out a repayment plan is too intimidating, if you're dealing with multiple collectors, if you just can't seem to communicate on money matters, or if you just want help getting started, a reputable credit counseling agency can help you create a spending plan. See Chapter 4 for help finding an agency.

Postdated checks: Good for the collector, bad for you

At some point in the collection process, a collector may ask you to send postdated checks. The logic here is that, with the postdated check, you demonstrate a firm intention to honor your payment agreement, and the collector doesn't have to call you to remind you to send in any payments you may have agreed to. This scenario also covers the collector in case you "forget" to send a check at the appointed time.

This practice is akin to putting a piece of bacon on your dog's nose and telling him not to eat it.

Giving a collector a postdated check is almost always a bad idea because the collector will likely be tempted to cash the check too early, even though he or she isn't supposed to. If the collector cashes the check early and the money isn't in the account yet, the check will bounce, and the collector will be upset. If the collector cashes the check early and the money is there but the collector gets it sooner than you planned, all your other checks may start to bounce.

Keeping your promise

Following through with whatever payment promise you make is essential. From the collector's perspective, you've already broken your original agreement to make payments. Breaking a second agreement places you squarely in the not-to-be-trusted category.

If you're in the military: Special help for special people

In Chapter 10, I discuss the rules of engagement between the financial system and military personnel. Generally speaking, some significant safeguards are built into the Fair and Accurate Credit Transactions Act (also known as the FACT Act or FACTA), the National Defense Authorization Act for Fiscal Year 2007, and a rewrite of the Soldiers' and Sailors' Civil Relief Act (SSCRA), now known as the Servicemembers Civil Relief Act (SCRA). Here's what you need to know about your rights when it comes to debt collection:

✔ **Delayed court hearings:** If a creditor summons you to court for a hearing, you can request at least a 90-day delay. The judge can grant additional delays as the case warrants.

✔ **Interest rate reductions:** The interest rates on pre-service loans and obligations can't exceed 6 percent; interest due in excess of 6 percent per year must be forgiven, not just deferred. But you have to ask the lender for the reduction in writing and include a copy of your military orders.

✔ **Interest rate caps:** Interest rates are capped at 36 percent for payday loans and refund anticipation loans. This cap includes all fees and charges.

✔ **Eviction protection:** You can't be evicted from rental property for not paying rent (if the monthly rent is $1,200 or less) without proper court action. The law gives you other special protections if the rent is between $1,200 and $2,400.

✔ **Lease termination:** You may terminate without penalty a housing lease that you enter into before you start active duty if you're under orders for a permanent change of station or are deployed for at least 90 days. You don't need a military termination clause in your lease.

✔ **Auto lease cancellations:** You can cancel automobile leases if your orders are for 180 days or more, even if the vehicle is for a family member.

✔ **Vehicle title loans:** Military personnel can no longer be asked to secure loans with their vehicle titles except as part of receiving an installment loan to purchase a vehicle.

If collectors attempt to contact you to collect debts, let them know your situation and ask for their cooperation in accordance with the SSCRA. If you have a spouse at home, you may have him or her follow up on your behalf; be sure to mention that in your initial letter.

Most military units have a financial specialist who may be able to help further. If that fails, contact a lawyer or an accredited credit counseling agency and ask the lawyer or agency to act on your behalf. A lawyer may be expensive but should be worth it. Credit counselors are free or low-cost, and most try to help you by e-mail or through their websites. See Chapter 4 to find a credit counselor.

To make sure that you and the collector are clear on what you promised, put everything you agree to in writing. Keep a copy of the names, addresses, and phone numbers of everyone you talk to and include a written copy of your agreement with the payment. Asking for an e-mail confirming the arrangement. This is a reasonable request. A letter is a little more challenging because the delivery time may cause you to delay acting on your promise for another five days or so. It's important to the collector that you act quickly, so confirm all agreements in a quick note with names and times (don't forget to keep your copy) and send it off with your payment — certified mail, return receipt requested, of course!

Identifying Escalation Options That Help

When you're dealing with a debt collector, you may arrive at a sticking point and recognize that the person you're speaking with doesn't have the authority to do what you're asking. Instead of stopping at that frustrating dead end, you're better off tactfully suggesting that you'd like to take your situation to a higher authority who's empowered to make decisions. This is known as *escalating* the issue. In this section, I show you how to do so, as well as how to contact other people who may be able to help you if the manager can't accommodate you.

Asking to speak to a manager

Collection representatives may have several reasons for not warming to your proposed payment plan. They may

- Not believe that you're offering your best effort to repay
- Have a quota to fill, and your offer won't do it
- Have strict rules regarding permissible payment options
- Be having a bad day and just don't feel like being helpful

A manager has more flexibility and may even see the bigger picture of a best offer. By asking to speak to a manager, you take the pressure off the little guy and free him (or her) to move on to another customer while you and the boss work things out. If you look at the situation as though you're helping everyone, you may have an easier time escalating the problem to management.

You can say something like this:

> I understand that you've done your best to try to resolve this issue satisfactorily. Thank you for helping. But I'd like to speak to someone who has the authority to make exceptions/waive policy/take my offer to a higher level. It's not fair of me to ask you to go against company policy and take the payment I'm offering, so please let me speak to a manager.

If the collector refuses to let you speak to a manager, say that you'll call back on your own and ask someone else. Thank the collector for trying and say good-bye, nicely. Going over the same ground with the same person quickly wears thin.

Approaching the creditor

My wife tells me that she doesn't like to revisit the past. Believing that what's done is done may be a good way to handle many things, but credit may be an exception. Your original creditor may be willing to cut a deal with you even after sending your bill to an outside collector. Much depends on how you left things with the creditor. If you left with bad feelings or you lost it with a customer service representative, you may not be welcomed back. But if the transition from inside collections to an outside agency was just a migration and not a stampede, the creditor may still be willing to talk with you.

So why would you want to approach the creditor directly? If you're not getting anywhere with the debt collector, the creditor may be willing to work something out with you. After all, the creditor just wants the money you owe.

Creditors either place a debt for collection (and pay a commission based on results) or sell the debt outright. The former scenario is more common unless your debt is really old. If your debt has been sold, calling the original creditor won't do any good. But this bit of bad news has a silver lining. You may well have more room to negotiate in a debt-sale situation because debts aren't sold at full value, so a smaller-than-owed payment may still be very profitable for the collector.

Fighting harassment

Getting harassed by a collection agency? You're not alone. If you complain to the Federal Trade Commission (FTC), which watches over the collection industry, you'll be among the more than 80,000 people who lodge collection complaints each year. Some consumers have even taken collectors who overstep the law to court, and some of them have won very large settlements.

To file a complaint against a collector who is harassing you, contact the FTC at www.ftc.gov or 877-382-4357. The FTC won't follow up on your specific case, but your complaint helps others by allowing patterns of possible law violations to surface. Enough complaints against the same collector and the FTC may act.

Here are some other things you can do about harassment or abuse:

- ✔ **Keep your cool.** Always be professional and as calm as you can manage, and never raise your voice.

- ✔ **Take notes during each call.** Be prepared with facts and dates, and know what you're going to say before you say it. After all, collectors do!

- ✔ **Get a name.** Always get the name of the person calling you, and ask for full contact information, including the name of the company and the office manager. Do so *before* things get out of hand.

- ✔ **Just say no.** If a collector goes over the top or breaks a rule (threatens, yells, uses obscene language, and so on), you can tell the collector to stop and call back when he or she can act in a businesslike manner. Keep a record of the call and the behavior.

- ✔ **Complain to the original creditor.** Even though you aren't in good graces at the moment, a complaint here can result in action. No business wants an abusive collector scaring away past or future customers. The original debt holder may take the debt back and deal with you directly if you make a good case.

- ✔ **Complain to the boss.** Remember, you were smart enough to ask for the manager's name when the collector first contacted you, so use it. Your complaint may be the one that gets the abuser canned. No collection agency wants to be sued because of a bully who can't be professional.

- ✔ **Tell the collector to deal with your lawyer.** This is a double-edged sword. After you tell the collector to contact your attorney, all contact with you ends. Usually, the collection agency sends the debt to its own lawyer.

Communicating with Customer Service Before Being Placed for Collection

Communicating effectively isn't always easy, and many people don't even know where to begin. If you're one of those people, keep reading. When dealing with creditors, communication can be even more difficult because of the associated guilt, anger, and other emotions; basically, you have a recipe for conflict and communication breakdown.

From your end of the phone line, the situation looks like this: You're a responsible adult who has been a good customer for a long time. A series of unfortunate, unexpected, and undeserved events has descended upon you like a flock of unwanted relatives. You've tried for months to overcome your payment problems before asking for help. You can't seem to catch up. You're at the end of your rope, dangling at the edge of a cliff. But with some help, you know that you can pull yourself out. The process is similar to the one outlined in the section "Preparing to answer collection calls" but the tone and your options are different.

From the customer service rep's point of view, the scenario looks like this: You made a promise and broke it. Everyone else is required to pay bills on time, so why shouldn't you? You may be overspending and living beyond your means. You need to catch up on your payments as fast as possible. If you don't come through, the collector's job performance and business will suffer, and if the collector gets fired, he or she will be unable to pay his or her own bills.

See how different people can see the same scenario so differently? And before you accuse me of being soft, let me reassure you — I *am* on your side! I just know that you'll be more successful in getting the outcome you want if you're able to see the situation from both perspectives. For whatever reason, you haven't been able to keep all the promises you made. Although this doesn't mean that you're a bad person, it does indicate that doing business with you may be risky.

So now it's *your* job to explain why the customer service rep should accommodate you. Is resolution possible here? Yes — if you do your homework, offer a solution, and follow through on your promises. Where do you start? What do you say? To minimize negative perceptions, be proactive from the start and follow the steps outlined in this section.

Contacting your creditor promptly

Putting off unpleasant tasks is human nature. However, when it comes to requesting assistance from your creditors, the earlier you make the request, the better. From the creditor's point of view, three types of customers exist:

- ✔ Good customers who pay as agreed
- ✔ Good customers with temporary problems who are willing to work things out
- ✔ Bad customers who have to be chased

You'd like to be the first type of customer, but sometimes life pushes you into the second category. What's really important, however, is not to be classed in the third group.

The best time to let your creditors know that you're in trouble is as soon as *you* know and have a solution to offer. Don't wait until you've missed a payment — or more than one payment — on that credit card or auto loan. Don't wait for the phone to ring or a letter to come and *then* give your story. Get in touch *before* the payment is late. By preempting the bad-news announcement, you increase the odds that your negative event won't show up on your credit report! Read on to find out what to say.

Explaining your situation

You may choose to contact customer service by phone, in writing, via e-mail, or through the creditor's website. In some cases, you can even communicate through an intermediary like an attorney or a credit counselor. Whatever method you use, you need to explain your situation as clearly and effectively as possible, assuring the creditor that, despite your temporary difficulties, you intend to get back on financial track as quickly as possible.

But what do you want to say? What can you do to increase your chances of getting the help you need and deserve? Here are some elements to communicate (using a phone conversation as an example):

- ✓ **Introduce yourself and ask for the person's name.** Why? Because doing so adds a human dimension to the dialogue and may help personalize your call. Don't say "you" or "you people." I suggest that you write the name down, because you're probably stressed out and may forget it easily. Plus, when you call again, you'll have a name to refer to.

- ✓ **Begin the conversation on a positive note.** Say something nice about the company and your relationship with it. For example, "I've been a customer for years, and I've always had great products/service from you."

- ✓ **Briefly (in a minute or so) present the facts.** For example, you lost your job, you have no savings, and you have only unemployment insurance for income. Skip the gory details and the emotional commentary.

Offering a solution

After you've succinctly laid out the situation, propose a solution that works for you, *before* you turn control of the conversation over to the customer service representative. Your goal is to make it as easy as possible for the rep to agree to what you need, and the best way is just to ask for what you need! This is a critical and very positive step in the communication process. The customer service rep may actually be pleased that you've come up with a workable plan. Doing so not only increases the chance that you'll get what you want, but may also shorten the call if the rep can agree to your request, thereby making the rep look like a very productive employee. Plus, by keeping more control over the outcome, you have a much better chance of getting a repayment plan that actually works for you. (You may even be able to negotiate a concession or two in your favor; see the section "Negotiating a payback arrangement" earlier in this chapter.)

Whatever your proposed plan, be sure to cover these bases:

- ✔ **Assure the rep that you're already taking steps to resolve the problem *now*.**

- ✔ **Offer a realistic estimate of how long you need to rectify the situation.** Not "soon" or "I don't know."

- ✔ **Propose a specific payment amount and plan that you can manage.** Don't ask the creditor to suggest an amount. You won't like the answer.

- ✔ **Offer specifics.** Avoid saying, "I can't afford the $300-a-month payment right now. You're going to have to accept less." That's not a plan. Instead, say, "I need to reduce the monthly payment to $150 for the next four months. I could even pay $75 twice a month. Then, in four months, I believe I can return to $300, which only extends the length of the loan by two months." Now *that's* a plan. It shows that you're sensitive to the creditor's situation and that you're making a fair effort to make good.

- ✔ **Don't overpromise.** You may feel intimidated or embarrassed, and it's only natural to want to give the creditor what the creditor wants. Don't be surprised if the creditor pushes back and asks for more. Stick to your offer if possible. In the end, though, remember that the creditor won't be happy if you promise a certain payment and fail to deliver. If you get stuck, ask to speak to a manager, who may be able to approve your offer.

If you prefer to handle things in writing, check out Partial Payment Hardship Letter Current at www.dummies.com/extras/creditrepair, along with other letters you may find useful as starting points.

Covering all the bases

After you propose your plan and agree to terms, ask for a letter outlining the new agreement to be mailed or e-mailed to you so that there's no chance for a misunderstanding. If that doesn't seem to be forthcoming from your contact, or if you don't receive written documentation of the new terms within a few days, follow up yourself, stating the agreement in writing.

Keeping Collectors in Check

Let me begin by demystifying the power of collectors. I'm told that collectors are people just like you and me, but with a tough job to do. My personal experience over some 20 years of helping people who are dealing with debt is that this is sometimes, but not always, the case. Although some professionals in the debt collection field see collections as no more than an extension of customer service to customers in trouble, others see collections as a power trip and an excuse to use unfair and abusive collection practices on people they think are vulnerable.

I cover dealing with the collection process and collectors in the section "Preparing to answer collection calls" earlier in this chapter.

Calling in a credit counselor

On your own, you can get to a customer service manager, but the manager can't get around policy that is set by corporate headquarters. Very often, the powers that be set a special collection policy that applies only to the legitimate credit counseling agencies with which they've established a working relationship. Thus, when credit counselors get involved, they may be able to deal with a special department that handles only credit counseling accounts and is much more sympathetic than the line collector or manager. So in one leap, you escalate to high-level corporate policymakers.

Talk to a credit counselor from an independently accredited nonprofit agency. Chapter 4 explains how to pick one from a crowded field. The cost to find out what the agency can do for you is zero, free, nada, and the professional analysis of your financial dilemma and your options is valuable. As an intermediary, the credit counselor can deal with your creditors on your behalf and may be able to administer a favorable workout plan (often referred to as a *debt management plan*) while you follow a fairly strict budget.

Fair Isaac's FICO score doesn't take points away for using a credit counseling agency.

Referring the matter to your lawyer

A good lawyer can work wonders with the more complex legal situations people face from time to time. Like showing up to a gunfight with the second-fastest gun, hiring a so-so lawyer isn't worth the effort. The best attorney for you is one who specializes in debt law. The drawbacks: Lawyers are expensive, and after *you* start down a legal path, so do the collectors.

Get an attorney who specializes in representing debtors. These lawyers know the routine, have the right letters on file, and may even know the collection agency or company. Besides sheltering you from having to deal with collectors directly, an attorney helps slow down the freight train of events heading your way. He or she knows what is acceptable to the collector, collection lawyer, and judge (if things get that far). Plus, in today's complex debt sale and resale environment, an attorney can review your loan documents to make sure that your debt is enforceable.

Freeing Up Money to Pay a Collector

You owe, you owe, you owe. Where are you going to come up with the money to pay what you owe? In this section, I explore ways to reduce expenses and free up some funds to satisfy those creditors and collectors. I'm not going to lie to you: Cutting expenses is no fun! But after you've done it successfully and have money to make payments, you feel much better. The short-term sacrifice of retooling your spending and changing some old habits turns out to be well worth the effort when you're able to reduce or even eliminate your debt challenge.

Utilizing a spending plan

The best way I know to get the most out of every dollar you earn and set yourself on the road to credit recovery is to develop a detailed *spending plan*. A spending plan puts you in control of your finances, allowing you to decide how much money to spend on the stuff you want. A spending plan tells you just how much available cash you have to meet your obligations and allows you to set some aside to have fun, too. More important for this chapter, your spending plan lets you know how much you can afford to offer a collector or creditor to rid yourself of problem debt. For more on developing such a plan, turn to Chapter 18.

Creating a spending plan is easy, but putting it in writing is critical in determining what you need to change! You can find forms to help you at www.dummies.com/extras/creditrepair. If you still feel overwhelmed, Chapter 4 offers advice on choosing a good credit counselor who can help you with this process for free. (Believe it or not, there *are* people who love putting together spending plans.)

Cutting the fat from your monthly spending

The simplest way to cut expenses is much like cutting calories when you're on a diet. When slimming down, you eat the stuff that's lower in calories and skip the cake. When cutting expenses, you do things that cost less (use more coupons at the grocery store and plan meals to match what's on sale) and lay off the expensive stuff (cancel that reservation to the hot new restaurant in town).

Eating out is one of the biggest entertainment expenses for American families. If you add up your monthly expense for restaurant food, you may be shocked. Even that $4-a-day latte on the way to work adds up to more than $1,000 a year. Instead of eating out, eat in more often, and pack a lunch for work or school. Make eating at home fun by involving the entire family in preparing some of the dishes you'd order at that fancy restaurant. You'll be surprised to see your monthly spending on food shrink by as much as 25 to 50 percent.

You're not giving up doing something you love forever; you're only giving up these things until you resolve your current financial situation.

Finally, take a look at your monthly expenses and determine whether you can trim back anywhere.

The savings from cutting back on expenses may seem insignificant at first, but they add up quicker than you realize. And before you believe you can go another day without a grande triple latte, you'll have reached your goal.

Avoiding Collectors Altogether

If you're reading this chapter, not paying your bills on time may be what got you into a bad-credit situation in the first place. But making on-time payments for the amount agreed is the most important thing you can do to keep bad credit from getting worse. This section lays out specific ideas to help you pay your bills on time and keep creditors off your back.

Getting organized

Nothing is quite as frustrating as getting hit with a $25 or $35 late-payment fee on your credit card statement when you're trying to cut expenses. The good news is that a late payment doesn't necessarily cost you any more than the fee. Thanks to the Credit Card Accountability, Responsibility, and Disclosure Act of 2009 (CARD Act), you no longer have to worry about getting hit with a penalty interest rate for being one day late with a payment. New rules require a payment to be 60 days past due before the penalty interest rate kicks in, but a fee for making a late payment can still be charged as soon as it happens. Find out more about how the CARD Act benefits you in Chapter 19. Don't get me wrong, I still don't want you paying late and getting hit with large fees, but at least the punishment now better fits the crime.

Getting organized is a surefire way to avoid unnecessary late payments. Here are some options for getting organized:

- **Pay bills as soon as you receive them.** Make a pact with yourself to get the mail, sit down immediately, and write checks or go online to pay any bills you receive *that day.*

- **Mark a calendar with the due dates for all bills.** Allow at least a week for bills that you mail and a few days for bills that you pay online. Place the calendar where you'll see it every day so you don't miss any due dates.

- **Set up a filing system.** Place bills in folders or in due date order, marked with the day of the month that they need to be paid. The trick is remembering to place the bills in the folders or organizer and to check the folders on a daily or weekly basis.

Experiment, find a solution that works for you, and get those bills paid!

Stopping the paycheck-to-paycheck cycle

If you live paycheck to paycheck, you may find it difficult to pay all your bills on time and in full every month because money is so tight, especially when an emergency crops up and you have to pay for it out of money allocated for another bill. Consider these tips:

- **Start a savings account.** What does starting a savings account have to do with living paycheck to paycheck? Plenty. Without emergency savings, you won't be able to stop living paycheck to paycheck. How else do you have the money to replace the muffler or pay your child's doctor bill? Find out more about the importance of savings in Chapter 18.

- **Ask your creditor to change your due date.** You can request that your due date fall when you have the money to pay the bill in full and on time.

✔ **Look to your job to free up extra cash.** If you want to increase your cash flow and can't get a second (or third) job, you may not have to look far. Here are a couple of things you can do regarding your current job:

- **Check your payroll deductions.** If you get a hefty tax refund each year, see your employer and add withholding allowances on Form W-4 to increase your take-home pay. But if you'll end up writing a check to the IRS, don't do it.

  For assistance in figuring out the right number of withholding exemptions you should take, see the IRS Withholding Calculator at `www.irs.gov/individuals/article/0,,id=96196,00.html?portlet=4`.

- **Free up some money in your retirement plan.** I'm not suggesting that you take money out of the plan; doing so would result in some ugly penalties! But you can temporarily reduce or suspend your contributions to help close the gap. You can always make them up later.

Chapter 6

Working with Collectors, Lawyers, and the Courts to Manage Debt Obligations

I'm a jazz fan, and I write about credit. If I were to combine my enjoyment of music with my writing, I might come up with a tune called "Take the A+ Credit Train" or "Kind of Blue: Credit Repair." Jazz is very much about the human condition and the emotions we all feel. Credit gone bad can be an emotional roller coaster for those trapped on that train. If the world of credit has you singing the blues, this chapter shows you how to deal with the most stubborn debt obligations — charge-offs, judgments, garnishments, student loans, child support, and IRS debt.

Because these debts are so troublesome, they attract hustlers and scam artists who promise to bring you relief for a fraction of what you owe. Claims of settling an IRS debt for pennies or removing valid charge-offs from your credit report are as bogus as those claims made by the endless stream of Nigerian millionaires who ask for your bank account information and promise to share their millions in return.

In this chapter, I give you the skinny on charge-offs, judgments, and debts that can't be wiped out, even by a bankruptcy. I tell you how to minimize damage to your credit (yes, you'll probably have some) and give you strategies for controlling and even eliminating those sour credit notes before they make your credit score sound flat. So have a seat and listen up — the music is about to begin, and you don't want to miss a beat.

Getting a Handle on Charge-Offs

During the collections process, you come to some significant stopping points where unresolved matters take a turn for the worse. It's important for you to know when you've reached these points, how important they are, and what comes next. In this section, I discuss unpaid charge-offs and paid charge-offs. Understanding how these actions work and what you can do about them may save you credit score points and money in the long run.

So what is a charge-off?

When a collector or creditor *charges off* your account, its accountants, regulators, or audit firm have decided that your debt is very unlikely to be collected, so they don't allow it to remain on the books as an asset. For accounting and tax purposes, the creditor considers your account a loss, and your account is charged off the company's books.

Some generalizations hold true for many types of unsecured debts like credit cards or personal loans:

- ✔ If you pay a bill after its due date, it's technically late.

- ✔ Paying up to 30 days late is usually no big deal.

- ✔ After you get to 60 days late, you may face some fees and maybe an interest-rate increase.

- ✔ Being 90 days late can cost you more and often brings on the serious players in the collection department.

- ✔ If your account is between 120 and 180 days past due, your debt enters a new phase known as the *charge-off*.

A creditor charging off a debt in no way means that the debt is canceled, nor does any interest associated with the account stop accruing. No one is happy about this turn of events, and among those who should be the least happy is you. Why? Because you still owe the bill while fees and interest continue to accrue and your credit damage grows.

The rest of this section covers the credit-reporting difference between unpaid and paid charge-offs and explains why paying a charge-off is worthwhile even though it stays on your credit report. I also talk about the role a spending plan plays in getting debts and collectors under control.

Making sense of unpaid charge-offs

A debt charges off when it gets so old (typically 180 days past due) that its value is called into question (as is your sincerity in promising to pay it). If your creditor reports account histories to the credit bureaus, and most major ones do, the charge-off is considered a very serious negative.

When a debt charges off, you still owe it, and the creditor or collector will still attempt to collect it. The charge-off means only that the creditor no longer counts the debt as an asset. An unpaid charge-off causes more damage to your credit report than a paid one.

Until you pay what you owe, the debt is labeled an *unpaid charge-off* on your credit report. When an account first charges off, you may experience a lull in collection attempts. The reason is that the debt is probably changing hands from the collectors who were unsuccessful trying to save the account to those who want to save at least some part of it.

The most experienced collectors typically deal with charge-offs. These collectors have heard it all a thousand times before and have lasted in this business because they're efficient and effective. Make no mistake, collectors will try to collect the money due; however, after they determine that you either can't or won't pay, your account may be sold many times for decreasing amounts to increasingly aggressive collectors or lawyers whom you really don't want to deal with.

Making charge-off payments

Collectors try to make you promise to pay your debt in full or in a series of agreed-upon payments. They take promises very seriously, so you don't want to make and then break one. I suggest that you know for sure how much you can afford to pay monthly or in a lump-sum amount before you make any promises. The best way to do so is to prepare a budget (see Chapter 18) that takes into account all your income and expenses. Using this spending plan, you can identify areas to trim so that you can put more money toward paying off your debt. Without a plan, you'll only be guessing.

The key steps to making and carrying out a plan (see the "Household Budget Plan" form at www.dummies.com/extras/creditrepair for a sample of a spending plan outline) are as follows:

- ✔ List all your income.
- ✔ List all your expenses.
- ✔ Cut out or decrease as many of the expenses as you can.
- ✔ Increase your income if possible.
- ✔ Repeat this process until you have enough money to pay the bill in a reasonable amount of time.

Don't promise more than your plan says you can afford to pay just to get off the phone. Be sincere, explain how you arrived at your payment amount, and request that the collector send you a written agreement for this amount. When you receive the agreement, send the payment, and do so on time, every time. You can ask for a reduction in fees and interest when you negotiate the payment agreement, but a reduction in the amount owed is harder to get (see the next section).

A delinquent debt that hasn't reached charge-off status and is paid becomes current on your credit report, but a charge-off never does. An unpaid charge-off becomes a paid charge-off. A paid charge-off is much better for your credit than an unpaid charge-off because it indicates that you had a problem — perhaps a serious one — but that you eventually paid the bill. Hallelujah! Now you can get a little boost on your credit report, as shown in Figure 6-1, and you're on the way to obtaining credit at a more reasonable rate. Why? Simple: You've established that, although you may be a high-risk borrower, you do pay your bills in the end.

Equifax Credit Report for **Melissa Carson**
As of: 08/07/2014
Available until:
Confirmation #: 123456789

Report Does Not Update
Print Report

Negative Accounts Show All Account Details

Accounts that contain a negative account status. Accounts not paid as agreed generally remain on your credit file for 7 years from the date the account first became past due leading to the current not paid status. Late Payment History generally remains on your credit file for 7 years from the date of the late payment.

Open Accounts

Account Name	Account Number	Date Opened	Balance	Date Reported	Past Due	Account Status	Credit Limit
XYZ BANKCARD Show Details	4873664803 16XXXX	08/2001	$0	07/2014	$287	PAYS 91-120 DAYS	$8,000

Figure 6-1: An example of a paid charge-off trade line on a credit report.

Closed Accounts

Account Name	Account Number	Date Opened	Balance	Date Reported	Past Due	Account Status	Credit Limit
ABC LOANS Show Details	31667XXXX	09/1997	$0	09/2010	$0	CHARGE-OFF	$0

Coming to a Debt Settlement Agreement

When a creditor allows you to pay off your debt for less than you borrowed, you're *settling a debt*. And because no one likes to lose money, settling a debt is rarely easy. Although you may not have stiffed the lender completely, your actions did result in a loss of profit for the company, which isn't an incentive to do business with you in the future. Settling a debt also has a negative impact on your credit report, so you may want to consider what's more important to you, the money or your credit history. This section focuses on what happens if you agree to a debt settlement.

Considering a debt settlement offer

Some businesses may offer you a debt settlement option if they believe that they may never recover what you owe, or continuing collections becomes uneconomical, or they think that they can recover more by settling than by selling the debt to a third-party collection agency. Although a settled debt is considered paid, the settlement appears on your credit report for seven years from the date of the delinquency leading to the account charging off, and you may have a tax liability if the creditor forgives more than $600 of the debt.

The IRS considers the difference between the amount you owe and the amount you pay as income. I know; this thinking defies logic. But if your settlement amount allows for more than $600 to go unpaid, you're responsible for paying income taxes on that amount. For example, if you owe $5,000 and you work out a settlement where you pay only $3,000, the $2,000 that was forgiven becomes taxable income on your next tax return. As the saying goes, only two things in life are certain — and one of them is taxes!

If you decide on debt settlement as a payment resolution, I strongly advise you to get the settlement terms in writing and read them carefully before you send in a penny. You need to be on your guard when you're negotiating a settlement or if you've been offered one. You're dealing with people who know settlements better than you do and who don't mind if you make a mistake that is to their advantage and results in more of what you owe being collected. After you send in the money, you have no leverage with the collector, and any promises that aren't in the written agreement are unlikely to be kept.

Hiring a debt settlement firm

You're likely to see and hear advertisements for debt settlement firms, and you may even be contacted by one. These companies have come to the attention of the Federal Trade Commission (FTC) because most of them charge large fees and provide limited results for consumers. New FTC regulations have curbed some of the abuses, but I still recommend that you try to settle on your own or use an attorney rather than a debt settlement firm. However, if you want to hire a settlement company, keep these points in mind:

- ✔ Make sure that the company is a member of the Association of Settlement Companies (TASC).
- ✔ Don't pay an upfront fee. Companies are required to settle at least one account before charging the consumer.
- ✔ Don't sign anything if you feel pressured to do so.

Consider running any offer by an attorney. Doing so will cost you money, but it may save you big if you avoid making a mistake or if only a bankruptcy can solve your problem. A consumer debt goes away in a bankruptcy; an IRS debt from a settlement doesn't.

Reaching expiration dates on debts

Sometimes, procrastination has a silver lining. When a debt reaches a certain age (as defined by the statutes of your state of residence), it's no longer collectible in a court of law. Each state has its own statute of limitations rules. Check out Chapter 5 for more on expired debts and statutes of limitations.

Finding Out about Judgments and What They Mean to You

An unpaid charge-off often makes its way to a lawyer sooner or later. A collection attorney may take your case to court, you may have a judgment entered against you, you'll lose a day to court and incur additional legal expenses, and maybe — if it's just not your day — your wages will be garnished for up to 25 percent of your take-home pay. This is about as much fun as a legal colonoscopy. If you get a court summons for a hearing on a debt issue, answer it! Read on for all the details.

The legal side of the collection process typically begins with a letter. After months of phone assaults, a simple mute letter is easy to ignore. Don't! The letter is a summons telling you that a court hearing will be held on a certain date in a certain place (see Figure 6-2). I strongly suggest that you show up with a plan and, if possible, an attorney. A good plan includes

- ✔ A short explanation of why you haven't paid
- ✔ Any disputes about the bill or collection process so far
- ✔ A plan to repay the debt on terms you can afford
- ✔ Documentation that shows why you can't afford more

SUM-120

ATTORNEY OR PARTY WITHOUT ATTORNEY (Name, State Bar number, and address):	FOR COURT USE ONLY *(SOLO PARA USO DE LA CORTE)*

TELEPHONE NO.:   FAX NO. *(Optional)*:

E-MAIL ADDRESS *(Optional)*:

ATTORNEY FOR *(Name)*:

SUPERIOR COURT OF CALIFORNIA, COUNTY OF

STREET ADDRESS:

MAILING ADDRESS:

CITY AND ZIP CODE:

BRANCH NAME:

PLAINTIFF:

DEFENDANT:

SUMMONS (JOINT DEBTOR) *(CITACIÓN (DEUDOR CONJUNTO))*	CASE NUMBER: *(Número del Caso)*:

NOTICE! You have been sued. The court may decide against you without your being heard unless you respond within 30 days. Read the information below.

  You have 30 CALENDAR DAYS after this summons and legal papers are served on you to file a written response at this court and have a copy served on the plaintiff. A letter or phone call will not protect you. Your written response must be in proper legal form if you want the court to hear your case. There may be a court form that you can use for your response. You can find these court forms and more information at the California Courts Online Self-Help Center (www.courtinfo.ca.gov/selfhelp), your county law library, or the courthouse nearest you. If you cannot pay the filing fee, ask the court clerk for a fee waiver form. If you do not file your response on time, you may lose the case by default, and your wages, money, and property may be taken without further warning from the court.

  There are other legal requirements. You may want to call an attorney right away. If you do not know an attorney, you may want to call an attorney referral service. If you cannot afford an attorney, you may be eligible for free legal services from a nonprofit legal services program. You can locate these nonprofit groups at the California Legal Services Web site (www.lawhelpcalifornia.org), the California Courts Online Self-Help Center (www.courtinfo.ca.gov/selfhelp), or by contacting your local court or county bar association. **NOTE:** The court has a statutory lien for waived fees and costs on any settlement or arbitration award of $10,000 or more in a civil case. The court's lien must be paid before the court will dismiss the case.

¡AVISO! Lo han demandado. Si no responde dentro de 30 días, la corte puede decidir en su contra sin escuchar su versión. Lea la información a continuación.

  Tiene 30 DÍAS DE CALENDARIO después de que le entreguen esta citación y papeles legales para presentar una respuesta por escrito en esta corte y hacer que se entregue una copia al demandante. Una carta o una llamada telefónica no lo protegen. Su respuesta por escrito tiene que estar en formato legal correcto si desea que procesen su caso en la corte. Es posible que haya un formulario que usted pueda usar para su respuesta. Puede encontrar estos formularios de la corte y más información en el Centro de Ayuda de las Cortes de California (www.sucorte.ca.gov), en la biblioteca de leyes de su condado o en la corte que le quede más cerca. Si no puede pagar la cuota de presentación, pida al secretario de la corte que le dé un formulario de exención de pago de cuotas. Si no presenta su respuesta a tiempo, puede perder el caso por incumplimiento y la corte le podrá quitar su sueldo, dinero y bienes sin más advertencia.

  Hay otros requisitos legales. Es recomendable que llame a un abogado inmediatamente. Si no conoce a un abogado, puede llamar a un servicio de remisión a abogados. Si no puede pagar a un abogado, es posible que cumpla con los requisitos para obtener servicios legales gratuitos de un programa de servicios legales sin fines de lucro. Puede encontrar estos grupos sin fines de lucro en el sitio web de California Legal Services, (www.lawhelpcalifornia.org), en el Centro de Ayuda de las Cortes de California, (www.sucorte.ca.gov) o poniéndose en contacto con la corte o el colegio de abogados locales. AVISO: Por ley, la corte tiene derecho a reclamar las cuotas y los costos exentos por imponer un gravamen sobre cualquier recuperación de $10,000 ó más de valor recibida mediante un acuerdo o una concesión de arbitraje en un caso de derecho civil. Tiene que pagar el gravamen de la corte antes de que la corte pueda desechar el caso.

1. TO THE DEFENDANT *(name)*:
    (AL DEMANDADO):
      You are hereby directed to file in this court, within **30 days** after this summons is served on you, a written response to the Declaration or Affidavit accompanying this summons, giving any legal reason why you should not be required to pay the unpaid amount of: $ on the judgment rendered by this court on *(date)*:
      against *(name each)*:

Date: Clerk, by   , Deputy
(Fecha)   *(Secretario)*   *(Adjunto)*

(For proof of service of this summons, use Proof of Service of Summons (form POS-010).)
(Para prueba de entrega de esta citatión use el formulario Proof of Service of Summons, (POS-010)).

(SEAL)

2. **NOTICE TO THE PERSON SERVED:** You are served
  a. ☐ as an individual defendant.
  b. ☐ as the person sued under the fictitious name of *(specify)*:

  c. ☐ on behalf of *(specify)*:
     under: ☐ CCP 416.10 (corporation)   ☐ CCP 416.60 (minor)
            ☐ CCP 416.20 (defunct corporation) ☐ CCP 416.70 (conservatee)
            ☐ CCP 416.40 (association or partnership) ☐ CCP 416.90 (authorized person)
            ☐ other *(specify)*:

  d. ☐ by personal delivery on *(date)*:

Page 1 of 1

Form Adopted for Mandatory Use Judicial Council of California SUM-120 [Rev. July 1, 2009]	**SUMMONS (JOINT DEBTOR)**	Code of Civil Procedure § 989 www.courtinfo.ca.gov

Figure 6-2: A sample court summons letter.

If the debt is valid (not in dispute or belonging to someone else) and hasn't been collected, the court generally issues an order confirming that you owe money and commanding you to pay it. This order is called a *judgment,* and it involves legal fees, public record information on your credit report, and dealing with a system that doesn't fool around. Figure 6-3 shows a copy of a typical judgment from a hearing on a debt issue. If you get one of these, you need to wake up and get a repayment plan going. If you *dishonor,* or ignore, a judgment, the next step could be wage garnishment. (Check out the section "Understanding Wage Garnishments" later in this chapter for more info.)

	CIV-130
ATTORNEY OR PARTY WITHOUT ATTORNEY *(Name, State Bar number, and address):*	*FOR COURT USE ONLY*

TELEPHONE NO.:   FAX NO. *(Optional):*

E-MAIL ADDRESS *(Optional):*

ATTORNEY FOR *(Name):*

SUPERIOR COURT OF CALIFORNIA, COUNTY OF

STREET ADDRESS:

MAILING ADDRESS:

CITY AND ZIP CODE:

BRANCH NAME:

PLAINTIFF/PETITIONER:

DEFENDANT/RESPONDENT:

NOTICE OF ENTRY OF JUDGMENT OR ORDER

CASE NUMBER:

(Check one): ☐ **UNLIMITED CASE** (Amount demanded exceeded $25,000)   ☐ **LIMITED CASE** (Amount demanded was $25,000 or less)

TO ALL PARTIES :

1. A judgment, decree, or order was entered in this action on *(date):*

2. A copy of the judgment, decree, or order is attached to this notice.

Date:

(TYPE OR PRINT NAME OF ☐ ATTORNEY ☐ PARTY WITHOUT ATTORNEY)   (SIGNATURE)

Page 1 of 2

Form Approved for Optional Use
Judicial Council of California
CIV-130 [New January 1, 2010]

NOTICE OF ENTRY OF JUDGMENT OR ORDER

www.courtinfo.ca.gov

Figure 6-3:
A sample court judgment letter.

The judgment itself doesn't force you to pay the debt. It does, however, set you up for execution — not execution as in the electric chair, but a *judgment execution.* If you receive a judgment and you still don't pay, the lender can go back to the judge and get an execution order. Depending on the laws in your state, the order allows the creditor to

- ✔ Garnish your wages up to 25 percent. (See the next section for more on wage garnishments.)

- ✔ Place a lien on your home or other property for the amount owed. A lien is like having another mortgage on the property. Before the property can be sold or mortgaged, the lien has to be paid off.

- ✔ Repossess any property involved with the debt you owe (for example, your furniture if it's a furniture loan).

Why some lenders don't care about your judgments — and why you should

Some lenders won't consider you for a loan unless you have great credit. Others don't care if you have judgments or a bankruptcy against you. You may consider such lenders saints to overlook a proven risk. Fact is, they probably don't mind the risk because they charge enough interest to make money anyway. Or they expect you to default and are prepared to take aggressive collection actions when you do.

Groucho Marx said it best when he quipped, "I don't care to belong to a club that accepts people like me as members." You really don't want a loan from a company that would lend money to people with active unpaid judgments against them.

A judgment is a very serious development in the collection process. At this point, many people seriously consider bankruptcy to wipe out their debts. Unfortunately, for many people who earn above the median income in their states, bankruptcy is no longer an attractive option (see Chapter 19). This is one of the reasons I think consulting a professional early in the game makes a lot of sense. If you don't have the option to file bankruptcy, you want to know as soon as possible.

Understanding Wage Garnishments

If you receive a judgment (see the preceding section) and still don't or can't pay the debt, your employer may be court-ordered to garnish part of your paycheck to pay off your creditor. After the court orders a wage garnishment, certain rules must be followed as defined in the Consumer Credit Protection Act (CCPA). This section focuses on the main points, including how you can avoid wage garnishments. Remember that state law can take precedence over federal law, but only if the amounts allowed for garnishment are lower.

Dodging wage garnishments

Before anyone can garnish your wages, a judgment from a court of law is necessary. You get a summons to appear in court to defend yourself against a suit for payment brought by the owner of your debt. If a judgment is issued and the debt remains unpaid, the creditor can go back to court and execute the judgment to push matters to the next stage, which may include having your wages garnished. You receive another summons if this happens.

Each state has its own debt collection laws. Some states permit a creditor to garnish your wages; others don't. Some states exempt large amounts or categories of assets from attachment or seizure by a creditor to pay your debt. Others may force you to sell possessions to satisfy a judgment. The best source for up-to-date information is your state's consumer protection office. You can find a Directory of State and Local Consumer Agencies at `consumeraction.gov/state.shtml`.

In many cases, you can avoid wage garnishments by doing the following:

- **Keep complete records of the collection process.** Be sure to keep a record of names, dates, copies of correspondence, summaries of conversations, and any agreements or disputes.

- **Show up in court when you're supposed to.** Go to the hearings and speak up! If you have a reasonable story to tell the judge and a reasonable offer to make, you may be surprised at the result. The judge won't be happy that a collector is wasting his valuable time with a case that should have been settled out of court.

State law may set garnishment limits lower than the federal maximum. In that case, the state law supersedes the federal law. The CCPA says that your boss can't fire you for having a garnishment. However, the CCPA doesn't provide this protection for multiple wage garnishments. You can find much more information on wage garnishments by calling the U.S. Department of Labor at 866-487-9243 or by visiting `www.dol.gov/dol/topic/wages/index.htm` and clicking on the Garnishment tab.

CCPA protections don't apply to the following types of nondischargeable debts:

- **Child support and alimony:** The court has little sympathy in matters of back support payments. The garnishment law allows up to 50 percent of your disposable earnings to be garnished for child support and alimony if you're supporting another spouse or child and up to 60 percent if you're not. An additional 5 percent may be garnished for support payments that are more than 12 weeks in arrears.

- **Debts owed to the government:** The garnishment restrictions don't apply to certain bankruptcy court orders or to debts related to federal or state taxes. A consumer debt such as a credit card or personal loan can be garnished up to 15 percent and a student loan up to 10 percent. If you're being garnished for more than one debt, you're subject to a 25 percent maximum. If a state's wage garnishment law differs from the CCPA, the law that results in the smaller garnishment must be observed.

Figuring out how much can be garnished

After your creditor is granted a judgment, you may wonder how much the court can order your employer to garnish from your wages. The court uses *disposable earnings* (the amount left after legally required deductions like taxes, FICA, mandatory retirement withholding, and unemployment insurance) to figure your garnishment amount.

Whether you have one or more garnishments, the law sets the maximum amount that your employer may garnish in any workweek or pay period. Exceptions are made for court-ordered support, bankruptcy, or state or federal tax. The amount may not exceed the lesser of two figures: 25 percent of your disposable earnings or the amount by which your disposable earnings are greater than 30 times the federal minimum wage (currently $7.25 an hour). See Table 6-1 for calculations of the latter.

Table 6-1 Maximum Garnishment of Disposable Earnings Under Normal Circumstances* for the $7.25 Federal Minimum Wage

Weekly	Biweekly	Semimonthly	Monthly
$217.50 or less: none	$435.00 or less: none	$471.25 or less: none	$942.50 or less: none
More than $217.50 but less than $290.00: amount above $217.50	More than $435.00 but less than $580.00: amount above $435.00	More than $471.25 but less than $628.33: amount above $471.25	More than $942.50 but less than $1,256.67: amount above $942.50
$290.00 or more: maximum 25%	$580.00 or more: maximum 25%	$628.33 or more: maximum 25%	$1,256.66 or more: maximum 25%

These restrictions don't apply to garnishments for child and/or spousal support, bankruptcy, or actions to recover state or federal taxes. Source: U.S. Department of Labor www.dol.gov/whd/regs/compliance/whdfs30.pdf.

Stating Your Case in Court

Asking for time off from work to go to court can be intimidating, embarrassing, and expensive. Most creditors count on this and are very happy if you don't show up. Why? Because without you there to object, they'll get just about anything they want from the judge. I strongly suggest that you show up and tell the judge your side of the story. Be sure to bring

✔ Statements from the account in question to make sure that the document filed with the court contains no mistakes or unwarranted additions.

✔ Records of phone calls and written correspondence with the creditor to document that you've been trying to come to an agreement.

✔ A budget of your expenses and income to support a payment plan you can afford so the judge can see that your offer is serious.

You can represent yourself, but you're at a disadvantage if you do. Trust me: Your creditor is intimately familiar with the ins and outs of the court process. If you can afford it, get an attorney. If you can't, go to court anyway; your presence and your genuine commitment to finding a workable way to repay your debt may be all you need.

Use your records to show the court that you've made a good-faith effort to propose the best settlement you can afford. Show that you've offered a reasonable repayment plan based on your means, but that it was refused. If you went to a credit counselor along the way, mention it; if you can say that the counselor thought your proposed settlement was reasonable, all the better. Of course, none of this reasonable stuff applies to overdue child support; unless your income has changed for the worse, you have to pay as agreed.

The following list shows the progression of the process for collections that have gone to an attorney for legal action:

1. **You receive a demand letter from an attorney demanding payment.**

   This letter comes in addition to all the letters you may have received from the creditor or collector. The demand letter gives you one last chance to try to resolve the problem before court action begins.

2. **A suit is filed in court, often within 10 to 30 days of the date of the demand letter.**

   This suit alerts the court to the situation and again demands payment.

3. **You get served with a summons.**

   You get a summons from the court to respond by a certain date and time.

4. **If you don't answer the summons, the attorney can file for a default judgment.**

   If the court enters a default judgment in the matter, the creditor wins. You lose.

5. **If you do file an answer, the discovery process begins, and a trial date is set.**

When you respond to the suit, be sure to explain any discrepancies in the creditor's claims. If you can't, then be sure to show up in court on the hearing date with all your documentation and your lawyer if possible.

6. **If a judgment is awarded and not paid by the due date, the attorney attempts to locate and verify your assets.**

The attorney initiates court-ordered bank levies, garnishment orders, liens, and so on to satisfy the judgment.

Understanding what happens may help demystify the process and remove one more obstacle that may keep you from reacting until it's too late.

Managing IRS Debts, Student Loans, and Unpaid Child Support

IRS debts, student loans, and unpaid child support are in a special class of debts that aren't dischargeable in a bankruptcy in most cases and must be paid. I cover them in the following sections.

Handling IRS debts

An IRS debt can be one of the easiest debt situations to deal with. First, the IRS knows that *you* know who's in control, so the IRS doesn't need to intimidate you with strong-arm tactics to get your attention. Second, the IRS isn't chasing down its own money — it's chasing down taxpayer money. And third, IRS employees don't get a bonus for collecting a debt. You can probably negotiate a reasonable repayment plan with the IRS that you can manage over time.

Figure 6-4 shows a sample IRS repayment form that covers repayment plans. The full version of Form 9465 is at `www.dummies.com/extras/creditrepair`. As you can see, it's not scary, so don't wait too long before you act.

If you have an accountant, I suggest that you bring him or her along when you meet with the IRS. Your accountant may be able to calmly explain why you shouldn't owe taxes on some income or why you should get certain deductions.

IRS debts just keep growing with age. In fact, if you delay too long, the IRS pulls any tax refunds you have coming and directs the money into the treasury until the debt is paid. Just what you wanted to hear, huh?

REMEMBER

It's not unusual for the IRS to be very slow in notifying the credit bureaus or clearing any liens on your property records when you've paid your bill. Keep good records of payments and discharges, and follow up by checking your credit report and, if appropriate, the property records at your local town hall. Make sure that the records are updated, or you may miss an opportunity to sell your home because it has a big fat lien on it that shouldn't be there.

Form **9465** (Rev. December 2012) Department of the Treasury Internal Revenue Service	**Installment Agreement Request** ▶ Information about Form 9465 and its separate instructions is at *www.irs.gov/form9465*. ▶ If you are filing this form with your tax return, attach it to the front of the return. ▶ See separate instructions.	OMB No. 1545-0074

Tip: If you owe less than $50,000, you may be able to establish an installment agreement on-line, even if you have not yet received a bill for your taxes. Go to IRS.gov to apply to pay on-line.

Caution: *Do not file this form if you are currently making payments on an installment agreement or can pay your balance in full within 120 days. Instead, call 1-800-829-1040. If you are in bankruptcy or we have accepted your offer-in-compromise, see* **Bankruptcy or offer-in-compromise,** *in the instructions.*

This request is for Form(s) (for example, Form 1040 or Form 1040EZ) ▶ _____ and for tax year(s) (for example, 2011 and 2012) ▶ _____

1 Your first name and initial | Last name | Your social security number

If a joint return, spouse's first name and initial | Last name | Spouse's social security number

Current address (number and street). If you have a P.O. box and no home delivery, enter your box number. | Apt. number

City, town or post office, state, and ZIP code. If a foreign address, enter city, province or state, and country. Follow the country's practice for entering the postal code.

2 If this address is new since you filed your last tax return, check here . . . . ▶ ☐

3 _____ Your home phone number   Best time for us to call
4 _____ Your work phone number   Ext.   Best time for us to call

5 Name of your bank or other financial institution:
Address
City, state, and ZIP code

6 Your employer's name:
Address
City, state, and ZIP code

7 Enter the total amount you owe as shown on your tax return(s) (or notice(s))
Note: If the amount on line 7 is greater than $25,000 but not more than $50,000, you **must** complete line 11. If you owe more than $50,000, complete Form 433-F and attach it to your request. See instructions . . . . | **7**

8 Enter the amount of any payment you are making with your tax return(s) (or notice(s)). See instructions | **8**

9 Enter the amount you can pay each month. **Make your payments as large as possible to limit interest and penalty charges.** The charges will continue until you pay in full. If no payment amount is listed on line 9, or the proposed payment does not meet our streamlined processing criteria, a payment will be determined for you by dividing the balance due by 72 months . . . . | **9**

10 Enter the date you want to make your payment each month. **Do not** enter a date later than the 28th ▶

11 If you want to make your payments by electronic funds withdrawal from your checking account, see the instructions and fill in lines 11a and 11b. This is the most convenient way to make your payments and it will ensure that they are made on time.
▶ **a** Routing number
▶ **b** Account number

I authorize the U.S. Treasury and its designated Financial Agent to initiate a monthly ACH debit (electronic withdrawal) entry to the financial institution account indicated for payments of my Federal taxes owed, and the financial institution to debit the entry to this account. This authorization is to remain in full force and effect until I notify the U.S. Treasury Financial Agent to terminate the authorization. To revoke payment, I must contact the U.S. Treasury Financial Agent at **1-800-829-1040** no later than 14 business days prior to the payment (settlement) date. I also authorize the financial institutions involved in the processing of the electronic payments of taxes to receive confidential information necessary to answer inquiries and resolve issues related to the payments.

Your signature | Date | Spouse's signature. If a joint return, **both** must sign. | Date

For Privacy Act and Paperwork Reduction Act Notice, see instructions.   Cat. No. 14842Y   Form **9465** (Rev. 12-2012)

Figure 6-4: A sample IRS repayment form.

Educating yourself about student loans

Student loan collections used to be a joke, but no one is laughing anymore. The bankruptcy law has granted student loans nondischargeable status, and lenders pursue delinquencies forever. Depending on how many loans are involved — you may have as many as one for each semester you were in school — the effect on your credit of being in default (*default* is defined differently for different types of loans; check with your lender to determine when your loan enters into default) varies from bad to nuclear meltdown. A lot of people ask me if they owe the money even if they didn't graduate or finish a semester. The answer is yes. You borrowed and spent the money, and you need to repay it. What you did with it is of no interest (no pun intended) to the lender. In fact, if you die while attending school, your estate (or your parents' estate if they cosigned the loan) often still owes the debt.

A student loan isn't secured with collateral in the normal sense of the word. When you leave school, whether you graduate or not, certain situations, such as economic hardship or unemployment, may enable you to defer payment for a period of time. See the section "Identifying the Best Repayment Option for Your Situation" in Chapter 22 for details.

However, after your student loan is in default, you lose your opportunity to defer payment. To make matters worse, you may have to pay back the loan all at once unless you come up with an acceptable repayment scheme. You're also unable to receive further student aid, your school may withhold your transcripts, your state and federal income tax refunds may be taken to offset the loan amounts, and your wages (if and when you get a job) may be *attached* or *garnished*. (See the "Understanding Wage Garnishments" section earlier in this chapter.)

Financial aid: The ultimate gamble?

It all seems so worthwhile: a college or tech-school education, the promise of a good job, and the great feeling you get from doing the right/smart thing. But a student loan is a big gamble, and I want you to understand that if anything goes wrong, you lose. Student loans are so high-risk that many have to be guaranteed by the government, and none of them are dischargeable in a bankruptcy under ordinary circumstances. If you fail to graduate for any reason, even because of illness or some other legitimate problem . . . if you can't find a job in your chosen profession or need to settle for a lower-paying job . . . if you decide that medical school isn't for you . . . no matter the reason, you still owe the money, and paying off the loan may take decades. That's a gamble that millions take every year. Some win and some lose. Look for alternative ways to pay for schooling, or consider community college before taking on the big debt of a big-name school.

Following are some repayment options:

- **Normal repayment:** You make principal and interest payments each month.

- **Graduated repayment:** You make lower payments at the beginning, and your payments increase at specified intervals for the life of your loan.

- **Income-based repayment:** Your monthly payments are based on a percentage of your monthly gross income (for Stafford, PLUS, and Smart loans and federally consolidated loans).

- **Extended repayment:** Your repayment term is lengthened.

- **Consolidation:** Your federal loans are refinanced into a single, fixed loan with a long payback period.

- **Serialization:** You consolidate only the payments into a single payment but retain the original terms and interest rates on all your loans.

See `studentaid.ed.gov/repay-loans/understand/plans` for more information.

If you can't pay back your loans as originally hoped, use all options available to you to defer your loans for as long as possible. However, after you've exhausted your deferments, you'll be in default if you don't agree to a new repayment plan. Depending on how your loans were issued, what may seem like a single loan may be as many as eight or ten individual loans (one per semester), because each loan is reported separately. So the loans may show up as eight or ten separate trade lines in your credit report. If you end up in default, you may get ten times the negative information on your credit report you expect, and your credit score may crash from all those negative individual loan entries.

For multiple student loans, consider the Direct Consolidation Loans program. The program provides borrowers who have at least one up-to-date federal student loan the opportunity to consolidate into a single monthly payment. You may also extend the repayment term on a student loan, which can reduce your monthly payment. Eligible loans include the Stafford, PLUS, Perkins, Health Profession, Health Education, and Nursing student loans. You may also be able to consolidate most defaulted education loans if you can make satisfactory repayment arrangements with the current holders or agree to repay the new Direct Consolidation Loan under an Income Contingent Repayment (ICR) plan. For information on the Direct Consolidation Loans program, see `www.loanconsolidation.ed.gov`.

Delinquent student loans can be a big hiring issue. Getting a job with bad credit is a lot harder if your employer pulls a credit report to see whether you're reliable and stable. If you have any unpaid loans, explain early in the hiring process why you haven't paid them and that you'll make good on a loan repayment plan as soon as you get a paycheck.

Working with a student loan creditor is essential to moving on with a normal life. Dealing with these folks is very much like dealing with the IRS: You need to get in contact, have a plan, make an offer to repay the loan, and follow through. See "Dealing with the Collection Process" in Chapter 22 for more information.

Putting your kids first: Child support

Unpaid child support is another category of debt that lives as long as you do. Under the bankruptcy law, child-support obligations can't be discharged. And the courts provide custodial parents the names of collection agencies that specialize in child-support debt, so your ex can easily work with a collection agency to come after you for what you owe.

Child-support debt can result in a criminal charge and jail time if you continue not to pay it. The decision whether to seek prosecution in nonsupport cases rests with your state's attorney general. Courts have no sense of humor when it comes to child-support debt. You really don't want such debt hanging over you. Plus, these debts make a very bad impression on employers. Make paying off such debt your number-one priority.

Part II

Reducing Credit Damage from Major Setbacks

Five Things to Consider Before Filing for Bankruptcy

- ✔ **Be sure that bankruptcy will solve your financial crisis.** Getting rid of all your debts and making collectors go away may solve one problem, but if the real problem is too much spending and not enough income, declaring bankruptcy won't help you for very long.

- ✔ **Understand bankruptcy's effects on your goals.** Ask yourself how this decision will affect your chances of buying a home, getting married or divorced, or getting a job. Bankruptcy is a big step, and its consequences affect you for years.

- ✔ **Consider all your options.** Make a list of other ways to deal with your debts. Can you increase your income? Reduce your expenses? Stretch out your payments? Sell some possessions to pay your bills until your situation improves?

- ✔ **Talk to a good credit counselor.** You have to meet with a credit counselor anyway within six months of filing for bankruptcy. Expect this visit to give you options, an analysis of your spending and income, and an action plan. This consultation goes a long way toward answering the question of whether bankruptcy will help you.

- ✔ **Talk to your creditors.** Seriously. If you're considering a bankruptcy, let your lenders know and ask if they can offer you a repayment plan. Keep in mind that you have to be able to afford this plan.

For more tips on avoiding bankruptcy, go to www.dummies.com/extras/creditrepair.

In this part . . .

- ✔ Understand how to recover from all-too-common credit catastrophes.

- ✔ Explore your options before, during, and after a foreclosure, and know where you can get help.

- ✔ Understand the pros and cons of bankruptcy.

- ✔ Recognize identity theft when it happens, and take steps to minimize the effects.

Chapter 7

Reducing Credit Damage in a Mortgage Crisis

In This Chapter

▶ Getting acquainted with the specific rules of mortgages

▶ Finding help for your delinquent mortgage

▶ Facing grave mortgage problems, including foreclosure

▶ Coping with a deficiency balance

▶ Beefing up your credit before a default

*L*ittle has changed more over the last few years than the economics and potential risks of homeownership. What about staying in a home that's worth less than what you paid for it? What are your options if it's worth less than what you owe on the mortgage? And what are the risks to your credit if you have a default? What used to be a no-brainer decision has become more complicated than anyone could have imagined. Millions of people are asking these questions today. This chapter helps you find the answers. Here I cover legal obligations, taxes, credit, and the long arms of credit scores and reports.

This chapter is an important one for every homeowner who's under financial stress. Money, credit, self-esteem, and the very roof over your family's head are at stake when a mortgage crisis looms. This chapter provides you with the advice you need to make the best decision for your situation. Getting help and getting it early is critical. Fortunately, help *is* available, and this chapter guides you through the process of getting what you need.

Assessing the Damage from a Mortgage Meltdown

Credit score misinformation is everywhere. What you don't know can and will hurt you if what you don't know is that your credit report and score have been seriously damaged. If you're trying to assess the damage to your score from a mortgage meltdown or even just a mild mortgage sunburn, having the best information available is important. That's what this section is all about.

Figure 7-1 illustrates the effects of various types of mortgage defaults on your credit score. These charts show the relative damage from mortgage problems, underscoring how important it is to resolve any problems as quickly and amicably as possible.

Impact to FICO Score

	Consumer A	Consumer B	Consumer C
Starting FICO® Score	~680	~720	~780
FICO® Score after these events:			
30 days late on mortgage	600-620	630-650	670-690
90 days late on mortgage	600-620	610-630	650-670
Short sale / deed-in-lieu / settlement (no deficiency balance)	610-630	605-625	655-675
Short sale (with deficiency balance)	575-595	570-590	620-640
Foreclosure	575-595	570-590	620-640
Bankruptcy	530-550	525-545	540-560

Estimated Time for FICO Score to Fully Recover

	Consumer A	Consumer B	Consumer C
Starting FICO® Score	~680	~720	~780
Time for FICO® Score to recover after these events:			
30 days late on mortgage	~9 months	~2.5 years	~3 years
90 days late on mortgage	~9 months	~3 years	~7 years
Short sale / deed-in-lieu / settlement (no deficiency balance)	~3 years	~7 years	~7 years
Short sale (with deficiency balance)	~3 years	~7 years	~7 years
Foreclosure	~3 years	~7 years	~7 years
Bankruptcy	~5 years	~7-10 years	~7-10 years

Figure 7-1: Credit score damage.

Note: Estimates assume all else held constant over time (e.g., no new account openings, no new delinquency, similar outstanding debt).

Courtesy of FICO

Note: The terms *default, delinquency,* and *negative event* tend to mean the same thing. Strictly speaking, being *delinquent* (late on a payment) leads to a *default* (based on the legal terms in your mortgage documents). Both are negative credit events that you don't want to experience.

People with great credit who default on a mortgage, like Consumer C, see a greater credit-score point drop than those whose credit isn't so great, like Consumer A. Why? Because a good score has to fall farther in order to end up at the lower point level that indicates serious credit problems. In general, the higher your starting score, the longer it takes for your score to fully recover from the damage.

A few items stand out in the list of credit and loan negatives in Figure 7-1. Delinquencies and some actions that result in your home being taken back by the lender *(deed-in-lieu)* or sold under distress (as in a *short sale*) cost you big points. However, there's no significant difference in credit-score impact between a short sale, a deed-in-lieu, and a settlement. Mega point drops in your credit score tend to occur when the lender loses money in addition to your being in default, such as in the event of a short sale or a foreclosure, both of which cost the bank money. But the worst and longest lasting of all injury to your credit occurs when you file for bankruptcy. Unlike the other, lesser defaults, a bankruptcy can stay on your credit report for up to ten years.

In addition to credit score penalties, you need to take the collateral damage into consideration:

- ✔ Although a score may *begin* to improve sooner, it can take up to seven to ten years to *fully* recover.

- ✔ Fannie Mae (the Federal National Mortgage Association) is the nation's largest mortgage buyer. It buys and then resells mortgages on Wall Street, helping to keep mortgage interest rates low. Fannie excludes borrowers who've gone through a foreclosure from obtaining a Fannie-backed loan for seven years.

- ✔ Fannie Mae won't accept a mortgage from a person who has had a mortgage delinquency in the last 12 months.

- ✔ If you can't get a Fannie Mae loan, you may have to take a nonconforming loan, which may require expensive mortgage insurance premiums and, for those with lower credit scores, higher interest rates and a larger down payment.

Understanding How Mortgages Differ from Other Loans

Mortgages differ from other consumer loans partly because of their size — a lot of money is on the line — and partly because they're backed by what historically has been the gold standard in collateral: your home. With more at risk, the stakes are greater. Furthermore, mortgages are not only underwritten differently from other types of credit but also have a different collection process, generally called the *foreclosure process*. When you default on a mortgage, the lender *forecloses,* or terminates the mortgage, and your house is taken away from you.

From a credit-score and credit-reporting standpoint, mortgage defaults and foreclosures are among the most serious negatives out there, with the exception of bankruptcy.

Obviously, a foreclosure puts a serious hit on your credit score and history. To help you minimize this hit, this section gives you an overview of how mortgages differ from typical credit and how mortgages and credit go hand in hand. Here you can find valuable information to help you understand when a late mortgage payment can quickly cause you problems and what you can do to get help.

Spotting a foreclosure on the horizon

A lender has a lot of money on the line with your mortgage, and the longer you're delinquent, the greater the risk that the lender will lose money on a defaulted loan. The result is that a mortgage lender has a much lower tolerance for delinquency than, say, a credit card issuer. For example, as long as you're less than 180 days past due on a credit card, it's not the end of the world. Generally, you can just pay the minimum due along with a late fee and pick up where you left off. If you're really lucky, you may get the lender to waive the late fee and not report the delinquency. For a mortgage, however, being just 60 days late puts you well on your way to the edge of a cliff, and you may not even be aware of it.

The key number to avoid in a mortgage delinquency is 90 days late. After 90 days, unless you get some help or work out an arrangement, the mortgage servicer generally requires the entire amount that is overdue (the *arrearage*) to be paid at once and may not accept partial payments. A 90-day mortgage delinquency on a credit report is very serious. To make matters worse, many people don't understand when the 90 days is up. The time frame isn't as simple as you may think, so I cover it in detail in the next section.

Mortgage servicers don't call you at work or at night, and they don't yell or threaten you over the phone. On the contrary, the tone of their messages (often letters) is concerned, low-key, and polite. If you ignore these messages, you could lose your home. But if you know where to get help, what to ask for, and what to avoid, your situation can change for the better.

Counting to 90

If you're 30 or 60 days late on your mortgage and you make a partial payment, the servicer usually credits your account with the payment. If you cross the 90-day mark and then send in a month or two's worth of overdue payments rather than the entire amount due, however, the servicer may send the money back and let the foreclosure clock keep ticking.

After you're late on your first payment, your grace period disappears. (Your *grace period* is the period of time specified in your mortgage loan agreement during which a default can't occur, even though the payment is technically past due.) The grace period applies only to loans that are up-to-date, or current. The following example illustrates how this works.

Say your loan agreement states that your due date is March 1. Assuming that you have a typical two-week grace period, your payment actually has to be in by March 15. If you don't submit your payment by March 15, you miss that window of opportunity and lose your grace period. Your April payment is now due April 1. April 15 is no longer an option. In other words, no more grace period in April. If you pay April's payment on or before April 1, you get your grace period back for May and thereafter, as long as you continue making your payments on time.

If you lose your grace period, the counting of the number of days you're late begins on the first of the month rather than the fifteenth. So if you don't send in a payment on March 15, April 1, or May 1, then on May 2, you need to catch up on the payments for March 1, April 1, and May 1, plus any fees and penalties (which can be hundreds of dollars or more), all at once. This sum is a huge amount for someone in financial difficulty. If you don't pay, then the formal foreclosure process can start on May 2, and you may incur fees for collection costs, attorneys, title searches, filings, and more. After the foreclosure process begins (it's up to the mortgage servicer when this process actually begins), the mortgage servicer can *accelerate* the loan, meaning that it can ask for the entire loan balance — not just the late part — to stop the foreclosure.

Knowing Where to Turn for Help

If you're having trouble making your mortgage payments, time is of the essence. Getting your mortgage issue resolved quickly is critical. Remember, the mortgage company doesn't want your house; it just wants to keep your loan *performing/up-to-date/current* (different terms for the same thing). But also remember that the mortgage company doesn't care whether it has to take your home. If the rules say to foreclose, the mortgage company will foreclose, without hesitation and without remorse.

Following are a few ideas on where to turn for help (along with some tips on who *not* to turn to!). The essential point, however, is not to wait but to take action. You can work directly with your mortgage servicer, but the servicer may offer you only what it thinks is the easiest solution, not the one you need, because the servicer doesn't know your situation in detail.

Finding good help for free

A number of housing counseling agencies are available to help you work out a solution. I strongly recommend that you use a third-party intermediary that's approved by the U.S. Department of Housing and Urban Development (HUD). These intermediaries are cheap, experienced, and knowledgeable and can help guide you through what can seem like an insurmountable problem. They're experts at getting the right information on the right forms and to the right person at the mortgage servicer — no easy task!

Although the contact information may change over time and new players are continually offering this service, you can look for resources through Fannie Mae's Know Your Options website, www.knowyouroptions.com, or HUD's website, www.hud.gov; or contact the Homeowners Hope Hotline at 888-995-4673 or HOPE NOW at www.hopenow.com. For the fastest service, I suggest that you call before you e-mail or visit an office. You can also get good help by contacting the National Foundation for Credit Counseling at www.housinghelpnow.org or 866-557-2227. Many credit counselors are also HUD-certified housing counselors. See Chapter 4 for additional sources of help.

Working with your mortgage servicer

If you're unable to make a mortgage payment on time, you can contact your mortgage company for help. If you believe that this may be the beginning of a serious problem that needs serious attention, ask for the *loss mitigation department,* which may be referred to as the *workout department* or the *homeownership retention department.* This department is able to go the extra mile to help you and can deal with complex issues better than the standard collection department, which usually offers only to make catch-up payment arrangements. To find the contact information for these departments, you can look in your mortgage loan documents, on your monthly statement, or in the correspondence you've received from your mortgage servicer. When you call, get names and extension numbers so that you can try to keep a single point of contact and continuity. Doing so may not be possible, but knowing who you talked to, when you talked, and what you agreed on is important in case matters get really serious. Take good notes!

Keeping the call simple is a blessing to everyone concerned, so I suggest that you do some homework before you call and have a written, well-thought-out proposal prepared that meets your needs and helps solve your problem. Be sure to include what concessions you need and for how long. I also suggest that you write down what happened, what changed, and how to contact you or your counselor if you're working with one. Writing down the facts and options before you call helps you keep from drifting during the conversation and keeps everyone focused on the task at hand. When you ask for what you need, be sure to ask what other options may be available beyond the one that's offered.

If you want some free help on figuring out what specific help you need to ask for, I suggest that you contact a counselor at the HOPE NOW Alliance (www.hopenow.com or 888-995-HOPE).

If you can't resolve your issue quickly or if you get transferred to multiple people, get expert help quickly. Time is precious, and mortgage servicers can easily pass the buck until you find yourself in a foreclosure situation. See the preceding section for information on where to find free help from experts.

Avoiding help that hurts

Some people make a living, and a good one, on the backs of folks in trouble. People who offer to help you with a mortgage problem for a fee are only trying to help themselves. So proceed with caution and consider the following tips as you evaluate any prospective source of help:

- ✔ Don't decide anything while in a panic.
- ✔ Be sure that you're dealing with a HUD-qualified nonprofit organization. Look them up at www.hud.gov.
- ✔ Don't make payments to anyone other than your mortgage servicer or its designee.

✔ Be wary of any organization other than your mortgage servicer that contacts you to offer help. It's fine if you call them, but not if they call you!

✔ Never sign a contract under pressure.

✔ Never sign away ownership of your property.

✔ Beware of any company or person who guarantees that they can stop a foreclosure or get your loan modified.

✔ If English isn't your first language and a translator isn't provided, use your own.

✔ Get a second opinion from a person or an organization that you know and trust.

If you're having trouble paying your mortgage, getting a high-risk, expensive second mortgage won't help. It will only keep you from finding real solutions by wasting critical time and money.

If you receive an offer saying that you've been preapproved for a loan, don't get too excited. It only means that you've been preapproved on a very cursory level and only for the offer, not the actual loan. Don't waste too much time chasing preapproved offers.

Alternatives to Going Down with the Ship

If you're having trouble making your mortgage payments, you may have a host of options to help you avoid the expense and upset of losing your home through a foreclosure. Even if you can't or don't want to keep your house, you can still lessen the damage to yourself, your family, and your credit by taking positive action.

Before you take any action, assess your situation as dispassionately as you can. If stress and anxiety make that impossible, I suggest that you seek help from a third-party professional such as a nonprofit HUD counselor (see "Finding good help for free" earlier in this chapter) or an attorney. Your situation may not be as bad as you think it is, or it may be worse. What's important is to know for sure where you stand. You need what's called *loss mitigation counseling,* which is help to develop a solution that enables you to afford to keep your home or lessen the damage caused by a foreclosure.

This section gives you some loss mitigation options to protect your credit.

What to do first

If you already have a plan to resolve your problem, catch up, or at least resume payments in three to six months, consider the following suggestions:

- ✔ **Find a good nonprofit housing counseling agency.** I recommend the Hope Hotline (888-995-4673) or HOPE NOW (www.hopenow.com) or a nonprofit credit counseling agency that has a HUD-approved housing counseling program. Expect an assessment of your overall financial picture and whether you can realistically afford your mortgage payments.

- ✔ **Ask your mortgage servicer about a repayment plan.** The servicer sets up a structured payment plan (sometimes called a *special forbearance plan*) that gets the mortgage back on track in three to six months by making up past-due amounts in addition to your regular payments. Get all the terms in writing so that you're both clear on the terms. The sooner you do so the less damage to your credit report and score.

- ✔ **Check the HUD (www.hud.gov) and Fannie Mae (www.knowyour options.com/options-finder) websites for resources and help.** Both sites have excellent referral resources, information on programs that might be right for you, and warnings to keep you from falling for scams.

- ✔ **Don't wait until it's too late!** Talk to your lender about your need for assistance, and do it soon. Some servicers have programs for those who are not yet delinquent and other programs for borrowers who already are delinquent. For the greatest number of options, get started as soon as you know that you have a problem making your mortgage payments as agreed, and be sure to ask for all the options your servicer may have for you.

What to do for more serious problems

For problems that may take longer than three to six months to remedy, ask for mortgage loan forbearance or loan modifications.

A *forbearance* temporarily modifies or eliminates payments that are made up at the end of the forbearance period. This option also prevents your credit from being damaged by a string of late payments.

A *loan modification* permanently changes one or more terms of the original mortgage in a way that addresses your specific needs. If this option seems intimidating, use a HUD-approved agency to deal with the servicer and offer solutions on your behalf. Clear communication is key here.

Modifications need to be in writing and approved by both the servicer and the borrower. Don't be surprised if the servicer asks for a fee to cover the costs of processing a loan modification.

What to do to end matters

Even when you can't solve your problem or just can't stand it anymore, you're better off staying in control of the process rather than just giving up. Doing so can lessen credit damage and expenses and keep your dignity — and maybe your sanity — intact.

The following are some of the many options available. And don't forget that another reason to use a free professional mortgage counselor is that newer options may be available to you as well. Be sure to check out the resources mentioned in the section "Knowing Where to Turn for Help," earlier in this chapter.

✔ **Sell your home:** You may be able to sell your home in a short sale if you have no equity left or a pre-foreclosure sale if the value of the house still exceeds the amount due on the mortgage.

• **Short sale:** You get your lender to allow you to sell your home for less than the mortgage value. This option is generally cheaper for the bank and less stressing for the homeowner than a foreclosure. Because it is good for the lender, you can negotiate a bit. Ask that the loan deficiency be reported to the credit bureau as a zero balance rather than a charge-off.

The Mortgage Forgiveness Debt Relief Act of 2007 exempts up to $2 million of forgiven mortgage debt, subject to certain conditions, from federal taxes. (The full text of the act is available at www.dummies.com/extras/creditrepair.) As I wrote this revision, it expired on January 1, 2014. It may be extended, but it may not. So be sure to find out what the consequences of a short sale or foreclosure may be before you proceed. If the act expires, you may have to pay income tax on that amount. Also check to see whether you may have state taxes due, as they aren't covered under this federal law.

• **Pre-foreclosure sale:** A pre-foreclosure sale arrangement allows you to defer mortgage payments that you can't afford while you sell your house. It also keeps late payments off your credit report.

- **Deed-in-lieu of foreclosure:** If the home can't be sold, you can sign the title over to the lender and move out. To qualify for this option, you usually can't have a second mortgage, a home equity loan, or another lien on the property.

- **Stopping payments as part of a plan:** Not my favorite option, but if your plan is to save money for rent or for the larger down payment you'll need for a new place to live, then setting aside the money you would have paid for your mortgage can accrue several months or even years of savings. The price can be high in credit damage and stress, however. See "Strategic default: Stopping payments" later in this section.

Managing a foreclosure

If you're being foreclosed on, you still may have the option to talk to the servicer and try to work things out, buy more time to come up with a solution, or at least make a more dignified exit from your home. But again, timing is very important, so don't wait!

- **Get a HUD-approved counselor involved and review loss mitigation options with your servicer.** Most want to help. (Check out "Knowing Where to Turn for Help" earlier in this chapter.)

- **Remain in contact with the servicer's loss mitigation staff until you get a solution you can live with.** If they don't offer workable suggestions, ask to speak to managers and vice presidents or higher. This is not a time to stand on protocol or accept "I'm sorry" for an answer.

- **See an attorney.** Ask for options. Review all the mortgage and foreclosure documents to be sure they were properly drawn and executed. The technical phrase used here is *truth in lending compliance*. Ask about bankruptcy options and timing so that you know all options available to you.

Strategic default: Stopping payments

A *strategic default* is an intentional mortgage default based on a plan or strategy. Here's an example: A person has a home whose value has fallen so far below what is owed on the mortgage that he will never realistically recover enough equity to break even on the home. Because the house will never be worth what is being paid, the homeowner stops paying the mortgage. This option is more popular in states with *nonrecourse mortgages* (meaning that the house is the sole security for the mortgage loan, and the homeowner isn't responsible for any shortage beyond what the house brings at sale).

For a chart that shows each state's recourse classification, as well as the typical timeline for foreclosure in each state, go to www.dummies.com/extras/creditrepair.

According to the Federal Reserve (www.frbatlanta.org/pubs/wp/13_04.cfm), strategic default among deeply underwater borrowers (those whose home values are way below what's owed on the mortgage) is less common than originally thought. Unemployment appears to be a bigger cause. Another consideration is that due to some local exemptions, collecting deficiencies is unlikely in some states.

Strategic default is a high-credit-damage strategy, but it may be cost-effective depending on your situation and plans involving loans or credit use in the future. Refer to Figure 7-1, earlier in the chapter, for details on the damage a foreclosure does to your credit score.

Strategic default is an unfortunate reality for many of the long-term unemployed. Thousands of homeowners are stopping payments on homes that they can no longer afford or that are deeply underwater. The argument goes: After all, this is business, and businesses routinely stop paying on debts that they can't afford or that are worth less than they owe. You probably have been told that you have to pay your bills, honor your obligations, and keep your promises, but many home buyers are taking a business rather than a personal approach to their homes and finances.

Most mortgages detail what happens if you don't pay. Either you pay or your home is taken away. So the question arises: If you tell the bank to go ahead and take the house, are you meeting your obligations? From the bank's perspective, clearly you're not. From your family's perspective, however, the answer may be different.

Some states require all mortgages to be *nonrecourse,* meaning that the lender has recourse to the defaulted property and nothing else. Also consider that the Mortgage Forgiveness Debt Relief Act prohibits the IRS from taxing as income any *recourse* mortgage debt forgiven up to $1 million ($2 million if filing jointly) from a foreclosure, short sale, or deed-in-lieu action until at least January 1, 2014.

Staying in a home you can't afford can deprive your family of your precious savings, empty your retirement accounts, and eventually ruin your credit when you finally default. Many people are willing to put up with the price of any shame or guilt in order to ensure a faster recovery with more money in their bank accounts.

Dealing with Deficiencies

When all is said and done, you may still owe some money. If your home sells for less than the amount you still owe on the mortgage, plus fees, then you may have what's called a *deficiency balance.* For example, say you borrow $500,000 to purchase a home, but you fall behind on payments or walk away from the home, and the bank forecloses. The home ultimately sells for $400,000. The $100,000 that the lender loses on the deal is called a *deficiency.* A first mortgage holder may or may not forgive this amount. Second mortgage holders often go after the borrower for deficiencies.

Your lender can get a deficiency judgment lien against your personal property and any other real estate that you own, giving it a security interest in that property. This means that the bank could foreclose on other real estate if you have enough equity for the bank to think that it might get enough money to make the effort worthwhile. However, just because the lender gets a deficiency judgment does not mean that it will try to collect. The lender may opt to write off the debt and issue you an IRS form 1099-C. If this happens, you might owe taxes on the forgiven amount. See the discussion of the Mortgage Forgiveness Debt Relief Act of 2007 earlier in this chapter.

If a lender comes after you for a large deficiency, consider speaking to an attorney about the benefits of filing for bankruptcy versus trying to work out a payment agreement with the lender.

The most important thing is to realize that your problems may not be over when you leave the home. You may need to deal with the IRS if you don't qualify for mortgage debt forgiveness under its rules.

The following are some potential, and I stress *potential,* situations you may face and what you can do to deal with them:

- **The lender may ask for a note.** Although this practice isn't current among first mortgage holders, I want you to be aware of it for the future, or if your second mortgage holder loses money on your loan. This note isn't written on monogrammed stationery; it's a promise to pay an unsecured amount to cover the mortgage deficiency after the sale. Use an attorney if your lender mentions this to you.

- **The lender may send a demand letter.** A mortgage lender may send a demand for payment of any deficiency following the sale of a home. The lender uses a *demand letter* if it doesn't want to give you an unsecured loan for the balance due. In essence, the problem is all yours, and you need to work out a way to pay the balance. Again, if this happens, get an attorney to advise you.

✔ **The lender may forgive what you owe.** More likely among first mortgage holders, forgiveness isn't required. This gesture is nice as far as it goes, but the IRS counts forgiven debt as income. Forms 1099-A and 1099-C, which are normally used to document unreported income, are also used to report forgiven debt. The amount of the forgiven debt becomes taxable income in most cases, unless you're covered by the Mortgage Forgiveness Debt Relief Act. Remember, the law is scheduled to end in 2013 and may not be in place in the future.

The law applies to debt forgiven in 2007 through January 1, 2014, only. Debt reduced through mortgage restructuring, as well as mortgage debt forgiven in connection with a foreclosure, may qualify for this relief. If you spent the forgiven debt money to pay a car loan, credit card bills, or for any non–real estate purpose, it's not covered, and you'll get a tax bill for it. Debt on second homes, rental property, and business property doesn't qualify.

If you are a foreclosed borrower faced with a sizable 1099, you still have hope. If you file IRS Form 982, "Reduction of Tax Attributes Due to Discharge of Indebtedness," and you're insolvent at the time of the forgiven debt, the IRS may forgive the liability. (You can find Form 982 at www.dummies.com/extras/creditrepair.) Again, see your attorney for the details.

✔ **The state you live in makes mortgages nonrecourse.** If you live in certain states, you may get a break relating to personal mortgage deficiencies. Some states have passed laws saying that you're not responsible for any mortgage deficiencies.

Preparing for "Credit Winter"

After a foreclosure, your credit will be severely damaged — in some cases and for some purposes, for years to come. Knowing that post-foreclosure credit is hard to come by, you are wise to give some thought to how you'll cope with the credit fallout that may seem like the equivalent of a nuclear winter. (See more in Chapter 17.)

Once you see that you may be getting in trouble with your mortgage, you can do some things to protect your access to credit in the "credit winter" that often follows a foreclosure. Like the biblical farmer who put aside grain for the lean years to come, you can store up some credit in advance. Here's how:

- ✔ Review your credit cards to make sure that you have enough credit available. Open new credit cards before you become delinquent on your mortgage. Doing so ensures that you can lead a more normal credit life while your credit is recovering. Plus, using and paying off multiple cards each month provides new streams of positive data to help repair your damaged credit report.

- ✔ Establish a personal line of credit at your local bank or credit union that is not secured by your home.

- ✔ If you are planning to make a large financed purchase such as a car (purchase or lease), major appliance, or furniture down the road, consider making it before you become delinquent on your mortgage, while your credit is still strong.

- ✔ Remember, your credit report is used for more than loans. Prepare a short explanation of why you defaulted and what you have done to make sure it won't happen again. Like an exit statement that explains why you left your last job in the best possible light, this explanation is useful if you need to find a new job, are up for a promotion at work, or are looking for new housing.

Chapter 8

Starting Over Again with Bankruptcy

· ·

In This Chapter

▶ Establishing the pros and cons of bankruptcy

▶ Discovering the eligibility requirements for filing bankruptcy

▶ Understanding the process of filing for bankruptcy

▶ Rebuilding your credit after bankruptcy

· ·

*B*ankruptcy used to be easy. You decided that you were too far over your head in debt, and you went to see an attorney, who made your debts disappear. Presto chango! Not anymore. Today's bankruptcy is less likely to rid you of all your debts. Plus, some chapters of bankruptcy leave you on a bare-bones, IRS-sanctioned spending plan for the next five years. Ouch.

Still, bankruptcy can be a cure for overindebtedness that threatens to deprive you and your family of the hope for a prosperous financial future. A fresh start is the intent of the law, and, when done correctly and for the right reasons, that's just what you get.

Equally important is assessing the role bankruptcy plays in your life for years to come as a result of damaged credit and long waiting periods before you can file again, should you need to. With credit playing an increasingly important role in most Americans' financial lives, the damage a bankruptcy can do to your future had better be worth it. But how do you know whether bankruptcy is right for your situation? How do you know which type or chapter of bankruptcy you qualify for and which bills you'll still be responsible for after you file?

This chapter gives you an accurate and unbiased picture of how bankruptcy law works. I help you figure out whether bankruptcy makes sense for you, which type of bankruptcy is best for your situation, and how you can minimize bankruptcy's effects on your credit. I've seen too many people use bankruptcy for the wrong reasons; instead of providing them with a fresh start, it placed them squarely behind the financial and credit eight balls. So if you're thinking about bankruptcy, this chapter can help you see past the legal fine print to consider what may be the most important financial decision you'll make in the next ten years.

Deciding Whether Bankruptcy Makes Sense for You

Declaring bankruptcy is a big decision that affects your life for up to ten years. It may affect your self-esteem and confidence for even longer. It's a condition that redefines your credit report, lowers your credit score, and remains an issue for future credit and employment.

Both financial and quality-of-life components may factor into your decision to file for bankruptcy. The benefits gained may outweigh the damage to your credit. If your wages are about to be garnished because of your inability to pay a bill — perhaps a totally unexpected medical bill — do you allow your family to suffer the financial consequences for years, or seemingly forever? More than half of those who file bankruptcy have large uninsured or underinsured medical expenses. In other words, bankruptcy is a major life event, so you want to consider it very seriously. Don't get me wrong — bankruptcy may just be the best choice if you've suffered some serious financial setbacks. But you need to invest time in carefully weighing all your options before you take the plunge.

Deliberating the bankruptcy decision

As you consider bankruptcy, take into account: Can you do anything more to help meet your obligations? Do you have hope of finding a solution that's acceptable to both you and your creditors? If you answered no to both questions, I think you're on the right track in considering bankruptcy.

Before you make the final decision to throw your credit and creditors off a financial cliff, I suggest that you review the following:

✔ **Be sure that bankruptcy will solve your financial crisis.** Getting rid of all your debts and making collectors go away may solve one problem, but if the real problem is too much spending and not enough income, declaring bankruptcy won't help you for very long. Likewise, bankruptcy won't help if you've been using credit to supplement your income for basic living expenses.

✔ **Understand bankruptcy's effects on your goals.** Ask yourself how this decision will affect your chances of buying a home, getting married or divorced, or getting a job. Describe your world as you'd like to see it over the next ten years, and understand the impact that a bankruptcy would have on that goal. Bankruptcy is a big step, and its consequences affect you for years. To make the decision based only on immediate events without considering the future impact would be a mistake.

✔ **Consider all your options.** Make a list of other ways to deal with your debts. Can you increase your income? Reduce your expenses? Stretch out your payments? Sell some possessions to pay your bills until your situation improves?

✔ **Talk to a good credit counselor.** You have to meet with a credit counselor anyway within six months of filing for bankruptcy. Expect this visit to give you options; an analysis of your spending and income, including a written budget; and an action plan. This consultation goes a long way toward answering the question of whether bankruptcy will help you. See Chapter 4 for more on credit counselors.

✔ **Get a professional legal opinion.** Find a lawyer who does a lot of bankruptcies. Find out whether you qualify for bankruptcy and, if so, which chapter. Make sure you understand what bankruptcy can and can't do for you. Ask about alternatives, including settlements and statutes of limitations. Also ask about the pluses and minuses of filing for bankruptcy on your own. Called *pro se,* the law allows you to represent yourself, and in some courts with sympathetic judges, doing so can be a money-saver. (In other courts, it can be a disaster.) An experienced lawyer is the best person to guide you here.

✔ **Talk to your creditors.** Seriously. If you're considering a bankruptcy, let your lenders know and ask if they can offer you a repayment plan. Keep in mind that you have to be able to afford this plan. Don't expect too much, but talking to your creditors is always worth a shot.

✔ **Consider the stiffer consumer rules in the Bankruptcy Abuse Prevention and Consumer Protection Act of 2005.** This change to the law was enacted because lenders convinced Congress (yes, the people you voted for) that a significant number of consumers had abused bankruptcy protection over the years. The act established restrictions to try to cut down on such abuse. Here's a brief summary of the main provisions that may help you decide whether a bankruptcy is worth pursuing in your situation:

- **Passing a means test is required to be eligible for Chapter 7.** Except in limited circumstances (check out the "Qualifying for and Filing for Bankruptcy" section later in this chapter to see if you qualify), your net income has to be below the median income in your state of residence to file for liquidation of your debts in a Chapter 7.

- **You're required to get credit counseling from an "approved nonprofit budget and credit counseling agency" before you can file.** The Executive Office of the U.S. Trustee provides a master list of approved agencies from which you may choose. You can find out who's on the list by contacting the clerk of the court where your bankruptcy is to be filed, by going to the U.S. Department of Justice website (www.justice.gov/ust/eo/bapcpa/ccde/cc_approved.htm), or by talking to your attorney. Counseling may be offered by phone, online, or in person.

- **After you file, you must complete a course in financial management before you're discharged from bankruptcy.** You may contact the same provider for this requirement as for the credit counseling requirement, or you can use a different provider. You can find a list of approved providers at www.justice.gov/ust/eo/bapcpa/ccde/de_approved.htm.

- **You're limited in what you can buy immediately before filing.** Having made the decision to file, you're prevented from going out and spending up a storm or taking out cash advances and then not having to pay. Generally, the limits apply to the 90 days preceding your filing.

- **You have to wait a long time after getting a discharge for bankruptcy before you can get another one.** The law requires eight years between Chapter 7 bankruptcy discharges, two years between Chapter 13 bankruptcies, six years between a Chapter 13 and a Chapter 7, and four years between a Chapter 7 and a Chapter 13.

- **Your *homestead exemption* (how much equity in your home you can keep out of your filing and keep for yourself) is limited by state law.** In addition, if you acquired your home less than 40 months before filing, you're allowed a maximum exemption of $155,675, regardless of your state's exemption allowance.

- **Under Chapter 13 bankruptcy, you're allowed to spend only what the IRS guidelines allow.** The rest of your disposable income must be included in the plan, and every year you have to document your income and expenses to see whether you can pay more (or less).

- **Your attorney must certify that what you say in the documents you submit to the court is true.**

- **You still may owe some past and future debts.** These debts include taxes (incurred in the last three years, unfiled, or filed late), domestic support, restitution and fines for drunk-driving injuries and other criminal offenses, and student loans. Courts are extremely reluctant to discharge student loans, and the general policy is not to discharge them. Rarely, some older student loans can be discharged; if an "undue" hardship condition exists, you file a separate motion with the bankruptcy court and then appear before a judge to explain your hardship.

- **Domestic-support obligations are a priority debt that you must pay.** A *priority debt* takes precedence over other debt payments you owe and is paid completely. However, the *bankruptcy trustee* (the person appointed by the court to administer your Chapter 13 plan) gets administrative fees before your spouse, ex-spouse, or kids get their money.

- **You may be evicted if you don't pay your rent after you've filed for bankruptcy.**

- **You must provide your most recent tax return to your creditors if they ask for it.** Before you can finalize your bankruptcy, you need to give your creditors information about your financial status so they can see that you can't afford to pay what you owe. If you're filing for Chapter 13, you must provide your tax returns for the last four years.

✔ **Visit with people who care about you.** Although these people may not be professionals, they know you and may offer important perspectives. Avoid visiting with someone who would be personally affected by your choice (such as a person you owe money to, someone who owes you money, or a dependent).

✔ **Look in the mirror.** Given your current financial state, how do you see yourself? Consider your goals; weigh the options offered by your creditors, your credit counselor, and your lawyer; and consider the advice of others who care about you. Now you're ready to decide what's best for your future and your peace of mind. If you don't like what you see, go through the process until you do, and then do what you think is in your best interest.

TIP

Locating a bankruptcy attorney

A qualified attorney is essential if you're considering filing bankruptcy. I always consider friends, family, or coworkers who've had a satisfying experience with an attorney as good sources of referrals. I'm not suggesting that you put a note up on the company bulletin board, but someone who has already been through the bankruptcy process may be a good referral source.

The Internet also has some good resources. Here are a few that you may want to check out:

✔ National Association of Consumer Bankruptcy Attorneys (www.nacba.org)

✔ Lawyers.com (www.lawyers.com)

✔ American Bankruptcy Institute (www.abiworld.org)

You can also find a listing of pro bono bankruptcy attorneys at probono.abiworld.org.

If you've used a lawyer to handle other issues, ask for a referral to someone who specializes in bankruptcy. Don't use your cousin, the real estate lawyer. Get a pro. You have to live with any mistakes made here for years.

Adding up the pluses and minuses

Like anything in life, bankruptcy is neither all good nor all bad. In the following sections, I explain bankruptcy's benefits as well as the harsh reality of bankruptcy's consequences.

The silver lining of filing bankruptcy

I'm always in favor of hearing the good news first. With bankruptcy, it's no different. Here are some of the positives that bankruptcy can do for you:

✔ **You get a fresh start.** The collection activity stops. The fees and penalty rates stop. In fact, in a Chapter 7 bankruptcy, virtually your entire debt may go away. Without the ability to put a stop to the madness of credit gone awry, some people would never — and I mean *never* — be able to live a normal life again. Bankruptcy can enable that to happen.

✔ **You get credit education.** The bankruptcy law says that anyone who files is required to get some credit education. This is an opportunity to look back at what happened and reset your financial and credit course going forward. If you take full advantage of this opportunity, you'll walk away with a much better sense of how to manage your financial life, which means that you'll be less likely to end up back where you started.

The darker side of filing bankruptcy

As you can probably guess, filing bankruptcy comes with some pretty heavy consequences, too. Here are the major ones:

✔ **You may still owe money.** Bankruptcy may not wipe out *all* your debt. Some debts don't go away, even though you'd like them to, and you must pay them in full. The debts that don't disappear are

- Federal, state, and local taxes
- Child support
- Alimony
- Student loans (except in very limited circumstances)
- Money owed as a result of drunk driving and other criminal offenses, such as willful injury or damage to people and property

✔ **Your credit score will be affected for years.** Bankruptcy is a major negative on your credit report that appears as a public record in your file as well as in your account history for up to ten years. Worse, it causes your credit score to stay depressed longer than a normal delinquency does. Good credit can plunge by 200 points. Declare bankruptcy and you're likely to see your score drop to the lowest 20 percent of all credit scores. Ouch! See Chapter 7 for more info.

✔ **Borrowing money becomes more difficult.** When lenders see a score in the lowest percentile, your interest rates and terms escalate. In a tight credit market, lenders may decline to give you credit at any price.

Some lenders, however, specialize in loaning to people with bad credit. They're delighted to see you; the fact that you've just gone bankrupt is a big plus in their eyes. Why? Because under the law, you can't file a Chapter 7 bankruptcy again for eight long years. So although lenders get to charge you high interest rates as a risky borrower, you can't avoid repaying them by playing the bankruptcy card. If you fall behind, you can run, but you can't hide. These lenders are very good at collecting overdue accounts. The bottom line: Avoid these lenders at all costs. If you must borrow shortly after a bankruptcy, use a reputable lender.

✔ **Renting an apartment may become more complicated.** Many landlords use credit reports to approve tenant applicants. They may refuse to rent to you, require a cosigner, or demand a larger deposit if they see a bankruptcy.

✔ **Insurance costs rise.** A bankruptcy may cost you more in insurance premiums, particularly for homeowner's and auto insurance. The insurance mavens and their actuarial elves love credit reports. All those dispassionate numbers lend themselves to justifying rate increases much more than real claims do. So even if you have no claims, expect your premiums to go up. Some states don't allow credit to be a factor in setting rates, but most do.

✔ **Employment searches may be more difficult.** Even under ideal circumstances, job hunting is extremely competitive and can be very stressful. When you consider the fact that many employers run a credit check before making a job offer, your stress level can increase as your opportunities decrease. As a practical matter, some licenses can't be given to people who've filed for bankruptcy, and security clearances can be denied.

The events, behavior, or judgments that resulted in your bankruptcy are concerns for prospective employers. They are the silent killers, because although you can't legally be denied employment because you filed a bankruptcy, a prospective employer rarely asks questions to find out the reasons. Going on to the next candidate is easier and legally safer. See Chapter 11 for more info.

✔ **Your self-image and confidence may suffer.** Bankruptcy can take its toll, because like it or not, a great deal of the way many people view themselves is wrapped up in their financial persona. Most people think of themselves as responsible adults, and they've been taught that responsible adults pay their bills and keep their promises. Even though you know that filing for bankruptcy is okay and that you have no choice in the matter, you may find that you have an unexpected internal conflict to deal with.

Considering a debt management plan first

One of the stops you're required to make on the road to getting help from the bankruptcy courts is a credit counseling agency. The court recognizes the value of the work done by these agencies by requiring that a court-approved agency review your financial circumstances (*before* you file). The idea is that you'll get an unbiased assessment of your financial condition and that you may, upon reflection, find other alternatives to handle your debt.

Understanding what a debt management plan is

One of the services provided by the credit counseling industry is the debt management plan. You begin with an individually tailored spending plan that you create with the help of a credit counselor. A *debt management plan* uses the equivalent of your disposable income after actual expenses and reallocates some or all of your income to pay your creditors. Many creditors require that you be able to pay off the balance in 60 months to allow the account to be placed under a debt management plan. The average plan is set up for three to five years but in practice tends to be completed in about two years. (For more on debt management plans, turn to Chapter 4.)

Seeing how a debt management plan differs from bankruptcy

Under a debt management plan, the money left (if any) after you've paid your living expenses and your creditors is yours to use as you see fit. If you file Chapter 13 bankruptcy, however, all your disposable income goes toward paying off your creditors. The amount you get to use for living expenses with minor adjustments comes from less-than-generous IRS guidelines.

Unlike the terms of a Chapter 7 or a Chapter 13 bankruptcy, a debt management plan is a voluntary arrangement between you and your creditors, using the credit counseling agency as an intermediary. You can walk away from a debt management plan at any time and still file for bankruptcy. Or, if you're on the receiving end of a windfall, you can pay off your creditors and be done with it.

Of course, your creditors don't have to accept the terms of the debt management plan, whereas they *have* to accept a court-ordered repayment plan if you file bankruptcy. That said, most creditors do accept debt management plans because they know that you'll be off to the courthouse to file bankruptcy if they say no. Additionally, if a creditor refuses to negotiate with a credit counselor, the court can order that the uncooperative creditor's debt get a 20-percent haircut.

Whereas a Chapter 7 bankruptcy liquidates many debts, a Chapter 13 bankruptcy forces creditors to accept a lower payment over a set period that may not cover all that you originally owed. The difference between what you owe and what you pay under Chapter 13 is what the creditors lose. They also can't charge interest or fees under Chapter 13. A debt management plan allows the creditors to collect interest charges, although many creditors reduce the rate to one that's more affordable and reflects your circumstances and your desire to repay the debt.

Perhaps one of the biggest differences between a Chapter 7 or Chapter 13 bankruptcy and a debt management plan is the effect on your credit score. Bankruptcy has a large negative impact on your score, which affects your ability to do lots of the things I mention earlier in this chapter for years after the *end* of your bankruptcy. A debt management plan, on the other hand, doesn't have the same negative impact on your credit score. In fact, many creditors don't report to the credit bureaus that your account is being handled by a credit counseling agency. Those that do report it to the bureaus report it as a description of the account (for example, credit card, real estate mortgage, or credit counseling), not as a payment history item (such as "pays as agreed" or "X days late"). Payment history items are included in calculating your credit score, but account descriptions are not. Further, your credit report shows the credit counseling account description only until you pay off the account or decide to discontinue the plan, at which point the notation is removed.

More good news: Even while you're enrolled in a debt management plan, the FICO scoring system doesn't subtract any points. That's right — your credit score isn't affected. A credit counseling notation on your file is perceived as neutral, not a negative or public-record item.

If you decide to try the debt management-plan route rather than a Chapter 13 and the debt management plan doesn't work out for you, you can always file for bankruptcy without a waiting period. I suggest that when you get your mandatory counseling on the road to bankruptcy, you explore making a debt management plan work for you. Your credit and score may be glad you did.

Understanding Bankruptcy, Chapter and Verse

Filing for bankruptcy is a very serious decision for which you need to be armed with all the information you can find. Why? Because for all the problems a bankruptcy solves, it can create many more if you make a mistake. As with many laws, bankruptcy laws may seem like a secret code. Besides being long and written in legalese, these laws contain mysterious chapters with numbers — 7, 11, and 13 — rather than names. What do the chapters really mean, and which one is right for you? That's what this section is all about.

In basic terms, the reason for filing bankruptcy is to seek the protection of the court from your creditors. It's that simple. If you can't pay what you owe on your own, now or in the foreseeable future, call in the judge, and the judge will handle your collectors.

The courts allow many different types of bankruptcy, identified as chapters with numbers. The variety of options reflects the variety of solutions needed for different situations. One size doesn't fit all. A farmer's problems and needs differ significantly from a corporation's. A Chapter 12 bankruptcy, for example, allows farmers to reorganize their debt and keep their farms.

Among all the various chapters, two are most commonly used by consumers who find themselves unable to come to agreement with or to meet contractual payments with their creditors:

- **Chapter 7:** Also known as *liquidation,* this is the most popular form of bankruptcy. It may require you to give up some assets (the liquidation part), but it gets you out of almost all your liabilities.

- **Chapter 13:** Often referred to as *wage-earner bankruptcy,* this form of bankruptcy allows you to keep most of your assets and pay back what the judge rules you can over a period of time, usually three to five years, under court supervision and protection.

Regardless of which chapter you file, my final advice is to make sure that bankruptcy will truly solve your problems — the problems you have today, the problems you'll have tomorrow, and the complications of dealing with the financial, employment, and insurance systems in the future.

Qualifying for and Filing for Bankruptcy

After reviewing the previous sections, you may determine that bankruptcy is the best or only viable solution for your financial situation. But you still need to see whether you qualify for bankruptcy. Both Chapter 7 and Chapter 13 bankruptcies have eligibility requirements, which I cover in the following sections.

For a look at the rules, refer to the document "Bankruptcy Code Filing Procedures Chart" at www.dummies.com/extras/creditrepair.

Qualifying for Chapter 7

Access to Chapter 7, the most popular form of personal bankruptcy in recent years, is restricted by the Bankruptcy Abuse Prevention and Consumer Protection Act of 2005. Chapter 7 has been so popular because of its ability to get rid of debts and collectors. Under a Chapter 7, you receive relief from virtually all your debts, with a few exceptions, and you get it fast — like the same day (unlike a Chapter 13, which may take years before you get a discharge).

Passing the means test

The first hurdle in moving forward with Chapter 7 bankruptcy is meeting the *means test.* If you have too many means (that is, too much money), you can't declare Chapter 7. And the courts won't take your word for it; you have to *prove* that your income really is what you say it is. If your income over the last six months is above the applicable median for your state of residence, you can't file for Chapter 7.

To find out whether your income is above the median in your state of residence, go to the U.S. Census website: www.census.gov/hhes/www/income/data/statemedian/index.html. See www.legalconsumer.com/bankruptcy/means-test/ for a good means-test calculator.

If your income is above the median, don't give up just yet. Next, you want to determine whether you have *excess monthly income* of more than $166.66 to pay $10,000 of debt over five years. So what counts as excess income? To find out, you have to use the spending guidelines approved by the IRS. Allowable expenses are shown here: www.justice.gov/ust/eo/bapcpa/20110315/meanstesting.htm. The IRS guidelines may be very tight for you. (I know from personal experience: My dad was an IRS agent, and his idea of a reasonable allowance was $5 a week, even through college!)

Using the IRS allowable expenses as a guide, if you *can* squeak the $166.66 a month out of your budget, the best you can do is to file under Chapter 13.

If you have less excess monthly income than the magic number of $166.66 after IRS expense allowances, you may proceed to the next hurdle: Do you have an extra $100 a month over the next 60 months? And will that $6,000 account for at least 25 percent of your debt? If the answer to both questions is no, you can pass go and file for Chapter 7. If not, go directly to Chapter 13.

Tithing — giving money to your church — is allowed in both Chapter 7 and Chapter 13 bankruptcies. You may donate up to 15 percent of your gross income and have it count as an expense that may lower your income. Donating to your church may just help you make the numbers work to become eligible for a Chapter 7 rather than a Chapter 13.

Receiving required counseling

At some point during the six months before you file for bankruptcy, you have to receive counseling and get a certificate from a court-approved nonprofit credit counselor.

The Office of the U.S. Trustee has a website (www.justice.gov/ust/) that lists approved agencies. Click the Consumer Information tab and then click "Credit Counseling & Debtor Education."

Credit counseling costs are on a sliding fee scale. They are free if your income is below 150 percent of the poverty level for your family size. Otherwise, up to $50 is considered reasonable.

Just because the court has approved the counseling agency doesn't make it the right one for you, so exercise caution when selecting. (See Chapter 4 for guidance in choosing a credit counselor.) You want someone who has a good track record and has electronic-certificate-issuing capability. Why? Because if the counselor makes a mistake or the certificate is delayed in getting to you, you could face costly delays in getting this matter successfully concluded.

Qualifying for Chapter 13

The strict guidelines to qualify for filing a Chapter 7 bankruptcy mean that some people qualify only to file Chapter 13. The requirements for counseling and proof of income are the same for both types of bankruptcy. Although you must take the same means test, the outcome leads to different results.

Chapter 13 differs from Chapter 7 in that, after establishing your income and deducting allowable expenses, you must use the remainder of your excess monthly income to repay your debt. *Excess* is defined by subtracting the IRS allowable expenses from your income (see the earlier "Passing the means test" section).

Just as with Chapter 7, those filing for Chapter 13 bankruptcy must establish that their family income is either below or above the median for their state. If your total income is above the state median, your excess income gets disposed of (paid to your bankruptcy trustee, who forwards it to your creditors) for the next five years, unless you can show that you can pay off 100 percent of the debt in less than 60 months. If your total income is below the state median, your excess income may be paid to your creditors over the next three years. The rest of the debt that you owe to your creditors goes unpaid, and no interest accrues on any of the accounts involved.

The current bankruptcy law is intended to require those who can afford to make payments toward their debt to do so.

Filing, then backing out

If you decide that bankruptcy isn't for you *after* you file your court papers, you can ask the court to dismiss your case before you get your discharge. For example, say you file a Chapter 7 and then find out that you have to give back that 3-carat diamond ring your sweetie gave you recently. Or in the case of a Chapter 13, maybe you've been making payments and eating peanut butter for a month and can't go on. Or, looking on the bright side, perhaps you get a windfall inheritance from a rich uncle and can pay off the Chapter 13 in one fell swoop.

No matter what the reason, you can call the whole thing off and get a dismissal. Keep in mind, however, that the credit-reporting bureaus pick up the record of your bankruptcy filing and report it, even if you stop the process without getting out of any debts. The bureaus must report that the filing was dismissed, but the record of your filing a bankruptcy stays on your credit report and continues to lower your score for the remainder of the reporting period (up to ten years). Both you and your creditors have the same rights and remedies as you had before you filed your bankruptcy case.

If you ask for a dismissal, you won't be the first to do so. In fact, the law has a specific section that deals with people who not only change

their minds but also change them back again. Perhaps after you back out of the bankruptcy to save the diamond ring, your creditors turn up the collection heat to the point where you'd gladly give them the ring and your grandfather's watch if they'd just leave you alone.

Here's how the change works the second time around: In your first filing, after you file the paperwork with the courts, you receive an automatic *stay* (or suspension) of collection activity on the part of your creditors. The length of time for the collection stay can vary depending on the type of debt or action pending, but generally it's in place until you discharge your debts (that is, get rid of them). But if you change your mind, ask for a dismissal, and then change your mind and refile a second time within one year of the original filing, the automatic stay (the stopping of all collection activity) is for only 30 days. So you have to get all your testing, counseling, and paperwork done in the 30-day period or the collectors and foreclosers return in force. If this is your third such filing in a year, you don't get *any* stay unless the court orders it.

In other words, when you file for bankruptcy, do your best to make sure that it's a decision you can live with for the long haul.

Managing Your Credit After a Bankruptcy

Declaring bankruptcy is more of a hassle than it used to be, and qualifying for relief is definitely harder. But if you take the bankruptcy plunge, don't think that you're out of the woods. You still have to live with the effects of bankruptcy on your credit report and your credit score, as well as the barriers that your new status creates. You're likely to discover that bankruptcy has an impact on your insurance rates and your ability to get hired or promoted. Your bankruptcy status remains on your credit report as the mother of all credit negatives for up to ten years, and that's a long time.

So how do you get a handle on your credit future post-bankruptcy? You rebuild your credit as quickly as possible, and you use credit carefully as you go forward. This section shows you how to do so.

Telling your side of the story

Now that your credit report shows a bankruptcy and will continue to show it for a long time, expect the matter to come up from time to time in a number of life's scenarios. You need to be ready with an explanation of what happened, what you did about it, and why it won't happen again. Work on a short statement that describes your valid reasons for filing for bankruptcy. Businesspeople and potential lenders who have access to your credit report want to know your reasons to help them decide whether to extend you credit or do business with you in general.

Note: This statement *isn't* the 100-word statement I discuss in Chapter 3 that you can attach to your credit report. This is a verbal statement that you make when you're doing anything that requires other parties to review your credit report (applying for a loan, applying for a job, and so on). Be proactive and tell them about your bankruptcy before they see your credit report, but only if you're sure they'll be looking at it. (Why raise the issue if they would never know about it otherwise?)

Like the statement you use to explain why you left your last employer, a tight and targeted statement explaining your bankruptcy is important. Whatever your circumstances were, your explanation always puts a positive spin on the truth. It's short, sweet, and rehearsed. Having it at the ready enables you to convey yourself as confident, professional, and reliable.

Although it's rare for one debt to push you over the edge, a single traumatic event such as a divorce, layoff, or illness is easier for a lender, employer, or landlord to accept. Something that's beyond your control is a plus. Your efforts to pay the debts or deal with collectors are only of interest to you. All you need to convey is that you reviewed all other solutions. End the short statement with some words of wisdom, like, "I've learned a lot from this experience" or "I've become better at saving money as a result." Here's an example of a tight little speech that takes less than two minutes to share:

> When you look at my credit report, I want you to know that you'll see a bankruptcy there. It's not something I'm proud of, but because of an illness, I ended up with $100,000 in medical bills. I felt terrible about having to declare bankruptcy, but I had no choice. I've increased my insurance coverage and savings so that this will never happen again. I certainly learned a painful lesson, but that's all behind me now.

Beware of solicitations

After you declare bankruptcy, you'll likely face a flurry of solicitations and telemarketing calls from companies that receive notices of your filing. Many businesses use bankruptcy notices as mailing lists for the high-cost credit products or scams that they sell.

Read the fine print on any solicitations, and be suspicious of a company that's eager to give you a new start. You're very vulnerable from both a personal and a financial perspective. This may be a good time to opt out of the credit bureau and direct marketing programs that a lot of solicitors use to send you preapproved offers. If you want your name and address removed from mailing lists obtained from the main consumer credit-reporting agencies, go to www.optoutprescreen.com or call 888-567-8688. The Direct Marketing Association can provide information about opting out of lists produced by companies that subscribe to their mail and telephone preference services. Contact the DMA at the following addresses:

✔ Direct Marketing Association Mail Preference Service, P.O. Box 643, Carmel, NY 10512

✔ Direct Marketing Association Telephone Preference Service, P.O. Box 1559, Carmel, NY 10512

You can also contact the DMA at www.dmaconsumers.org/consumer assistance.html. Include the following information with your request:

✔ The date

✔ Your first, middle, and last name (including Jr., Sr., III, and so forth)

✔ Your current address

✔ Your home phone number (only for the telephone preference service)

Check out the Credit Bureau's Sample Opt-Out Letter at www.dummies.com/extras/creditrepair, which is recommended by the Federal Trade Commission. Be sure to send your letter to all three credit bureaus.

It wouldn't hurt to make sure you're included in the Federal Trade Commission's National Do Not Call Registry as well: www.donotcall.gov.

Reaffirming some debt

As part of your bankruptcy rights, you can request to keep some of your debt if you can show the court that you can afford to pay it. After all that trouble to relieve yourself of the terrible burden, isn't keeping some of your debt sort of like going through a knock-down divorce and remarrying your spouse? Well, people do both, and here's why.

Believe it or not, keeping some debt (and its associated credit lines) has some benefits. This is technically called *reaffirmation*. For starters, having some ready credit available when you walk out of the courthouse may be a good idea. Also, a chunk of your credit score is based on longevity of accounts. Keeping an old account with a positive credit history may help you rebuild your credit score.

If you decide to keep some of your debt, make sure that you really *can* afford to pay. And more important, if the debt is in the form of a credit card, be sure that the terms of the card, including your original unused credit limit and interest rate, don't change because of the bankruptcy.

Repairing your credit score

Your credit score is likely to suffer dramatically from a bankruptcy. The better your score originally, the more it drops. If you had terrible credit before, a filing may not cause such a big drop. Either way, you'll likely have a very low credit score for a very long time unless you take positive action to improve it.

In Chapter 13, I explain the factors that influence your credit score. Here's how those factors are influenced by a bankruptcy:

- **Timeliness of payments:** This category may be heavily affected, especially if yours is among the nearly half of all bankruptcies that happen with no prior delinquencies. After you get new credit, be sure to make all your payments on time, every time.

- **Amount and proportion of credit used:** In a bankruptcy, you or your lenders close most of your accounts. Your available credit drops to $0 in most cases. As you reestablish credit, expect low limits at first. Try not to carry balances over 50 percent of your limit for best results.

- **Length of time you've been using credit:** Here again, your score is damaged, because the history on your open accounts stops at your filing. Negative accounts drop off your record in seven years, although the bankruptcy record may remain for up to ten years. Positive accounts are reported for at least ten years and sometimes longer.

- **Variety of accounts:** Chances are you're left with only secured debt such as mortgages, student loans, or car loans. All your revolving and retail accounts may be gone, which means that you don't have the variety of accounts that helps boost your credit score. Consider a secured credit card or a passbook loan to restart your revolving or installment credit history.

- **Number and types of accounts you've opened recently:** After the bankruptcy, you may have more activity here than usual as you attempt to reestablish your credit. And your score will fall. (The more inquiries you have for new accounts or changes, the lower your score.) To minimize damage, don't apply for more accounts than you need.

A helpful tactic is to take steps to improve your credit in each of these five areas. And don't forget that creditors don't necessarily report to all three credit bureaus. Now more than ever, you want to make sure that your good creditor experiences get onto *all* your credit reports. Ask a potential creditor whether it reports all your information to all three bureaus. If it doesn't, try to get credit from another creditor that does.

Follow the tips below to increase your credit score as much as you can in the aftermath of your bankruptcy:

- ✔ **Keep one or two of your older and lower-balance cards or lines of credit open by reaffirming them.** See the preceding section for more information.

- ✔ **Apply for a secured credit card.** This type of account uses a deposit to secure or guarantee that you will make the payments. Most report to the credit bureaus as any other credit card would, but be sure to ask the issuer whether the card you choose is reported.

- ✔ **Open a passbook savings account, and then borrow against it to demonstrate that you can make those fixed payments on time every month.** Again, make sure that the lender reports the loan to the credit bureaus.

Establishing new credit

Yes, you can probably get new credit soon after you come out of bankruptcy. In fact, establishing new lines of credit could be the first step in improving your credit score. You'll face some challenges as you pursue new credit opportunities. For example, you'll discover that the best loans at the most attractive terms and interest rates may not be available to you. Instead, you may find that you're being pursued by loan-shark types that make Jaws look like a guppy (see the earlier sidebar, "Beware of solicitations").

Be extra careful about committing to new lines of credit. Not only are you a target for unscrupulous lenders who specialize in post-bankruptcy loans, but also — now more than ever — you're vulnerable to slipping back into an out-of-control borrowing situation. You don't want to get trapped in debt again. New credit is okay as long as it's part of a plan to rebuild your rating, you're 100 percent confident that you can handle the payments, and it fits into your spending plan.

Moving forward with a game plan

Moving forward with a plan is very different from moving forward *without* one. Although plans may not always work out exactly as you want them to, plans give you the direction, motivation, and tools to achieve your financial ends, and they help you realize when you're drifting.

Begin by paying close attention in the post-bankruptcy education class you must attend as a springboard for your future. You may feel that this class is a waste of time, but it isn't. Then, if you didn't create a spending plan when you went to the credit counseling agency (as you were required to do before filing for bankruptcy), work with your counselor to develop a detailed spending plan that includes saving for financial goals.

A credit counselor will work with you to craft a spending plan that not only fits your current needs but also enables you to set aside money for emergency savings and savings for those goals you want to achieve in the future. This plan tells you how much money you can comfortably spend each month and helps you make sure that you're spending only on those things that you've consciously decided to spend your money on. No impulse buying for you. That money will be allocated to other choices you make — like a college fund, a vacation fund, or a retirement account.

Chapter 9

Repairing Credit Damage in the Wake of Identity Theft

In This Chapter
▶ Knowing who to inform when your identity has been stolen
▶ Taking steps to minimize further damage
▶ Recovering from identity theft and reestablishing your credit

Recovering from identity theft is almost always more difficult and time-consuming than most people think. If you're a victim of identity theft, you need to act quickly and comprehensively. Don't rely on others to resolve this mess. You have the biggest interest in getting this situation stopped, fixed, and behind you, and you need to assume all responsibility for doing so. This chapter tells you who to contact, what to do, and, most important, how to minimize the damage and move on.

Taking Fast Action When Identity Theft Occurs

If your identity has been stolen or you believe that it has (you don't need a smoking gun, video, or a ransacked room to act), do everything I recommend in the following sections as soon as possible. Most of the places you need to contact are open 24 hours a day, so a late-night call won't bother anyone.

Communicating with the right people

You may read different advice on who to call *first* when you believe your identity has been compromised or stolen. Some sources say to begin by reporting the crime to the police to establish a formal record, others suggest that you call your creditors, and still others say to notify the credit bureaus. My advice is to begin in one of two places, depending on your circumstances:

- ✔ If your existing bank or credit accounts have been compromised, call your bank or creditors first.

- ✔ If you find out about accounts you've never heard of and didn't open, call the credit bureaus first.

Either way, don't wait long between the two calls.

Before you pick up the phone, do one more thing: Start recording everything that happens from now on. You want dates, times, names, badge numbers, phone numbers, and so on. Documentation is critical because, unfortunately, this situation may go on for a long time and require a lot of calling and writing to resolve. Don't trust your memory or count on people to call you back when they say they will. You'll help yourself out by writing down the facts and promises.

The online material includes a handy worksheet called "Chart Your Course of Action," courtesy of the Federal Trade Commission, that you may find useful (go to www.dummies.com/extras/creditrepair). You can use it as is or use it to generate ideas for creating a customized chart of your own. I also like the booklet available from the Federal Trade Commission at www.idtheft.gov/probono/docs/i.Table of Contents.pdf. Originally intended for lawyers helping clients deal with theft issues, it is a great self-help guide.

Canceling your cards

If your credit or debit cards have been compromised, call the card issuers, ask for the fraud department, and have the cards cancelled immediately. You can find the phone number on your monthly statements, in your terms-and-conditions brochure, or on the card issuer's website. If you're away from home when you find out the bad news, use a business center computer — don't wait until you get home to call. If you have the card, look for the toll-free customer service number on the back of the card.

A small comfort: Your liability on stolen credit card accounts is relatively low — just $50 maximum per card. Even so, you need to contact all your creditors as quickly as possible so that the thief doesn't continue to rack up charges in your name or open new accounts.

For ATM and debit cards, your maximum liability is $50 if you report the loss within 48 hours of noticing it, but the liability can be $500 or even the full amount of your accounts (including any overdraft protection) if you delay too long.

Getting in touch with the credit bureaus

If you call just one of the three major credit bureaus (Equifax, Experian, or TransUnion) to report identity theft, a 90-day *fraud alert* is placed on all three of your credit files within 24 hours. A fraud alert can make it more difficult for a thief to get credit in your name because it tells creditors to follow certain procedures to protect you. (See the section "Sending out a fraud alert" later in this chapter for more info.)

Fraud alerts aren't foolproof, and compliance by lenders can be spotty. I prefer to lock a door rather than just close it. So consider putting a *credit freeze* on your credit reports until you know how severe the identity theft damage is (see Chapter 20 for info on how to place a freeze). A "frozen" credit report can't be pulled to issue new credit without your express permission, shutting off access to your information much more completely. You can always thaw your accounts later.

You can also add a *victim's statement* to your credit report. This statement informs the people who view your report that the information in your file has a potential problem and that they should be wary of making any decisions based on that information. Most creditors take strong notice of this fact and won't issue new credit in your name.

Adding a victim's statement to your report may motivate creditors to suspend existing accounts that weren't affected until they can determine that you're safe again, which may keep you from using your accounts until you can speak with the creditors.

After you notify the credit bureau of your situation, you'll receive a free credit report from each of the bureaus. Be sure to keep a copy of all reports. (Store them with those copious notes you're taking.)

Contacting the Federal Trade Commission

The Federal Trade Commission (FTC) is the nation's number one consumer protection agency and supports an entire department that handles identity theft issues. The folks in the identity theft clearinghouse don't follow up on individual cases, but they play an important role in looking for patterns and accumulating statistics that help everyone concerned with stopping identity theft.

Call the FTC's Identity Theft Hotline at 877-438-4338 (877-ID-THEFT). From a purely self-serving perspective, contacting the FTC bolsters your claims regarding unauthorized credit card charges or accounts opened by thieves in your name. It has a comprehensive written Theft Affidavit form (`www.ftccomplaintassistant.gov/FTC_Wizard.aspx?Lang=en#last`) that you can print out and use as evidence that a thief misused your information and that you are not responsible for the fraud. While many companies accept this affidavit, others may have their own forms. The FTC Complaint Assistant (`www.ftc.gov/bcp/edu/resources/forms/affidavit.pdf`) is an electronic version that walks you through a detailed form to use when disputing accounts or charges with creditors or when filing a police report in addition to giving the FTC information about the theft.

Notifying the police

If you call the sheriff, will he flip on his blue and red lights and tear around town to find the thief? Not exactly. But a crime has been committed, so you need to call the police and report it. Plus, some of the people you'll be dealing with may require a police report to take action.

The police report is also a way for others in the process to get a straight, consistent story from a third party about what happened and when. You'll have less difficulty convincing a collector if you can send an official police report to bolster your story. Be sure to get a copy of the report as soon as it's available, or at least get the report number for reference.

Here's how the police reporting process works:

1. **Contact your local police station if you suspect that someone is using your identity.**

   You don't need legal proof or a smoking gun to prove your claim; it's your identity, and your suspicion is enough to file a police report.

2. **File the report, providing all the facts and circumstances.**

   Supply all account numbers and other relevant information (see the preceding section regarding the FTC Identity Theft Complaint Assistant or Theft Affidavit). No standard form or procedure exists; each police department has its own.

3. **Get the police report number with the date, time, police department, location, and name of the officer writing the report.**

   You'll likely need to provide this info when dealing with insurance claims, credit card companies, or lenders or collectors to clear your account.

4. **Be persistent but polite if the police seem reluctant to take your statement.**

   Most states require police departments to file reports for identity theft victims, but some police departments may not be required to do so. If your local police are reluctant to file a report, you can remind them that, without a police report, credit bureaus may not block fraudulent items on your credit report, and the lack of a formal police report may inadvertently help a crook.

   If your police department still doesn't want to file a report, contact your state's attorney general's office (you can find contact info at www.naag.org) for assistance.

Alerting the post office

Many identity theft cases result from unauthorized and illegal access to information via the U.S. mail. Tampering with the mail is a federal crime. If you're a victim of identity theft and think that your mail may have played a role, contact the U.S. Postal Inspection Service and report your concerns. Call 877-876-2455 or go to postalinspectors.uspis.gov/forms/IDTheft.aspx.

Protecting your identity through the FACT Act

The Fair and Accurate Credit Transactions Act (the FACT Act or FACTA) has numerous provisions for businesses, credit bureaus, and you. An entire book could be written on the topic, but in essence, the FACT Act was designed to bolster the Fair Credit Reporting Act (FCRA) and address issues surrounding incomplete or inaccurate credit reporting, including new safeguards for identity theft. The following list highlights the consumer-oriented, identity theft–related provisions of the act that I believe are most informative or useful; go to www.dummies.com/extras/creditrepair for a copy of the full act:

- You're entitled to at least one free credit report each year from each of the three credit bureaus. You can often get more than one report if you file a fraud alert (see the next section) or an active-duty alert. Specialty reporting agencies, such as insurance and landlord reporting services, must also give you a free report if you ask. (See Chapter 13 for more info on specialty bureaus.)

- Information based on an account that you've reported as fraudulent or that you've shown to be inaccurate or incomplete cannot be reported to a bureau.

✔ Businesses must cooperate with you to help clear your name in the event of identity theft. They must provide copies of records about goods or services that they provided to the thief. Businesses may require a police report and may take up to 30 days to comply.

✔ You may place a 90-day fraud alert, a 7-year extended fraud alert, and a 1-year military active-duty alert on your credit file.

✔ You may block any fraudulent trade lines on your credit report if you've reported the crime to a police department or law enforcement agency. (See "Blocking fraudulent credit lines" later in this chapter.)

✔ You may request that your Social Security number be truncated (shortened) on your credit report and communications in case it falls into the wrong hands. And credit report users can't just throw your used reports into the trash. They have to dispose of the reports in a legally sanctioned manner.

✔ Businesses must truncate your credit card number on credit card receipts. In other words, your restaurant receipt shouldn't show your entire credit card number — just the last four or five digits.

Sending out a fraud alert

As I mention earlier in this chapter, contacting the credit bureaus is one of the first steps you should take when you discover an identity theft. When you contact them, you have the opportunity to place a fraud alert and a victim's statement in your file. These two items indicate to those who view your report that the request for credit they received recently may not actually be from you. The creditor should contact you before approving a subsequent request for a new account or a change to an existing account.

A fraud alert is placed on your account for 90 days. Any new activity, including your own, is researched and reported to you. So if you open new credit lines during this time, you may notice a slower-than-normal approval process. It's worth the extra red tape to ensure that you and your identity are protected.

If you aren't sure whether your identity has been stolen but you know that the information necessary to steal it has been compromised, consider an *extended alert* on your credit report. An extended alert lasts seven years. Why use an extended alert? Say that your hospital's computer is hacked, and the hacker gets access to patients' Social Security numbers, birthdates, and credit information. The thief may not sell or use your information right away; he may save it for future use. The extended alert covers a long enough period to prevent the information from being used to open an account, say, next year.

An extended alert can be a bit of a nuisance. After you place an extended alert on your credit file, potential creditors are required to contact you, or meet with you in person, before they issue new credit in your name. Still, an extended alert warns you of any suspicious activity even after you've forgotten about the original event that triggered you to establish the alert in the first place.

A small silver lining: After you put an extended fraud alert on your file, you're entitled to two more free copies of your credit report from all three bureaus at any time during the next 12 months.

Blocking fraudulent credit lines

"Block that line" may sound like a football cheer, but blocking can be a powerful tool. Be sure to request that the bureaus block any lines of credit that you believe are fraudulent. You'll have to provide information about the account you want blocked and a copy of your valid police report or state-approved identity theft form. The block prevents those accounts from being sold, transferred, or placed for collection. In addition, ask the credit bureaus to remove any inquiries on your record as a result of those fraudulent lines. Those inquiries can hurt your credit score.

Finally, ask the credit bureaus to notify anyone who may have received reports over the last six months with the erroneous information and inquiries on them. Doing so helps alert creditors and other interested parties to the situation — and can save your reputation.

Getting and Using Credit After Identity Theft

As with any theft, break-in, or personal attack, as a victim of identity theft you likely feel traumatized, fearful, and angry. You may want to avoid any experience with credit and borrowing in the future.

But my advice is to recognize these feelings for what they are — feelings — and not give up altogether. After all, credit — though it certainly can be abused and exploited — is a powerful and sometimes indispensable tool that can help you achieve personal and financial goals that you may not be able to achieve otherwise. I strongly suggest that you adopt a strong offense and move forward with your personal goals. Whether you're planning to buy a house or a car or you're simply taking advantage of a retailer's offer for

10 percent off with a new credit account, don't be afraid to use credit to your advantage. This section outlines some steps that you can take to get your credit going again without putting yourself at renewed risk for identity theft. See Chapter 20 for more ways to protect your identity.

Closing and reopening your accounts

Whether your accounts were broken into, stolen, or just sniffed at, change all your user IDs, passwords, and account numbers. You'll probably have to close the accounts and reopen them. Doing so may be a hassle, but if you've been a victim of identity theft, you already know the meaning of *hassle*.

Here's a list of which accounts to close and reopen:

- ✔ **Bank accounts:** When your information is compromised, you never know if or when trouble will pop up. Changing the account numbers results in dead ends for a thief. Place an alert on the new accounts so that you're informed when certain transactions occur or when dollar amounts are exceeded, such as a debit of more than $1,000.

- ✔ **Credit card accounts:** When you contact the card companies, they'll ask you for proper identification. (This is good — you *want* them to be suspicious!) They're used to closing accounts and reopening new ones quickly and painlessly. I suggest that you reopen only those accounts that you use. As a rule, if I haven't used a card in two years, I begin to wonder why it's taking up space in my wallet or sock drawer.

- ✔ **Other accounts:** Contact your Internet service provider, telephone service provider, and utility companies to alert them of the identity theft and to get new account numbers.

Altering your PINs, passwords, and radio transmissions

When you reopen your bank accounts, change your personal identification numbers (PINs), too. And when you access money at ATMs or in public places, make sure that no one can see you enter the PIN. Getting close to the machine may block the sight of someone across the street using binoculars or a camera with a telephoto lens. (Yes, thieves really *do* go that far.) Using ATMs located in bank lobbies is better for your security.

Some newer credit cards use technology that allows you to make a charge by tapping your card on a reader rather than swiping it. It is very popular in Europe, where our magnetic-strip-only cards are considered relics. If you have this newer type of card, a thief with a sensitive reader can get your credit card information via a radio transmission from the chip in your card. Be sure to use a transmission-blocking sleeve. See Chapter 20 for more identity-protection measures.

For online access to bank, credit card, bill-paying, and investment accounts, switch to a *pass phrase* instead of a password. A pass phrase uses a short series of words like "Mauiis#1" instead of a single password. Pass phrases tend to be longer and harder to crack. Include some capital letters, numbers, and non-letter characters for additional strength.

Changing your Social Security number and driver's license number

If you can't seem to shake the damage done by identity theft (because new occurrences keep popping up or collectors keep landing on you like mosquitoes), you may need to take more serious action. Consider contacting the Social Security Administration to inquire about getting a new Social Security number.

Getting a new Social Security number is a huge pain for everyone. Imagine all the places you've used your old number. If you go this route, you need to change all your records yourself. For more information, visit the Social Security website at `www.socialsecurity.gov` or `ssa-custhelp.ssa.gov/app/answers/detail/a_id/79/session/L3RpbWUvMTM3NjMzNjcONy9zaWQvV0pUcllCeGGw=`, or call 800-772-1213 (800-325-0778 TTY for the hearing impaired).

You won't be the first person who had to take this step. Besides the storied federal witness protection program, Social Security numbers are changed for domestic violence victims and others when warranted. But with all the emphasis on national security, changing your number isn't easy.

A few circumstances can prevent you from changing your Social Security number. You can't get a new Social Security number if

- ✔ You've filed for bankruptcy.
- ✔ You intend to avoid the law or your legal responsibility.
- ✔ Your Social Security card is lost or stolen, but there's no evidence that someone else is using your number.

Be sure to document everything. This dog can have a very long tail. You may need to dig up documentation a year or two after you thought all the dust had settled. Good written records, with names and dates, are a godsend.

While you're at it, go to the Department of Motor Vehicles and get your driver's license number changed, especially if someone is using yours as an ID.

Part III

Rebuilding Credit, No Matter Where or When You Begin

Five Money-Related Issues to Discuss Before You Say "I Do"

- ✔ Discuss your current annual income and your income hopes for the future. This is a chance to show support, not to criticize.

- ✔ Talk about your debts and how you plan to handle them. Will you each pay your own debts? Will you pool them together and split them 50-50? Or will the bigger earner pay more?

- ✔ Discuss your spending habits (whether you're frugal, indulgent, or don't even know how to budget). The frugal one may be the better choice to handle your bill paying.

- ✔ Discuss your personal approaches to budgeting. Will you count every penny or go for estimates instead? Yes, you need a budget!

- ✔ Discuss your financial goals. Make this exercise fun. After all, it is about dreams and hopes. No wet blankets allowed!

Find ways to get the best terms on a new credit card at www.dummies.com/extras/creditrepair.

In this part . . .

- ✔ Create good credit for couples, and shelter your credit in a split-up.

- ✔ Establish credit if you are an immigrant or a first-time credit user.

- ✔ Maintain your good credit after losing your job so it won't limit your new job opportunities.

- ✔ Handle debt incurred because of medical bills or the death of a spouse.

- ✔ Know the special credit rules for students and military service members.

Chapter 10

Starting (or Restarting) Your Credit in Real Life

C redit isn't an American invention. It's been around in one form or another since ancient Roman times. Modern consumer credit, however, is as American as apple pie. Taking off after the GIs returned from World War II, credit has been among the most prolific of financial services. Life without it is almost unimaginable today, but if you're among those starting over or just getting started, getting the credit you need may be easier said than done. Those starting over because of divorce or death can find the process to be a stressful endeavor, while credit newbies such as recent immigrants and high school or college graduates may wonder where to start. You may find yourself feeling like you're looking through a shop window but can't find the door to get in.

This chapter is your point of entry. I help you understand why a good credit history and financial-services relationships are essential to getting the credit you need. Your confidence gets a boost when I show you the size and importance to lenders of the underbanked market (meaning people like you, whose financial needs aren't being met), so you know just where you stand. I also debunk some credit myths that you may have brought with you from another country or may have been taught right here at home by well-meaning but misinformed friends. I include help for young people as well, with sections for students, grads, and military members. Take your seat at the table and help yourself to a big piece of the American dream: credit.

Debunking Misinformation about Banking and Credit

Depending on your culture or what your friends and family may have told you, you may not have an accurate understanding of how credit really works. However, with a few tips, you'll find that using credit can increase your enjoyment of life and all it has to offer. The following list debunks some commonly held misconceptions about banking and credit:

- ✔ **Banks aren't safe places to put money because they can fail, causing you to lose all your money.** Not so. All depository institutions (like banks) are insured by the full faith and credit of the U.S. government for up to $250,000 per depositor. No one has ever lost a penny of money that was insured in an FDIC or NCUA federally insured depository account.

- ✔ **Bank accounts are unsafe because currency can decrease in value or become worthless overnight.** When you deposit money into a U.S. bank, it's deposited in dollars. The dollar, though subject to fluctuations in value, is the most stable and trusted currency in the world. So it's safe!

- ✔ **The government may nationalize your bank and your account.** If the financial crisis taught people anything, it's that the government wants to support, not own, banks.

- ✔ **You need to be rich to be treated well at a bank.** Not so. Adding new customers is a top priority for banks, and the size of your account, no matter how small your deposits may be, doesn't determine your value as a customer. Banks know that many big depositors start out small and increase their deposits over time. If a bank doesn't respect you on your terms, take your money to a competing bank.

- ✔ **Using cash is safer than using credit or debit cards.** A lost or stolen card is protected against misuse by another person (most have a liability of $50 or less); lost or stolen cash is gone. Plus, purchasing with cash never builds the credit history you need for a credit score.

- ✔ **You can't build a credit history if you have only a consular ID or a green card and not a Social Security number.** Not true. You can establish a credit history and use credit without a Social Security number.

The following sections explain why you need credit and why it's safe. I hope that this information eases any anxiety you may have.

Why you need credit

What's your definition of the good life? A good job, a safe place to live, a car, some financial security, and a good education for your kids? The reality of life in the U.S. is that having good credit is important in accomplishing goals like these.

Building from checking to credit to a business

A solid credit report and a good credit score help you gain employment, borrow money, and get a credit card, a decent apartment, and insurance. They can also form the first building block in starting a new business. With good credit, savings, and the stability that savings bring, you're a prime candidate to step up to that business you may have always wanted.

Good personal credit is essential. If you want to start a business, you can't be financially successful in doing so unless you move from the underbanked to traditional banking. That big piece of the American dream called credit is now yours to enjoy. Be sure to bring the family! For more information about starting your own business, check out *Small Business For Dummies*, 4th Edition, by Eric Tyson and Jim Schell (Wiley).

Let's start with that good job. Chances are that you have to compete with others for a good position. Many employers check your credit history to see whether you're reliable or you have distracting financial issues at home before making an offer. People can lie about their experience (ADP Screening and Selection Services says that about half of applicants lie on their resumes), and they can pretend to be nice during an interview, but a good credit history is tough to fake. As one employer put it, "When you think about it, people who have good credit keep their promises and are responsible, so it makes sense that if their credit is good, they may be more honest." So, all other things being equal, the job may go to the candidate with the best credit history.

The same thing happens when you try to rent an apartment, buy insurance, apply for a college loan, or vie for a promotion at work. In all these circumstances, the person making the decision may check your credit history as part of the qualification process. Being underbanked and relying on cash may knock you out of the race. It pays to understand how to build good credit and use the banking and financial system to your advantage.

Why credit is safe

The credit industry didn't become the huge and powerful entity that it is today without addressing the question of safety. The federal government has put many regulations and safeguards in place over the last several years to ensure the safety and fair treatment of credit users. As a result, you have access to one of the fairest and most market-driven credit systems in the world. The following laws play a major role in protecting borrowers in the U.S.:

- ✔ **The Fair and Accurate Credit Transactions Act (FACT Act or FACTA)** gives you lots of rights when it comes to how your credit is reported and what you can do to correct mistakes. It also gives you rights and remedies in the event of identity theft.

- ✓ **The Fair Debt Collection Practices Act (FDCPA)** spells out what third-party bill collectors can and can't do when they try to collect a debt. If they step over the line, you can sue them.

- ✓ **The Equal Credit Opportunity Act (ECOA)** prohibits credit discrimination on the basis of race, color, religion, national origin, sex, marital status, age, and whether you get public assistance. Creditors may collect this information, but they can't use it to decide whether to give you credit or how to set your credit terms.

- ✓ **The Credit Card Accountability, Responsibility, and Disclosure Act (CARD Act)** protects you from unfair credit card billing practices. Major protections spell out notification requirements, grace periods, fees, interest rate changes, restrictions on student cards, and more.

- ✓ **The Dodd-Frank Wall Street Reform and Consumer Protection Act** established an independent consumer financial protection bureau within the Federal Reserve to protect borrowers against abuses in mortgage services, credit card services, payday lending, and credit counseling.

- ✓ **The Truth in Lending laws** ensure that you won't find any hidden surprises when you borrow money. All the costs of borrowing must be spelled out for you before you sign a contract.

Recognizing what's not in your credit history

With all the information available to companies, the government, and others, you may think that your credit report houses a huge dossier about your every movement. To clarify: A credit history is nothing more than a snapshot of your financial life to date.

Keeping track of the information that can make or break your chances of getting credit may seem mind-boggling. The good news is that only the information sent to the credit bureaus by people with whom you choose to do business ends up in your file. And even then, not all your information is reported. Some companies and service providers, like doctors, hospitals, and grocery stores, don't report credit activity at all. Turn to Chapter 14 to read about other items that aren't included in your credit report.

You have the right to dispute out-of-date or inaccurate information in your credit report. These provisions are detailed in the FACT Act, which is spelled out at www.dummies.com/extras/creditrepair. Check out Chapter 14 for more info about what appears in your credit history.

Obtaining Credit: Starting Out on the Right Foot

You're ready to begin building your own credit, but you're not quite sure where to start. They say that a journey begins with a single step, which just goes to show how wrong people can be. The journey actually begins when you have a destination in mind. Then, after packing your lunch and other essentials, you take that first step. You build up a credit history over a period of time. How much time depends on how active you are and which scoring model is used to rate your credit file.

Don't fret, though. This section walks you through the steps to help you begin your credit journey down the right path.

Establishing a credit file without a Social Security number

You don't need a Social Security number to start building your credit report. In fact, a frequent misconception is that to establish a credit history, and thereby a credit score, you need a Social Security number, a driver's license, or a voter registration card. None of these items is required to establish a successful and envious credit record.

Why banks want to do business with you

Why do banks do anything? To make money, of course. With hundreds of millions of dollars in profits at stake, some of the biggest and best names in the financial-services industry would love to have you as a long-term customer. Why do they like long-term customers? You guessed it: They're more profitable. Selling something new to someone you know is much easier than selling to a stranger. So banks really do want your business, although at times you may not know it from the way they act.

Now that you know you're a valued and valuable customer in a large market segment that banks want to do business with, you should expect to be treated well, respected, and, yes, maybe even spoiled just a little. Anything less and you can just move on to the next player, who may know better how to treat a valuable customer like you.

When a credit bureau receives a new data line, the bureau matches the data with the following items, in the order shown:

1. Your name
2. Your birthdate
3. Your address
4. Your Social Security number

No number? No problem. The bureaus can use plenty of other matching points to get your information into the right file. But being consistent is important! For example, make sure to spell your name exactly the same way every time you apply for or use credit.

Setting goals before you set out

Figuring out what your goals are prior to seeking credit is an important step, especially for the underbanked and those new to credit. Writing down your goals enables you to see what you need to do financially to achieve success.

To begin setting goals, I suggest that you (and your partner, if you have one) follow these steps:

1. **Set aside some uninterrupted time to dream about the future you want.**

   Allow at least an hour, and set an end point so that you finish before you are exhausted. You can always come back to this step later after some reflection.

2. **Write down some short-term (one year or less), intermediate-term (one to five years), and long-term (more than five years) goals.**

   Typical goals include beginning to save this year, beginning to save next year, getting out of debt within a year, and rebuilding bad credit. Others would like to receive guidance on financial topics such as bank accounts, certificates of deposit (CDs), children's college savings accounts, and retirement accounts.

   Writing down your goals serves two purposes: It clarifies what you're talking about, and it makes your goals seem more real.

3. **Make a list of the actions you need to take to reach each goal.**

   For example, if you want to get a better apartment and a new job, how do you do so? Good credit can help. A smart first step is to get a copy of your credit report at www.annualcreditreport.com and make sure that it's accurate. Dispute and remove any inaccuracies or out-of-date items to improve your credit. Then make sure to make your payments on all your accounts on time. It's simple, but it works. Chapter 18 has more suggestions about budgeting and goal setting.

A real-life couple: How goals can help

I love using examples to illustrate and clarify concepts. To help me, I invented Roland and Carlotta, two recently engaged young people who are new to credit and want to get a head start on their life together. They begin by spending an hour one evening imagining what they want their futures to look like and then setting goals to make it happen.

Roland and Carlotta want to get married in a year, and they agree that they want a better apartment and eventually a small house for

the family they'd like to start as soon as they're able. Roland wants a better job than the hourly one he currently has, and he would really like to buy a better car. Carlotta wants to decorate their new place and buy some new furniture for it. She also wants to establish credit for herself, and Roland needs to repair his credit.

You don't need to be in complete agreement on all the specifics as long as you can agree on the concept. You can make adjustments as you get closer to your goals.

	Roland's Goals	Carlotta's Goals
Short term	Get married	Plan a wedding and get married
	Open savings and checking accounts	Establish credit
Medium term	Get a better apartment	Get a bigger apartment
	Repair credit	Furnish and decorate apartment
	Get a better job	
	Buy a car	
Long term	Buy a big house	Buy a house
	Have six children	Start a family

4. **Track your progress.**

   Reviewing your progress toward your goals periodically is not only an incentive to keep up the good work but also an opportunity to celebrate your interim successes.

Establishing a relationship with a financial institution

The saying "That's as good as money in the bank" means that it's as good as it gets. Having money in the bank is a good thing; it is the situation you want to be in. If you don't have a relationship with a bank or credit union, I can't stress enough how important this relationship is to your ultimate success. You want to develop a relationship with a bank by setting up at least a savings or checking account, not just so you have a place to take out a loan or get a titanium credit card to impress your friends, but because you need a place to put the money you earn but don't spend right away. Saving is essential to your success.

Spending everything you make or using credit to supplement your income is a recipe for disaster. There's no substitute for savings when life throws you a curveball. Chapter 5 has details on what you can do when times get tough. But without savings, even life's little bumps are enough to hold you back on your journey to financial success.

Why you need to save

Everything is going okay. The money that comes in goes out, and your debt is under control. You may be a little short at the moment and your credit card balances may be building, but you figure that will end as soon as you get that promotion in six months. Then your car muffler falls off and costs $500 to repair, your tooth breaks at lunch and you need $900 for a crown, and your roommates tell you that they're moving out and you have to pay the rent on your own. Where does the money come from if you have no savings?

You can use credit if you have any left. But if you do, you may be paying a high interest rate and getting closer to your card limit, and your minimum payment is now huge.

Without access to credit or savings, you have fewer choices. You may have to carpool, have the tooth removed rather than crowned, and be forced to move to less-expensive housing. That's why you need savings; credit and good luck are never enough for you to be financially successful.

How to get started saving

Fortunately, starting to save is easy and painless once you get going. The key is not to focus on how you're going to save six months' worth of living expenses, which could test even a saint. (For your information, St. Matthew is the patron saint of money managers.) What I want you to do is start with a small savings program but make it automatic.

To get started saving, take the following steps:

1. **Go to a nearby bank or credit union and ask about automatic deposit savings and checking accounts.**

   You probably don't have much to put away, at least right now, but that's okay. Limited funds are no excuse for not saving. Tell the bank that you don't want to pay any fees because you'll be using automatic deposit. If the bank charges a fee, go to another bank or credit union. Banks and credit unions usually waive all fees for people who save regularly through payroll deductions.

2. **After you open two accounts, one checking and one savings, go to your human resources or payroll department at work and say that you want your pay automatically deposited into these two accounts.**

   For example, you want all your take-home pay minus $5 (or more if you can) put into checking and the remaining $5 put into your savings account. At the end of the first pay period, you will have saved $5. Not a huge sum, but you're starting a habit that will grow and add up with time.

   If direct deposit isn't available through your employer, you can have your bank automatically transfer money monthly from your checking account to your savings account.

3. **When you get that next raise or promotion, have half the increase automatically deposited into your savings account.**

   Now you're making a smart financial move — increasing your savings by putting away the extra money from your raise before you have an opportunity to spend it! Do the same thing for tax refunds and other windfalls. In no time you'll have a cushion that can get you over life's bumps without stretching your credit or damaging your credit history!

To secure your financial future, stop cashing paychecks and start automatic savings. You owe it to yourself, your family, and your future.

Using prepaid and reloadable cards

While you are building your credit, you may want to consider using prepaid and reloadable cards as alternatives to using cash. They're neither credit cards nor debit cards; rather, they exist somewhere in between. You deposit money onto the cards at locations throughout the nation and then use them as you would a credit or debit card. But they don't build your credit history or score.

The following list outlines the major advantages of prepaid and reloadable cards:

- ✔ You can use money without getting mugged for the cash in your pocket.

- ✔ You need no credit record or credit check — just your name, address, and phone number and the ability to pay a one-time fulfillment fee. Non-U.S. citizens can provide an alternative form of ID, such as a driver's license, passport, or alien registration. Funds may post to your account within 30 minutes.

- ✔ Prepaid cards offer convenience, easy availability, guaranteed approval, and other features that can make them ideal substitutes for credit cards.

- ✔ You can use prepaid cards online, over the phone, and in many other places, just like a credit card or debit card.

- ✔ Prepaid cards can help with financial discipline and the building of good financial habits.

Fattening up your credit file

If your credit file is underweight, you're not alone. Today, up to 50 million U.S. adults — nearly 25 percent of credit-eligible consumers — come back from credit inquiries to the major bureaus either as no-hits or as *thin files* (files with too little data in them to receive a credit score).

If you fit this category, don't worry. You can take action to build your credit muscle. The following options work well for credit newbies and underbanked individuals:

- **Continue using your foreign credit card if you have one.** You may be surprised to find out that foreign credit history doesn't carry over and can't be imported into your U.S. credit file. However, you can still use your impeccable overseas credit experience to your advantage. You can either continue to use your foreign credit card or get a letter from a multinational bank extolling your virtues so that the local underwriters will approve you for an American credit card that is reported to the American credit bureaus.

  Global scoring is expected in the future; in fact, FICO claims a proven global score that's accurate in every country in the world except France *(quelle surprise!)*. However, while the global score is being used in many countries, it isn't used in the U.S. yet.

- **Ask that an expansion score be used to score your application for credit.** This is a one-time snapshot of about 90 noncredit databases that tell whether you pay your obligations as agreed. Reporting real-time information rather than keeping a warehouse full of dated material may be the future of credit reporting. (Check out Chapter 3 for more info.)

- **Take out a passbook loan:** A *passbook loan* is a loan the bank makes to you using your own money. It may sound strange, but if you open a passbook savings account at a bank or credit union and then borrow the money back, the bank gladly charges you interest (low interest, thank heavens) and reports your loan repayment history to the credit bureaus. You use your money in place of credit for the loan until you can build enough credit to get an unsecured loan. Faster than you can say "Super Prime," you're adding positive history to your file and improving your score.

  Check with your bank or credit union to make sure that it reports the loan to at least one, and preferably all three, of the major credit-reporting bureaus. If it doesn't, request that it do so. If the bank is unwilling to report the loan to at least one of the bureaus, take your business elsewhere.

✔ **Get a secured credit card.** A secured card is a cross between a credit card and a prepaid card. After you establish a savings account and build up the balance, you can ask the bank to give you a credit card backed by your deposit in the bank. You may qualify for a credit line in excess of the amount you have in savings.

Many credit issuers eventually move you to a traditional credit card after a period of successful payment. The best part is that, unlike most prepaid cards, many secured cards are reported to the three major credit bureaus and can help you build a history and a credit score. Shop around for the best terms; many secured credit cards have high interest rates and fees.

Here's how to get and use a secured card:

1. **Contact your bank or credit union to find out whether it offers secured credit cards, or look online for an issuing bank.**

   Watch out for annual processing or maintenance fees. You can get secured credit cards for free — you just have to look around for banks or credit unions that offer them.

2. **Deposit the funds to be used as security for the card.**

   Be sure that the account is FDIC or NCUA insured.

3. **Use the card for purchases, making sure that you can pay the balance each month.**

   You don't need to use the card a lot. Just make a few purchases each month.

4. **Make on-time payments every month.**

A last word about credit scores and access to credit

Getting a credit score takes a few months or more of credit use. The two major credit score providers, FICO and VantageScore, require different amounts of payment history to generate a score. (See Chapter 14 for more information on credit scores.) Also, you need more than a score to, well, score a card! Lenders are hyper-nervous about potential losses. New accounts are an unknown, so the lender will look at your credit report and income information in detail to decide whether it should grant you credit.

Avoiding high interest, fees, and scams

Unfortunately, being new to something leaves you vulnerable to abuse by people who know the rules better than you do. Abuses perpetuated on immigrants and credit newbies have been around forever and aren't about to go away. This section lists several that you're likely to run into, along with some guidelines on how to handle them.

Payday loans

When you don't have savings or credit but you have an unexpected expense, what do you do? An entire industry has arisen to answer this question. *Payday lenders* charge a very high interest rate or fee for a short-term loan guaranteed by your next paycheck. The fee is based on the amount of your paycheck, and you must supply the lender with a signed check for the date the loan is due.

It's not unusual for a person seeking such a loan to need additional money after the lender cashes the postdated check. This can start a vicious cycle of high-fee, high-interest loans rolling over or piling up with no practical way to pay them off. Payday lenders don't report your loan experience to the credit bureaus, so you receive no credit history–building benefit. If you must use a payday lender, look for one that's a member of the Community Financial Services Association of America (www.cfsaa.com). Members subscribe to a code of conduct and may offer extended repayment terms if you can't pay back a loan as scheduled.

Refund anticipation loans (RALs)

Refund anticipation loans (RALs) are high-fee loans secured by your tax refund that may, and the operative word here is *may*, get you your refund a week or so earlier than having it direct-deposited after filing your return electronically. The real downside of these loans is that the person who sells you the loan has an incentive to inflate your tax refund to get you to take out a higher loan.

If your actual refund is less than what you borrow, you owe the difference plus a hefty interest rate. A much better idea is to open a bank account and have any refund direct-deposited. You get it fast, free, and with no surprises.

Check-cashing for a high fee

Going to a check-cashing place instead of a bank or credit union is like shopping at the most expensive store in town in the worst possible neighborhood. Check cashers are often located in places that are rife with crime. Why? Because everyone coming out has a pocket full of cash. A bank or credit union with which you have an account won't charge you to cash your check, and you don't have to take all the cash with you when you leave — you can deposit it in your savings and checking accounts.

Instant credit rating

Credit repair companies may offer you a new identity or a repaired credit rating for only a few hundred dollars. Don't spend the money. The new identity is often illegal, and the instant credit repair doesn't exist.

Foreign bank accounts

Occasionally, you may receive a letter or e-mail saying that you've been chosen (lucky you!) to help a rich foreign person get some money into the U.S. and that you'll receive a fat percentage of the amount for your small trouble because you're trustworthy. Most of these communications come from Nigeria, but they can originate anywhere. Don't do it!

Overcoming Credit Fears and Mistakes

Everyone makes mistakes, even lenders and credit bureaus. A mistake needn't be a big deal if you deal with it quickly.

As a person new to credit and maybe even new to the United States, you may be a tad scared of having to deal with credit and the problems that can come along with it. Bill collectors aren't above using threats of deportation or imprisonment if they think that doing so will help them collect a bill. The truth is, they can't legally do either. You won't be deported and you won't go to jail, no matter what they say. How do I know for sure? Well, these companies only get paid for collecting the money due their employers. If they actually deported you or put you in jail, they wouldn't get their money!

You can find complete copies of the FACT Act, the CARD Act, and the Fair Debt Collection Practices Act, all of which spell out your rights, at www.dummies.com/extras/creditrepair.

If you're a credit newbie or have had a problem with your credit (including checking overdrafts), keep these basic tips in mind for dealing with mistakes:

- ✔ **Don't delay.** Credit and debt problems, unlike my wife, don't improve with age. If you're proactive and make an effort to resolve a problem before you receive a call, you'll get a much better reception and improve your chances of a favorable resolution.

- ✔ **Open your statements when you get them and challenge anything you don't understand or remember.** You can correct errors, but often there are time limits. And what may look like an error may turn out to be the beginning of an identity theft.

If you overdraw your checking account, be sure to contact the bank as soon as you find out. The objective is to work out a solution before the bank reports the overdraft to one of the credit bureaus. Having this kind of a black mark on your report can make it difficult or even impossible to open a checking account for up to several years afterward.

- ✔ **Do everything in writing.** You may resolve simple problems over the phone, but to protect your rights in a dispute, you need to make your case in writing. If you really want a problem fixed, do it in writing and keep good records.

- ✔ **Keep track of contacts.** Keeping notes on who promised what to whom not only keeps you from making more mistakes but also tells the other person that you know what you're doing. So when the manager says that this is the first time you've called, you can say, "You are mistaken; I called on these occasions, and I spoke to these people, who told me these things."

- ✔ **Keep cool and calm.** Nothing can derail your effort to resolve an error faster than raising your voice. After you escalate the volume, you'll be directed to someone who does "loud" professionally, or you'll be politely ignored. Either way, you lose. Call back if you need to, but don't lose control.

- ✔ **Safeguard your identity.** Newbies to credit often come from a culture of sharing. Whether you shared with your family in Mexico or you shared with your roommate at Harvard, the time for sharing information and credit is over. Identity theft is a serious and growing crime that can take years to unravel and cost thousands of dollars to fix. Chapter 9 tells you how to safeguard your identity, but in brief, guard your personal identification, mail, computer passwords, and bank account information. Shred financial mail. If you invite people into your home, be sure to put away your financial statements and checkbook. You wouldn't leave $20 bills all over the floor and furniture. The same applies to financial information.

Chapter 14 has more information on what to do if you run afoul of the credit-reporting system. If you do end up owing more than you can pay and you have to deal with collectors, Chapter 5 has the advice you need.

Qualifying for First-Time Cards and Lending

This section looks at how credit impacts two major and basic consumer credit instruments that most people need when they get started on life's journey: credit cards and loans. You may think that you know how these instruments work, but things have changed because of regulations like the CARD Act and the financial meltdown that threatened banks with failure due in large part to lax underwriting standards.

Getting a credit card

Getting credit for the first time used to be easy. All you had to do was drive to your nearest gas station and fill out an application for a gas card and then wait for the mail to arrive with your new plastic. If you were a city dweller who didn't drive, the trip may have been on foot to a department store, which would often grant credit on the spot. Both types of credit were relatively easy to get, and they reported your credit history to the three bureaus so that you built a credit history quickly. More and more department store and gas cards are tightening their standards to reflect tightened credit conditions. You can try for cards issued by banks that use a national transaction network such as Visa. Though these cards are more versatile and powerful than their earlier counterparts, they're also harder to get. Getting that first card now requires a new approach.

To begin with, you need a credit history. But how do you get a credit history without credit? Two of the most popular ways are to use someone else's credit or to use a secured credit card.

Using other people's credit

In most instances, when you use another person's credit, the other person is a family member or a person with whom you have an emotional attachment. Why? Because using someone else's credit can be dangerous to that person if you mess up. Only someone who really likes you is willing to risk helping you get started.

You can piggyback on another person's credit in two ways. The most popular way is to be added to the person's account as an authorized user. The other way is to have the person cosign for you.

Becoming an authorized user

Being named an *authorized user* on someone's credit account enables you to have his or her credit history reported on your credit report while you use a card for which the other person is solely financially responsible. The card statement goes to the account owner, he or she pays the credit card company, you pay the card owner, and the card's credit history is reported in both your and the owner's files. Problems with this approach can arise if the account owner defaults or is late with payments, because then those negative marks go on your credit history, too. Another common pitfall is that you overcharge and the account owner has to ask you for more money than you have available, which can cause a rift between you.

Cosigning

Cosigning on an account is more often than not a recipe for disaster, and I usually don't recommend it. The cosigner's credit history doesn't show up on your credit report. Instead, all that shows up is your own payment history. The statement for a cosigned account doesn't go to the cosigner, so unless you share the information, the cosigner has no idea what's happening to the account. Often, the cosigner first hears of a problem when a collector calls and demands an overdue payment. Unfortunately, if you make late payments, the delinquency history appears on the cosigner's credit report, and negative information stays on the cosigner's credit history for a full seven years.

If you decide to go the cosigning route, I suggest that as the borrower, you commit to paying this bill before almost any other. You also need to have the courage to keep your cosigner informed of any changes in your financial picture, especially if you may be late on a payment.

Using secured cards

A secured card looks and works just like a credit card but is backed by a cash deposit at the bank that issues the card. Typically, your deposit qualifies you for a credit card with a limit equal to that deposit amount. As a result, limits on secured cards tend to be low, but the real value here is to establish a credit history so that you can get an unsecured card and reallocate your deposit to a better purpose, like your emergency savings account.

You can find and compare secured cards on a number of websites. My favorites include www.bankrate.com and www.creditcards.com. You want to balance services, fees, and interest rates to find the best card for you.

Using savings for credit

Most banks and credit unions are happy to lend you your own money. If you accumulate some savings in a passbook account, you can use the savings to secure an installment loan of the same or a lesser amount. Needless to say, with 100 percent collateral in cash for the loan, the interest rate should be very low. Make sure that the loan is reported to the credit bureaus so that you build your credit as you pay the money back.

Considering Credit for Students and Military Members

At first blush, students and military members may not seem similar. However, as a credit grouping, they share some commonalities. For example, both have relatively limited means, a high number of younger members, a susceptibility to scams, and laws designed to protect them. And bankruptcy doesn't work as well for students or military members as it does for the general population.

In this section, I show you the protections offered under the CARD Act and Dodd-Frank legislation, as well as the impact of the Servicemembers Civil Relief Act. I also offer practical advice tuned to the unique needs of students and military members.

Giving credit to students

Most young people entering college or technical school have been brought up using their parents' credit cards. They'd sooner be without their cell-phones than do without a credit card. But after they cross that line from authorized son or daughter user to customer, they're exposed to all the pluses and minuses of the credit industry.

Imagine new drivers getting behind the wheel with no driver's education, no insurance, no speed limit, and no police to tell them to slow down. Not a pretty picture, is it? This scenario applies to students and credit, and this section helps you avoid crashing your credit and maybe your immediate future with some insights and suggestions for students and their parents.

Checking out the CARD Act

The Credit Card Accountability, Responsibility, and Disclosure Act of 2009 (CARD Act) aimed to bring about more responsible lending and borrowing and foster more accountability in debt management. The CARD Act set rules to stem the tide of heavily indebted students who often have to drop out of school, work full-time jobs while studying to pay off credit card debts, or enter the job market with damaged credit that can interfere with finding a job. Key provisions include

- ✔ **Proof of income:** Under the law, if you're under the age of 21, you must show proof that you can repay any credit card debt you may incur.
- ✔ **Cosign requirement:** If you don't have sufficient income, you need to find someone who does to cosign on the account.

✔ **Credit limit regulations:** Card companies can no longer offer a preapproved credit limit just because you're a student. Limits have to be based on your independent ability to repay, or you need a cosigner. And if you have a cosigner, the cosigner must approve limit increases in writing.

✔ **Fewer sign-up incentives:** Card issuers can't turn your head with sign-up rewards such as free T-shirts, pizza, or electronics. The law also prohibits credit card companies from hitting you up on school property. They must remain a specified distance away from campuses. However, they can set up shop at other locations favored by students.

✔ **Practical financial education:** Though not a part of the CARD Act, you may find some financial education programs at your school. Many schools require freshmen to attend sessions on credit and debt management.

Practicing student credit etiquette

No, you don't need white gloves or a tie to practice credit etiquette. But if you're new to having your own credit and being responsible for the consequences, here are some basic rules for keeping your credit neat and tidy, regardless of how messy your roommate is:

✔ Don't apply for a credit card you don't need. Every time you apply for a card, it counts against your credit score, whether you're approved or not.

✔ It's okay to leave your socks lying around, but not your credit cards or billing statements. Misuse and identity theft happen to students, too!

✔ Lend a shirt, your car, or your date to a friend, but never lend your credit card. You're fully responsible for anything your friend does with your card. Anything!

✔ Decide what you consider to be an emergency worthy of using your credit card before one happens to you. If you can wear it, eat it, or drink it, it isn't an emergency!

✔ Stick to one low-interest-rate card and charge only what you can afford to pay in full each month. If you must use more than one card, pay off the card with the highest interest rate first, and make at least the minimum payment on the other(s), on time.

✔ Before you charge an item, reflect on whether you can pay it off at the end of the month. If you know that you would have to carry the balance over, estimate how long you would need to pay it off before swiping. If the answer is more than 90 days, seriously reconsider buying the item!

Student credit loopholes to watch out for

Any law has its loopholes, and the CARD Act is no exception when it comes to protecting students from credit card schemes. The CARD Act doesn't allow credit card issuers to market their cards on campus, but they may operate just over the edge of campus. Older students have been buying beer for younger students forever, so cosigning for a student under 21 is nothing new. Students need to show income to get a card, and some applications may allow student loan proceeds to be counted as income. Income verification beyond filling out the application can be spotty for young adults who may not file their own tax returns.

Following military credit rules

America owes a tremendous debt of gratitude to those who volunteer to defend this country and way of life. Not surprisingly, Americans take a dim view of those who take advantage of soldiers and sailors during their term of service. Life is complicated enough in the service without having financial concerns distract you from your mission. This section discusses some of the rules of engagement between the military and the financial-services sector.

Enlisting with credit issues

In addition to meeting rigorous moral character standards, those seeking to join the military undergo a background check that includes a review of their credit history. Uncle Sam doesn't want to give you a loan; he wants to make sure that you don't have existing financial problems, because you're not likely to overcome those difficulties on junior enlisted pay. See Chapter 2 for ways to get your credit under control before you walk into a recruiting station and raise your hand.

Serving with credit issues

Credit problems happen in the military as well as in civilian life. Military personnel have extra protections under the law known as the Servicemembers Civil Relief Act. They're entitled to enhanced protection from eviction, auto lease cancellation penalties, high interest rates, and being summoned to a court hearing while serving. For more information, see Chapter 5.

A program sponsored by the U.S. Department of Defense, Military One Source offers financial counseling if you're having financial difficulties. Military One Source also offers confidential resources and support for service members and their families on a wide range of topics. Twelve financial counseling sessions are available at no cost to active duty, Guard, and Reserve members and family members, as well as deployed Department of Defense civilians and their families. Financial counseling is available in person and over the phone in partnership with a vetted nonprofit organization (currently the National Foundation for Credit Counseling, or NFCC).

Counseling includes education and coaching in the areas of

- Budgeting
- The creation of a realistic action plan using specific, manageable steps
- Housing (prepurchase, foreclosure prevention, and reverse mortgage)
- Credit and active-duty alerts
- Debt management
- Debt collections
- Financial-related deployment issues
- The Servicemembers Civil Relief Act (SCRA)
- Payday loans, title loans, and rent-to-own

To reach Military One Source, call 800-342-9647 from inside the U.S., 800-342-6477 from outside the U.S., or 484-530-5747 for an international collect call, or go to `www.militaryonesource.com`.

Advice for non-English speakers

If you're new to the United States and new to credit, you may be new to English as well. Although many companies offer financial services in other languages and most documents are at least bilingual, the language of finance is English. Period. Having to do business in another language limits the number of people you can do business with and thereby limits your access to competitive products and services. For example, my daughter-in-law's parents are Korean. They do business only with a financial planner who is and speaks Korean. As a result, their selection of advisors and products is severely restricted. My advice is to become fluent in English as soon as possible.

Chapter 11

Ending Life's Negative Credit Surprises

In This Chapter

▶ Seeing how negative credit hurts your job opportunities

▶ Leveraging your credit with landlords and lenders

▶ Using your credit to get the best deal on a car

▶ Knowing credit's role in insurance matters

*I*n my experience working with consumers since the early 1990s, I've learned that life, happiness, and credit are intertwined. Not to say that better credit or more money makes you happier, but financial failure takes a toll on the rest of your life and your relationships with others. So rather than look at your life in one place and your credit in another, I invite you to look at the two as highly correlated.

You would probably define a successful and fulfilling life as one that includes a job, a place to call home, a car to get you to your job and elsewhere, and, of course, insurance. In all these life scenarios, a good credit record is important. Employers often check credit reports before making job offers. Landlords and mortgage lenders require you to pass a credit review. To get a car, you need both credit and a down payment. And insurance involves a credit check that may determine your premium or eligibility.

Bad credit doesn't just deny you these things. Oh no, it can be much worse. What do you get with bad credit? Job problems, eviction or foreclosure, and debts and collections.

In this chapter, I offer you credit insights into some of what I call life's structural events and give you strategies to help you make the most of these credit-challenging situations. I show you ways to manage your credit for your maximum benefit as you step out in your early years. In Chapter 12, I continue this theme with credit's effects on the more personal areas of your life, such as marriage, divorce, and more.

So how important is good credit to your life? Very! How can you make sure that you have the credit you need as you set up the structure of your life? That's what I show you in this chapter.

Keeping Your Credit from Hurting Your Job Prospects

Most people dislike searching for a job, be it a first job or a fifteenth. I've been through the job-search process more times than I would have liked, and I understand the angst that many suffer as they take stock of their credentials and gear up to enter the job hunt. The role of credit in a job competition is sometimes overlooked, but it can be important and even critical if the competition is stiff enough.

Why? Because as part of the hiring process, employers frequently pull credit reports on candidates before making an offer. Before you get outraged at this possibility, you should know that you've probably given the potential employer permission to review your credit report thanks to some obscure language in the job application. If your report contains disturbing data, the employer can ask you to explain or simply move on to the next candidate. After all, passing on a prospect, if a number of other candidates are available, is safer and less confrontational.

As you can see, keeping your credit clear when you're looking for a new job — and even when you're up for a promotion — can be a big deal. Following are two simple steps you can take to help you keep your credit clear, whether you're new to the job market, looking to make a change, or trying to get back into the workforce:

- ✔ **Get copies of your credit reports from the three major credit bureaus.** The good news is that you're entitled to one free copy of your report from each of the bureaus (Equifax, Experian, and TransUnion) per year, plus an additional report if you're unemployed. To find out how to order your copies, head to Chapter 14.

- ✔ **Read your reports to make sure that no one else's negative history has been placed on your record by mistake.** Credit bureaus get millions of pieces of data each month that they have to apply to the right files. Sooner or later, one goes to the wrong place because of an address mix-up, a misspelled last name, a dropped suffix, and so on. If you see anything on your report that doesn't look familiar, you need to dispute it immediately; I explain how to do so in Chapter 14.

Correcting inaccuracies in your reports can take a few months, so be sure to start the process well in advance of when you need your reports looking good for a potential employer's judging eye. If you ask after the errors are fixed, the credit bureau will send a copy of your updated report to any employer who has requested it in the last two years, or to any business that has requested your credit report. That way, those employers and businesses get the most accurate and up-to-date info in your file.

If you're new to the credit game — perhaps you're just entering the workforce or you've immigrated to the United States from another country — flip to Chapter 10 for pointers on creating a personal credit history.

If the negative information in your reports is accurate, be sure to see my advice in the section "Repairing Bad Credit" in Chapter 1.

Dealing with Rental Application Checks

Apartment living used to be a great way to start out on your way to homeownership. Today, however, more people choose apartment living over homeownership because selling a home can be difficult and the long-term outlook for home prices is uncertain. Others have been foreclosed on and then rent as a result. If you're looking to call an apartment home sweet home, forever or just for a while, you need to understand how credit plays into the rental process.

Credit reports figure prominently in a landlord's decision to rent to you. They show how you handle routine payments, but they generally don't include any rental-specific information (unless you've been evicted and a judgment for unpaid rent or damages was ordered). Recently, Experian began showing limited rental history on a small percentage of its reports. Landlords also rely on data available through some national, specialty reporting bureaus that focus exclusively on rental information. Rental data, when available, is reflected in your VantageScore credit score, but not in your FICO score. (See Chapter 14 for more on credit reports.)

The type of information a rental report may contain includes eviction filings from local court records and other tenant history information from landlords who report their experiences with tenants. Unlike credit reports, specialty bureau reports can pick up evictions without monetary judgments; they can even note a pending eviction. They also contain information about when you moved into or out of your rentals and can include landlord reports on lease violations and ratings. The goal of all this data? To help landlords identify good, as well as problem, tenants.

So what happens when you finally find a great apartment, only to hear from the leasing agent that your background check has revealed problems? Is it time to move on? No way! This section offers some effective ways to address credit and background concerns so you can move into the apartment of your dreams.

If you're trying to rent an apartment after a mortgage foreclosure, you definitely want to be upfront about what happened, because the foreclosure *will* appear on your credit report. If you find yourself hitting a brick wall when dealing with large apartment complexes, which can have less-flexible renting criteria, try a smaller complex, or even a house, condo, townhome, or duplex. Individuals (versus big rental companies) and owners of small complexes may be less likely to run a credit check on you; at the very least, they may be more flexible about your situation if they do run a check.

Knowing what's on your reports

First things first: Pull your credit reports (ideally before you begin searching for an apartment) and look them over carefully. If your reports contain negative data that's out-of-date (over seven years old) or accounts you don't recognize, quickly dispute the inaccurate or out-of-date items with the credit bureau(s). Next, if you find any erroneous negative items, explain to the leasing agent that you're in the process of correcting the errors and ask the agent to repull your report. Disputed items come off your report until they can be checked out further.

Landlords can still say no to your application; however, if you can explain what happened, what you did about it, and why it won't happen again, many may be willing to work with you.

To find out what information is contained in the specialty bureaus' databases and whether it's correct, I suggest that you ask the leasing agent or landlord which specialty bureau he or she uses and then get a copy of that bureau's report by using the contact information I provide in Chapter 14. Dispute errors just as you would for a credit report; instructions for doing so come with your free report.

Taking action

If clarifying that certain information on your report is incorrect isn't good enough for the landlord, you may need to take additional action. Here are some suggestions that may help you get past such a sticky credit situation:

- ✔ Write a letter explaining the circumstances from your point of view. Submit this letter *with* your application (not later), and be sure to say why the problematic situation won't happen again.

- ✔ Offer a larger deposit. Remember, you get the money back when you move.

- ✔ Offer more than one month's rent upfront.

- ✔ If you're renting now, get a letter of recommendation from your present landlord saying that you're a good tenant (you pay on time and in full each month and take good care of the apartment).

- ✔ Find a roommate who has good credit or who can help you with a larger deposit. Agree to have a roommate for a year. When you renew the lease, you can go your separate ways if you like.

You could get a *cosigner* (essentially, a person who guarantees your performance), but I don't recommend doing so if you can avoid it, largely because it can put a strain on relationships, especially if you run into money problems. If you do decide to go ahead with a cosigner, family members or even friends may be willing to help.

Qualifying for a Mortgage

If you've done your homework and you come out on the buy side of the rent-versus-buy decision, then you're ready to dig into the next phase of the mortgage-qualification process. But first it helps to know what you need in order to be successful in your quest:

- ✔ Steady, reliable income

- ✔ Good credit

- ✔ Documentation to verify savings

- ✔ Savings to get through a temporary setback such as an unexpected loss of income or a home-maintenance emergency, in addition to your down payment and closing costs

If you're already having credit or financial difficulties, I strongly suggest that you do what's necessary to resolve these issues before you start the home-buying process.

The subprime mortgage market collapse of 2007 will live on in lenders' memories for the next two decades, and it should! The upshot is that lenders are being more intelligent in their decision making. What does that mean for you? Simply that you need to adopt the same critical approach to your credit. In this section, I help you understand the essentials you want to master *before* you start looking for a home and the mortgage required to purchase it.

Ordering your credit report and score

When you apply for a mortgage, the quantity and quality of the accounts on your credit report are incredibly important. They ultimately affect your *credit score,* the three-digit number that lenders use to figure out what interest rate and other deal terms to offer you. You're entitled to a free copy of your credit report from each of the three major credit bureaus every 12 months, but you have to fork over some cash to find out your credit score. Of course, if you've already received a copy of your credit report from each bureau within the past 12 months, then you may have to pay for another one as you begin the mortgage application process unless you live in a state that allows you more than one annual free report (you want the most current report). Either way, I explain how to order your report and score in Chapter 14.

Because your credit score makes a big difference in the interest rate you get for your loan — and that interest rate can make a difference of tens of thousands of dollars over the course of the loan — you need to have a solid understanding of the components that make up the two main types of credit scores (FICO and VantageScore) so you can try to get the highest score possible. I reveal the breakdown of the components for both types of credit scores in Chapter 13.

So do you need a perfect credit score to qualify for a mortgage? No way! Although lenders are certainly very hesitant to lend to people with low scores, they also understand that perfect credit is virtually a myth given all the moving parts to your score and reports. What you really need is good enough credit to quality for a mortgage and get the best deal. Because what's considered "good enough credit" changes with the financial markets, I suggest that you check respected sites like www.bankrate.com and www.myfico.com to see the prevailing rates for various credit score tiers.

Your credit score varies with each credit report because each bureau may have different information or errors. Chances are a mortgage lender will check all three reports, so you should too.

Looking at your credit file like a lender

When a lender looks at your loan application, he or she wants to see more than just your credit score. You can expect any lender to look at the following items, all of which determine whether you're a good risk:

- ✔ Your income, employment history, and monthly debt payments

- ✔ Your savings and assets, such as investments and properties that can be sold relatively quickly for cash

  Lenders love to see money in the bank, otherwise known as *cash reserves.* The mere fact that you have a cash reserve speaks volumes about how you manage your money and your life.

- ✔ Your credit history

If you believe that you may come up short in any of these areas, be sure to have a plan to address the shortcoming with your lender during the loan origination process. For instance, if you have a short employment history, point out to the lender how stable your company and job are and that you just received a great performance review.

The process called *underwriting* looks at many factors and applies seasoned judgment to what's there. The term itself explains what happens. In earlier times, when a risk was reviewed and approved, the person responsible would write his name below the application — hence, underwriting.

Preparing to Purchase a Car

A car dealer (or any lender, for that matter) wants to know three things about you before deciding whether to make you a loan. They call them the three Cs of credit:

- ✔ **Your character:** To a dealer, your character boils down to whether you'll make the payments as agreed. Sometimes a person can have great income, low fixed expenses, and a fat down payment but just be too lazy, disorganized, or distracted to pay on time. So the issue here is not *can* you make the payment, but *will* you!

- ✔ **Your capacity:** *Capacity* refers to how large a loan you can handle. Car dealers take into account all your other financial obligations in addition to the monthly car payment relative to your income.

- ✔ **Your collateral:** *Collateral* is something a lender can take away and sell if you default on your loan, such as your car. The more equity you have in your car, the better the dealer will feel about financing your purchase.

Although purchasing a car is a big step, credit doesn't have to be a major consideration if you prepare beforehand. This section details what you should take care of before you set foot onto the lot and offers insight into what you should consider after you pick the car you want.

Arming yourself with information

Unless you plan to pay cash, your credit has a lot of say in what kind of a car payment and maybe even what type of car you end up with. Naturally, you want to follow the process I describe in Chapter 14 to obtain copies of your credit reports from all three major bureaus and pore over those reports to see whether you can spot any errors. If you find any, dispute 'em (Chapter 14 also has advice on correcting inaccuracies).

If you're smart, you'll also look into your credit score, a tool that helps a lender predict how risky your loan is likely to be. In modern America, lenders can't ask your friends or enemies if you're reliable. They can't make decisions based on anything that may be discriminatory, such as how you look or sound or where you live. This is where the credit score shines. Your credit score looks at your credit history plus any public record items on your credit report, such as being taken to court for defaulting on child support or alimony payments. Using a complex set of formulas, your score predicts the likelihood of your defaulting on your next loan.

Find out your credit score before you approach a lender or dealer about an auto loan. Most lenders use a score developed by either FICO or VantageScore. If you know in advance if your credit is great or horrible, you'll be prepared to hold out for the best rate you qualify for rather than just accepting an offer that may have a higher interest rate tacked on to see whether you're paying attention.

If you're considering a specific car dealer for your purchase or a certain bank or credit union for your car loan, I suggest that you find out which credit bureau's report and score the dealer or bank uses to determine eligibility. Then you can go to that site and order just what you need.

After you know your score, you can check www.bankrate.com to determine what your interest rate will be for a car loan from a traditional bank or credit union. This is good information to have before you ever set foot in a dealer's finance department. Sure, you may still want to use a dealer incentive and opt for a loan through the dealer, but this way you can make a valid comparison.

Reviewing what to consider when you're at the dealership

It's easy to get overexcited when you're finalizing your car deal. The thrill of a new car and the prospect of getting a bargain can lead you to miss a fine point or two in your decision-making process. To keep your passion in check, consider the following points before you pick up a pen and sign anything:

- **Think about dealer financing if your credit score isn't the best.** A dealer may have more flexibility than a bank or credit union when making a loan. Why? Because dealers make money on the cars they sell, so loaning you money is worth more to them than it is to a bank, which profits only from the loan and not the car sale.

- **Remember that when you sign a lease, your credit will impact your monthly payment and overall cost.** With a lease, you agree to pay the lease monthly, keep the car insured, and take good care of the vehicle for the term of the lease. From a credit perspective, you're essentially taking out a loan for the amount by which the car is expected to depreciate (decline in value) over the lease term. Your credit report and score are big determining factors in what interest rate is applied to the term of the lease and your resulting monthly payment.

- **Don't fall into the trap of weighing monthly payments more than the overall price.** A common car dealer tactic is to talk to you about a vehicle's cost in terms of what you're willing to pay per month instead of the actual price. Though the monthly payment amount is an important part of your budget, don't lose sight of the total amount you'll pay over the term of the loan. A longer payment period (five years versus three years) costs you more overall than a shorter one.

If you're unhappy with your loan payment or interest rate for your new car purchase, don't despair. Instead, follow my advice in Chapter 3 to polish up your credit. Within six months to a year, your score may have improved enough that you can look into refinancing your balance at a lower interest rate and a lower payment! Leases, however, can't be changed later.

Another thing you can do to help your credit is to pay off your existing car loan early, provided the loan doesn't have a big prepayment penalty. A credit report with a good payment history and no outstanding car loan scores higher than one with a good payment history and a large balance due.

Where to go for car info

You can find out car values, interest rates, and other critical car-buying information from a number of good places before you walk onto a lot to begin negotiations. To find info on interest rates and the scores that track with them, check out www.bankrate.com. Cars.com, Edmunds (www.edmunds.com), and Kelley Blue Book (www.kbb.com) all offer free information about car models, features, prices, and more. You can even find owner ratings, vehicle suggestions, and reviews on sites like www.cartalk.com. *Consumer Reports* also offers a good service for a fee that helps you understand what a car costs the seller so you don't end up overpaying.

Unveiling the Relationship between Your Credit and Your Insurance Premiums

Credit plays a significant role when you're looking for car insurance, renter's insurance, or homeowner's insurance. A thin credit file, inaccuracies in your credit reports, or just plain bad credit can hurt your chances for coverage, and insurance will likely cost you a small bundle. Perhaps you already have blemished credit and think that being charged more for insurance before a fender's ever dented or a window's ever broken just adds insult to injury. Well, the Federal Trade Commission (FTC) agreed that this situation might be unfair (or worse, a proxy for discrimination aimed at overcharging policyholders). So it did some investigating and issued a congressionally mandated report examining credit-based insurance scores (www.ftc.gov/opa/2007/07/facta.shtm). The good news and the bad news is that these scores really do predict claim experience and often result in lower prices for people who are better risks — as in people who are smart about their credit. The FTC also found that credit scores have virtually no discriminatory bias.

But just what is a credit-based insurance score? And how can you get your hands on your score? This section not only answers these questions but also reveals what you can do to make sure you get the best insurance rate you can.

Understanding insurance scores

Understanding how your credit history affects your insurance options can be a challenge. When evaluated with other information like your claims history and driving record, your credit-based insurance score (also known simply as an *insurance score*) helps insurance companies determine whether you qualify for coverage based on their underwriting guidelines and what rate you'll pay.

Your insurance score is a snapshot of your insurance risk at a particular point in time. It's a number based on the information in your credit report that shows whether you're more or less likely to have claims in the near future that result in losses for the insurance company. As with other scores, the higher your insurance score, the better off you are.

Another way to look at this score is to contrast it with your credit score. An insurance score is a credit-based statistical analysis of a consumer's likelihood of filing an insurance claim within a given period in the future. A credit score, on the other hand, is a credit-based statistical analysis of a consumer's likelihood of a credit default within a given period in the future.

Note: Neither your insurance score nor your credit score is adversely affected if you contact several insurance companies for quotes.

Getting a copy of your insurance score and insurance claim report

Fair Isaac Corporation, the provider of FICO credit scores, and ChoicePoint, owned by LexisNexis, are the most well-known developers of insurance scores. Fair Isaac insurance scores range from 300 to 900, and ChoicePoint scores range from 300 to 997. To find out where you stand, you can ask your insurance company for your number. You may find when you ask that your insurance company considers this information to be proprietary, but in the land of the free, you can almost always get someone to sell you your score.

For a small fee, you can get a copy of your LexisNexis Attract insurance score by going to `personalreports.lexisnexis.com/lexisnexis_attract_score.jsp`. While you're on the LexisNexis website, you can get a copy of your C.L.U.E. personal property and auto reports at no charge under the annual disclosure rules of the Fair and Accurate Credit Transactions Act (FACT Act or FACTA; I explain the basics of this act in Chapter 19). If you don't have Internet access, you can order your reports by mail at C.L.U.E. Inc. Consumer Disclosure Center, P.O. Box 105295, Atlanta, GA 30348-5295, or by calling toll-free 866-312-8102. LexisNexis also offers what's known as a full file disclosure that covers your insurance, employment, and tenant histories all in one swoop. Get a copy by following the instructions at `personalreports.lexisnexis.com/access_your_personal_information.jsp`.

Figuring out what to do with your newfound knowledge

After you have a copy of your insurance claim report, take the time to check it out. If you believe that any of the information on your report is incorrect or incomplete, you can file a dispute, just like you would with one of the credit-reporting agencies, by following the instructions included with the report. All claims are verified or removed. You can also include an explanation regarding any information that's factually correct but may warrant further discussion. Send disputes to LexisNexis Risk Solutions, LLC, P.O. Box 105295, Atlanta, GA 30348; or call 866-820-8976.

A small but still bright spot in the insurance underwriting process is that if you don't get the best rate available because of information contained in your credit report, you must be told about it, and you can get a free copy of the credit report used (in addition to the free annual credit report you're automatically entitled to). Be sure to check the report carefully for errors and out-of-date information. Dispute any mistakes you find and then ask your insurer for a premium recalculation.

Taking other factors into account

Be aware that insurers have no responsibility to take into account catastrophic events that may damage your credit score either directly or indirectly. Consider adding a statement to your credit report and contacting your insurer for a rate review if, for example, you were unable to pay bills on time because

- You were injured or seriously ill and hospitalized.
- You live in an area hit by a natural disaster such as a hurricane and were unable to pay your bills on time because of the storm's effects.
- Your company closes and you lose your job.

Insurers may use more than your own credit history to adjust your rates or deny you coverage. They may order the reports and/or scores of other people living at the same address, even if those people aren't listed on the policy. For example, insurers may consider unnamed persons' driving records at the same address. If you purchased an item or property with a former spouse and that person defaults or pays late, even if the property and debt responsibilities have been reassigned by court order, your credit history and score may be adversely affected, which in turn may affect the cost of your insurance premiums. For more on the credit impacts of divorce, see Chapter 12.

Chapter 12

Protecting Your Credit During Major Life Challenges

*L*ife is full of surprises. You may plan to get married, but few of us plan to get divorced. You may plan to get a job but end up unemployed. You may plan time at the gym to be healthy, but you may not plan for illness and subsequent medical debts. And have you planned how to handle your credit when your spouse passes on?

That's what this chapter is all about. Building on Chapter 11, which links your life goals to your credit, here you find what you need to know to survive the surprises that life events bring. No matter what life throws at you, you're better able to cope if you maintain good credit. In marriage or divorce, in employment or unemployment, in sickness or health, knowing how to keep your finances under control makes your recovery faster and stronger.

In this chapter, I offer you credit insights into some of life's personal events and offer strategies to help you make the most of these often credit-challenging situations. I show you ways to manage your credit for your maximum benefit as you journey through your own personal odyssey. Whether you are embarking on the sea of life for the first time or the last, this chapter's for you.

Tying the Knot in Life and in Credit: A Couples' Guide to Building Good Credit

Nothing is more hopeful than deciding to get married. And nothing can be as potentially dangerous to your finances. Keeping your credit in its best shape can be tricky enough when you're making financial decisions on your own. Add another person's emotions and excitement to the mix, and the process can get out of hand unless you're careful. In this section, I offer you my very best hopes for the future, along with advice to match.

Engaging in prenuptial financial discussions

Understanding and communicating with your spouse is critical in all aspects of married life, but especially when it comes to financial issues. I advise all engaged couples to spend significant time discussing and exploring how they plan to handle their finances, what their credit looks like, how they'll pay their bills, and what their long-term financial goals are. After all, new couples want to continue the honeymoon phase as long as possible, and arguing over finances does nothing to achieve that goal. This section helps you begin the communication and budgeting processes.

Looking ahead to "dessert"

When my wife, Barbara, and I go out to dinner, she always looks at the dessert menu first. In the beginning of our courtship, this behavior baffled me. As a typical linear-thinking man, I approached my meal choices in the order I planned to consume them — starter, salad, entrée. In fact, I typically wouldn't even think about dessert until I was sopping up the last of the marinara sauce from my plate.

Finally, I got up the nerve to ask her about this display of, in my view, backward behavior. She explained that dessert, for her, was the most important part of the meal, and she wanted to plan ahead to accommodate what for her was

a priority. If she saw bread pudding (her favorite) on the menu, she'd go for a light entrée or salad and skip the sticky rolls. If the dessert choices were just so-so, she'd order a heartier main course and perhaps take an extra piece of bread.

Although my wife's logic, as always, is different from my own (and usually right), her approach to dining out is a great way to look at household budgeting. Focus on the goal (like traveling to an exotic destination or buying your dream home) instead of zeroing in on all the mundane bills and expenses of everyday life. This approach has served our relationship well.

Identifying and agreeing on your major money issues

If you're soon to be married or partnered (or even if you already are and haven't yet talked money), you need to openly discuss a range of money issues, including your current credit and financial status. If you could live on love, the conversation would be unnecessary, but if you two pool your resources, you need to determine together how your credit and your money plans will affect your lives as a couple.

Here's a list of ten things to do before your "I do" day. If you've already taken the plunge and you haven't yet discussed these issues, do it now!

- **Show each other your credit reports and credit scores.** Discuss what you see, but don't judge.

- **Discuss your current annual income and your income hopes for the future.** This is a chance to show support, not to criticize.

- **Determine your financial style — are you a saver or a spender?** Find out the same about your partner.

- **Talk about your debts and how you plan to handle them.** Will you each pay your own debts? Will you pool them together and split them 50-50? Or will the bigger earner pay more?

- **Tell each other about any major negative financial events in your past.** These events may include outstanding (or defaulted) student loans; for those in second marriages, the effects of a bankruptcy may be around longer than the kids, and you wouldn't forget to talk about *them*.

- **Discuss your spending habits (whether you're frugal, indulgent, or don't even know how to budget).** The frugal one may be the better choice to handle your bill paying.

- **Talk about whether you've cosigned any loans.** Cosigning for an old flame may be forgiven, but hiding it won't.

- **Discuss your personal approaches to budgeting.** Will you count every penny or go for estimates instead? Yes, you need a budget!

- **Discuss your financial goals for the next five years.** Make this exercise fun. After all, it is about dreams and hopes. No wet blankets allowed!

- **Talk about your long-term financial goals and how you'll fund them.** Will you retire at 50? Sail around the world? Give all your worldly possessions to charity?

I strongly advise that you get copies of your credit reports when your relationship turns serious. Credit is a critical relationship factor, and bad credit can be a deal breaker. You may have bared your heart and soul to your sweetie, but until you bare your credit, the job's not done. Flip to Chapter 14 to discover how to get copies of your credit reports.

Building a budget for your new life together

I strongly recommend that you and your partner sit down and make out a budget for your new household. Budgeting is among the most important first steps you can take together to strengthen your relationship and reduce the risk of a split due to financial stress and spending incompatibility.

Explore together and agree on what you want to save for, such as a family, a house, a cat or two, or early retirement. This discussion paves the way for all the saving steps you want to establish in order to reach your goal. You also need to budget for the everyday stuff (utilities, transportation, food, housing, and the like). If you find that you just aren't able to get the numbers to add up, consider a credit counselor. Good credit counselors aren't just for credit, debts, or problems — they can help you plan a budget before disaster strikes. (See Chapter 4 for more on credit counseling.)

Chapter 18 is all about how to budget. The material at `www.dummies.com/extras/creditrepair` includes a number of resources that can get you going.

When working on your budget, always start with the fun part: your future goals. What could be more inspiring than describing all the things you're going to do and the adventures you'll share together over the years? For example, my wife and I are planning an extended road trip to look for the perfect piece of blueberry pie.

By committing to maintaining communication, establishing common goals, and working together for mutual benefit, couples can achieve financial bliss.

Considering joint accounts

If your sweetheart has a less-than-glowing credit history, it begins to affect *you* as soon as you apply for credit together and open joint accounts. Why? Because the bank reviews both of your credit histories. You keep your own history, but your new joint accounts appear on both of your credit reports. So if you're concerned that your spouse may not be as diligent as you are in paying bills on time, paying the bills yourself is a good idea.

Many couples decide to merge their accounts because consolidated accounts often make for easier record keeping and enhance that feeling of togetherness. But beware: Both of you are equally responsible for all debt incurred in any joint credit accounts. Regardless of which one of you takes the credit card out for a joy ride, a missed payment on a joint account negatively affects both of your credit records. Also, if you miss a payment on an individual account, that missed payment may affect your ability to open joint accounts because both credit histories are considered.

In states with community-property laws, you may be responsible for your spouse's debts even if you aren't on the account. As long as the debt is incurred during the marriage, you're liable, even if you receive no benefit from it or don't even know about it. Currently, 9¾ states fall into this category: Arizona, California, Idaho, Louisiana, Nevada, New Mexico, Texas, Washington, and Wisconsin. Alaska has an opt-in provision (so I count it as half), and Puerto Rico has community-property laws but isn't a state (so I count it as a quarter).

Even if you decide to consolidate your accounts with your spouse, always keep at least one credit account in your own name as a safeguard in the event of an emergency. Keeping an individual account can also be a good thing in the event of divorce or the untimely death of a spouse; having your own account can help you reestablish credit on your own.

Keeping separate accounts

If you have a credit-challenged spouse or partner or if you're merely cautious and want to take the credit sharing slowly, you can always keep separate accounts and allow each other to be authorized users on your accounts. Both of you can charge on the account, both of you get the credit history reported on your credit reports, but only one of you is responsible for the bill.

Although this strategy can safeguard your credit score from a late payment, it also exposes you to the potential of at least one bigger-than-expected bill (if your spouse or partner is a dangerous shopaholic, this setup won't protect you from his or her spending). But if you can trust your sweetheart not to go crazy with the credit card, this method allows him or her to add credit history while you keep responsibility for and control of the account in your hands. (And, of course, if your

sweetie gets out of control with the credit card, you can always remove him or her from the account.)

Provided you don't live in a community-property state (see the "Considering joint accounts" section for a list), separate accounts can really make sense, especially if you and your spouse or partner come together later in life and each of you has substantial assets of your own. As long as you both agree, this sort of financial independence can keep you looking attractive to your sweetie long after your personal charms have become less charming. It can also help each of you feel the independence and vigor that only money of your own can provide. For my birthday one year, my wife took me, at her exclusive expense, to Walt Disney World. If we had merged all our finances, she couldn't have done so without spending at least some of my money. Happy birthday to me!

Managing joint debt

Talking to your creditors is hard, but talking to your sweetie about money may be even more daunting. Dealing with joint debt isn't necessarily twice as difficult as dealing with debt alone — it can be 20 times harder! If you're trying to keep your bad credit from getting worse and you have some joint debt, you may feel as though your situation is out of control. And it may be.

The most helpful tool at your disposal is communication. Here's what you and your partner need to discuss:

✔ **Agreeing on goals:** Starting here is important. This conversation is about the future, and setting goals gives you a shared future that you both buy into as the impetus to make some changes. Goals may include saving for college tuition, retirement, or vacations. In the goal-setting process, you don't have to be specific the first time around. After you get through all the steps that follow, go back to the goals and put a price tag and date on each. Then rework the plan to see how many goals you can fit in and what needs to be cut or delayed. Keep in mind that goals change over time. Refer to these shared goals as you continue talking.

✔ **Eliminating debt:** You're trying to keep bad credit from getting worse, so determining the best way to eliminate debt is a priority. How much can you allot each month to paying off debt? While paying down debt, agree that neither one of you will add to credit card balances.

✔ **Paying bills:** If possible, pay bills together so you both know how much you owe each month and where your money is going. Decisions that need to be made, such as how much to pay on a particular credit card balance, can be made together.

✔ **Keeping track of payments:** Make sure that you both record all checking account transactions (including checks you write, electronic checks, and automatic debits) in one place so that you can keep up with your balance. The same goes for using your ATM or debit card; you both need to record expenses. If you have separate accounts, decide who pays what and let each other know how things go with your respective bills.

✔ **Saving:** Come to an agreement as to how much you can afford to put aside in savings each month. Early in your financial life, you may save only $5 or $10 a paycheck. But the key is to start a habit; savings *do* add up over time.

With good feelings flowing and a plan in place, make a commitment with your partner to track your progress, communicate regularly about your finances, and avoid making large purchases without discussing them first.

Avoiding money conflicts

The moose on the table. The elephant in the room. These are just a couple euphemisms I've heard to describe those huge, looming issues that couples or families pretend don't exist. But ignoring credit and money conflicts is done at great peril to a marriage. You can pretend it's not there, but it will still wreck your home.

Too often, couples who thought they were in perfect — though unspoken or assumed — agreement find out after the wedding that they're polar opposites when it comes to spending, borrowing, and saving. If you talk with your spouse about finances, you shouldn't run into credit conflicts — certainly none that could destroy your marriage. But money seems to be a taboo topic, even among married couples. Couples often don't discover money conflicts until a bounced check, late payment notice, or mammoth-sized credit card balance shows up, and by then, the discussion may not be pretty.

Lack of careful and constant communication about money can lead to irreconcilable differences that result in divorce. When divorce is on the horizon, the fighting can escalate. Here are some of the pitfalls I hope you can avoid:

- **Not being open with each other about how you see and value savings, money, and credit:** Silence is your enemy. The list in the "Identifying and agreeing on your major money issues" section earlier in the chapter can help you start a money-focused discussion.

- **Pooling your funds, earnings, and credit:** Keeping some credit in your own name is important. The same goes for money. How much? Enough that you feel comfortable!

- **Surprising your partner with a big expenditure (a car, boat, home theater system, designer shoes, donation to a cat-rescue fund, and so on):** Spending joint money without consulting your spouse is a big no-no. Determine together a spending limit, such as $100, and agree to discuss beforehand any purchase exceeding that amount.

- **Criticizing your partner's money style in front of others:** No one wants to be ridiculed in front of others, even in good humor. If you're uncomfortable with your mate's spending behavior, talk about it when the two of you are alone.

- **Failing to set mutual goals:** Discuss your goals and agree on a plan for achieving them. (Turn to Chapter 18 for budgeting advice.)

- **Not meeting your financial obligations:** If you're unable to pay a bill that's your responsibility, let your partner know as soon as possible.

- **Letting kids set the rules:** Kids know how to play you against each other to get what they want. This time-tested strategy can lead to discipline issues, overspending, and fights between Mom and Dad. If you have a blended household (kids from different marriages), establishing rules and standing together as a united front are especially important.

Protecting Your Finances in a Divorce

Marriage is the ultimate expression of hope for the future. When that hope goes unfulfilled, you may be faced with the prospect of a divorce, which can impact your credit and finances. If your financial life was challenging as a married couple sharing a common future, in divorce it may become even more so. To add to the stress, you may find that some of your expenses increase as you separate into two households; for example, you may have two mortgage or rent payments every month. The financial fallout from a divorce can also include difficulties in opening new accounts and obtaining new loans in your own name. This section outlines the steps you can take to protect and, if need be, restore your good credit in the event of a divorce.

Taking precautions when a split-up looms

If you suspect that a divorce may be in your future, consider the following. Even if things end up working out, these strategies are still worth considering.

- ✔ **Keep good credit in your own name.** A couple different types of accounts — such as revolving (credit card), installment (car loan), and retail (department store card) — should be sufficient.

- ✔ **Build your own credit while you're married.** Remember that your credit score is made up mostly of the amount you owe and whether you pay on time. (For the scoop on all the components that make up your credit score, turn to Chapter 13.)

- ✔ **Open your own bank account with checking and savings features.** Overdraft protection can be a plus, especially if it's free.

- ✔ **Keep track of your joint credit accounts by checking your credit reports frequently or by enrolling in a credit monitoring service.** Doing so may provide you with an early warning that your partner is having some issues. At a minimum, check one of your three credit reports every four months. (Chapter 14 explains how to obtain copies of your credit report from the three major credit bureaus.)

Preparing your credit before heading to court

If the possibility of divorce becomes a reality, you want to ratchet up your credit protection action. Quickly separating your financial selves to the best of your abilities is important. Here's how:

- **Inform your spouse that you're closing joint accounts, and then send a letter to each joint creditor asking that the account be closed to any new activity.** Closing accounts protects you. Telling your spouse in advance allows him or her to make other plans and is the decent thing to do. Just don't wait too long to send the letters.

- **Attempt to agree on how joint or community property accounts will be paid and who'll be responsible for making the payments.** If you can't reach an agreement, make the minimum payments yourself so that your credit doesn't deteriorate. You can always recoup the money in a reconciliation or divorce settlement; just keep track of what you pay.

- **Transfer joint balances to individual accounts if possible.** Also, include a division of joint debts as a stipulation in your divorce decree, with specific amounts assigned to each person.

- **Build individual credit as soon as possible.** Start small and build up gradually if you have to. If your credit is damaged already, start with a credit card that has a small credit limit — perhaps a card from a local department store, gas station, or credit union. After paying your bills on time for six months or so, apply for another card and continue paying bills consistently. (Check out the section "Getting new credit in your own name" later in the chapter for more info.)

- **Check your credit more frequently than normal.** Consider subscribing to a credit monitoring service or freezing your credit to prevent the addition of any new accounts.

Even if your prospective ex is uncooperative, keep paying at least the minimums on all joint bills on time. Don't listen to uninformed but well-meaning friends and relatives who may tell you to stop making payments or run up debts to spite your ex. Missed payments generally stay on your credit reports for seven years, making it hard or more costly to obtain new credit, employment, insurance, and maybe even a new spouse or partner.

If you change your name, be sure to write to all your creditors and the three major credit bureaus to let them know. Doing so helps keep errors based on name mix-ups from affecting your credit history.

Your joint credit history may outlast your marriage

From the time you open your first joint account, you and your mate link your credit futures together. Your personal credit history and credit score are now influenced by the behavior of your partner. A blemish on his or her part is a blemish on yours, too.

How long do you have to suffer from your ex's joint-account misadventures? Conventional wisdom says seven years, but what if I told you it could be longer? Maybe *much* longer. Just look at the numbers: Negative credit items are reported for seven years in most cases. Your ex's credit may be part of your credit report for seven years from whichever event happened last:

- Your honey first forgot to pay the credit card bill.

- You got that notice saying that your ex was 60 days late.

- Your ex's loan was charged off after going six months past due.

  If the bill goes to court after the six months of charging off, and if the creditor goes for a wage garnishment (which precipitates a bankruptcy filing), the original account is reported for seven years, as is the public record of the court action. The bankruptcy overlaying that, however, is reported for up to ten years.

It can get even worse in certain situations, but I think the point is made. Your spouse's debts may be with you for a long, long time after you go your separate ways.

Protecting your credit in a divorce decree and beyond

When the judge rules in your divorce decree, be sure that all joint debts are clearly and specifically assigned and that both you and your ex understand that these debts must be paid on time. Close all remaining joint accounts by the date on which the divorce is granted. In the case of joint real estate that will eventually be sold, the party living on the property has more interest in making sure that the payments are made and should ask the judge to rule that the person in the house will send in the payments, even if the money comes from the other party.

A divorce decree doesn't end either party's responsibility for joint debts incurred, including individual debts in community-property states (see the section "Considering joint accounts" earlier in the chapter for a list). After all, you both promised the lender that you'd repay the loan. The fact that the judge says only one of you has to make the payments from now on doesn't change your contract with the lender. Each person is fully responsible for the entire balance of joint accounts, from credit cards to car loans to home mortgages.

This section helps you figure out your next steps after your divorce is finalized.

Overcoming your ex's defaults on your joint accounts

Given the stress associated with divorce, the fact that your ex may miss a payment or two is almost understandable. I said *almost*. Although you may be understanding of such a mishap, keeping your credit record as clean as possible is critical in rebuilding a positive credit history as a single person.

Because you want to address any missed payments as soon as possible, you need to stay up-to-the-minute on payment status. You may find out about a delinquency in a number of ways: a letter, a phone call, a duplicate billing statement (you can request one), a website visit, or a credit monitoring service. As soon as you know that a payment wasn't made, take action.

- ✔ **If your relationship allows, contact your ex to find out whether the bill has been paid.** If trust is a concern or if your relationship precludes direct communication, let your lawyer handle it. Instruct your attorney to notify your ex's attorney that the court order has been violated, and ask for a response.

- ✔ **If the situation isn't resolved, you can always go back to court.** You can ask the judge to reorder your ex to pay as agreed or face the not-so-pleasant legal consequences of contempt of court, which can include jail time. Returning to court to enforce the paying of assigned accounts is a lengthy and expensive course of action, so consider making the payments yourself if you think the two of you can resolve the issue. Making the payments costs you money, but perhaps less than bad credit (not to mention attorney fees) costs you.

By now you've probably figured out two things: Life isn't fair, and paying a bill yourself may be easier than dealing with your ex and may be beneficial to you in the long run.

Repairing the damages

Credit damage from divorce isn't unusual, but you can take the following steps to lessen the negative impact to your credit report and score:

- ✔ **Pay your bills on time.** Paying on time adds positive credit history on top of any negative history. Over time, your credit score gives a large number of new, positive reports more weight than older negatives. As your credit report ages, older items count for less, so make the most of new credit going forward.

- ✔ **Add a 100-word statement to your credit report.** Through this statement you can explain circumstances that a prospective lender or employer may not know about when considering your application.

Be careful not to leave this statement on your report longer than you need to, because it may draw attention to a past problem that's no longer a factor in your credit score.

✔ **Review your credit reports frequently.** Getting copies of your credit reports can help you control unexpected negatives, especially if your ex is still paying off joint or community-property debts. If your ex winds up not paying on a joint account, you'll probably be subject to collection activity and have to pay, or you may end up in a different court. (The rationale here is that creditors shouldn't be made to suffer just because your marriage failed.)

You can pay for credit monitoring services that alert you to any negative entries as soon as they occur, allowing you to take immediate action to reduce the damage. See Chapter 15 for the scoop on credit monitoring.

Getting new credit in your own name

The first step in getting credit in your own name is to find out where your credit stands. Begin by obtaining your credit report and your FICO score or VantageScore (I tell you how to get both in Chapter 14). The national average score is around 675. If you're at 780 or above, you're in Super Prime territory!

If you have a good credit score

If your score is 675 or above, you probably have a good chance of getting new credit in a normal credit environment.

Credit standards tighten or loosen from time to time. In loose credit periods, a good score gets the job done. In a tight credit environment, a good score may not be enough to get the terms or even the credit you want. I suggest that you apply for the following in your own name; this diversity of credit helps you respond to most financial situations that arise and helps build your credit score with on-time payments:

✔ Checking account

✔ Savings account

✔ Small installment loan (use the savings account for collateral if you must)

✔ Retail store credit card

✔ Major bank credit card

✔ Library card (because it saves you money on books, videos, and more)

If you have a borderline credit score

If your score is 660 or lower, your journey toward establishing credit in your own name may be a bit slower. Begin with the following:

- ✔ Checking account
- ✔ Savings account
- ✔ Passbook loan (secured by your savings account)
- ✔ Major bank credit card (if you qualify)
- ✔ Secured credit card (if you don't qualify for an unsecured credit card)

  A secured card gives you a line of credit based on a savings deposit to secure the credit line. This card shows up on your credit report just like an unsecured card; no one but you and the issuing bank will know!

- ✔ Retail store credit card (you're likely to qualify if you qualify for a bank credit card)
- ✔ Library card (no kidding)

If you apply for a credit card from your credit union or bank and you aren't sure whether you'll qualify, bring your credit report into a branch and have the bank employee look at it rather than asking the employee to pull your report. Why? If the bank declines you, a credit report inquiry won't show up on your credit report and lower your credit score unnecessarily.

If you have a sympathetic parent or relative with decent credit, you may be able to speed up the process of reestablishing credit by having that person cosign for you, but I don't recommend it. Too often this arrangement fails, and relationships are damaged along with credit.

Keeping Credit Strong While Unemployed

The job market fluctuates just as the stock market does. The economy has good years and bad years. During bad years, you may find yourself laid off or downsized. During good years, you may decide that the time is right to change jobs on your own and for good reasons (higher pay, for example).

The reality is that you can expect that your employer to make the decision to say farewell at least once in your career. I can tell you from experience that the event will arrive at the least advantageous time possible. In this section, I help you through this almost inevitable fact of modern life — temporary unemployment.

Employment information isn't regularly reported as part of your credit report. The credit bureaus don't keep track of where you work or what you earn. So any unemployment impact doesn't show up on your credit record unless you fail to make your payments on time, exceed your credit limits, or do something silly, like opening a lot of credit lines just in case you need them.

Preparing your credit for the worst-case scenario

The following suggestions help you protect your credit in case of unemployment:

✔ **Start an emergency savings account if you don't have one already.** Fund it regularly so it grows to between six months' and a year's worth of living expenses (not income — your expenses should be less than your income). Six months to a year is how long you're likely to be unemployed if you're caught by surprise.

✔ **Keep one or two credit cards or lines of credit open.** Many employers view your credit report when hiring, so you want your report to look its best even if you're unemployed. To do so, continue to pay your bills on time and keep your credit card balance at less than 50 percent of available credit if possible. (See Chapter 14 for more on what you can do to avoid raising any hiring-related red flags on your credit report.)

Using credit when you don't have a job

If you're unemployed, don't beat yourself up. You're in good company. Many people lose their jobs, often more than once. But if you've established savings and you have some available credit, you have two tools to help get you through this time without damaging your credit or your employment prospects. You can put together a new plan that includes finding a new job and a budget that works while you do so. This section tells you how.

Stay away from using cash advances on your credit cards! Spending money this way is much more costly than simply using the credit card to pay for items. Cash advances incur an extra fee, usually have a much higher interest rate than purchases, and often have a lower limit than your credit limit.

Looking at credit differently

When you're unemployed, you move from spending resources to *conserving* them, a situation that calls for you to change your credit use priorities and start looking at credit differently. While you were employed and earning a regular income, you may have used credit differently than cash. You also may have used it for larger purchases that you needed some time to pay off.

When you're unemployed, possibly for longer than you anticipate, you don't have those earnings coming in (you may have funds from a severance package or unemployment benefits, but they're only temporary, and they may not last as long as your unemployment does). With little to no funds coming in, you may need to use credit for basic living and job-hunting expenses only. This is just about the opposite of what most people advise, but you'll do it for a limited time and for a specific, worthy purpose. If it helps, think of this approach as borrowing money for a surefire investment: you and your future.

Preserve your cash for as long as possible by using credit first. You want to keep your cash because you can't replace it after it's gone. This advice may contradict what you've heard in the past. Conventional wisdom says to control expenses by paying cash for as many things as possible. But when you're unemployed, within reason and as part of a plan, the opposite is true. Use credit *for essentials* and save the cash. You can limit your overall spending to just the essentials by closely following a budget.

Refiguring the family budget

With your reduced resources, cutting back your spending to only basic needs is essential. Begin by sitting down with your family and discussing the situation and the need to reduce expenses temporarily. Don't be embarrassed in front of the kids. This situation is an important lesson in reality for them. And you can show them how adults face difficult issues and win.

The material at www.dummies.com/extras/creditrepair includes worksheets that are helpful in putting together a spending plan. For additional budgeting pointers, whether you need to start a budget from scratch or revise a budget that you've already created, turn to Chapter 18.

If your severance is being paid out over time or you haven't yet received it, ask your employer to raise your tax deductions to the maximum allowed. The IRS wants a report of anyone with more than ten deductions, so you should generally ask for ten (after all, you don't want the IRS looking at you unnecessarily). This strategy results in more cash flowing through to you now, when you need it. Yes, you may owe some taxes on this money in April (though your deductible job-hunting expenses and reduced earnings for the year may offset that). But you want to maximize today's income at the possible expense of tomorrow's demands.

Getting credit counseling to help

If you're overwhelmed and think you can benefit from some professional perspective or guidance, go to an accredited credit counselor. You can get information on credit counselors and where to find them in Chapter 4.

Protecting your credit lines

The downside to using your lines of credit for your basic living expenses while unemployed (a strategy I recommend) is that you *may* do some damage to your credit. Here are some tips for protecting your credit status while you leverage your available credit to help you get through this challenging time:

- ✔ **Keep balances at less than 50 percent of your available credit limit.** If it becomes necessary, spread your credit use over several accounts to keep your balance on each card at less than 50 percent. For example, rather than have a $2,000 balance on one card and a zero balance on three other cards, consider spreading the amount over all four cards equally, with each balance at $500.

- ✔ **Make all payments on time.** Remember that 35 percent of your credit score has to do with whether you make payments on time. (For the full scoop on the various components of your credit score, see Chapter 13.)

- ✔ **Pay the car loan first.** A car can be repossessed in as little as two weeks. Then how will you get to work when you do find a job?

- ✔ **Pay your mortgage a very close second.** Not all bills are created equal, and your mortgage is the most unequal of all. Partial payments don't work, and falling behind 90 days begins a very-difficult-to-stop foreclosure process. (See the section "Counting to 90" in Chapter 7.)

Don't contact your creditor unless you *know* you're going to miss a payment. If you just *think* you may miss a payment, it's none of their business. If you *know*, however, telling the creditor before it happens is important. Why? Because you'll have more options if you do.

If you have any income, ask for a *hardship program* — a special repayment arrangement that may be offered to a good customer in need of some extra help. Such programs tend to last for no more than three to six months. Most creditors have them, but the hardship has to be real and imminent, and you have to ask for it.

If the hardship program isn't sufficient to bridge the gap between what you can afford to pay and what the creditor insists you pay, send a letter stating that you can't make any payments but that you intend to do so in the future, as soon as you find employment. An example of this type of letter appears at www.dummies.com/extras/creditrepair.

What to do when you run out of credit and options

If you aren't able to make any payments on maxed-out credit cards or credit lines and you still have no job on the horizon, something has to give. This triangle has only three sides: income, expenses, and credit. If credit isn't an option, income and expenses are the only things you can alter.

Take out that budget you prepared when your unemployment started and consider some extreme moves to cut expenses. Can you move to a smaller home? Can you move in with a friend? Can you sell things to raise some cash? On the income side, have you considered taking a job to tide you over until something in your field opens up? The goal here is to generate some income, not move a career forward. *Remember:* Given time and perseverance, you *will* come out of unemployment stronger than you went in.

Curing Medical Debt

Little in life can seem more unfair than medical debt. You didn't ask for it, you got no pleasure from it, but you owe it just the same. Medical debt isn't much different from any other type of unsecured debt except that it tends to come quickly and in large amounts. The key to curing medical debt is to be proactive by negotiating discounts before a service is provided or, in the case of overwhelming debt, to cut your losses early.

If you have health insurance coverage, your approach to maintaining your credit is different from the approach you'd take if you didn't have insurance, at least initially. Even if you're insured, dealing with health insurance and how it covers your medical bills can be complicated and stressful. Not to worry, though. This section covers the relevant issues concerning medical debt and your credit.

Reviewing your options for paying medical bills

When faced with a pile of medical bills, you have five main options:

- ✔ You can work with the healthcare provider to pay the bills over time.
- ✔ You can seek assistance from a patient advocate resource.
- ✔ You can seek medical debt consolidation.
- ✔ You can attempt to negotiate your bills down (this works just like when you settle credit card debt — see Chapter 7).
- ✔ You can file for bankruptcy.

If you know in advance that you'll be incurring uninsured medical expenses and you don't know whether you can afford them, I suggest that you speak to your service providers as soon as possible. Ask if discounts are available for underinsured/uninsured patients. (Note that you may have to provide financial disclosures to qualify for these discounts.) Be sure to get all agreements in writing so there's no misunderstanding.

Applying for medical financial aid

Many hospitals provide charitable or financial aid to patients who qualify. Many clinics and doctors' offices also consider helping those who can prove that they're under unusual financial duress because of escalating medical bills or decreasing incomes. However, if you decide to apply for assistance, you may be better off doing so as soon as possible because many providers have time limits on aid applications (usually 6 to 12 months). Although you have to complete a substantial amount of paperwork and supply a lot of information, you may wipe thousands of dollars off your financial ledger.

Getting professional help

Help is available to consumers in the form of advocates. A number of organizations, some nonprofit, help you negotiate fees and payments or just get through the process of filling out the forms you're likely to encounter in the bill-negotiation process.

Here are some of the advantages to using an intermediary:

✔ They know the industry, the laws, and the regulations.

✔ They're not emotionally involved.

✔ They've done this before, and you may not have.

✔ They may help you identify benefits, grants, and entitlements.

✔ They may have developed existing relationships that can be helpful in resolving issues more quickly.

The Patient Advocate Foundation is a national nonprofit organization that has provided mediation and arbitration services since 1996. It offers assistance to patients dealing with the effects of chronic, debilitating, or life-threatening illnesses. Its free services include resolving insurance-access issues, helping patients with employment issues, and assisting with medical-debt crises. Reach the organization at 800-532-5274 or www.patientadvocate.org.

You can find fee-for-service advocate organizations on the Internet but you may want to check out:

✔ **Healthcare Advocates, Inc.,** knows the industry, laws, and regulations to help you get the best healthcare: `healthcareadvocates.com/index.html`.

✔ **Medical Billing Advocates of America** helps you cut your medical costs by manually reviewing each charge to verify that your insurance payments are not shorted: `www.billadvocates.com`.

Negotiating your debt down

Believe it or not, you can negotiate medical expenses. Most providers have more than one rate for the same service or product — the insured price and the uninsured price. Because they negotiate prices in advance, many insurers get much lower prices than individuals paying out of pocket do. Asking for a discount is nothing new, and asking for insurance company pricing shouldn't cause any heart rates to rise at your provider's office.

If you're not comfortable attempting to negotiate medical charges yourself, try working with a patient advocate group that has experience in this area.

Financing your medical debt

Having one bill to deal with may be easier than keeping track of many service provider payments. Here are the two ways to consolidate your medical debts:

✔ **Pay with credit cards:** Putting your medical debt on a credit card may seem like a way to make the problem go away, if only for a billing cycle. But what you're really doing is borrowing money from a lender to pay a medical provider. You may be better off making a deal with the provider than with a lender if you have a hardship.

If you opt to use plastic to cover your bills, be sure that you can afford your payments, you know what interest rate your card charges, and you're aware of any possible issues paying with credit may cause, such as affecting your eligibility for Medicaid (medical debt on a credit card may no longer qualify as a medical expense).

Be sure to consider a new card or one that has a balance transfer option with a long, low introductory interest rate to keep payments affordable.

✔ **Pay with installment loans:** Another option is to get an installment loan from your bank or credit union. This type of loan has a fixed interest rate, term, and payment. Under the Fair and Accurate Credit Transactions Act (FACT Act or FACTA), lenders can't use your medical condition against you when they decide whether to give you credit and when they establish terms. To help ensure enforcement of this requirement, your copy of your credit report shows the name of the creditor so you can identify the debt. To protect your privacy, others ordering your report see only the generic descriptor "medical payment data."

What to do when your insurance company denies payment

If your insurance covers only a portion of a bill and you can't afford the balance, you have a couple alternatives to letting the bill go to collections, which damages your credit:

✔ **Ask for a discount.** Big insurance companies ask for discounts all the time, and hospitals grant them. Don't be afraid to ask your provider.

✔ **Ask the doctor to accept the insurance payment amount as payment in full.** Doctors do this all the time. Doctors in a network get whatever the insurer pays. The doctor agrees to this arrangement upfront in order to become a member of the network and get referrals. You may be able to get the same deal if you ask.

Filing for medical bankruptcy

You may hear the term *medical bankruptcy* touted as though it's different from a regular bankruptcy, but technically the two are the same. Personal bankruptcies are generally either a Chapter 7 or a Chapter 13. A Chapter 7 eliminates many but not all debts, and to qualify you have to pass a means test based on your state's median income. A Chapter 13 bankruptcy allows you to repay what you can from current earnings, typically over a five-year period, and is not income restricted.

A medical bankruptcy is brought on by medical bills that are either so large or owed to such aggressive providers or collectors that they can't be satisfied. No one I know of is happy when forced to consider bankruptcy. However, in the case of overwhelming medical debts, you need to

✔ Be realistic in assessing whether you'll ever be able to repay what you owe.

✔ Know the full extent of what you owe and to whom you owe it.

After you know that your bills are insurmountable and providers won't accept reduced payments that you can afford, see an attorney to assess your legal options and plan your best strategy. To ensure that a bankruptcy is in your best interest, use an attorney who specializes in debt problems. A nonspecialist may leave debts out of a filing or expose your assets to claims. Income, recentness of debt acquisition, and homestead exemptions are examples of items that can be overlooked.

Going without medical treatment isn't an option just because you can't afford to pay for it.

Settling medical debts

You or your attorney may be able to settle your medical debts rather than declare bankruptcy. In a settlement, a partial repayment that you can afford is negotiated and agreed to. Upon payment of the less-than-full balance, the remainder of the debt is forgiven. I recommend using an attorney for the negotiations and to handle the payments. Using a legal professional can be much cheaper and faster in the end. The forgiven portion of the debts may be considered taxable income, so be sure to consider this in a decision whether to settle or file bankruptcy. Tax debts aren't usually dischargeable in bankruptcy.

Discovering how insurers get your medical information

Whether you like it or not, insurers have access to your medical records and prescription drug records, thanks to the MIB and the newer prescription drug databases. When I say MIB, I'm not referring to the Men in Black but to the even more mysterious Medical Information Bureau, which maintains a database that's home to health-related information on millions of people. Four hundred fifty member insurance companies use and share the MIB's information to supplement their underwriting before pricing their services or issuing life, disability, or individual health insurance products. And that information isn't always accurate.

Not everyone has an MIB file. You need to have applied for life, disability, or individual (not group) insurance from an MIB member company. Information about your health or longevity is sent to the MIB by the member company in an encrypted format. The data identifies medical conditions or tests and a few nonmedical codes. Those codes report potentially hazardous avocations or hobbies or a motor vehicle report showing a poor driving history.

Insurers also rely on prescription drug databases, such as those operated by Ingenix and Milliman, primarily when you're seeking private health, life, or disability insurance. Prescription drug databases can go back as far as five years, detailing drugs used as well as dosage and refills — and they aren't always error-free, either.

 You're entitled to copies of your records at the MIB and both prescription drug databases. Simply call the organizations (I provide contact information in Chapter 14) and ask how to obtain your free copies. To dispute any inaccurate information, just follow the instructions on your report. Should the dispute not be resolved to your satisfaction, you can submit a statement of dispute, which becomes part of your MIB file. From that point forward, any MIB member that receives your MIB file also receives a copy of your statement of dispute.

Monitoring insurance claims for errors

You may be tempted to ignore the whole medical-payment process and assume that the insurance company and the doctors will handle everything satisfactorily. But you know better — what can go wrong often does. Claims payments and treatment-authorization communication between doctors and insurance companies are coded, and one misplaced digit can make a big difference in what medical care is paid for or allowed. Catching small errors early is important, and you, as the party responsible for the bill, have the most at stake.

Between the insurance companies — which have a better day when they don't pay a lot of claims — and the underpaid staff in medical offices and hospitals who code all the procedures, errors are common, and legitimate claims are sometimes rejected. If your claim is rejected, ask for the bill to be resubmitted and for an explanation of why it was rejected the first time.

You don't have to be a claims whiz to keep track of the insurance process. Familiarizing yourself with your coverage limits is worth your time. Read through your insurance contracts (sorry, it's not the most scintillating reading). Get a copy of your coverage if you don't already have one. It may be a policy, a booklet, or something called a *summary plan description*. (The insurance policy itself is the best and most complete source.) The health plan description is 20 to 30 pages or more. The devil is in the definitions; terms you want to pay attention to include the following:

- ✔ **Schedule of benefits:** This section explains what the insurance company pays and what you pay — deductibles, percentages, co-pays, and so on.

- ✔ **Covered benefits:** Often separate from the schedule of benefits, this section is a laundry list of what's covered.

- ✔ **Exclusions and limitations:** This section tells you what isn't covered, as well as items that are covered but with limits.

- ✔ **Claims procedures:** This section explains the steps for filing claims and appealing denials. You may want to read all the way through this part, as it usually includes important time limits and details.

Reviewing these key components should give you a good idea of your coverage. If bills and statements start showing up and you find that keeping track of expenses and reimbursements is just too stressful, consider a *daily money manager (DMM)*. Relatively new on the scene, a DMM is similar to a personal financial advisor — someone who can provide a wide range of services depending on your needs. This individual can also keep track of medical bills and insurance forms. The best way to find a good DMM is through a referral. If no one you know can direct you to a good DMM, contact the American Association of Daily Money Managers (AADMM) at www.aadmm.com or 877-326-5991.

Dealing with denied medical claims

Most doctors and hospitals don't report payment histories to credit bureaus. They don't like to pay the fees, and some of them don't like to think that they're in the credit business. However, if a debt moves from a medical provider to an outside collection agency, odds are it will hit your credit report. The message here is that you have more wiggle room with a medical provider, but be sure to ask whether the provider reports your payment history to one of the credit-reporting agencies.

Keep in touch with the hospital billing people, who assume that if the insurance company denies a claim, you'll pay the difference. Communicating that you don't consider the claim settled and that you need their help to resubmit or appeal a decision makes them a part of the process and keeps their expectations in line with yours. Just as you take an active role in your care and treatment as a patient, you also have to take an active role in the payment of your medical costs.

If you have a hard time getting your bills covered and you think the insurance company is wrong, take the following steps:

1. **Complain.**

   Insurance carriers, believe it or not, don't like complaints. Here's a list of people to complain to, starting with the lowest one on the totem pole:

   • Claims adjuster

   • Supervisor

   • Unit manager (over several supervisors by line of business)

   • Assistant manager (over unit managers, but not in all offices)

   • Claims manager or claims vice president (in charge of a local office)

   • Regional claims vice president (in charge of several offices in a region)

   • Home office claims, senior vice president

   Despite how frustrated you may be feeling, always be polite and direct. Nasty complaints are easily dismissed or sent to a lawyer.

2. **Maintain detailed records.**

   When dealing with insurers, keep records of conversations (times, dates, and what was said), as well as copies of any documents you receive. If you write to an adjuster, copy the supervisor and request a written response within a set time frame.

3. **File a written complaint.**

   If you reach an impasse, write to your state insurance regulatory agency. Don't go into great detail; just explain the basic issues that are in dispute. To find your state regulator online, go to www.naic.org. Complaining to your state regulator is likely to motivate the insurer to pay better attention to resolving your claim.

Managing expenses to avoid credit repercussions

If, when all is said and done, you're left with medical expenses that you're responsible for paying, you have some options:

✔ **Suggest a reduced repayment amount either in a lump sum (ask the service provider to consider an ease-of-handling discount for cash) or a set payment every month.** Do so before you get billed. When third-party billers get hold of a debt, they're tenacious, and the providers generally don't want to get in the middle. Deal with the provider first if you can.

✔ **Find out whether your hospital is covered under the federal Hill-Burton Act, which prohibits discrimination in providing services.** In 1975, Congress amended

the Hill-Burton program, which established federal grants, loan guarantees, and interest subsidies for certain health facilities to require that they must provide uncompensated services forever. The U.S. Department of Health and Human Services at the Health Resources and Services Administration has information about where to find the 170 facilities covered under Hill-Burton. Check out `www.hrsa.gov/gethealthcare/affordable/hillburton/facilities.html`. There are no such facilities in Alaska, Indiana, Minnesota, Nebraska, Nevada, North Dakota, Rhode Island, Utah, or Wyoming, and all the territories except Puerto Rico.

If you have no insurance, let the doctor or hospital know this fact early in the process. Then ask about discounts and payment plans, but be sure you can afford the payment plan before you agree to it. (You may want to follow the process I recommend in the "Keeping Credit Strong While Unemployed" section earlier in this chapter, which involves resetting your spending priorities until you have the new bills under control.) Being willing to pay a reasonable bill over time is the best course of action to keep collection activity off your credit record. Communicating with your doctor and hospital is the key.

Resolving Credit Issues After the Death of a Spouse or Partner

If you've lost a spouse or partner, you're already going through one of life's most emotionally draining experiences. Unfortunately, in the midst of the often debilitating experience of losing a loved one, numerous financial matters surface, including credit and debt issues.

For one thing, thieves may use the deceased's Social Security number and identity to open fraudulent credit accounts. Promptly sending a copy of the death certificate to the credit bureaus can help deter this crime:

✔ **Equifax,** P.O. Box 105069, Atlanta, GA 30348

✔ **Experian,** P.O. Box 9701, Allen, TX 75013

✔ **TransUnion,** P.O. Box 6790, Fullerton, CA 92634

Stabilizing your credit in the event of a death can be difficult, especially if your spouse held all or most of the credit in his or her name. A creditor wants a copy of the death certificate and typically asks the estate to pay the bill. As a rule, you aren't personally responsible for credit held in the deceased's name alone unless the two of you lived in a community-property state.

In community-property states — Arizona, California, Idaho, Louisiana, Nevada, New Mexico, Texas, Washington, and Wisconsin — credit accounts opened during a marriage are automatically considered joint accounts. That means you're responsible for any debt your deceased spouse incurred during the marriage. This may also be true in Alaska if you opted for community-property status when you moved there. Although Puerto Rico is an American territory and not a state, it has community-property laws, too.

This section tells you how to protect your credit when the debts belong to a deceased spouse.

Understanding what happens to joint credit when you're single again

By law, a creditor can't automatically close a joint account or change the terms because of the death of one spouse. Generally, the creditor asks you, the surviving spouse, to fill out a new credit application in your own name. If your creditor doesn't approach you with this option, close the joint account and open a new individual account in your name alone. The creditor then decides whether to continue to extend credit or alter the credit limit. *Remember:* You don't have to deal with this issue the day after your spouse's death, but sooner is better than later, because a major change to your account has occurred.

Knowing exactly what your liability is

If you're a joint account holder on a credit card, or if you live in one of the community-property states noted earlier, you may owe the debts of the deceased. In a community-property state, as long as the debt was incurred during the marriage, you are liable, even if you received no benefit from it or didn't even know about it.

Terminating the deceased's preapproved credit offers

Credit bureaus automatically update records with periodic reports from the Social Security Administration. When the update is made, your spouse's credit history is flagged, and his or her name is removed from any preapproved credit offer mailing lists. This reduces the mail you get in your spouse's name. You can speed up this process by notifying the three major credit bureaus (use the information provided earlier in this section).

In non-community-property states, credit card debts and other debts that are solely in the name of the deceased aren't passed on to surviving spouses or children. However, notifying creditors is still a good idea, even if you aren't liable. They generally request that a certified copy of the death certificate be forwarded to them to close the account. If the estate has assets, creditors may try to collect any balance due from the estate's executor. If the estate doesn't have enough cash and has few assets that can be sold, the issue generally ends there.

Some people feel that they should pay their deceased spouse's debts, whether out of a sense of obligation or honor or just to set the record straight. Paying the debt of your deceased spouse isn't necessary unless you're required to do so by law. Creditors understand risk very well and factor it into their fees and interest rates. In that regard, they've already been paid. If a creditor tries to pressure you into paying a debt that you aren't obligated to pay, I recommend telling the creditor to take a hike.

Building your credit record on your own

If your spouse or partner has died and you shared financial matters, you need to reestablish yourself as an individual. Your first task is to come up with a spending plan that covers your expenses as a single person. This plan helps you understand how your financial situation has changed, for better or worse. I offer pointers on creating a spending plan in Chapter 18. When setting goals, I suggest that you stick to short- and intermediate-term goals until your life has settled down.

When you know where you stand financially, you can begin deciding how you want to use credit. Because your credit score determines what you pay for credit and under what terms it may be available, I suggest that you get your FICO score from www.myfico.com, along with copies of your credit reports. The better your score, the less you have to pay to borrow or use credit. (For guidance on reviewing your reports, flip to Chapter 14.)

Don't close old accounts with positive credit histories unless you have to. The length of time an account is open counts in your favor for credit scoring purposes. Having a variety of accounts also helps your score. If you have a mortgage or a car payment and you can afford to pay it off, you may want to consider keeping it open for a short while to keep new positive information flowing into your credit file.

Fitting Credit into Retirement

Until a certain point in their lives, most people think of their kids or their home as the most expensive part of their financial environment. Then they hit retirement. Retirement may not last as long as your kids or your home, but it does require more saving and planning. The sooner you begin to plan, save, and invest for your exit from the workforce, the better.

Credit can be a help or a hindrance in retirement. On the positive side, using credit rather than cash can be a great convenience and can add value in your later years if done wisely. But because credit essentially allows you to use tomorrow's income today, you may wind up overusing credit, which can be difficult to rebound from when you stop getting paychecks and raises and find that your income is more or less fixed. To avoid falling into a credit crunch in retirement, make sure that you have a solid budget. You need to know what you're spending and what you have coming in each month. In this section, I present the basics on creating a budget that can set you up well for retirement, and I help you understand how the use of credit changes in this phase of life.

Budgeting on a fixed income

Following are the essential ingredients for successful budgeting. (Chapter 18 goes into detail about constructing a budget that works for you, not against you.)

✔ **Set short-term and long-term goals.** Whether you're 55 or 95, you need a reason to get up in the morning. Goals provide this motivation and more. Although they may differ from those you had earlier in life, goals, especially around spending, keep you looking forward to tomorrow. They may include traveling to places you've always wanted to see, making a difference in your community, or just seeing more of family.

Short-term goals for your stage of life should be in the 6- to 12-month range, while longer-term ones may go out to 5 years.

✔ **Know your monthly income and expenses.** After you settle on your goals, you need to fund them. Don't guess; know what you can afford. Make sure that you can cover basic, recurring monthly expenses, and don't forget to keep an emergency fund. You don't need the standard 12 months of expenses because you won't have to fund a period of unemployment. But you will need to meet any unexpected out-of-pocket expenses like home repairs, major car repairs, or insurance deductibles. Know what your exposure is and set funds aside for it.

✔ **Protect your cash.** When your cash is gone, it's gone! Be sure to control your urge to spend for items not in your budget. Don't use tax-deferred retirement funds to pay off debt if you have any other choice. Although you may be beyond the age of early-withdrawal penalties, taxes take a big chunk out of withdrawals. Use excess cash flow to pay down debt gradually whenever possible. Home equity loans or reverse mortgages may be sources for interest-deductible or tax-exempt funds if they fit your goals and plan.

✔ **Control debt payments.** Any new debt payments must fit into your budget. Try to match the time it takes you to pay off a debt with the time you'll be using an item. For example, the debt you incur by paying for a meal out with a credit card should be paid off at the end of the month. The debt you incur for a car should be paid off over the useful life of the car or before you plan to buy a replacement. The debt you incur in buying a home that you intend to live in for the rest of your life need not be paid off until you die.

Using credit for convenience

Although your income may decrease when you hit retirement, your credit history keeps on growing. Great reasons to use credit rather than cash include reward points and easier tracking of expenses. These conveniences add value to the money you spend.

With some simple caveats, credit can be as big a boon to seniors as it is to the population as a whole. Here are three easy and simple safeguards to consider:

✔ **Never lend your good credit to someone else.** Adding an authorized user to your account to help a friend with bad credit or cosigning on a loan usually ends in disaster. Giving someone else access to your credit gives that person access to your cash and your future well-being; it's absolutely not worth it.

✔ **Don't put yourself in a position to become a victim of credit card fraud.** To avoid becoming another statistic, be on guard when you use credit. When shopping online, look for the padlock icon in the address bar or *https* in the web address; both indicate that the connection is secure. And never give your credit card information to anyone who contacts you first.

✔ **Check one of your free credit reports every four months, alternating requests among the three credit bureaus.** Staying on top of your credit reports is one of the most effective ways to catch credit card fraud early. Be sure to dispute any accounts you don't recognize. See Chapter 3 for details on disputing credit report errors. They could mean identity theft! For guidance on getting free copies of your credit reports from the three major credit bureaus, head to Chapter 14.

Part IV

Big Brother Credit Is Watching You: Credit Reporting and Scoring

Five Easy Ways to Monitor Your Credit on Your Own

- Get a free copy of your credit report every 12 months from each of the three major credit-reporting agencies (Experian, Equifax, and TransUnion). Stagger the ordering so that you get a different report every four months. Review them and dispute any inaccuracies.

- Monitor your bank and credit card accounts online weekly. If something funny is going on, you'll know about it sooner.

- Set up free alerts on your accounts that tip you off when certain types of transactions are made or if a dollar limit is exceeded.

- Get a free report if you're turned down for credit or applying for a job. Within the first six months of seeking employment, you can have a freebie.

- If you apply for a mortgage, you're entitled to a copy of the credit report and score the lender uses.

For a letter you can use to contact a creditor about an error on your credit report, visit www.dummies.com/extras/creditrepair.

In this part . . .

- Discover how credit reporting, scoring, and monitoring work.
- Uncover the differences between FICO and VantageScore.
- Order free copies of your credit reports from the big-three credit bureaus.
- Find out which specialty bureaus report your medical, check writing, and gambling histories.
- Follow a detailed plan to clean up your credit reports.

Chapter 13

Discovering How Credit Reporting Works

Some people who use credit sparingly (or not at all) think that knowing their credit history is unimportant. But your credit history doesn't just come into play when you want to borrow money. Landlords, insurers, and even employers review credit reports and make decisions about you based on the information contained in your credit history. Heck, even a particularly finance-conscious romantic prospect may want to review your credit history before saying yes to moving in or tying the knot! A poor credit history can cost you thousands of dollars and deny you opportunities you never even knew you missed.

Anytime lenders and others take a look at you to determine your credit risk — but especially in a tight credit market — knowing what they'll see is important. Your credit report and credit score, the two pieces that reveal your credit history, can make a difference in whether you qualify for a loan, as well as how much you pay in interest or other terms of the loan and how much you pay for your auto and homeowners/renters insurance. Don't worry, though. In this chapter, I help you understand why you need to be on intimate terms with your credit report and credit score, what these pieces of info actually are, and how they're compiled.

After you're up to speed on credit reports and scores, challenge your friends to the credit score quiz found at www.creditscorequiz.org. Hint: This quiz was co-authored by VantageScore and the Consumer Federation of America!

Grasping the Importance of Your Credit Report

Perhaps you're wondering where all the data about your credit history comes from. Would you think I've seen too many spy movies if I told you that your personal information is being accumulated every day? Or would you think that the NSA, FBI, or CIA is overstepping its boundaries again? Well, the truth is that your credit history is being compiled courtesy of credit issuers, banks, insurers, pharmacies, and landlords with whom you do business. Chances are they're reporting your financial transactions to the three major credit bureaus (Equifax, Experian, and TransUnion) and many other specialty bureaus that store information.

When you pay your car payment, mortgage payment, and credit card bill each month, your creditors report your payment history to the credit bureaus. If you miss a payment, your creditor reports that as well. Creditors review the information in your credit report or other specialty reports to determine the terms they may offer you for a credit card, loan, apartment, or insurance policy.

Clearly, what you don't know *can* hurt you. Consider two hypothetical life situations to illustrate my point:

- ✔ Say you sign up for an Internet dating service in hopes of meeting that special someone. Now, what if all the information available to your prospective dates was given to them by the people you've dated in the past? What if the quality of the dates you get in the future was directly tied to what all the people you've dumped (or have been dumped by) say about you? Starting to get concerned?

- ✔ Say you're applying for a job. Your salary, job title, and office size are tied directly to what's on your résumé. But what if your past employers wrote your résumé for you, and what if they mixed up your personnel file with the file of a person who was fired for punching the boss in the nose? Can you imagine walking into that job interview without having any idea what your former boss may have reported or whether it was accurate?

I'm not saying that you're guaranteed to *like* the outcome of your date or the job interview, but at least you know that it's based on accurate and timely information. Likewise with your credit report: You can't report your own credit history to the bureaus, but you *can* be knowledgeable about what your credit report says and anticipate how it may influence others as you try to negotiate your way through the financial universe. You *can* head off situations that could cost you thousands of dollars or deny you opportunities. And you *can* catch inaccuracies on your report (a fairly common situation) and correct them.

You have no excuse for not knowing what's in your credit report because you can get a free copy of your report annually from each of the three credit bureaus. Getting the information is fast and easy. Simply visit www.annualcreditreport.com or call 877-322-8228 to order your reports.

What Is a Credit Report, Exactly?

In its most basic sense, your credit report is your financial life history. Credit-reporting bureaus manage, maintain, and share this information. As many as 20 credit-reporting bureaus are out there; most are specialty reporting agencies (I introduce you to some of them in Chapter 14). The following three are considered the biggies:

- ✔ **Equifax** (www.equifax.com; phone 800-685-1111)
- ✔ **Experian** (www.experian.com; phone 866-200-6020)
- ✔ **TransUnion** (www.transunion.com; phone 800-888-4213)

You can rest assured that your rights are protected in the reporting process because of the Fair and Accurate Credit Transactions Act (the FACT Act or FACTA). You can find more details on the FACT Act in Chapter 19 and read a copy of the law at www.dummies.com/extras/creditrepair.

The following sections explain what your credit report reveals about you.

Revealing the facts about your financial transactions

You may think that your credit report contains the intimate personal details of your life, ferreted out from interviews with your neighbors, your ex, and your business associates. Not true! You can rest assured that your credit report doesn't reveal whether you tend to drink too much at office parties, whether you sport a tattoo, or any other information about your personal behavior.

The information in your credit report is specific, factual, and limited to your financial transactions. What it lacks in scope, however, it makes up for in the sheer volume of detail and the length of time it covers. When I talk to high school, college, or technical school students, I tell them that if they cut one class, chances are no one will notice, but if they fail to pay a single bill on time, the creditor will notice and report the late payment, and that info will be available to everyone considering doing business with them for the next seven years!

Here's the short take on what's in your credit report:

- ✔ **Personal identification information:** This info includes your name, Social Security number, date of birth, addresses (present and past), and recent employment history.

    Be consistent with your personal information, especially how you spell your name and address. Name, address, and date of birth are the most common sources used to identify your file; Social Security number is fourth. If you're a woman and you take your husband's name when you get married, your files should be automatically updated when you get a reissued credit card or a loan in your new name.

- ✔ **Public record information:** Your credit report includes info on tax liens, judgments, bankruptcies, child-support orders, and other official information.

- ✔ **Collection activity:** If you've had accounts sent to collection agencies for handling, your credit report contains that info.

- ✔ **Information about each credit account (or *trade line*), whether open or closed:** Your credit report includes details on all your credit accounts, including

    - Type of account (such as a mortgage or installment account)
    - Whether the account is *joint* (shared with another person) or just in your name
    - How much you owe
    - Who you owe
    - Your monthly payment
    - Your payment history (whether you've paid on time or been late)
    - Your credit limit

    Experian, one of the three main credit-reporting agencies, also keeps a record of rental data over the last two years.

- ✔ **A list of the companies that have requested your credit file for the purpose of granting you credit:** Requests, known as *inquiries,* are one of two types:

    - *Soft inquiries* are made for promotional purposes (for instance, when a credit card issuer wants to send you an offer). These inquiries don't appear on the version of your credit report that lenders see, but they do appear on the copy that you get.
    - *Hard inquiries* are made in response to a request from you for more or new credit. These inquiries *do* appear on the lender's copy of your credit report.

✔ **An optional message or ten from you:** You can add a message of up to 100 words in length that explains any extenuating circumstances for your report overall or any negative listings on your report. One message may be enough, but if you have different explanations for more than one account, you can add individual 100-word messages to specific trade lines. See Chapter 3 for more on adding these messages to your credit report.

✔ **An optional credit score and reason code:** Your credit score is, strictly speaking, not part of your credit report but an add-on that you have to ask for. Your score is different for each credit report because the data that each bureau has may vary slightly, and each bureau may offer a proprietary score of its own. You get reason codes with each score to help you understand why your score is what it is. (I cover the importance of your credit score later in this chapter.)

Credit reports are easy to read, although they still have room for improvement. Each of the three major credit-reporting agencies reports your information in its own unique format. The credit-reporting agencies compete with one another for business, so they have to differentiate their products. (Chapter 14 highlights the differences in each agency's presentation.)

Among the list of items *not* included in your credit report are your lifestyle choices, religion, national origin, political affiliation, sexual preferences, medical history, friends, and relatives. In addition, the three major credit-reporting agencies don't collect or transmit data on your checking or savings accounts, brokerage accounts, business accounts (unless you're on record as being personally liable for the debt), bankruptcies that are more than ten years old, charge-offs or debts placed for collection that are more than seven years old, or your credit score (although your credit score is generated based on information in your credit report, it's not part of the report itself).

You can view sample credit reports from each of the three major credit-reporting bureaus at www.dummies.com/extras/creditrepair.

Providing insight into your character

Many entities use your credit report to predict your potential behavior in other areas of your life. The fact that you have a history of making credit card payments late tells a prospective landlord that you may be late with your rent, too. A history of defaulted loans may suggest to a potential boss that you don't follow through with work commitments. A home foreclosure in your file may indicate that you take on more than you can handle or that you're just one unlucky duck. If you've declared bankruptcy because your finances are out of control, perhaps you're out of control in other ways, too.

This financial snapshot, which brings into focus the details of your spending and borrowing and even hints at patterns in your personal life, also paints a *bigger* picture of two important factors that are critical to employers, landlords, lenders, and others:

- **Whether you keep your promises:** Your credit history is an indicator of whether you follow through with commitments, a characteristic that's important to most people, whether they're looking for a reliable worker, a responsible nanny, a dependable renter, or a faithful mate. Needless to say, a person or company that's considering extending you a loan, apartment lease, insurance policy, or job wants to know the same.

- **Whether you fulfill your obligations in a timely manner:** Following through with your obligations in a timely manner is the other half of the credit-reporting game. Tight lending standards make a history of past failures to pay on time harder to accept for lenders who can't afford any more defaults.

In the lending business, the more overdue the payment, the more likely it won't be paid in full — or paid at all. That's why, as you get further behind in your payments, lenders become more anxious about collecting the amount you owe. In fact, if you're sufficiently delinquent, the lender may want you to pay back the entire amount at once rather than as originally scheduled. So the longer you take to do what you promised, the more it costs you and the more damage you do to your credit and credit score.

The Negatives and Positives of Credit Reporting

Whether you're new to the world of credit or you're an experienced borrower, you may be mesmerized by the amount of information on your credit report. Fortunately, it all falls into one of two categories: negative (information that makes you look like a potential financial risk) and positive (information that makes lenders want to throw money at you, or at least not turn you down for a loan). In the following sections, I zero in on the differences between the two so that you can focus on what matters and let go of what doesn't.

The negatives

I hate to have to be the one to tell you, but if you aren't married, someone has to: You aren't perfect. And neither is your credit report. The good news is that you don't need a flawless credit report to qualify for financial products and services at competitive rates and terms, nor do you need to have a financial record that entitles you to canonization for credit sainthood. Confused? Never fear. Here are the answers to some common questions about the negative data found on the vast majority of Americans' credit reports:

- ✔ **How long do bad marks stick around?** Most negative data stays on your credit report for seven years, although a few items are different, such as a Chapter 7 bankruptcy, which stays on your report for ten years, and IRS debts, which stay on until you fully repay them. Even though the negative info is out there for a long time, as the months and years roll by, this info becomes less important to your credit profile. For example, most creditors aren't concerned by the fact that you were late in paying a credit card bill one time three years ago.

- ✔ **Just how much does one mistake cost you when it comes to your credit report?** That depends on the rest of the items on your report that make up your credit history. Lots of positive information can lessen the impact of negative items, and the size of the mistake counts, too. A default on a credit card is less serious than a mortgage default. Along with your credit report, lenders can also access your *credit score,* a number that's calculated based on the contents of your credit report. This three-digit score comes from a mathematical equation that evaluates much of the information on your credit report at that particular credit bureau. By comparing this information to the patterns in zillions of past credit reports, the score tells the lender your level of future credit risk. (Check out the section "Cracking credit score components" later in this chapter for more info on credit scores.)

- ✔ **How do those who view your report interpret bad marks?** Think of it this way: Say you loan your significant other $5,000 for a worthy cause. Your honey promises to pay you back monthly over two years but stops paying after four months, with no intention of repaying the full amount. You, not wanting to see your friends suffer the same fate, then mention the negative experience to any who are thinking of floating this person a new loan. In business, as in love, trust and faithful performance are keys to success. Basically, any delinquencies or charge-offs definitely count against you. However, a creditor tends to look at your bill payments in the creditor's specific area as most important. A car lender, for example, scrutinizes your car payment history more closely than a credit card issuer. Other concerns include how much credit you have available (too much is not good) and how much you've used (maxing out what you have is not good).

Some unscrupulous lenders may use negative information from your distant past as a reason to put you into a higher-cost (and potentially more profitable for them) loan, even though you may qualify for a less-expensive one. If you don't know your score, you may be duped into a higher rate than your imperfect credit deserves. This is just one example of a situation in which understanding your credit score can save you money. The scenario can go something like this: You're looking for a loan for a car or some similar big-ticket item. The lender you contact reviews your credit report and offers you a loan at terms that are "a great deal considering your credit history."

Translated, this means that the lender is charging you a higher-than-market rate because of your imperfect credit report.

TIP

If a lender offers you a loan at less than the best terms or denies you a loan, the lender must provide you with a *credit score disclosure exception notice* that includes a free copy of the credit score used to make the decision. The notice includes the score range and how your score compares to other U.S. consumers. You're also entitled to a free copy of the credit report that was used to obtain that credit score.

The positives

Positive information — the good stuff that everyone likes to see — stays on your report for quite a while. In fact, some positive data may remain on your report for 10, 20, or even 30 years, depending on each bureau's policy and whether you keep your account open.

The more positive information you have in your credit files, the less effect a single negative item has on your credit score. So if you're an experienced credit user with a long credit history, one missed payment won't affect you much. If, however, you're a young person or a new immigrant with only a few trade lines and a few months of credit history, a situation that's sometimes called a *thin file,* a negative item has a much larger effect because you have fewer positive items to balance things out. For pointers on beefing up (or just plain starting) your credit history, flip to Chapter 10.

Your Credit Report's Numerical Offspring: The Credit Score

Your credit score is a three-digit number that rules a good portion of your financial life, for better or for worse. But where did this all-important number come from? Starting back in the 1950s, some companies, including FICO (formerly known as Fair Isaac) and more recently VantageScore, began to model credit data in hopes of predicting payment behavior. (A *model* uses a series of formulas based on some basic assumptions to make predictions about future behavior. A weatherperson uses models to predict the weather. Usually, the credit folks are more accurate because they predict the likelihood of something bad happening in the next year or so.)

Until recently, the three major credit bureaus offered different scoring models created for them by FICO, the developers of the *FICO score*. Each bureau called the score by a proprietary name, and each had some differences in how it handled your data. Now, they all also offer a single credit scoring model called the VantageScore that's exactly the same across all the databases.

The following sections take a closer look at the two main types of credit scores — FICO and VantageScore — to help you understand their components and ensure that your credit score is the best it can be.

Cracking credit score components

In order to have a credit score, you need to have at least one account open and reporting. FICO requires at least one account to be open for at least six months and to have been updated in the last six months. VantageScore requires the account to be open for at least three months before generating a score. For those who have been out of the credit market for a while, VantageScore can generate a score using data that is up to 24 months old. VantageScore can also develop a credit score based on rent, utility, and cellphone history when it is included in your credit bureau report. You can find out more about both main types of scores in the next sections.

Although having no credit history makes it difficult to get credit initially, building credit for the first time is a lot easier than repairing a bad credit history.

What makes up a FICO score?

The most widely used credit score is the FICO score, which ranges from 300 to 850. The higher the number, the better the credit rating and the better terms you get when looking for your next loan or credit card. Your FICO score changes over time as your credit history changes.

FICO takes into account more than 20 factors when building your score, and the importance of each one is dependent on the other factors, the volume of data, and the length of your history. Your FICO score is made up of five components (see Figure 13-1):

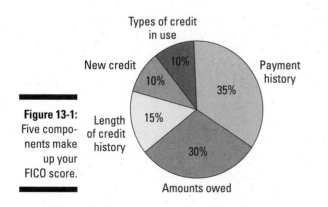

Figure 13-1: Five components make up your FICO score.

✔ **Payment history (35 percent):** Payment history is the most significant factor when determining whether you're a good credit risk. This category includes the number and severity of any late payments, the amount past due, and whether you eventually repaid the accounts as agreed. The more late payments, the lower your score.

✔ **Amount and type of debt (30 percent):** The amount you owe is the next most important factor in your credit score. This category includes the total amount you owe, the amount you owe by account type (such as revolving or installment, which for FICO includes mortgage debt), the number of accounts on which you're carrying a balance, and the proportion of your credit lines that you're using. For example, in the case of installment credit, *proportion of balance* means the amount remaining on the loan in relation to the loan's original amount. For revolving debt, such as a credit card, proportion of balance is the amount you currently owe in relation to your credit limit. The less you owe in relation to the amount of credit available, the higher your score. Having credit cards with no balances ups your limits and your score.

✔ **Length of time you've been using credit (15 percent):** The number of years you've been using credit and the type of accounts you have also influence your score. Accounts that have been open for at least two years help increase your score.

✔ **Variety of accounts (10 percent):** The mix of credit accounts is a part of each of the other factors. Riskier types of credit mean lower scores. For example, if most of your debt is in the form of revolving credit or finance company loans, your score is lower than if your debt is from student loans and mortgage loans. Also, a lender is likely to give greater weight to your performance on its type of loan, meaning that a credit card issuer looks at your experience with other cards more closely and a mortgagor pays closer attention to how you pay mortgages or secured loans. An ideal mix has a positive credit history with a variety of different types of credit, such as installment and revolving credit lines.

✔ **Number and types of accounts you've opened recently, generally in the last six months or so (10 percent):** When you apply for new credit or ask for a raise in your credit line, the creditor makes an inquiry into your credit report. A high number of inquiries for these actions has a negative effect on your credit score. The reasoning is that if you apply for several accounts at the same time and get approved for them, you may not be able to afford your new debt load.

What makes up a VantageScore?

VantageScore has been around since 2006. It uses the same score range as FICO: 300 to 850. As with the FICO score, the higher the number, the better the score. As you can see in Figure 13-2, your VantageScore is made up of six components (note that VantageScore reviews its scoring factors annually, so their weightings may change every year if large changes occur in economic conditions or consumer behavior):

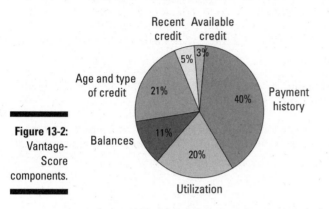

Recent credit

Available credit

Age and type of credit

Payment history

Balances

Utilization

5% 3%

21%

40%

11%

20%

Figure 13-2: Vantage-Score components.

✔ **Payment history (40 percent):** Paying on time (satisfactory), paying late (delinquent), or not paying at all (charge-off) show up here. Payment history is not only one of the most significant factors in determining whether an individual is a good credit risk, but also the most influential component of the VantageScore.

✔ **Age and type of credit (21 percent):** Another highly influential category, this includes the length of your history and types of credit you've used. A long history with mixed types of credit (mortgage, car loan, credit cards, retail stores, and so on) is best.

✔ **Utilization, or percentage of credit limit used (20 percent):** The percentage of credit available to you that you've used or that you owe on accounts is highly influential in determining your score. Using a large proportion of your overall available credit is a negative.

✔ **Balances (11 percent):** The amount of recently reported current and delinquent balances. Balances that you've increased recently can be an indication of risk and lower your score.

✔ **Recent credit (5 percent):** The number of recently opened credit accounts and all new inquiries counts but is among the less influential scoring components. New accounts initially lower your score because creditors may be unclear on why you want more credit. However, after you use the accounts and pay on time, the accounts help raise your score by adding positive information to your credit report.

✔ **Available credit (3 percent):** The amount of credit available on all your accounts. Using a low percentage of the total credit available to you is a good thing.

If you're trying to build a credit history for the first time, here are two things to look for. First, seek a lender that uses VantageScores to grant credit because VantageScore can give you a valid score using less data than FICO can. Plus, VantageScore can give you scoring credit for rent payments if that information is in your credit report. Second, consider a lender that uses the FICO Expansion score (see the next section), which uses boutique credit databases and information verified by the lender, such as utility payments, to give a one-time score.

For examples of ways to start a credit history, including using a secured card or a passbook loan, check out Chapter 10.

There is more to a credit decision than score component weightings. Consider the weighting factors as directional indicators rather than a guarantee of great credit rates and terms.

The reasoning behind reason codes

When you see your credit score for the first time, you may say: "They must be wrong; my credit is better than that!" If so, you're not alone. As a result, the two scoring companies, FICO and VantageScore, have developed reason codes and brief statements to help you know what went wrong with your credit that resulted in your particular credit score. VantageScore recently reduced the number of reason codes to fewer than 80 and simplified the reason code statements by using rent, utility, and telecom data when it is present in a consumer's credit file. It also set up an online resource, www.reasoncode.org, that goes into more depth than the simple reason codes and corresponding reason statements that you get with your score by providing details about what each reason code means in plain English. Features of ReasonCode.org include

 ✓ A primer on what reason codes are and how they are used

 ✓ Searchable and interactive reason code definitions and explanations

 ✓ A glossary of common reason code terms

See Chapter 14 for additional information about reason statements.

Allowing for acts of God

Sometimes things happen to people that are so far beyond their control that even lenders don't want to hold them responsible. I put what I call acts of God in this category. Lenders may indicate that an account belongs to a natural disaster victim when reporting account activity to the credit bureaus. Reporting an account with the natural disaster reporting code means that the account is not counted in the calculation of your credit score. When this happens, both positive and negative information is potentially invisible to your credit score. In the case of VantageScore, only negative information is "set to neutral" so that you can continue to benefit from positive information even though you have been the victim of a natural disaster.

Chapter 14

Understanding Credit Reports and Scores

*W*hether you agree with the concept or not, people in your life make an increasing number of decisions about you based on your credit information. Therefore, knowing the what, when, where, why, and how of your credit information is in your best interest. In fact, I'm not sure why the need to understand your credit history and what it means for your financial life isn't included in the many instructions people receive as children. "Do your best to maintain good credit" is just as valuable a lesson to impart as "Eat your vegetables."

The majority of the credit information collected about you is contained in your credit reports from the three major credit bureaus. Getting copies of those reports and reviewing the information in them is as easy as it is important, and doing so gives you a good idea of what most people or programs evaluating your credit see. In this chapter, I explain how to get your hands on your credit report, and I walk you through the process of reviewing your report from each bureau and making sense of all the industry jargon. I also reveal how you can dispute inaccurate information included in your reports. Of course, the three major credit bureaus aren't the only ones compiling financial information about you. I introduce you to a growing number of specialty reporting agencies in this chapter as well.

Credit scores are also a part of the credit-reporting picture, so I share how to obtain and make sense of your score. By the time you're done reading this chapter, you'll be armed with the information you need to discover exactly how potential employers, lenders, landlords, and insurance agents see you when viewing you through the lens of your credit history.

Getting Copies of Your Credit Reports

The three main collectors of credit information in the credit industry today are Equifax, Experian, and TransUnion. These major credit bureaus are basically huge databases of information. (I reveal where all that information comes from in Chapter 13.)

Given the billions of pieces of data that flow in and out of the bureaus every month, some of your information may be inaccurate or out-of-date. Getting copies of your credit reports from the three credit bureaus to make sure that the information in your files is a true representation of your credit use is therefore essential. By reviewing your reports, you'll also know if someone has stolen your identity to establish fraudulent credit accounts.

Any incorrect information included in your credit report has the potential to be very costly to you. For example, erroneous info could mean that you don't get the loans or terms you want or that you have to pay a much higher interest rate than you should have to pay. The catch is that the companies reporting information to the credit bureaus don't always report to all three, so checking your credit report with just one bureau isn't good enough. The information that Equifax has may be slightly different from the information that Experian has, and the information that Experian has may be slightly different from the information that TransUnion has. Also, you can have a perfectly clean Experian report while your TransUnion report contains some negative items in error, or vice versa.

The good news is that you don't have to do much heavy lifting to get your hands on all your credit reports thanks to the Fair and Accurate Credit Transactions Act (commonly referred to as the FACT Act or FACTA). This act entitles every American to at least one free credit report from each of the three bureaus every 12 months. You're also entitled to an additional free report from each of the bureaus if you

   ✔ Were denied credit in the last 60 days

   ✔ Are unemployed and planning to seek employment in the next 60 days

   ✔ Are on welfare

   ✔ Are a victim of fraud or identity theft and have reported it to the police

In the following sections, I explain how to get your reports, what kind of information you need to provide, what to watch out for, and when you should check your reports.

Where to get your reports

To obtain your one free credit report from each of the three major credit bureaus each year, simply visit the website www.annualcreditreport.com. Or, if you prefer, you can request copies by phone or mail:

> Annual Credit Report Request Service
> P.O. Box 105281
> Atlanta, GA 30348-5281
> Phone 877-322-8228

You need to fill out a request form if you use the mail to get your free copies from the central source. The form is included at www.dummies.com/ extras/creditrepair.

Many different websites with similar-sounding names have cropped up since the central source for free credit reports was established. These sites advertise free credit reports, but the fine print is that your free report costs you something because you must purchase another product or service to receive it. You shouldn't have to purchase anything to get your free copies. If the site requires you to provide payment information, you're on the wrong site.

Note that your credit score isn't provided with your free annual credit reports when you use www.annualcreditreport.com. If you want to know your score, you need to contact the credit bureau directly for a copy of your credit report and credit score, for a small fee. You can get things started with a phone call, a visit to the bureau's website, or through the mail. Here's the contact information for the three major credit-reporting bureaus:

- **Equifax,** P.O. Box 740241, Atlanta, GA 30374; phone 800-685-1111; www.equifax.com

- **Experian,** P.O. Box 2104, Allen, TX 75013-2104; phone 866-200-6020; www.experian.com

- **TransUnion,** 2 Baldwin Place, P.O. Box 1000, Chester, PA 19022; phone 800-888-4213; www.transunion.com

What you need to provide

Whether you contact a credit bureau directly to get a copy of your report or you go through the free central source to get all three at once (see the preceding section), you need to provide information that lets the powers that be know that you are who you say you are. So be ready to give all the information you've always been told not to give to a stranger over the phone or Internet. In this one case, it's okay.

The information requested varies from one bureau to the next, but the following is a list of some information you're likely to be asked for:

- ✔ Your Social Security number
- ✔ Your credit card account numbers
- ✔ Your former addresses and the dates you lived at each address
- ✔ Your employment history

When you order your credit report, the bureaus may try to sell you a credit score as well. See the section "Ordering your score," later in this chapter, for more information.

When to get copies of your credit reports

Because you're entitled to a free copy of your credit report from each of the big-three credit bureaus every 12 months, reviewing your credit reports at least once a year makes sense.

I recommend that you order a report from one of the three bureaus every four months, rotating through the bureaus so that you have three separate chances, at evenly spaced intervals, to see whether something unexpected has shown up. To make it easy to remember when to reorder each report, I suggest that you pick three times during the year that stand out and are roughly four months apart. Consider New Year's, a birthday or anniversary, and Labor Day, for example.

A couple of exceptions: if you believe that a problem may be lurking on your report from an error or identity theft, or if you are going to be applying for a large credit addition for a major purchase. In these cases, get all three reports at once in addition to your normal free annual report rotation.

Who else has access to your report?

Anyone can get a copy of your credit report if the person has a *permissible purpose* — in other words, a valid business reason to review your report — *and* if you give that person your permission to do so. The permission part is often buried in the fine print of a credit card application or at the bottom of a job application.

What counts as a permissible purpose under the law? Here are some examples:

- ✔ **Apartment rental:** It only makes sense that a landlord would want to know whether you're likely to pay your rent on time before giving you the keys to a piece of real estate. For that reason, most rental applications ask for permission to access your credit report and any tenant history information that may be available.

- ✔ **Credit approval:** When you apply for credit (whether you're filling out a credit card application or applying for a car loan, student loan, or mortgage), creditors and lenders have the right to get a copy of your credit report. They need to know whether you have a history of defaulting on loans or whether you're overextended on credit already and about to miss your next payment.

- ✔ **Court order or subpoena:** If a court orders you to appear before the court or subpoenas information about you, the court can also get access to your credit file.

- ✔ **Employment:** When you apply for a job, the prospective employer can get a copy of your credit report. Why? Because your financial history says a lot about what kind of employee you might turn out to be. If you use poor judgment with money, the logic goes, you may show poor judgment at work as well.

- ✔ **Insurance:** Depending on the type of insurance you apply for and the state in which you live, the insurer may get a copy of your credit report and use the information in it to help predict the likelihood of your filing a claim. Insurers and their actuaries believe that a strong relationship exists between past credit performance and future claim experience. So when you apply for car, homeowners, renters, medical, or any other kind of insurance, in most states, your insurance company has the right to get a copy of your credit report.

- ✔ **IRS debts:** If you owe the tax man and don't pay on time, the IRS looks in your credit report to find out if you have assets to attach or sell, like real estate, cars, or bank accounts.

- ✔ **Professional license:** Licensing authorities take their responsibilities very seriously. Before allowing you to become licensed — in other words, approved to perform a specific job — they want to know all they can about your background and how you've conducted yourself. If you want a license to be a financial planner and deal with someone else's life savings, for instance, it makes sense to see how you handle your own money. Want a gambling license? Same thing applies.

- ✔ **Review or collection of an existing account:** If your account is overdue and sent to collections, the collector wants to know who else you owe money to and what kind of payer you are. If you move a lot, the collector uses the information in your credit report to find a current address or phone number. (The industry term for this practice is *skip tracing*.) However, even if you're current in your payments to your credit card issuers, mortgage company, or other creditors, your creditors may look at your account from time to time to determine whether your credit quality is deteriorating or, on the brighter side, whether they should increase your limits.

Get copies of your reports from all three bureaus at the same time when you're planning to

✔ Buy or lease a car

✔ Buy or rent a house or an apartment

✔ Refinance a mortgage

✔ Apply for a job

✔ Be up for a promotion

✔ Apply for a professional license (such as to sell securities or insurance)

✔ Apply for a security clearance

✔ Join the military

✔ Get married or divorced

✔ Switch insurance companies or buy new insurance

Real estate closings can be delayed, mortgage rates can go up, and job opportunities can be lost if your credit report contains incorrect negative information. So give yourself time to correct your reports before going forward with your plans. I recommend getting your reports up to six months in advance of your plans so that you have time to dispute any errors (like information belonging to someone whose Social Security number is one digit off from yours). As you get within a month or two of applying for credit, insurance, or a job, consider getting copies of your reports again in case new errors have slipped into your files.

Tracking Down Specialty Reports: From Apartments to Casinos to Prescriptions

Specialty reporting agencies, as the name implies, gather information for specific industries. They often gather more detailed information than the big-three credit bureaus do in areas such as gambling, checking accounts, medical claims, insurance, and rental and employment history. If you're being checked out because you're applying for a loan, insuring your car, finding a new apartment, or being considered for a promotion at work, the person reviewing your application has the option to request a report from a specialty agency in addition to a traditional credit report from one of the big-three credit bureaus (Equifax, Experian, and TransUnion).

Who's reporting you to the specialty bureaus?

Included in the growing list of companies that report on you are those that specialize in your rental history, workers' compensation claims, prescription drug purchase history, and gambling history.

Until recently, use of prescription drug use databases was unheard of. Insurers' use of these databases was first publicized when the Federal Trade Commission sued two owners of drug databases. (See `www.ftc.gov/opa/2007/09/ingenixmilliman.shtm`.) Like the Medical Information Bureau reports, these reports are used primarily when you're seeking private health, life, or disability insurance. Rx drug databases can go back as far as five years, detailing drugs you've used as well as dosages and refills.

Among the better-known specialty report providers are the following:

✔ ChoiceTrust, which sells its C.L.U.E. products based on your auto and homeowners insurance claims history, as well as information for background employment and rental checks

✔ The Medical Information Bureau (MIB), which accumulates and sells your medical-insurance claims history report

✔ ChexSystems, SCAN, and TeleCheck, all of which keep records of bounced checks and sell various check-verification products

Many people aren't aware of these specialty reporting agencies or the fact that you have the right to request and obtain free copies of your credit reports from these agencies annually, just as you do with the traditional credit bureaus. Some reports contain only negative information, or they may have absolutely no information about you at all. I suggest that you get your free report annually just to make sure that the information in the report is yours and is accurate. You may not be aware that one of these databases is being checked because they aren't as top of mind as the three main credit bureaus.

Table 14-1 provides the contact information for the major specialty bureaus to get you started. Call any bureau you want a report from and ask how to order a free copy.

Table 14-1	Specialty Credit-Reporting Bureaus	
Category	*Bureau Name*	*Phone Number*
Casinos	Global Cash Access (Central Credit)	888-898-8021
Checking accounts	Certegy	866-543-6315
	ChexSystems	800-428-9623
	Early Warning Services	800-325-7775
	SCAN	800-262-7771
	TeleCheck	800-366-2425
Employment	Accurate Background	800-784-3911
	American DataBank	800-200-0853
	EmployeeScreenIQ	800-235-3954
	First Advantage	800-321-4473
	GIS	800-265-4917
	HireRight	800-381-0645
	Infocubic	877-360-4636
	Intellicorp	866-202-1436
	LexisNexis	866-312-8075
	Pre-employ.com	800-300-1821
	Trak 1 Technology	918-779-7000
	Verifications Inc.	877-884-1313
	The Work Number	866-604-6570
Identity	ID Analytics	Web only
Insurance	C.L.U.E. Auto History	866-312-8076
	C.L.U.E. Homeowners' History	866-312-8076
	Insurance Information Exchange	866-560-7015
	ISO's A-Plus Auto and Property Databases	800-709-8842
Medical information	Medical Information Bureau (MIB)	866-692-6901
Supplementary credit report	Innovis	800-540-2505
	L2CInc.	866-268-7156
Payday lending	Clarity Services	Web only

Category	Bureau Name	Phone Number
Prescription drugs	DataX	Web only
	Factor Trust	866-910-8497
	Microbilt	877-772-2123
	Milliman	877-211-4816
	Teletrack	877-309-5226
Rental information	Accufax	800-256-8898
	Advantage Tenant	800-894-9047
	American Tenant Screen	800-888-1287
	Contemporary Information Corp.	800-288-4757
	Micobilt	877-772-2123
	Resident History Report	877-448-5732
	Core Logic Safe Rent	888-333-2413
	Leasing Desk	866-934-1124
	LexisNexis Resident History	866-312-8075
	National Tenant Network	800-228-0989
Property tax filings	Tenant Data Services	800-228-1837
	CoreScore Credit Report	877-532-8778
Utilities	National Consumer Telecom and Utilities Exchange	866-343-2821

Perusing Your Credit Reports

When you get copies of your credit reports from Equifax, Experian, and TransUnion, you're ready to walk through what can be, at times, a confusing landscape of codes and language that may seem as foreign as Swahili to you. Perhaps the best way to get a handle on how a credit report comes together is to take it apart, starting from the outside and working in.

Each credit report contains the following generic elements:

- ✔ Personal profile
- ✔ Accounts summary
- ✔ Public records

- ✔ Credit inquiries

- ✔ Account history

- ✔ Your 100-word statement(s) (optional; see Chapter 3 for info on writing a 100-word statement)

- ✔ Credit score (optional; see the section "Getting and Understanding Your Credit Scores" later in this chapter for details)

The following sections cover each of these parts of your report in detail. Bear in mind, though, that the three credit-reporting agencies use slightly different names for each of these sections.

For samples of Equifax, Experian, and TransUnion credit reports, go to www.dummies.com/extras/creditrepair.

Personal profile: It's all about your details

This section of your credit report may be labeled "Personal Profile" or "Personal Information," depending on which credit bureau issues the report.

Appearing first in the order of credit report elements, your profile section contains the key components that help you verify that the report is actually about *you:* your name (and any of your previous names if you're married or divorced or if you use multiple spellings or nicknames like Steve instead of Stephen), Social Security number, address(es), and current and previous employers.

Be sure to check the personal profile section and verify that all the information is correct. Something as simple as a transposed number in an old address can cause someone else's credit history to end up on your report.

Accounts summary: An overview of your financial history

Each of the three bureau reports has a summary of your credit or accounts that shows you a broad history of what's included in your credit report. It includes open and closed accounts, credit limits, total balances of all accounts, payment history, and number of credit inquiries. If you have a short attention span, the summary provides a one-page snapshot of your credit history. But don't worry: If you're hungry for painstaking detail, you can find it in the Account History section, which I describe later in this chapter.

A quick review of the summary section lets you know whether you need to scrutinize something in more detail that appears to be inaccurate or isn't related to your account at all. For example, if you don't have a mortgage, finding a mortgage account listed in your summary is an immediate red flag.

Public records: Tallying up your legal losses

Ideally, the section of your report dealing with public records is blank. Public records are negative items that come from — you guessed it — a public record. You have a public record if you've been the object of a court proceeding, filed for bankruptcy, received judgments or tax liens, or (in some states) defaulted on child support.

Credit inquiries: Tracking who has been accessing your file

Knock, knock. Who's there? The section listing inquiries into your credit file shows who's been knocking on the credit bureau's door, asking if you're home. People who are legally allowed to view your credit information and have requested copies of your report are listed here. They include businesses and individuals you've given permission to, such as employers, insurance companies, and lenders, as well as yourself. (For more information on this topic, see the earlier sidebar "Who else has access to your report?")

This section also shows the date of each inquiry and how long the inquiry will remain on your report. An inquiry that you initiated to, say, shop for or obtain credit stays on your report for two years.

Your own copies of your credit reports have information about credit inquiries. When you request access to your own credit file, you get some extra information in a separate section. Inquiries from creditors who looked at your credit report for the purposes of extending preapproved credit offers show up for you and only you to see. These inquiries aren't revealed to others who request your report and don't count against you.

Account history: Think of it as a payment CSI

Your account history section, sometimes titled "Account Information," is the heart of your credit report. It shows all open and closed accounts with near forensic detail about payment history, balances, and account status over the last seven years. Each credit bureau displays these details in its own unique way, as outlined here. If you see negative items that you don't recognize or that are more than seven years old, dispute them using the instructions included with your report and they'll be removed.

Equifax's version

Equifax reports account history by type of account, such as mortgages, installment accounts, and revolving accounts. Under each account type, open accounts are listed first, followed by closed accounts. A short summary at the beginning of each account includes your account status, which indicates whether you have paid as agreed or are late (and if so, how late).

Go to www.dummies.com/extras/creditrepair for a sample Equifax credit report.

Here's a list of all the information Equifax reports for each account in its Account History section:

- ✔ **Account name:** A brief description of the account type and creditor. For example, 123 Mortgage Co., Address, Phone Number.

- ✔ **Account number:** That long, alphanumeric string that's unique to your card or loan. Note, though, that account numbers are shortened for the protection of your account information.

- ✔ **Account owner:** Indicates whether the account is an individual or joint account.

- ✔ **Type:** Here are the account types you may find:

    - **Mortgage account:** First mortgage loans, home equity loans, and any other loan secured by real estate.

    - **Installment account:** Loans that are for a set amount of money and often for a set period. A car loan is an example of a common installment loan.

    - **Revolving account:** An account that has a credit limit and a minimum payment and doesn't have to be paid off in a set amount of time. Credit cards fall into this category.

- **Other account:** Includes those accounts that don't fit into the set categories, such as charge accounts that must be paid in full each month, like some American Express cards.

- **Collections account:** An account that has been sold or turned over to a collection agency, usually when the account is more than 180 days past due.

- **Negative account:** A past-due account that is less than 180 days late, or a debt that was written off because you couldn't pay it and is now a collections account.

✔ **Term duration:** The total number of payments you're expected to make (for example, 60 payments for a five-year car loan).

✔ **Date open:** The date on which you opened the account.

✔ **Date reported:** The latest report from the lender, whether provided monthly, quarterly, or less frequently.

✔ **Date of last payment:** The date listed here may be different from the date reported. If you're past due, your last payment may be from September 2013, and the last date reported may be December 2013. If you had no activity on a credit card account for six months, the last payment date may be June 2013, and the last reported date may be December 2013.

✔ **Scheduled payment amount:** Information that applies only to install-ment accounts, in which a set amount of money is due at a set time every month.

✔ **Creditor classification:** The type of creditor.

✔ **Charge-off amount:** Debt or portion of debt that the creditor wrote off because of nonpayment and inability to get the money from you. For example, if you don't pay your credit card for 180 days, it will be listed as charged off. You want this amount to be *zero*. Any amount — no matter how small — is not a good thing to have on your record.

✔ **Balloon-payment amount:** The big lump-sum payment at the end of some loans. Your loan may or may not have one.

✔ **Date closed:** The date you or the lender terminated an active account.

✔ **Date of first delinquency:** Any late payments recorded during the seven-year reporting period.

✔ **Comments:** Additional information about the closed account. Some examples are "Account Transferred or Sold," "Paid," "Zero Balance," and "Account Closed at Consumer's Request."

✔ **Current status:** Whether you've paid or are paying as you said you would. You may see terms such as "Pays," "Paid as Agreed," or "X Days Past Due."

- ✔ **High credit:** The highest amount of credit you have used.

- ✔ **Credit limit:** Your maximum limit for this account.

- ✔ **Term's frequency:** How often your payment is due (weekly, monthly, and so on).

- ✔ **Balance:** The amount owed to the creditor.

- ✔ **Amount past due:** The amount you owe that should have been paid by now but hasn't been.

- ✔ **Actual payment amount:** The amount of your last payment.

- ✔ **Date of last activity:** The last time you used the account.

- ✔ **Months reviewed:** How many months are in the payment history section (up to 81).

- ✔ **Activity designator:** A description of account activity, such as "Paid" and "Closed."

- ✔ **Deferred payment start date:** Some accounts have no payment for a year or other promotional terms.

- ✔ **Balloon-payment date:** When that big lump-sum payment at the end of some loans is due. Your loan may or may not have one.

- ✔ **Type of loan:** For example, auto or credit card.

- ✔ **81-month payment history:** Equifax shows each month's status for the last seven years of payment history. Terms used in reporting the status include the following:

  - • Pays as agreed

  - • 30 (30 to 59 days past due)

  - • 60 (60 to 89 days past due)

  - • 90 (90 to 119 days past due)

  - • 120 (120 to 149 days past due)

  - • 150 (150 to 179 days past due)

  - • 180- (180 or more days past due)

  - • CA (collection account)

  - • F (foreclosure)

  - • VS (voluntary surrender)

  - • R (repossession)

  - • CO (charge-off)

Experian's version

On Experian's credit report, potentially negative items are listed first and include both public records and credit accounts. The remainder of your accounts in the Account History section are listed as accounts in good standing. You of course want all your accounts to be listed as being in good standing.

You can find a sample Experian credit report at www.dummies.com/extras/creditrepair.

Here's a list of the information that Experian reports for each account in its Account History section:

✔ **Address of creditor and account number**

✔ **Status:** Open or closed and paid or past due by X days.

✔ **Date open:** The date you opened the account.

✔ **Reported since:** First reported date.

✔ **Date of status:** Last time the status was updated.

✔ **Last reported:** Last time the update (which may be new or old) was reported.

✔ **Account type:** Installment account, revolving account, and so on.

✔ **Terms:** The total number of payments you're expected to make (a 30-year mortgage would be 360 payments, for example).

✔ **Monthly payment:** The last reported minimum payment you owe(d). This typically applies for installment loans such as auto loans and mortgages, if reported at all.

✔ **Responsibility:** Individual, joint, authorized user, and so on.

✔ **Credit limit/Original amount:** The highest credit limit you've ever been approved for.

✔ **High balance:** The most you've ever owed on the account.

✔ **Recent balance:** The amount you owe. Sometimes balance information is on the report and sometimes it's not. This isn't because the credit bureau wants to save trees but because some creditors don't want their competition to know what a big spender and great customer you are.

✔ **Recent payment:** Your most recent payment amount.

✔ **Account history:** Whether you've paid late, and if so, how often.

✔ **Your statement:** This is where you tell your side of the story. For example, you may contest an account that shows you haven't paid as agreed if you contend that you didn't receive the services for which you were charged.

✔ **Account history for collection accounts:** Comments that the creditor may have sent to the bureau, such as when the account was placed for collection.

TransUnion's version

TransUnion reports public records and collection accounts first. The Account History section for all other accounts is listed under Trades.

You can find a sample TransUnion credit report at www.dummies.com/extras/creditrepair.

Here's a list of the information that TransUnion reports for each account in its Account History section:

- ✔ **Account name:** Name and address of the creditor.

- ✔ **Account number:** Only a partial account number is included.

- ✔ **Account type:** Automobile, credit card, and so on.

- ✔ **Credit limit:** The maximum amount of credit approved by the creditor. The creditor doesn't always report this information if your limit isn't firm (such as with American Express) or if you're allowed to exceed your limit under the terms of your agreement (such as with Visa Signature accounts).

- ✔ **Balance:** The balance owed as of the date of verification or when closed.

- ✔ **Date opened:** The date the account was opened.

- ✔ **Responsibility:** Individual, joint, authorized user, and so on.

- ✔ **High credit:** The highest amount ever owed on the account.

- ✔ **Past due:** Amount past due as of date verified or closed.

    - **Terms:** Minimum payment amount.

    - **Pay status:** Whether you are paying as agreed.

    - **Account type:** Open or closed.

- ✔ **Date paid:** The date the account was last paid.

- ✔ **Remarks:** Explanation of dispute or account credit condition as reported by the creditor. Includes account closed by consumer.

- ✔ **Terms:** Number of payments, payment frequency, and dollar amount agreed upon.

- ✔ **Date closed:** If the account is closed, the date on which it was closed.

- ✔ **Date verified:** The date of the last update on the account.

- ✔ **Loan type:** The type of loan and/or the collateral used for an installment loan. Includes home equity loan, mortgage, and automobile.

- ✔ **Late payments:** A graphical representation of all paid months being reported as agreed or late.

- ✔ **Payment pattern:** A numerical indicator 1–9 indicating paid as agreed (1) to charged off (9).

What's not in your credit report?

Before you get too comfortable with what's not disclosed in your credit report, be aware that the big-three credit bureaus do their best to limit *indirect disclosures* — that is, some of your personal information getting passed on inadvertently — but such disclosures can be tough to avoid. Medical information is one example. Even though credit bureaus don't report medical history, specifics on your credit report may give away information that indicates that you have some type of medical condition. Say you fall behind on a hospital or other medical bill and you're paying a collection agency under an agreement. The account noted on your credit report may read "Medical Collection." Now say that you apply for a job. As part of its background check, your prospective

employer requests a copy of your credit report. The employer can see that you have (or had) a medical condition. A week later, you get a letter saying that the position has been filled. As you can see, without disclosing medical reports or particulars about a health condition, the details on your credit report *can* reveal personal information that's legally restricted from your file.

Some other indirect disclosures that can happen include employment history you forgot to mention to a prospective employer, frequent changes of addresses (which may make you look unstable), and multiple inquiries from Central Credit Services for gambling lines of credit (which may raise a question for a lender or an employer).

 If you have an account that doesn't show a credit limit, FICO assumes that your highest monthly balance reported is your max for the purposes of calculating your credit score. To increase your score (if you can afford it), charge close to your real max for one month and then pay it off the next month to avoid interest charges and minimize point losses in the future. For more on how your credit score is calculated, see the section "Getting and Understanding Your Credit Scores" later in this chapter.

Your optional 100-word statements: Getting the last word

You have the right to add statements of up to 100 words to your credit report that can help explain any extenuating circumstances that may have led to negative information being included. You can add an overall statement that covers all your accounts, and you can add a statement for one or more trade lines with which you disagree. For example, a general statement describing a temporary job loss can explain why many of your accounts were 60 days late. A trade line or individual account statement can explain why a particular account is being reported negatively and why you disagree. The credit bureaus are required to include these statements whenever anyone accesses your credit report. On the flip side, lenders may not always pull a full credit report when ordering a score for screening, so keep in mind that your statement may not always be seen.

Use the 100-word-statement privilege with care, and be sure to circle back to request that the statement be removed after any negative information that it explains is more than two to three years old. If you don't request that it be removed, your comments may stay on the report as long as the account does and may draw unwanted attention to an old credit complaint.

Correcting Any Errors You Find

With any luck, the information on your credit reports is accurate. However, mistakes happen. The good news is that those mistakes don't have to remain a part of your file.

Credit-reporting agencies are required to investigate all disputed listings. They must verify the item in question with the creditor *at no cost to you,* the consumer. The law requires the creditor to respond to and verify disputed entries within 30 days, or the information must be removed from your credit report. The credit bureau also has to notify you of the outcome. If information in the report is changed or deleted, you get a *free* copy of the revised report.

You have two options for fixing errors that you find on your credit reports: contact the credit bureau or contact the creditor who reported the incorrect information. I walk you through both processes in the sections that follow.

Contacting the credit bureau

If you notice incorrect information on your credit report, contact the credit bureau that reported the inaccurate information. Each of the three major bureaus allows you to dispute information in your credit report on its website, or you can call the bureau's toll-free number (I provide contact info for the big-three credit bureaus in the earlier section "Where to get your reports"). If you make your dispute online, you need to have a copy of your credit report available, because information on the report enables the bureau to confirm your identity without a signature. If you opt to call the toll-free number, you're unlikely to get a live person on the other end, but you'll be told what information and documentation you need in order to submit a written request. Either way, after you properly notify the credit bureau, you can count on action.

Contacting the creditor

Another way, and sometimes a better way, to remove inaccurate information from your credit report is outlined under the FACT Act: Deal directly with the creditor who reported the negative information in the first place. Customer service contact information appears on your billing statements from that creditor, and the general address and phone number are on your credit report. After you dispute the information, the creditor must look into the matter and can't continue to report the negative information while it's investigating your dispute. This approach is more direct and eliminates the possibility that a bureau employee may not follow up with a creditor as aggressively or as quickly as you would.

I recommend that you contact the creditor directly, in writing and through the mail, requesting a return receipt for every piece of correspondence you send.

For new delinquencies, the FACT Act requires that you be notified if negative information is reported to a credit bureau. That said, you may have to look closely to even see this new notice. Anyone who extends credit to you must send you a one-time notice either before or not later than 30 days after negative information — including late payments, missed payments, partial payments, or any other form of default — is furnished to a credit bureau. This includes collection agencies, as long as they report to a credit bureau. The notice may look something like this:

- ✔ **Before negative information is reported:** "We may report information about your account to credit bureaus. Late payments, missed payments, or other defaults on your account may be reflected in your credit report."

- ✔ **After negative information is reported:** "We have told a credit bureau about a late payment, missed payment, or other default on your account. This information may be reflected in your credit report."

Receiving notification about what a creditor has reported about you to the credit bureaus isn't a substitute for your own close monitoring of your credit reports, bank accounts, and credit card statements.

Getting and Understanding Your Credit Scores

Getting your hands on your credit reports is one thing, but getting copies of your credit scores isn't as straightforward as you may think. (And a misstep here can cost you more money and give you less-than-accurate information.) Your three-digit credit score is an additional component used in most credit reviews. When a lender orders your credit report, it often also orders a credit score, which summarizes your risk of default.

The two major credit scores that lenders use are the FICO score and the VantageScore. Not all the credit bureaus can offer you the trademarked FICO score that most lenders use, but they *can* all offer you the VantageScore. Four of the top five financial institutions, all credit card issuers, and two of the top five auto lenders use VantageScores for lending decisions. Both scores range from 300 to 850.

Don't get hung up on a number. Be as good as you can be, but don't get excited and yell at the cat over a score of 820 instead of 850. The most important thing is to know what your *lenders* know about your credit score and what's in the credit report they look at. On this topic, you want to be on the same page.

The main points to keep in mind regarding credit scores are as follows:

- ✔ Your score is different for each credit bureau report, if only because each bureau has slightly different data about you in its files.

- ✔ Be sure you know which score you're getting: a FICO score, a VantageScore, or a proprietary bureau score (which may be called a *TrueScore* or a *PlusScore* or some other name).

- ✔ You can only improve your credit score by improving your credit history, not the other way around.

- ✔ Because about 25 percent of credit reports contain errors and about 11 percent of errors are serious enough to affect your score, you may receive a faulty credit score. Dispute errors and outdated items to get the most accurate score possible.

With a grasp of the essentials about credit scores, you're ready to take the plunge and get your score. Of course, once you have it, you can count on me to explain what it means for you and what you can do about it. Read on!

Ordering your score

The Fair Access to Credit Scores Act that was bundled into the massive Dodd-Frank Wall Street Reform and Consumer Protection Act (the law's wording is at www.dummies.com/extras/creditrepair) allows you free access to your credit score if you've been denied credit or if some other "adverse action" (denial of insurance or utilities, for example) was taken as a result of your credit score. You don't have to request your credit score if such an adverse action is taken based on that score; a copy of the score used to make the decision is automatically sent to you.

To get your current score, you need to order a credit report at the same time, because your score is figured based on the information in your credit report at the time you order the score. Generally, unlike your credit report, you have to pay for a copy of your credit score.

If you want to order your FICO score, keep mind that you can get it from only two places:

- **Equifax** (phone 800-685-1111; www.equifax.com)
- **myFICO.com** (phone 800-319-4433; www.myfico.com)

The other credit-reporting bureaus — Experian and TransUnion — offer consumer credit scores but not the FICO credit score. (FICO developed slightly different score models for them in order to enable the bureaus to offer unique products and make some more cash.) Also, the credit bureaus jointly developed the VantageScore (a fierce competitor of FICO), so they have an interest in you buying a VantageScore rather than a FICO score. Oh, and all three credit bureaus compete with one another every chance they get.

So how do you know which credit score is the right one for you? My advice is to try to get the same score that your lender uses. How do you know which one that is? Ask! Your lender will tell you if it knows. Surprisingly, many don't. If, however, you aren't working with a specific lender and you just want to know where you stand (good, bad, or ugly), either score will do.

When you are ordering scores, most sites try to get you to sign up for a credit-monitoring service. You should be able to get your one-time credit report and a score without signing up for a long-term service; just read the fine print before you hit Enter. I discuss credit-monitoring services and their benefits and costs in Chapter 15.

Telling a good score from a bad one

Good score ranges (for example, a FICO score of 760 to 850) change over time as the history of the population changes. And I don't mean history as in ancient Greek or Roman (who used credit, too!), but your personal history of using credit and paying bills. During the aftermath of the most recent recession, the poor economy, high unemployment, and punishing defaults and foreclosures have caused a lot of people who had high scores to move much lower on the scoring ladder. While scores seem to be returning to pre-recession levels, yours may be ahead of or behind the trend.

So is your score a good one? What's a good score, anyway? Essentially, a good score is one that's good enough to get you what you want at a price you can afford.

FICO likes to give you a picture of where you stand in comparison to others using an eight-bar graph and an eight-column chart, as shown in Figure 14-1.

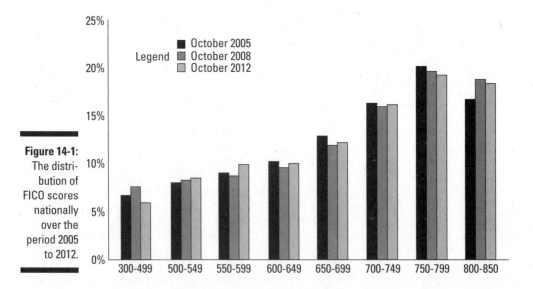

Figure 14-1: The distribution of FICO scores nationally over the period 2005 to 2012.

Another useful way to understand score dynamics is to look at score movement over time. Figure 14-2 shows how the scores of different pockets of consumers fared between October 2011 and October 2012. As you can see, it's hard to move out of the bottom tier. Six out of ten people in the bottom tier of 300–499 stayed there during the year, while nearly eight out of ten people in the top tier stayed on top. While it may be hard to move your score, 30 percent managed to move up a tier to 500–549. What's the best way to do so? With a plan and over time! As you can see, anyone who claims that he or she can turn your credit score around overnight is not telling the truth.

		October 2012 – FICO® B Score							
		300–499	500–549	550–599	600–649	650–699	700–749	750–799	800–850
October 2011 FICO® B Score	300–499	59.5%	29.9%	9.7%	0.8%	0.0%	0.0%	0.0%	–
	500–549	17.8%	46.0%	28.5%	6.9%	0.6%	0.1%	0.0%	0.0%
	550–599	6.2%	19.0%	43.9%	25.8%	4.2%	0.8%	0.1%	0.0%
	600–649	1.7%	6.7%	16.7%	45.1%	25.5%	4.3%	0.5%	0.0%
	650–699	0.7%	1.9%	4.5%	13.7%	50.3%	24.8%	3.8%	0.4%
	700–749	0.1%	0.5%	1.2%	2.9%	14.2%	56.2%	22.2%	2.7%
	750–799	0.0%	0.1%	0.1%	0.7%	2.7%	16.9%	58.3%	21.9%
	800–850	0.0%	0.0%	0.0%	0.2%	0.6%	2.4%	20.2%	76.6%

Figure 14-2: FICO score migration over time.

Courtesy of FICO

In the current credit environment, where lending is fairly tight, the difference in loan terms between a score of 750 and a score of 800- (the top two groups) may be small, but those with a score of 650 or lower may not be eligible for credit at all. However, not all lenders view risk the same way. One lender may consider a credit score of 650 to be a high risk, while another lender may not consider such a score to be all that risky and may have a special program to take advantage of — er, accommodate — lower-scoring consumers.

What shape is your credit in?

VantageScore recently described the U.S. population according to its scoring scale, with the shocking result that almost 20 percent of Americans are in less than good shape. Using this scale, you can estimate your place in the credit pecking order:

✔ **Excellent:** The top 22.86 percent of the population is in this category, with scores ranging from 781 to 850.

✔ **Great:** 16.88 percent of the population. Great scores range from 721 to 780.

✔ **Good:** 15.30 percent of the population. Good scores range from 661 to 720.

✔ **Fair:** 13.16 percent of the population. Fair scores range from 601 to 660.

✔ **Unfavorable:** 25.21 percent of the population. Unfavorable scores range from 500 to 600.

✔ **Deficient (formerly called High Risk):** 6.59 percent of the population. Deficient scores range from 300 to 499.

A bad credit score and history can make you a target for unscrupulous lenders. If your credit is damaged, read the fine print on any credit agreement carefully and understand all fees, penalties, and interest rates before you act.

So how high is high enough? In a time of relatively easy credit, such as before the last recession, the saying was that all you needed was a pulse to get a loan. Although this may not have been entirely true, getting a loan with a lower score in good times was certainly easier than it is today. The credit market has tightened up considerably since the most recent financial crisis and is only beginning to loosen up. Over time, the standard for lending tends to swing like a pendulum from easy to tight and back again. So keeping your credit as clean as you can is all the more important, because today's record will be there for at least the next seven years, while tomorrow's credit market will surely change.

Connecting pricing to your credit score

Most lending today is done on a modified version of *risk-based pricing.* Risk-based pricing used to mean that rather than saying "no" to a bad-risk customer, a lender would say "yes" and still make money on the risky loan because it would charge a high interest rate and fees. This model allowed more people with low scores to get more loans, albeit at a higher cost. That approach ended when the subprime mortgage mess turned risky loans into huge losses at any interest rate. So although your credit score may get you a higher or lower interest rate, if it's too weak under tight credit conditions, you may get a "no, thank you" instead.

To get the best deals on credit, you need to have a good credit score as well as a good credit report. Having a perfect credit score (a FICO or VantageScore of 850) is extremely rare. I've never seen a validated case. Fortunately, a perfect score has very little influence on loan approval; what you need is a good enough score for the credit for which you're applying.

For each type of credit — such as revolving (credit cards) or installment (car loans and mortgages) — credit grantors divide customers into different score ranges or buckets and offer them different rates and terms based on where they fall. For example, the rate for a 30-year mortgage may be the same for people with scores between 760 and 850, all other underwriting criteria (such as income and job stability) being equal.

What do credit-score groupings look like in the current market? As an example, say you have a $300,000 30-year fixed-rate mortgage. (Keep in mind that I'm using numbers from late 2013. The rates for loans today may be different.)

This example is meant to illustrate the magnitude of difference between scores and rates. The interest rates for each grouping for this particular loan look like this:

FICO Score	Rate	Monthly Payment	Interest Paid
760–850	4.133%	$1,455	$223,924
700–759	4.355%	$1,494	$237,955
680–699	4.532%	$1,526	$249,276
660–679	4.746%	$1,564	$263,119
640–659	5.176%	$1,643	$291,440
620–639	5.722%	$1,745	$328,339

Courtesy of Informa Research Services

Using this table, a person with a FICO score of 639 and an interest rate of 5.722 percent pays out a total of $628,339 over the term of the $300,000 mortgage, whereas a person with a FICO score of 760 and an interest rate of 4.133 percent pays only $523,924. That's a difference of $104,415! As you can see, maintaining the highest credit score possible can save you hundreds a month and tens of thousands in mortgage payments over the term of the loan.

Although the amount of money you save on smaller loans may not be as high as that associated with a mortgage loan, a high credit score saves you money in interest charges for any amount you plan to borrow. In addition, in a tight credit market, a low credit score may mean that you don't qualify for credit at any price.

Your goal is to get into the best bucket you can by the time you need the type of credit in question. How? By building a plan that gets you to your goal of good enough credit. Take some time and include everyone with whom you share your life. List your credit-oriented goals, and then check a resource like www.bankrate.com to find out what credit score will get you into the next-highest tier of borrowers. Unless you're in the top tier, come up with actions to take based on what you find in your credit report. You can find details on how a credit score is built in Chapter 13.

Another way to pump up your credit score is to remove any errors or out-of-date information you find on your credit report. Because credit scores normally look back over a two- to three-year period to develop an accurate picture of your risk profile, overcoming any negative data that may be hurting your score takes time. Removing errors or out-of-date information, however, has an immediate effect on your score.

Avoid companies that promise to improve your score by removing accurate negative information from your credit report. They can't do what they claim, and they may get you into even more trouble if, for example, you're approved for a loan based on a fraudulently altered credit report.

Knowing the reason for reason statements

Along with your credit score, you get up to four reason statements on your credit-score report. A *reason statement* is a simple explanation of why your score is less than perfect. What's the reason for reason statements? Well, a lender can't make money turning down business, so if a poor score is keeping a lender from making a buck, knowing the reason why your credit is in a hole can help identify how to dig out and get those fees and loans flowing again!

Creditors get what's called a *reason code,* and you get the interpreted version of that, which is called a *reason statement.* For example, if a reason code reveals that your lower-than-it-could-have-been score is because of too many open accounts used to the max and not because you never pay on time, you can focus on reducing balances and using less of each credit line to raise your score.

Some 60 different codes give you and your lender a hint about what's causing your credit to sag. In addition, the codes may help you determine whether your credit report contains errors and where the errors exist, because the codes highlight areas that lower your score.

The credit bureaus generate the reason codes. Typically, immediately following whatever section your credit score is in, your credit report lists both positive and negative reasons for your score, with tips to help increase your score muscle.

According to FICO, the most frequently used reason statements are as follows (although the specific wording may vary):

- **Reason code 10:** "Proportion of balances to credit limits on bank/national revolving or other revolving accounts is too high." This code tells you that you're using more of your limits than the scoring model thinks is safe. A high percentage of usage — say, 50 percent ($10,000 on a $20,000 credit line) — is inherently riskier than 25 percent (or $5,000).

- **Reason code 14:** "Length of time accounts have been established." This code is great for senior credit users but not for first-timers. Clearly, someone with 20 years of account history has the advantage here.

VantageScore's most frequent reason statement, which shows up about 44 percent of the time, is, "Available credit across all open, recently reported accounts is too low." If you see this reason statement in your credit report, it's time to slow your charging and increase your payments. This statement tells you that you're using more of your credit lines than the scorers at VantageScore are comfortable with. VantageScore recently launched a microsite to help you better understand this little-known feature of credit reporting. See `www.reasoncode.org` for more info.

Chapter 15

Monitoring Your Credit Reports and Scores

I received my car insurance renewal recently, and for a hefty premium my insurance company offered to monitor my credit report for identity theft and fraud. What does my car insurer have to do with credit monitoring? Two things: First, bad credit (which can be caused by errors or identity theft) can raise my car insurance premium; and second, my car insurer wants to make money on a hot product add-on whether I need it or not. So I asked myself, do I need credit monitoring or don't I? To find out whether I do and you might, I created this chapter. After all, it's your credit and your money, and you want to protect them both!

Don't confuse credit monitoring with identity theft protection. Credit card fraud can be caused by the larger problem of identity theft, or it can happen on its own. Credit monitoring won't stop someone from stealing your identity or using your Social Security number, but it may enable you to detect a potential problem in its earlier stages. I deal with identity theft in detail in Chapters 9 and 20.

In this chapter, I discuss how credit monitoring works and what you get for your monitoring dollar so that you can decide whether you should pay someone for this service or handle it on your own.

How Credit Monitoring Really Works

Hiring a company to monitor your credit means that you give the company access to your credit reports. You may wonder just how this monitoring takes place. Each service provider has a series of programs that it runs against databases to which it has access (some, like Experian, have their own credit database but also buy access to others), looking for changes, updates, or patterns that indicate something may be amiss in your world.

Some services monitor only one credit bureau, others monitor all three, and still others monitor some of the many national, specialty, consumer-reporting bureaus (see Chapter 14) for activity or changes to your reports such as

- The opening of new accounts

- Larger-than-normal charges

- Unusual account activity, such as a change in the frequency, location, or type of charges appearing on your credit reports

- A surge in balances

- Other changes to your accounts, such as payments, late payment notices, credit inquiries, public records, employment, addresses, and fraud alerts

Some monitoring services produce detailed reports about your credit score and even suggest ways to make it more attractive to lenders and improve your creditworthiness. Most also give you free credit reports and scores (they may be proprietary scores or a FICO or VantageScore; see Chapter 13 for the differences between score types). Lastly, monitoring services check your data with differing frequency. Some check daily, others weekly, and others quarterly, depending on their service level.

Understanding the Types of Monitoring Services Available

A universe of services is available to help you monitor or safeguard your credit.

Before I get into the details, let me add that in my experience, you can handle most of the monitoring on your own *if you have the time and inclination.* For instance, you're entitled to a free credit report from each of the three major bureaus annually. You get another free credit report under certain circumstances, such as if you think you've been the victim of identity theft or if you don't receive the best rates available for a loan or insurance policy based on information in your credit report. So, with at least one opportunity to get a free look at your report every four months, you can do a credible job of monitoring your credit at no cost. You just have to remember to order your report and then examine it to see what's changed. (For more on monitoring your credit yourself, see the section "Monitoring on your own" later in this chapter.)

If you're interested in having someone else do the monitoring for you, here's a look at each type of service in more detail:

- ✔ **Credit report monitoring:** This service notifies you about changes to your credit report(s). It often provides frequent access to your credit report upon request. Some services monitor only one credit report, while others monitor reports from the three major credit-reporting agencies (Experian, Equifax, and TransUnion) as well as some of the national specialty-reporting bureaus. Credit report monitoring may provide limited help in giving you an early warning about identity theft, but because such services monitor only the data in your credit report, an identity theft that involves noncredit or unreported areas won't be addressed.

- ✔ **Credit score monitoring:** This service may include all or some of the credit report monitoring services, but it also includes checking your credit score. You may get access to your credit score; which score depends on your service provider.

- ✔ **Identity theft monitoring:** This service may include additional monitoring areas beyond credit. It focuses mainly on financial databases and not on criminal or law enforcement data, medical billers that don't report to the credit bureaus, or government data.

- ✔ **Credit freeze products:** These products, offered by the credit bureaus, work by freezing access to your credit report. No one may view your credit report without your express permission. Typically, a lender reviews your credit file before issuing a new loan or credit card. The inability to do so may prevent the issuance of new credit to criminals. For more info, see the section "Setting Alarms, Alerts, and Freezes" later in this chapter. Also, www.idtheftcenter.org/id-theft/state-resources.html outlines credit freeze laws and other resources by state.

- ✔ **ID theft recovery products:** By definition, recovering from identity theft requires a clearing of all fraudulent records and charges created by an identity thief. You can find companies to do all the research and restoration work for you.

✔ **Data sweep services:** Data sweep companies monitor the Internet for listings of your personal identifying information that may expose you to identity thieves. They may also monitor specific websites known for questionable activities. If your personal data is detected, these services alert you. They may also offer insurance if they fail to perform.

✔ **Virtual account numbers:** Superman used Clark Kent, Batman had Bruce Wayne, and you have a virtual credit card number to protect your identity from being discovered and misused by evil forces! These one-time computer-generated surrogate numbers enable you to better limit what personal information of yours — such as billing address, account number, or e-mail address — appears when you're online shopping, paying bills, or registering at websites. It does so by replacing your real information with anonymous data that has a very short life span and is useless after your transaction is completed. It works for almost any type of purchase except for items to be picked up later that may require you to match your credit card number to the receipt. Movie/game tickets fall into this category. If your number is stolen, you have to cancel only that number instead of your main account number.

✔ **Identity theft insurance:** ID insurance may be a stand-alone policy or an add-on to one of your existing policies. It helps replace out-of-pocket expenses you may incur after your identity is stolen and misused. Note that ID insurance doesn't keep you safe from theft itself. Collecting legal costs used to defend yourself against a crime committed by an ID thief may require an acquittal or a dismissal of charges.

Making a Case for and against Third-Party Credit Monitoring

During up periods of the stock market, people used to check the values of their 401(k)s like they were bank accounts. But the reality is that the value of your 401(k) counts only when you make a withdrawal for a specific purpose. Hiring someone to monitor your credit or score without a specific purpose is an equally empty exercise and one I don't think is worth paying much, if anything, for. If you're trying to improve your credit or get to a certain credit score so that you can make a large purchase like a home or a car, however, then laying out some dough for a professional monitoring service makes more sense. Also, if you are a "credit worrier" and can't sleep soundly without all the safeguards and early warning bells in place, then a monitoring service may be right for you.

Your lender's score may well differ from the one you get because it may come from another company (FICO, VantageScore, a credit bureau, and so on) or because the lender applies its own algorithms based on proprietary factors that it weights based on its specific business experience.

No credit monitoring service can offer you complete protection. If a lender or vendor doesn't report to the credit bureaus, or if it does report but not to the bureau monitored by the service you've chosen, you won't know whether a bogus account has been opened in your name until a problem arises down the road and a collector or the authorities call. Furthermore, because not all reporting creditors report daily, you're likely to experience a delay in catching fraud.

Monitoring on your own

You can monitor your credit on your own by taking these simple actions:

- ✔ Get a free copy of your credit report every 12 months from each of the three major credit-reporting agencies (Experian, Equifax, and TransUnion). Stagger the ordering so that you get a different report every four months. Review them and dispute any inaccuracies.

- ✔ Be sure to get a free credit report if you dispute an item on your report. You're entitled to a free report to make sure that the mistake has been removed.

- ✔ Get extra free copies of your credit reports directly from the bureaus (not from www.annualcreditreport.com) if you live in Colorado, Georgia, Maine, Maryland, Massachusetts, New Jersey, or Vermont. These states require that you be allowed an additional free report annually — except you lucky Georgia residents, who get a total of three free reports a year from each bureau. Puerto Rico, not a state (yet), requires that residents be given free credit reports as well.

- ✔ Get a free report if you're turned down for credit. Anytime you are turned down for credit, you're guaranteed a free report.

- ✔ Get a free report if you're looking for a new job. Within the first six months of seeking employment, you can have a freebie.

- ✔ If you apply for a mortgage, you're entitled to a copy of the credit report and score the lender uses.

- ✔ Order your free national, specialty consumer report annually (see Chapter 14). Doing so may give you many more free looks into your cyber files.

- ✔ Need to add a fraud alert or an extended fraud alert to your credit report? You get one or two additional free reports, respectively, over the next 12 months from each bureau.

- ✔ Every time your insurance renews, look at the disclosure language, which is usually in the front of your policy, to see whether your insurance company used a credit report to set your rates. If so (and it's very likely), follow the instructions and get another free credit report.

- ✔ Monitor your bank and credit card accounts online weekly. If something funny is going on, you'll know about it sooner.

- ✔ Set up free alerts on your accounts that tip you off when certain types of transactions are made or if a dollar limit is exceeded.

When paid monitoring may be worth the time and money

Depending on the depth of your wallet and your degree of credit nervousness, paid monitoring may be for you. Here are some circumstances when paid monitoring makes sense:

- ✔ Your credit is damaged and you've been trying to improve it for some time. Rather than ordering your report frequently at a premium price, a service that gives you more frequent access for a low monthly or annual fee may make sense.

- ✔ You're planning on making a large purchase that requires your credit score to be in primo condition. You can take your scoring temperature often so you know when the time is right to see the man.

- ✔ You've been the victim of identity theft and accounts are being opened in your name. After you slap on a credit freeze (see Chapter 20), monitoring may help you sleep better at night.

- ✔ You're slightly obsessive-compulsive about your identity or credit file. Monitoring may give you a sense of security.

Credit report or score monitoring isn't done in real time. Information can be days, weeks, or months old. In addition to the fact that monitoring companies report at differing frequencies, not all credit issuers (small credit unions, medical providers, utilities, and so on) report to the credit bureaus. Credit monitoring alerts you only after you have a problem.

If you decide to try a monitoring service, check to see whether it offers a free trial period. Most do. Just don't forget to cancel before the trial period ends if you're not going to stay with the service.

Recognizing the protection you have already

You and your credit card are already protected against fraud under federal law. (See Chapter 19 for more on your legal protections.) Unless you fail to notify your credit card company about erroneous or questionable charges on your statements within 60 days, your total liability for fraud is a whopping $50 per card. And if you have homeowners insurance, the $50 charge is probably a covered peril for which you can get reimbursed. Debit card liability also begins at $50 but can escalate after two days have passed from the time you find out about the fraud. Where debit card fraud is concerned, act in haste or you may repent at leisure!

Many of the major creditors have adopted zero-consumer-liability policies to further limit your exposure and increase your confidence in being able to use your cards safely.

Here's an example from my own experience with one card issuer. American Express (and I'm sure the same goes for some other card companies as well) monitors every transaction through a screening process, using models and patterns to look for charges that match known fraud trigger alerts. This process enables AmEx to leverage information on a real-time basis (as charges are presented for approval) so that the company can identify fraud and stop it quickly. If a certain type of fraud becomes popular, AmEx can tighten up its approval for that type of transaction. Its system is so good that if you go on vacation overseas, you have no need to tell AmEx about it. The company knows that it's you and recognizes where you are to allow purchases. Recently AmEx began offering free real-time notification through smart-phone apps.

Other card issuers may still appreciate your help in letting them know when you're traveling away from home. Be sure to check on their policies by calling customer service and asking whether you need to notify them.

AmEx also offers some optional alerts that you can set up on its website. (Your credit card may offer similar alerts.) AmEx will notify you by e-mail or on your mobile phone if

- ✔ A cash withdrawal is made.
- ✔ A purchase exceeds a limit that you set, is made outside the United States, or is made online or over the phone.
- ✔ Someone tries to reset your password or billing address.
- ✔ AmEx sees a questionable transaction.

Getting Your Money's Worth from Monitoring Services

If you decide that monitoring is a good fit for you, you may need some help to cut through the huge volume of providers. I can't analyze each one, but I can provide tips to help you make your decision.

Asking the right questions before you buy a service is important. Here are some questions you should ask before you sign on the dotted line, or sign up online, to be sure you get the most for your credit monitoring dollar:

✔ **What are the total costs and fees?** Set a limit that you're willing to pay and stick to it. Weigh the possible $20 to $50 a month charge against your odds of suffering a credit card fraud that you'd be liable for. Any liability is likely to be low. Also, banks, insurers, and the big-three credit bureaus all offer products to detect fraud and give you a credit score. Shop around for the best price. You may get a better price from someone you already do other business with.

✔ **What is the monitoring company's reputation and track record?** Like nearly everything else today, you can get reviews of services online. Sites like www.nextadvisor.com and www.fightidentitytheft.com offer user ratings that you can compare.

✔ **Exactly what will you get for your money?** Know how comprehensive you want the monitoring to be. Be sure that you're getting the type of score you want; many services offer proprietary or bureau scores that lenders don't use. These scores may be okay for reference, but not if you're using them to estimate the loan interest rates or deal terms you'll get. Here are some common safeguards you can expect:

• Frequent or unlimited access to your credit report

• Frequent or unlimited access to a credit score of some type

• Monitoring of one or more credit reports

• Alerts when critical changes are made, including address changes

• Alerts if your credit score deteriorates into a lower lending category

• Alerts if personal information like your Social Security number or your credit card number starts showing up on public websites

• Warnings if patterns of credit use change or multiple applications for credit occur within a short time span

• A periodic statement summarizing your credit report changes, score, and alerts

• Assistance in restoring your identity if it's stolen

✔ **What is the monitoring company's cancellation and renewal policy?** Avoid automatic renewals. They require storing your credit card data.

✔ **Can you get help from a live customer service person when you want?** Be sure to check the hours the service reps are available. If you need help, you don't want to have to wait until Monday morning.

✔ **What exactly will the company do to restore your identity if your identity is stolen and misused?** The service should pay for and perform all the tasks needed to restore your identity. The service shouldn't push this time-consuming, expensive, and difficult process off on you.

If a company makes unrealistic claims or offers unlimited guarantees, chances are it may not be able to deliver. Be sure to check user reviews and industry ratings.

Setting Alarms, Alerts, and Freezes

In one of my favorite Three Stooges clips, the lads put a bucket of water above a partially open door. When someone comes through the door, a big crash and splash announces the intruder. You may not be able to set up buckets of water to warn you of credit or identity intrusions, but you do have access to an array of early warning tools.

Alarms

You can set an alarm to go off with your bank or credit card company by establishing certain parameters for notification. For example, if a check for over a certain amount hits my checking account, I get an e-mail. You can do the same and more for your credit card accounts easily and for free. Check out your card's website and look for options. You can use texts or smart-phone messages if e-mail is too slow.

Fraud alerts

You can place a fraud alert on your credit file if you think that someone may be trying to compromise your information. Say you're notified that your personal information was accessed in a data breach. You may or may not have anything to worry about, but a fraud alert requires anyone using your report for new accounts or limit changes in the next 90 days to exercise extra caution and make sure that you're actually the one doing the asking. You also get a free credit report from each bureau.

✔ **Extended fraud alerts:** These longer-lasting alerts give you seven years for fraud alert protection and two additional free annual credit report reviews. You need to give the credit bureau a copy of the police fraud or identity theft report you filed. See Chapter 9 for details.

✔ **Active-duty alerts:** If you're an active-duty military person, there's an alert just for you. An active-duty alert lasts for one year on your credit report.

✔ **Widget alerts:** Norton, the antivirus software company, has a free widget tool called the Norton Cybercrime Index that sits on your desktop or phone and warns you about real-time cyber crime so you can take preventative measures. The tool also provides in-depth information on cyber crime trends and patterns. Think of it as a traffic report that alerts you to trouble spots, areas and streets to avoid, and potential hazards on the road. I expect others to follow suit and offer this type of service soon.

Credit freezes

More serious than alerts, a freeze on your credit report locks your report. In order to review your report, a lender or other party would need to ask you to unfreeze your account. This request tips you off about any unauthorized inquiries right away and prevents new accounts from being opened without your permission. You may incur a small fee to unfreeze an account; it varies by state.

The Consumers Union website has state-by-state rules on credit freezes at `consumersunion.org/research/security-freeze/`.

Part V
Never Have Bad Credit Again! Successful Credit Management for Life

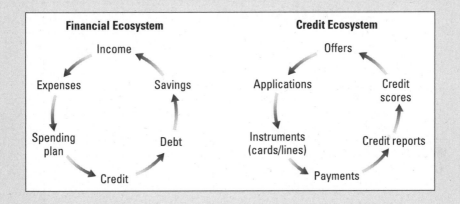

In this part . . .

- ✔ Make a firm foundation to build good credit in today's unforgiving and very tight credit environment.

- ✔ Understand your consumer protections in the CARD Act, Dodd-Frank legislation, FACT Act, and Fair Debt Collection Practices Act.

- ✔ Spot early signs of identity theft, control access to your identity, and keep your personal information safe.

- ✔ Give your credit score a boost by identifying your credit style and achieving balance with your spending and savings.

- ✔ Get a new and easy way to understand the role of credit as a renewable resource in your balanced credit ecosystem.

Chapter 16

Putting Yourself in Control of Your Credit

. . . .

In This Chapter

▶ Identifying your credit style

▶ Achieving balance in your spending, savings, and credit use

▶ Discovering how essential planning really is

. . . .

*W*hen Henry Ford decided that you could have any color you wanted for your new Model T Ford, as long as it was black, it wasn't because car buyers liked black. It wasn't even because Henry liked black. It was because drying the paint on cars coming off the assembly line took the longest of all the operations, and black dried the fastest of all the colors. By sticking with black, Ford could ship more cars each day and make more money, faster.

Credit issuers operate pretty similarly; they care more about making money than about meeting your needs. They shovel out credit offers by the truck-load based on cursory reviews of your relative creditworthiness. Sure, some of the things they tell you may be true (for instance, you may indeed have earned the right to exclusive privileges and benefits), but the only thing you can be sure of is that the offer is good for them. Whether you need the credit product in question, or whether it's even remotely advantageous to you, is just not a question that the marketers of the credit world consider. Like the black paint on a Model T, you get what makes the most money for the lender. Unless, of course, you put yourself in control of your financial and credit future.

This chapter is all about helping you take the control of your credit away from the issuers. I unmask the plans others have for your financial future and introduce you to the tools you need to chart your *own* course to success. I also help you figure out how to perk up your credit score; gauge your credit style; and balance your spending, savings, and credit use.

Determining Your Credit Style

Lenders, particularly banks, divide their credit card customers into two main categories: *transactors* and *revolvers*. The people in these categories need different things from their credit, so identifying your type is important in the process of picking a credit product that fits your lifestyle.

Transactors, also referred to as *convenience users,* are pretty straightforward in their credit use. You fall into this category if you use your credit cards primarily for convenience in place of cash. Doing so reduces your need to carry a wad of bills with you. You pay your balances in full every month and avoid fees and interest charges.

If you think that you may be a transactor, focus on the incentives that a card offers you for using it, like airline tickets or hotel stays, rather than a low interest rate. No balance means no interest, so who cares if it's 19.8 percent over prime; if you don't carry a balance, the interest rate is irrelevant to you.

Be sure that you use the card enough to benefit from it. For example, if you choose an airline mileage card that requires you to charge $25,000 annually to get a free ticket, and you plan to spend only $10,000 a year on the card, it may not be a good choice. You may want to consider a cash-back card instead. Some cash-back cards have an annual fee. Again, be sure you get more out of the card than you pay into it.

Revolvers frequently carry a balance from month to month. If you're one of these more desirable customers (from a lender's point of view), you consider your credit card a line of credit to use to pay for purchases over time. You make your payments on time, and often pay the minimum or more, but you rarely pay the balance in full. You pay interest every month and may not look too carefully at what the interest costs you over the long haul. Your bank could only love you more if you missed a payment or two and racked up even more interest and penalty charges!

A revolver's best choice is a card that offers a low interest rate. A low rate does a lot to help keep your balance down because your interest charges are included in the minimum payment you make each month. If your rate is high and you make minimum payments, you carry debt for much longer. Shopping for a zero-percent-interest card makes sense, but expect to change cards more often, as these rates usually apply for limited periods.

Be careful about incurring a 3 to 5 percent fee for transferring the balance from an old card with an expiring rate to a new one. Changing cards often has a negative effect on your credit score (see the list of score components in Chapter 13).

In addition to the usual card user categorizations, I have a few of my own that you may find helpful in identifying yourself:

✔ **The quicksand charger:** You qualify as a quicksand charger in my book if you spend on impulse and don't notice that you're slowly sinking into debt. Using credit without knowing how or when you'll be able to pay the bill is a bad habit that usually leads to an unhappy ending.

Use short-term installment loans for expenses that you plan to carry for six months or more. The fixed payment helps you pay off the debt more predictably, and the additional type of credit use can help your credit score. Plus, every time you apply for a new installment loan, you get a free reality check from your lender.

✔ **The clueless charger:** If you continue to find unpleasant surprises on your credit card statements (like unexpected balance transfer fees and penalties), you may be a clueless charger. Students and other credit newbies tend to find themselves being taken advantage of because they don't understand how their cards work and lack a plan for using credit.

Read and understand the terms that come with your credit card. Believe that you have to make payments on time as your card agreement says, and not what other clueless chargers may tell you. For example, you can and eventually will be sued in court if you don't make the minimum payment required by the card issuer, even if the lesser payment you're making is all you can afford. Get some financial education from a responsible provider. Lenders and credit counseling agencies can help you make an affordable plan to get out of debt.

✔ **The great pretender:** With apologizes to the Platters, who released the hit song "The Great Pretender" in 1955, this category includes millions who extend their income or lack thereof by using credit as if it gave them additional money to spend. This approach may help you make ends meet in the short term, but it is often a disaster in the end.

The tighter your finances, the tighter you need to control your use of credit. Start with a budget, trim your expenses, increase your income, and use credit only when you know that you can pay it off in a reasonable length of time (90 days or less is best). If you can't say when you will be able to pay off a charge, don't charge it. It's better to cut back now rather than later, when your credit is trashed.

Balancing Spending, Savings, and Credit Use

An orchestra is beautiful to hear. A gourmet meal is a delight to eat. What makes each experience a pleasure is balance. Whether it's the balance of instruments or the balance of ingredients, each component must be in harmony with the others. If the balance is wrong, the outcome can be a disaster.

The same idea of balance applies to your finances. Your spending, savings, and credit use must work together for the most pleasing results. The next sections show you how to take baby steps toward achieving that all-important balance. (For details about crafting your future vision into achievable goals, turn to Chapter 18.)

Spending on your terms

If your spending is under control and you have money for periodic expenses, chances are you've built a strong foundation for your financial house, and your credit will be safe and strong when you need it. Say your car has a mechanical problem; where does the money come from to fix it? If you plan your spending, then you should have a category for periodic auto maintenance and repairs. So the money comes from there and not your available credit on a credit card.

When you use credit, you use tomorrow's money — money you haven't yet earned and may not earn. Look at it as using tomorrow's money today. When tomorrow comes, how are you going to pay if you've already spent tomorrow's money yesterday? The more you shelter your credit from surprises or overuse by planning where and how to spend your money, the stronger your credit history, credit score, and financial future will be.

Saving for financial emergencies

If a spending plan gives you a firm foundation on which to build, then emergency savings provide the roof for shelter. Saving for emergencies and goals is essential to financial success. Let me say that again. If you don't save, you'll fail, becoming more and more vulnerable to money shortages and the stress they bring.

I'm sure you don't *want* to live paycheck to paycheck, but perhaps money is tight and you're wondering how on earth you can possibly save enough. Here are four essential ways to save your hard-earned moola:

- ✔ **Make saving painless.** Use direct deposit to put money from every paycheck into a savings account. Start small with what little you can afford — even $5 a week. The amount doesn't matter.

- ✔ **Make saving a habit.** Automatic deposits build slowly. Your confidence in seeing savings where there were none before will build faster. Soon you'll have enough saved to handle a small emergency or even just a part of one.

- **Add to savings with money you don't have yet.** Put half of new raises, tax refunds, and other windfalls like birthday money into the account. This is money you never had, never counted on, and won't miss.

- **Consider joining a savings club or organization.** Groups like America Saves (www.americasaves.org) and the Women's Institute for Financial Education (www.wife.org) offer valuable ideas and support to keep you on track. Local banks or credit unions may offer savings clubs tailored to specific expense categories like Christmas, taxes, and vacations, with incentives. Check them out.

Using credit to enhance your life

With your spending under control and money in the bank for emergencies and expected big-ticket items, you can use your excellent credit to get the best offers. You get the best terms on loans and credit cards thanks to a solid credit history and score. Even better, you free up thousands of dollars for trips, school, and other expenses when you get the lowest interest rates on mortgages, car loans, and more. Great credit also gives you lower insurance rates, access to better housing, and even an edge at work. Hiring and promotional decisions often involve credit report reviews. Your good credit can give you a competitive edge over other applicants or coworkers who have blemished credit.

Remembering the Importance of Planning When It Comes to Your Credit

Imagine a football quarterback saying that he plays the big game based on how he feels that day. If he sets no goals, practices no plays, and doesn't monitor his performance after each practice, would you bet on him leading his team to a win? In the sport known as credit, you need to follow a plan if you want to succeed.

But you don't have any competition, you say? Wrong! Lenders, credit grantors, insurers, landlords, and employers are constantly measuring your credit performance, and the cost of a substandard performance can be higher interest rates and fewer opportunities. These players and others use your credit profile as a gauge of your potential for success or failure, so having a plan and goals for your credit makes real sense.

The following sections reveal the plans that others have for your money and introduce you to the steps you can take to take control of your funds so that you don't fall prey to plans that benefit only credit issuers.

Zeroing in on the plans others have for your money

People constantly try to get you to spend money that you don't really need to spend. Just think of the credit offers you receive. These offers may ebb and flow with the economy and lenders' appetites for new customers, but inevitably they continue to show up from banks, investment companies, and even strangers. Rest assured that the issuers design these offers to be great for them without regard for your particular situation. If you answered many (or all!) of the offers you receive, your credit score would take a hit each time your report was reviewed for an offer, and you'd get a further score reduction every time you were approved for new credit. Trust me, the issuers don't care that their plans are winning at the expense of your credit.

If credit issuers' hidden goals seem a bit nebulous to you, consider what happens when you set foot in your local grocery store. The fact that the milk is located on the opposite side of the store from the door is no accident. This setup forces you to walk through the entire store, past an array of tempting products, to get to the one thing you need. The potential for an impulse buy is greatly enhanced, to the delight of the store owner and at your expense.

The bottom line is that if you have no plan for your finances and others do, you're more likely to fail and they're more likely to win.

Developing your own plans for your future

To avoid being a pawn in some credit issuer's chess game, you need to craft a plan for your finances. Specifically, you need to identify what you want to spend money on (goals), develop a spending and savings plan that reflects your goals, and then determine how credit fits into those plans. Chapter 18 presents the process of developing a spending and savings plan in detail, but the key tasks are as follows:

- ✔ Set and prioritize your financial goals.
- ✔ Take simple steps to create a workable plan.
- ✔ Adjust your plan as you go along.

The same process applies to your credit, but with a few differences. Yes, you need to set credit goals, but they can be simpler. For example, perhaps you want to buy a home in three years. If you had to wait until you saved up, say, $300,000 to purchase your dream house in cash, you might be ready for assisted living before you moved into your first home. Borrowing on future income to move in today makes sense and may well improve the quality of your life for years to come. You need to save for a down payment, and you need to have good credit to get a good mortgage interest rate and terms. This won't happen overnight, so you need to plan to make it happen.

Setting goals is easy. Just keep these steps in mind:

1. **Do a little prep work.**

   Set aside an evening or a weekend afternoon, sit down alone or with your partner, without distractions, and look into the future. No need to pull out a crystal ball; simply describe what you want your future to look like. Consider the short term (generally from a few months to a year), intermediate term (two to five years), and long term (five years and beyond). Your goals may include such things as getting a car, buying a home, having a family, saving for college or weddings, and going on a fabulous vacation. In no time, you'll be imagining all those things you've always wanted to do.

2. **As you identify goals, write them down.**

   Documenting your dreams is important because doing so makes them seem more real. Better yet, cut out or print out pictures that illustrate your goals — maybe a picture of a cruise ship or a tropical island surrounded by blue waters, or just you relaxing without fiscal worries.

To begin your planning, first, find out where you stand by obtaining free copies of your credit report and ordering your credit score; I explain how to do both in Chapter 14. Review your report for inaccuracies and then dispute any errors or out-of-date items you find using the pointers in Chapter 14.

After you take care of the inaccuracies, you can use the correct information in your report as a starting point for building the credit you want. Make adjustments to your credit usage based on your credit-score report's four statements about how you can improve your credit, called *reason statements*. They may indicate that you have too many active cards or that you have too much credit available. Both situations can hurt your credit.

VantageScore thinks understanding reason codes is so important that it has devoted an entire site to them. Check out www.reasoncode.org.

Next, use your spending plan to determine which of your goals (say, buying a home or taking a cruise) need to be funded using credit. Then find out the credit criteria for a low-interest mortgage rate and determine what kind of credit card you want to use on your cruise. Consider a card that gives you points toward a cruise as an incentive. Now you're making decisions about which credit offers to accept or turn down instead of just accepting the preapproved offers that show up, whether or not they fit your needs.

When you match your spending goals to a credit or lending need, you take charge of your own finances.

Now that you've taken the critical steps toward creating a successful plan, you've established a powerful reason to save a portion of your income. And you have the motivation to get your credit standing back on track to help you achieve those goals. Believe it or not, achieving your goals is generally not the problem. Knowing where you're going — and, for couples, agreeing on mutual goals — is the trickiest part.

Take the list of goals you made when creating your plan and reference it when things get a little rocky. Doing so can be a big help in getting you through difficult periods (for example, when something *not* on your list of goals is calling your name).

Chapter 17

Taking a Sustainable Approach to Your Credit

*N*ot everyone is comfortable with numbers. I know this from personal experience. My wife is one of those non-math types. Don't get me wrong; she can count her change and has money in the bank, but she sees the world differently than I do. So for the large number of people who don't see the world through a financial lens, I want to offer another way to understand credit. I gave a keynote address on this topic to 200 teachers, and they agreed that their students need a better way to relate to credit that isn't just dollars and cents. Everyone understands the environment, so why not draw a parallel? Well, I did. And I call it the ecology of credit, or green credit.

Not long ago, Americans didn't understand the connection between their actions and their environment. They didn't get that something as seemingly minor as spraying for mosquitoes could upset the ecological balance of nature, or that throwing trash into the ocean could harm sea creatures and endanger whole species. Today, we see the connections, and although we can disagree about whether humankind is experiencing climate change, everyone understands that actions have consequences, sometimes for years to come.

Most people don't see these types of connections in their use of credit, but the reality is that credit decisions can create both negative and positive feedback loops, just like you see in the environment. For example, paying only the minimum payment on a credit card means that you pay more interest, which means that you have less money to deal with emergencies, which may make it more likely that you accumulate more debt as you go along.

In this chapter, I help you better understand credit by drawing parallels between your natural environment and your credit environment. My "green credit" point of view advocates a sustainable approach to managing your financial resources and the stewardship of your credit ecosystem through self-interested individual behavior. I help you recognize that credit is an integral part of modern life, not just an accessory. So come along with me as I take you on a field trip to the wilds of credit and beyond.

Going Green: Treating Credit as a Renewable Resource

Looking at credit as a renewable resource changes your perspective: You want to better understand how it works so you don't unknowingly harm it. It also makes you responsible for not overusing or abusing this important resource to the point of endangerment or even extinction. To be a good steward of your credit, you need to understand how credit coexists with all the other parts of your financial ecosystem and how it fits into the rest of your life. In this section, I show you how to recognize the parts of your credit environment, their relationships to one another, and ways to keep them all in sync so that they complement one another.

Recognizing your credit environment

You've heard about ecology or ecosystems at one time or another. What is an *ecosystem,* really? It's a unit consisting of a number of factors that function together in an environment. Each participant in an ecosystem depends on the others to survive. Together, they sustain one another in a routine pattern of give and take. The balance can be delicate and easily upset. Major disruptions to the ecosystem can be disastrous to all the participants and can take years to undo. For example, in nature, if too many fish were born, they would use more than their share of water and plants, affecting the delicate balance.

Similarly, your credit ecosystem has a number of parts — lines of credit, emergency savings (to fund unexpected expenses without relying solely on credit), mortgages, credit cards, car loans, a payment history, and so on — that function and interact together. If one part is out of control, it impacts the others. A late payment on a bill can cause a ripple effect throughout your credit ecosystem, as sure as a forest fire damages more than trees. Each factor in your credit ecosystem has an effect on the rest of your life, such as your job, insurance rates, borrowing capabilities, and housing options. Central to the credit ecosystem concept is the idea that your credit, savings, and spending are continually engaged in an interrelated set of relationships with other financial elements that need to be kept in balance to be healthy.

When you take a walk through any environment, you like to know what to look for. If you're at the beach, you look for footprints in the sand that tell you whether seagulls or terns have been there recently. The presence of horse-shoe crabs, clamshells, or broken lobster pots tells you other things about the tide, currents, or passing storms. The same applies in the world of credit. Does your financial beach have excess income? Is your credit score rising or falling, like a barometer indicating a brewing storm? Does your credit report show healthy activity or signs of stress? The signs are there for you to read if you know where to look and what they mean. In the sections that follow, I help you predict tomorrow's financial weather and your long-range forecast.

Taking a closer look at the parts that make up your credit ecosystem

The major components of your credit ecosystem include your net income, your debts, the types of credit you have available, your payment history, and any major financial missteps (toxic spills) that you've made over the last seven to ten years. You may think that some of these items, like your income, aren't strictly credit related. And you're right in a narrow sense, but as in any ecosystem, all the parts influence one another and their environment, both positively and negatively.

On the left, Figure 17-1 shows the interdependencies of a typical financial eco-system. Beginning with income, this figure visually depicts the relationships among the financial factors that make up your ecosystem. The right side of Figure 17-1 details the credit portion of your ecosystem. If any part of the system is out of whack, the others are compromised, beginning with offers of credit and building to credit scores.

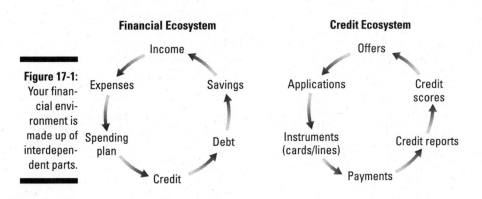

Figure 17-1:
Your finan-
cial envi-
ronment is
made up of
interdepen-
dent parts.

Counting your income

Income is always my favorite topic, so I want you to start there. Every biosystem needs nourishment in order to support its inhabitants. Krill are a type of small shrimp that form the basis of a food chain. The krill found at the South Pole nourish migrating fish, birds, and mammals. No krill? No chain of life as we know it.

Your credit ecosystem's nourishment is income. Because you have income, you can support spending, debt, and credit. Knowing how much income you have tells you what you have to work with and what you can support. If you don't know what your spendable income is, you can only guess and hope that you don't harm your environment by overspending or overtaxing your resources. Surprisingly, many people don't have a clear picture of how much income they have available or whether they're losing income through leaks in their paychecks. You can find examples of leaks and things you can do to maximize your income in Chapter 18.

Balancing your expenses

If income is your fertile resource, then your expenses represent what you take out of your environment. If you're a farmer, you need to balance the types of crops you grow or the types of animals you graze on your fertile land; too much of either and you won't be successful. If you're a fisherman, knowing how many fish you can catch and what kinds you need to leave behind for balance is important for a sustainable ecosystem.

Knowing what you're spending and how fast you're depleting your income enables you to manage your income resources so that they're healthy and productive for a lifetime. For tips on focusing your expenses, see Chapter 18.

Managing your resources

How can you be sure that you're managing your resources for maximum yield? It's easy. You use a plan that accounts for all your income and all your expenses. I call it a *spending plan.* Making and sticking to a spending plan — sometimes called a *budget* — assures that you don't overextend your income resources. Doing so also enables you to be in charge of the resources you use and how fast you use them so that you stay in control of your environment. Just like knowing how many fish a pond can support, you want to know how many expenses you can afford before you commit to them. Failure to plan may result in an ecosystem collapse!

You can find help and tips on creating a spending plan that works for you in Chapter 18.

Introducing credit

Using credit in your environment can be a powerful way to increase yields in the present. Credit can be a great thing as long as you don't overstress your environment to the point of doing long-term damage. A farmer may add fertilizer to the soil and growth hormones to cattle feed. Doing so can enhance growth and yield, but too much of either can damage resources and cause a failure down the road. Knowing the right time to use credit and the right amount to borrow to improve, rather than harm, your credit environment is your goal.

Sustaining Your Credit Ecosystem for Life

In this section, I show you how financial goals and planning help keep your ecosystem in balance. I talk more about goals in Chapter 18, but in brief, you want to set goals for life's major credit-related financial milestones and then create a plan to reach those goals. Among your goals may be paying for college, buying a home, or purchasing a car. Here I take an ecological look at each of these goals.

Funding college

Unless you're fortunate enough to have a trust fund, you and/or your parents may have to take out a student loan to pay for your higher education. For the purposes of this example, I'm going to assume that you'll have to make at least some, if not all, of the loan payments in the future. How does this type of loan fit into your overall financial environment and credit ecosystem? Be sure that it fits well, because, like an invasive species, this type of loan can't be eradicated by ordinary means.

Student loans are exempt from most bankruptcy proceedings, so you need to understand what your payments will be and what income stream you can expect from your chosen career field. If this loan is going to eat up too much of your future income — if, say, you're studying to be a modestly paid social worker — you may want to supplement the loan by working part-time. Or you could pass on that expensive Ivy League school in favor of a lower-priced community or state college to lessen the future stress on your income.

Balancing your current spending with your future ability to make payments keeps this loan sustainable. This advice works for parents as well as students. How much would you pay for a mystery item hidden in a box? Not much, I bet. How much would you borrow to fund an education leading to an unknown job with an unknown income?

Home sweet home

In the past, millions of Americans bought a home as soon as they were able. Today, with home value appreciation no longer a certainty, the goal of homeownership warrants a second look to see how it fits into your credit and overall financial landscape. Beyond making sure that you can afford the payments on a mortgage and that your job is secure enough to enable you to make a long-term commitment to those payments, consider this: Homeownership isn't a good fit for everyone. Changes to employment and income and opportunities to move or travel can make a long-term commitment less certain today. Owing more than your home is worth (referred to as being *upside down* on a loan) can keep you from relocating for an opportunity. Having your own place is great, but it may not be all roses for your career, finances, or credit. Homeownership complements and fits best into a stable credit environment.

Credit on wheels

You will probably use credit to make a purchase as large as a car. Making a down payment that's large enough to keep you from owing more than your car is worth when you drive it off the lot keeps your options open. Too small a down payment prevents you from selling your car unless you have savings to make up the difference between the sale price and what you owe. If you owe more than the car (or any asset) is worth, you're upside down on your loan. You don't want to turn a big part of your credit ecosystem upside down — it's as uncomfortable as it sounds!

Steering Clear of Credit Pollution

Your credit report offers you a graphical representation of your credit ecosystem. Each account listed on your report is like a tree growing in a forest. The older it is, the better it is for you and your credit score because its age indicates strength and stability. As negative items appear on your report, they can spread from one account to another as defaults increase your cost of credit. Late payments can cause damage that weakens your credit and its ability to play its role in supporting your goals. This damage is the equivalent of pollution seeping into your natural ecosystem. Just as too much pollution can create a toxic environment, too many negative items on your credit report can cause major credit problems before you realize what has happened. So how do you recognize this situation, and what can you do to restore your credit to a healthy balance? Read on!

Endangering your payment history

In most cases, credit card or loan payments are reported to one or more of the credit bureaus. A payment that is on time and for the amount due helps your credit report and score grow stronger. Missing a payment or paying too little dumps toxic data into your credit file. The effects can go far downstream in your financial environment. Bad credit can cost you a new job or promotion, licenses in some fields, higher insurance costs, and the opportunity to buy or rent decent housing. After damage is done to your credit forest, regrowth may take from two to seven years — or even ten years, as I explain in the next section.

Paying off a delinquent account or bringing it to a current status doesn't undo the damage already done, but it does prevent future damage and enables you to begin to rebuild your credit over time.

Your payment history can harm your credit environment in many ways:

- ✔ Overspending by using credit means higher payments. Higher payments limit the amount of money you can devote to savings and place a strain on your credit from overuse and lack of replenishment.

- ✔ Drying up your savings can cause a damaging cash-flow drought that weakens your ability to respond to new or unexpected challenges.

- ✔ Although creditors can no longer raise your interest rates on existing balances if you miss a payment on another loan, you damage your payment history as soon as you're 30 days late, and creditors can raise the rate on new purchases (see Chapter 19 for more information).

- ✔ If you miss two payments on a credit card (in other words, you're more than 60 days late), your existing-balance interest rate will explode like a wind-driven wildfire and consume more of your income than you can imagine when you can least afford it.

Clear-cutting your credit in bankruptcy

Among the most damaging things that can happen to a forest is overlogging — clear-cutting all the trees and leaving a wasteland behind. When you're forced to declare bankruptcy, you're clear-cutting your credit. All those credit accounts and lines that had been strong and growing trees on your credit report are chopped down. The resulting wasteland takes years to regrow, just as in nature.

Despite the devastation of a credit clear-cut, you may still owe a lot of money. Bankruptcy may not wipe out *all* your debt, and the debt that remains can be the most tenacious and longest-surviving of all. Like plastic bags and inorganic products that can live on in the environment for years and years, some debts just don't disappear, including

- ✔ Federal, state, and local taxes
- ✔ Child support
- ✔ Alimony
- ✔ Student loans
- ✔ Money owed as a result of drunk driving

Some bankruptcy-resistant debts continue to grow and consume precious resources. For instance, unpaid student loans can result in the seizure of tax refunds or even part of your Social Security payouts until they're satisfied.

Some lenders specialize in giving new loans to people with damaged credit. Why? Because they can charge super-high rates, and because, under the law, you can't clear-cut your debt with a second Chapter 7 bankruptcy filing for eight long years. My experience with these types of bottom-feeding lenders is that they verge on predatory, and you're better off not doing business with them. They make risky loans all the time, so they're ready, willing, and very able to hammer you for any delayed, missed, or short payment.

Living in a post-bankruptcy wasteland has other challenges. See the section "The darker side of filing bankruptcy" in Chapter 8 for more info.

If you need to wipe out all your debts because you're overwhelmed, be sure that this extreme measure will solve your problems. For example, if your defaults were caused by overuse of credit to supplement your income for basic living expenses, a bankruptcy won't solve your problem.

People tell me it's unfair that they're penalized for the damage they've done by filing for bankruptcy. After all, they had no choice, and the situation genuinely may not have been their fault. Still, the trees are all gone, and it takes time to regrow your credit and convince lenders and others that you'll take better care of your environment next time.

Outlasting a long, cold credit winter

As if the damage you can do to your credit ecosystem isn't enough, I want you to consider one more aspect of your financial environment. You're in an environment that has seen a major shift in climate. No, I'm not talking about climate change, but about credit change! Like the dinosaurs, millions of people have had a meteorlike meltdown hit their financial lives. Beginning in late 2007, the economy tanked, housing prices dropped, and unemployment gushed like an angry volcano spewing darkness over the sky. The result? A "credit winter." Credit remains frozen in many places and has been slow to thaw. It may take years before credit flows as it did before the last bubble.

You can avoid a dinosaur-like fate for your financial dreams by adding new credit only when you need it, by making payments on time and for the full amount due, and by keeping balances low to remain nimble.

Surviving and Reviving After a Credit Catastrophe

Whether your credit has taken a toxic hit from delinquencies or has been wiped out in a clear-cutting due to a bankruptcy, you can minimize ongoing damage and foster a recovery. I have three suggestions to help speed your credit ecosystem's revival and some tips to get you through the rough spots until your credit has healed.

Understanding what happened

The first thing you need to do is to understand what happened and why. For most people, the problems can seem like a blur. But credit problems can usually be traced to two main causes: gradual accumulation of debt by an extended period of overspending, or an event such as an illness or accident.

Planning for your next challenge

You can remedy the slow and easy overspending trap by developing a spending plan that accounts for all your income and expenses. A spending plan helps you make conscious decisions about where you spend your money and keeps you from slowly sinking deeper and deeper into debt. Chapter 18 goes into the nuts and bolts of setting up a spending plan that works for you.

A number of different tsunami-like events can wash out your finances. Illness, even if you're insured, can deluge you with huge amounts of debt. An unexpected and uninsured or underinsured calamity like a house fire or a car accident can make a serious dent in your finances. The way to avoid a repeat is to insure for what you can and save for the rest. Be sure that your auto, home, and disability insurance policies are adequate to protect you in the event of a loss. Establish a plan to save between six months and a year of living expenses in an emergency account to last you through income interruptions from a job loss or to fund deductibles and expenses not covered by insurance.

Minimizing the damage as you move forward

You still need to live through the months that follow a credit crisis despite the complications that damaged credit can cause. It's important to recognize and to be proactive about situations where your damaged credit may hurt you when someone checks your credit report. Realize that your credit ecosystem is part of your larger financial environment and that each one affects the other.

Damaged credit can affect you far beyond being unable to get a credit card. Some events trigger a review of your damaged credit report while you're in the process of restoring your financial environment. These events include getting a new job, being considered for a promotion, moving to a new apartment, and buying a car. Here are some details about these events:

- **Employment/promotions:** Employers commonly pull a credit report as part of the hiring or promotion process. If you're up for a new job or a promotion, be sure to have an explanation of what happened in your credit history and what you've done since to ensure that it won't happen again. Mistakes are common; showing that you learned from them is not.

- **Moving:** Landlords want to know if you *will* pay your rent, not just if you're able to. Bad credit is cause for concern unless you can explain what happened. You may want to offer a larger security deposit to set your landlord's mind at ease.

- **Car financing:** A reliable car is an essential part of making a living for many people. If you're buying a car with damaged credit, be prepared to put down more money than usual so that the financing company is protected against a default. Be careful of dealers who charge high interest rates and penalties for prepaying your loan. Establishing a relationship with a credit union can be a good way to get a loan at a reasonable rate, even with blemished credit.

Rebuilding your credit ecosystem

Is rebuilding a damaged credit ecosystem a chicken-or-egg puzzle? Or is it a catch-22 situation, with the catch being that you can't do what you want from where you are? It's neither, although it can sure seem that way.

Following an oil spill or other disaster, environmental experts show up and analyze the damage. They come up with a plan for what needs to be done to restore balance, and they predict how long it will take for the ecosystem to heal.

Your credit score indicates the health of your credit ecosystem. A low score means that your credit environment has had some damage that will take time to repair. In times like these, getting new credit to show that you can handle it can be challenging. But if you heed the following simple steps, you'll be growing healthy credit lines and a garden full of blooms in no time.

When oil was spilled into the Gulf of Mexico, experts predicted that it might take years for the fragile coastal ecosystem to recover. They began working to clean up the damage and built berms to protect against future damaging events. A toxic credit report and score take time to restore as well. Slowly rebuilding your report with fresh accounts that you pay on time and as agreed leads to a thriving credit ecosystem again. Showing that you can handle different types of credit can favorably impact your score, too.

Try the following for diversity and a speedy recovery:

- ✔ **Secured credit card:** Using a secured credit card may help you rebuild your credit and boost your score over time when other products aren't available. No one will know that you have a bank account securing this card. Secured by a cash deposit, many of these cards report every on-time payment to the credit bureaus, just like an unsecured card does. Confirm that the secured account will be reported to the credit bureaus before you open the account.

- ✔ **Passbook loan:** Open a savings account and borrow the amount that you have on deposit. Just make all your payments on time. This personal loan is inexpensive and grows your credit.

- ✔ **Retail store cards:** Usually easier to get than an unsecured bank card, a revolving credit line from a retail store can even get you discounts. But use it only when you're shopping for a need, not when you feel the need to shop.

Checking your credit report and score periodically can offer you a simple measure of your progress. You can get a free copy of your credit report annually at www.annualcreditreport.com. For measuring growth in your credit saplings, I suggest that you check one report every four months; that way you can have three free looks each year.

Chapter 18

Safeguarding Your Credit with a Spending Plan

*I*magine that you're competing in the Olympics. The other athletes entered in your event have trainers and training plans to keep them focused and on track. You'd be at a severe disadvantage if you just made up your training as you went along instead of following a comprehensive plan that builds on a series of steps, each of which makes your workout more effective. Well, consider this book your trainer and this chapter a training regimen to help you develop spending and savings plan muscles for financial success.

So what does a spending plan have to do with credit? Everything! Your credit is a financial reflection of your life. If your life is out of control, chances are your finances are, too, and your credit isn't far behind. But if you successfully manage your spending and savings, your credit will never get overextended, you'll be able to pay the full balances of all your bills on time every month, and your credit score will be great as a result. Without a plan for your finances, you're destined to fail, but if you make a plan and follow it, you'll succeed big time.

In this chapter, I show you how some simple planning helps focus your spending and credit use to achieve the goals you set for yourself and your family, to protect and build your credit, and to sleep soundly at night. This plan isn't about sacrifices that keep you from doing the things you want to do and can afford. It's a plan that will make your dreams a reality. Plus, it will keep others from diverting your financial future into their pockets. I take you through the process of figuring out how much you're spending and where your money is going now and how you'd like to spend your income in the future. You accomplish this task by allocating your income to spending areas that you choose and by selecting the most advantageous types of credit for your needs. I help you get your plan in shape so you can win the gold in your financial Olympics!

Appreciating the Benefits of a Solid Spending Plan

A *spending plan* (formerly known as a budget) is a powerful tool that lets you decide how to spend your money to your greatest advantage and build your credit at the same time. It's your personal road map for spending your income, building up your savings, and using credit to save money and to enhance your credit profile. A spending plan can be as detailed or as general as you want it to be. To create a plan, you need to know your income and expenses and have a general idea of your financial goals. Your plan helps you organize your financial life and attain your goals in the near and long term.

Many people incorrectly think that a spending plan is restrictive and may cramp their style or their ability to be spontaneous. In many ways, a spending plan is to a budget what planning a balanced, satisfying, and healthy menu is to going on a diet. You get to enjoy *exactly* what *you* want. How is this possible? You discover how to eliminate spending money on things that others (friends, marketers, and so on) want you to buy while focusing your hard-earned money on those things you really want.

As I explain in Chapter 17, credit is a tool. It doesn't give you more money to spend; it simply allows you to spend the money you haven't earned yet. If you borrow to cover emergencies or big-ticket items, you're spending money today that you won't earn until tomorrow.

So what happens when you get to tomorrow and find that you spent all the money that was supposed to be there? Nothing pleasant, I can assure you. You can't use credit to extend your income indefinitely. Sooner or later, overusing credit catches up with you. Why do people keep spending money they don't have? For many reasons, one of which is that they listen to other people's ideas regarding what will make them happy instead of relying on their own plan and goals. But not you. You are going to develop a winning plan that helps you attain all *your* goals!

Here's a short list of things that a good plan can help you do:

- **Reach your financial and personal goals:** Your plan is a GPS that keeps you on track, helping you put aside money to reach your goals without getting sidetracked. Whether your goals include an exotic vacation, an addition to your home, or a new car, a plan assures that you get there.

- **Master your finances:** Deciding in advance where to spend your money helps assure that you spend it on those things that are most important to you. In addition, your plan builds your credit record and score with timely payments for those items you purchase with credit. For everything you need to know about credit reports and credit scores, including how to improve your score, flip to Chapters 13 and 14.

- **Save more than you thought possible:** You may notice when you begin the planning process that your expenses equal — or, in some cases, exceed — your income. Spending less than you make is a great way to ensure that you don't become overextended, because the money you don't spend can be saved for inevitable unplanned expenses and emergencies.

One of the best ways to live within your means is to have a plan for what you do with extra money you don't currently have, but expect to have in the future, such as tax refunds, raises, and promotions. When a chunk of cash shows up, save half and spend half. Before you know it, your bank account will be buff!

- **Uncover extra cash:** The best part of having a spending plan is that you end up with more money to spend on what you want. Eliminating waste puts more money in your pocket every month. Instead of spending money on things you don't really want or need, you can use that cash any way you want, from buying new toys to building savings.

- **Share common goals:** An effective spending plan pertains to your entire family. For example, your children are much more likely to go along with watching Netflix movies rather than going to the movie theater for several months if they understand that doing so will give them an extra day at Disney World! The same is true of your sweetie: If the two of you decide that an update to your home is your top financial priority, you'll be on the same page when it comes to making the necessary financial adjustments.

- **Be as prepared as an Eagle Scout:** As part of your plan, you set up and grow an emergency savings account. This account covers unexpected expenses such as major car repairs, large appliance replacements, or big medical bills.

- **Keep debt in its place:** Because planning helps you bring your expenses in line with your income and builds savings, you don't need to use credit unless it's in your best interest to do so.

 ✔ **Manage your credit:** Keeping your debt down improves your credit and builds your credit score. Your score improves with lower amounts owed, fewer accounts with balances, and a smaller proportion of your credit limit being used. For details on your credit score and how to manage it successfully, check out Chapter 14.

 ✔ **Give yourself peace of mind:** Being in control of your money helps you avoid the financial stress that causes sleepless nights, reduced productivity at work, and even physical symptoms like headaches or ulcers. You'll have a smile on your face instead of worry lines.

Deciding on Goals: Imagining Your Future as You Want It to Be

Imagining your future is the fun part of building a spending plan. Many people wander through life without goals, letting events take them where they will. Well, there's a better way, and setting goals is a key first step. The first part of managing your finances and credit is to decide what you want to do and when. Don't worry — this isn't a test, and you can't fail. In fact, you can change your goals as often as you want.

Setting the stage for planning

Set aside an hour or so — more if you can — to envision your future as you'd like to live it. If you're sharing your life with another, be sure to involve that person in the discussion. Heck, make it a date! Over a glass of wine or a cup of tea, get comfortable and dare to dream. Or go to a favorite quiet place — a nearby park, the steps of a monument, a scenic overlook — and let your surroundings inspire you.

At this point, the sky's the limit! Dream as big as you want. Have you always wanted to take a year off and sail around the world? Jot it down. Do you yearn to go back to school or launch a new career? Add it to the list. Buying a home, owning a sports car (or just a reliable one) — this goal-setting stage is your opportunity to indulge in *all* your financial fantasies. Getting them down on paper and discussing, assessing, and prioritizing them is an important part of the process of tailoring your spending plan to meet your personal goals.

Be sure to include some details. For example, you may have written down, "Go to Disney World." But to flesh it out a bit more and bring it alive, be more specific. Will you stay at the Grand Floridian or the Days Inn? Will you go for a weekend or a week or two? Try to be as specific as possible. This level of detail not only gives you a clearer target but also keeps communication about your goals clear.

Wherever you do your planning, record your goals and put a date next to each one. If you're in the mood, you can have some fun with this step: Get out the scissors (or your mouse) and cut and paste pictures from magazines, calendars, and other sources to illustrate your goals. These images can be powerful motivators. Put them up on your refrigerator or turn them into a screensaver so that you can refer to them as you go along.

Categorizing your goals

I like to say that you eat an elephant one bite at a time. I suggest that you separate your goals into categories to keep from being overwhelmed. Otherwise, you may focus only on short- or long-term goals. For the best results, I recommend that you use four general categories:

- ✔ **Short-term goals** are no longer than one year. They may include taking that vacation to Disney World, starting a retirement plan or an emergency fund, or even repairing your credit.

- ✔ **Intermediate-term goals** require one to five years to accomplish. These may include saving enough money to buy a new car, to begin a family, to purchase new furniture, or to pay off your debts.

- ✔ **Long-term goals** are at least five years down the road. These may include saving for your kids' education, starting your own business, or buying a home or boat.

- ✔ **Life goals** don't have a time frame, because you'll probably never *fully* achieve them. These goals aren't necessarily money-driven but capture the imagination. For example, you may want to have less stress in your life. Imagine what it would take and write it down. Have at least one goal you can pursue that may be unattainable through money alone. Who knows? You won't succeed if you don't try.

Pay attention to how many goals you have in each category. Are all your goals focused on the short term? If so, spend some time thinking a little further into the future. Also, remember that not all goals require money to realize. Adding some nonmonetary goals to your list can help take some of the financial pressure off the ones that do. For example, spending more time doing a shared activity, such as volunteering to assist the elderly or help out at the local library, may offer a nonfinancial respite — and can be a great exercise in togetherness. Look for other opportunities to work "free" into your future.

Putting your goals in order

After you list all your goals and sort them into categories, the next step is to prioritize them. I suggest that you assign a high priority to short-term goals that you think you can reach easily or that are particularly motivating. That way you can experience the thrill of victory early on and gain momentum for tackling the next goal.

If you have goals that you know will be difficult to achieve or will require a lot of saving, I suggest that you segment them. By breaking large goals into smaller chunks, you're better able to see your progress. Plus, you'll have more reasons to celebrate.

This process shouldn't be a slog to the finish. You need to have fun along the way. It's important to celebrate every milestone. And don't be afraid to make adjustments as you go. An unexpected bonus can move up a timeline; a layoff or illness can set it back. Adjust your plan accordingly.

Building Your Vision of Your Future

Setting and prioritizing your goals establishes a powerful incentive for turning easy immediate gratification into a plan that puts you, not others, in control of your finances and your life. Now what you need is a tool, or a series of tools, to help you achieve your goals. That's where the spending plan that I discuss in detail in this section comes in.

You're creating a plan not to *restrict* your spending, but rather to put yourself in charge of directing your money to where you want it to go.

Identifying resources and eliminating waste are great places to begin. Start with your current income and expenses. After all, you can't decide how much money to spend and where to spend it until you know how much you have to go around.

Step 1: Counting up your income

Figuring out how much you earn in a year can be easy or tricky depending on how you're paid. If you earn a regular salary or work a set number of hours per week, the task is easy — just multiply your regular pay by the number of pay periods in a year. On the other hand, if you earn commissions or tips or if you're, say, a fisherman or a landscaper, you need some basis on which to project your income. Perhaps your work is seasonal (you sell ice cream or prepare tax returns, for example) and you bring in more income at certain times of the year, or maybe you work extra hours at inventory time and that affects your income. I suggest that you look at last year's income as a starting point. Your old tax return should have most of the information you need.

Whatever your situation, try to estimate a year's worth of income. If you find it helpful to come up with a monthly average, start with a high-earning month rather than a low-earning one. That way you can save some of that month's extra income to tide you over in a low-income month.

Use Table 18-1 to list all the sources of income you expect each month. Be sure to use your take-home, or *net,* pay rather than your *gross* pay (your salary before taxes and other deductions). For example, if you earn $60,000 a year, your gross income is $5,000 a month — but you probably take home about $3,600 after Social Security, federal and state taxes, and other deductions. You may also want to list the expenses that are deducted from your paycheck. Be sure to consider ways to reduce or eliminate deductions.

Table 18-1	Income Worksheet		
Source of Income	*Planned*	*Actual*	*Difference*
Salary 1			
Salary 2			
Bonus			
Interest			
Dividends			
Other periodic income			
Child support/alimony			
Rental-property income			
Gifts			
Deduction changes/other			
Total Income	$	$	$

For income items that are uncertain, use the Planned column. Put a value you know you can count on in the Actual column and then record the Difference as you receive payment. If an amount in the Difference column is bigger than you feel comfortable with, you may want to pare down your Planned number. Here's an example: Your current (Actual) take-home pay is $4,000 a month. In a few months, you expect a 10 percent raise, which takes it to $4,400 (Planned). The Difference is $400. If the raise doesn't come to pass, ask yourself if your plan will work without the extra $400 in income.

You can print out a copy of this worksheet at www.dummies.com/extras/ creditrepair. If you prefer to use computer-based budgeting tools, see the section "Budgeting websites" later in this chapter.

Many people over-withhold for taxes. If you got a $2,400 tax refund last year, that money was an interest-free loan to the IRS that you could have put to better use. I suggest that you reduce your withholding by half the amount of your refund. For a $2,400 refund, you're overpaying $200 a month in taxes. Reduce your withholding by $100 a month. That still leaves you a cushion with the tax man but adds some extra cash to your budget.

You may have income from other sources besides your regular paycheck. Don't forget to include child support, alimony, overtime pay, bonuses, investment income, royalties, or rental-property income. If you have income from a part-time activity such as playing in a band or selling stuff on eBay, add it to the pile!

After you list all your income sources, come up with an average monthly income. Why monthly? Because you pay most of your major expenses on a monthly basis — mortgage or rent, utilities, phone, and even many charitable contributions are often portioned out in monthly increments.

Step 2: Tallying what you spend

After you know what's coming in, you need to calculate what's going out — and where it's going. Determining your monthly spending isn't difficult, but for some people it requires a little digging. Many of your major expenses — mortgage or rent, credit card bills, utilities, car loans, and so on — hit monthly. If you have an expense that occurs other than monthly, prorate it to a monthly amount. For example, a $2,000 homeowner's insurance bill due once a year is $166.66 a month. For frequent yet varying expenses such as electricity and entertainment, gather several months to a year of history and then determine a monthly average.

Table 18-2 helps you get started. Using your checking and savings account statements, credit card statements, cash receipts for significant purchases, other financial records, and/or a financial planning program such as Quicken, enter and categorize all your expenses to figure out what you spend each month. If you don't have complete financial records, don't worry — just use your best estimates to fill in the blanks.

Table 18-2	Expenses Worksheet		
Expense	*Planned*	*Actual*	*Difference*
Rent/mortgage			
Property taxes			
Renters/homeowners insurance			
Home maintenance			
Water			
Sewer			
Garbage			
Gas/oil for heating			
Electricity			
Telephone			
Car payment			
Car insurance			
Gasoline			
Car repairs/maintenance			
Clothing			
Groceries/household supplies			
Doctor/dentist			
Prescriptions			
Health insurance			
Life/disability insurance			
Childcare			
Tuition/school expenses			
Child support/alimony			
Personal allowance (small, out-of-pocket expenses)			
Entertainment			
Eating out/vending			
Cigarettes/alcohol			
Newspapers/magazines			
Hobbies/clubs/sports			
Gifts			

(continued)

Table 18-2 *(continued)*

Expense	Planned	Actual	Difference
Donations			
Work expenses			
Cable/satellite TV			
Internet service			
Cellphone			
Student loans			
Pet/veterinary expenses			
Other:			
Other:			
Total Expenses	$	$	$

Here, use the Planned column for your best guesses of expenses that are not fixed, like electricity, and then record the Actual amounts as bills roll in. If an expense is fixed, like rent, put it in the Actual column. Fill in the Difference column as you track your Planned expenses and find out the Actual Amounts.

You can print out a copy of this worksheet at www.dummies.com/extras/creditrepair.

If you're like most people, you'll be able to account for around 80 to 90 percent of where your money is spent. But you're likely to find that a fraction of your income seems to vanish into parts unknown. I call these items "money gobblers" — small cash expenditures that never seem to register in your memory, let alone make it to the checkbook register or any other account ledger. I've assembled a list of some of the more common of these expenses. You may be able to save in some of these areas if you decide that you'd rather consciously reallocate the money or reallocate the expense to personal allowance:

- ✔ **Allowances:** Your kids will hate me for this, but you don't have to give them set allowances.

- ✔ **Bank fees:** There is no reason to pay fees for a checking account if you take the time to shop around. You may need to have your paycheck direct deposited or have a certain number of transactions each month, but you could save $300 a year. You can save even more by using electronic bill pay rather than ever more expensive postage stamps.

✔ **Babysitting:** See if you can work out a deal with friends or neighbors to watch their kids one day in exchange for them watching yours the next. Or take shameless advantage of the grandparents — most are only too happy to volunteer their services.

✔ **Salon:** Instead of going to a high-priced salon, look for a beauty school in your area. You may be able to get your hair done for free (or for a nominal charge), and the attention to detail you get is phenomenal — the students are supervised by teachers, and they're working to impress.

✔ **Beer, wine, and soda:** For some people, giving up brewskis, a favorite cabernet, or soft drinks may seem like a real hardship. But when you add up how much money you're spending, it may be enough of a motivation to abstain or cut back if you can attain a goal with the proceeds.

✔ **Fast food and vending machines:** The stuff is bad not only for your body but also for your wallet. Shop at the grocery store instead; use coupons for amazing savings.

✔ **Books, magazines, newspapers, CDs, and movies:** One of the greatest resources at your disposal is your public library. You can get all the books, magazines, and newspapers you want — free of charge. Most libraries also lend audio books, e-books, music CDs, and movies for free.

✔ **Car washes:** Now, I'm not suggesting that you never wash your car. I'm just suggesting that, when you need to do it, you do it yourself or toss a sponge, some soap, and the hose at your kids and set them loose. They have fun, your car gets a little cleaner, and you save significant dough.

✔ **Lottery tickets and other forms of gambling:** A dollar in the bank is much more valuable than a dollar spent gambling. End of story.

✔ **School fundraisers:** When the neighbor kids come a-knockin', just say no. If you want to help your local school, you can volunteer at the library, coach a sports team, or lead a scouting troop.

✔ **Entertainment (concerts, movies, sporting events, and so on):** Look for ways to entertain yourself and your family free of charge. Instead of going to a professional baseball game, go to the park and toss a ball around with your kids or your friends. Instead of going to a movie, check out a DVD from the library.

✔ **Health foods:** Eating healthfully is important, but health foods can be pricey. Shop the produce department of your grocery store, stick to whole grains and lean meats, and you and your spending plan will be fine.

✔ **Hobbies:** Most hobbies cost money, and although they're fun, so is saving money. Make *that* your new hobby.

✔ **Eating out:** Even if you're eating at fast-food restaurants, eating out costs a lot. You can save big money by preparing your food at home.

✔ **Pets:** If you're in financial trouble, getting a new pet isn't a good idea. (Let me tell you about my free cat!) Even healthy pets cost money, and if your pet gets sick, you're in for more expenses. If you already have pets, stick to the necessities (food, vaccinations, hugs) and avoid store-bought toys. You can make a rope bone out of old T-shirts or throw a tennis ball around in the yard — all your pet cares about is you (and food).

✔ **Tobacco:** You already know that you shouldn't be smoking. Add up the financial costs, and you can see the damage it's doing *beyond* the damage to your health.

✔ **Yard sales:** If your idea of a fun Saturday morning is going from one yard sale to the next looking for bargains, wash the car instead. Most people think that they're getting bargains, but they usually end up buying things they don't really need.

Are you an average spender?

You may be looking for guidelines to tell you whether your spending is in line with that of others. Look no further. The nice people at the Bureau of Labor Statistics (BLS) have been hard at work adding up grocery store receipts and watching how often people fill up at the gas station. Their report is available at www.bls.gov/news.release/cesan.nr0.htm. They have their ways of getting the stats on what Americans are spending. The latest data is a year or so old but is probably fine for your purposes.

To help simplify your spending plan discussions, I summarize some of the main items as percentages of expenditures for a "consumer unit" (sort of like a modern incarnation of a family). See the BLS website for the full details. I arrived at the percentages by taking an average individual expense as a percentage of overall average annual spending. I'm not suggesting that you plan according to these percentages, but you may find them useful as guidelines to see whether your estimates are way out in left field. For example, your family may spend more on housing and less on entertainment, and I may do the opposite. The key to remember is that *you* get to decide.

✔ **Housing:** 32.8 percent of annual overall expenses

✔ **Transportation:** 17.4 percent (includes vehicles, gasoline and motor oil, and other transportation)

✔ **Food:** 12.8 percent (at home: 7.6 percent; away from home: 5.2 percent)

✔ **Personal insurance and pensions:** 10.9 percent (includes premiums for whole life and term insurance; endowments; income and other life insurance; mortgage guarantee insurance; mortgage life insurance; and premiums for personal liability, accident and disability, and other nonhealth insurance other than for homes and vehicles, pensions, and Social Security)

✔ **Healthcare:** 6.9 percent

✔ **Entertainment:** 5.1 percent

✔ **Apparel and services:** 3.4 percent

You don't have to cut all these items out of your life. Just be aware that you're spending discretionary money and consider how important each item really is. For example, you may not be willing to scrimp when it comes to Fido's super-premium dog food — if that's the case, just make sure to budget for it every month.

To identify that last 10 to 20 percent of expenses, track your daily expenditures. Record all those cash expenses that are such a part of your routine that you hardly notice them — the morning paper, coffee, snacks, and so on. Again, I'm not saying you shouldn't *have* them — the goal is just to be aware of where your money is going so you can decide whether that's the best use of your funds.

The really good news about this tracking is that you need to do it for only two months to catch almost everything. After that you'll have a good handle on what's gobbling up your extra cash, and you can either plug the hole or include it as an expense in your budget.

Step 3: Making savings part of your spending plan

How can *savings* be part of a *spending* plan? Easy — consider savings an allocation of your available money. Then it becomes an expense, even though you aren't actually spending it.

Most people don't budget for savings, and that's a huge mistake. To be successful, you need to save money for emergencies beyond your identified goals. Add up what you need to save in a year to reach your prioritized financial goals and divide by 12. That's the monthly amount you need to include in your plan. If you don't have that much to allot to savings, you have a decision to make — spend less in another area(s), increase your income, or rearrange your goals.

The old saying "Pay yourself first" is a wise one indeed. If you save only what drifts to the bottom line, you're shortchanging yourself and losing out on an essential way to protect your credit — an emergency savings cushion.

Taking the direct (deposit) approach

The best way I've found to save is to have money from your paycheck directly deposited into a savings or checking account. After you get into the habit, it will become self-reinforcing. Seeing that balance rise will inspire you to do more when you can. You won't think to spend money if you can't see it. I do this myself and have found it to be painless.

Have your paycheck set up so that the money you need to run your household (your monthly budget minus savings) goes directly into your checking account every pay period. I suggest that half of any pay raise, bonus, or left-over money above that amount be left to go directly into your savings. You never see it and never spend it — unless, of course, you want to. You get half and the savings account gets half. What could be more fair?

Your savings plan is really two-pronged: You're saving to achieve the goals you've set for yourself, and you're saving so that you have money in case of an emergency. I cover both in the following sections.

Saving the easy way: The grown-up version of a piggy bank

Remember when saving consisted of getting change and putting it into a piggy bank? Remember the happiness you experienced as those quarters and dimes clinked into your personal treasure chest? Well, you will have that feeling back and more once you start a savings plan that works for you. Security, confidence, and the sheer potential of a pile of money waiting for you to transform it into your fondest wish make your childhood excitement pale in comparison. All you need is a little encouragement and a tip or two and you'll have savings for emergencies and the good things in life in short order.

A technique that helps me make the most of my spare pennies is to roll change. No, I don't mean pretending that you're someone else. At the end of the day, I place my loose pocket change into a neat little bank that separates the coins by denomination so I can put them in those cute little tubes you can get (for free) at the bank. Stay away from the machines that change coins into dollars for a fee. For guys, gathering change is easy, as the coins usually fall out onto the floor when you hang up your trousers. Ladies will not only save money, but also save the expense of physical therapy to address the damage caused by purses weighted down with coins. Expect that this exercise will yield about $200 a year per person.

Another way to save is to use your credit cards less. Paying with cash helps reinforce the link between spending, earning, and the cost you're paying. Paying for a $100 item is easy with a swipe of your favorite mileage-accruing credit card. If you have to peel off ten $10 bills, the experience is different. It's real money — and a lot of it! Plus, when your roll of cash is nearly gone, you may find yourself thinking twice about a purchase.

Give yourself a fat raise by bagging your lunch. Going out to lunch every day costs you thousands! Check out the math: With 260 business days in a year, a $10 lunch special becomes $15 per lunch (including tax, tip, and gas/transportation), which equals $3,900 a year. If you pay 25 percent federal income tax, 7 percent state income tax, and 7 percent Social Security, bringing your lunch to work and saving $3,900 after taxes is the equivalent of nearly a

$6,400 pre-tax raise [$6,400 – $1,600 (25 percent of $6,400) – $448 (7 percent of $6,400) minus another $448 (7 percent of $6,400) = $3,904 take-home]. Think of the goal you can realize with that money! The same math works for breakfast, too.

Finally, buy a Sunday paper and cut coupons. I know, newspapers are dying. So you'll be saving jobs and doing a public service in the process. Or visit a website such as www.coupons.com where you can browse for coupons that you need. If you can put in a half-hour and come up with $20 in savings every week, you've made a great trade. How much? How about the equivalent of a $1,445 raise!

Managing to save for a goal

After you've agreed on your goals, you know your income, and you've tracked your spending, the next task is to break down a goal into bite-sized pieces to make it more easily attainable. If you can do so with *all* your goals, you'll be closer to a plan that works for you.

Take an intermediate-term goal as an example. Say you want to take a trip costing $2,000. If your goal is to go in 18 months, divide the $2,000 by 18 months. The result — $111.11 — is what you must put aside each month to pay for the trip by the time you're waving goodbye to the cats and driving to the airport.

But $111.11 a month isn't chopped liver. So where will the money come from? You need to either increase your income or reduce your expenses. For example, if you can get overtime at, say, $20 an hour, you'll need 100 overtime hours in the next 18 months, or 5.55 hours a month. On the expense side, you're looking to redirect $5.13 per workday ($2,000 ÷ 390 days) or $3.65 per day ($2,000 ÷ 548 days). Maybe your trip really is as easy as passing up that coffee and doughnut on your way to work!

With some longer-term plans, it's fair to apply income that you're pretty sure will show up but hasn't yet. Say you expect a 4 percent raise in six months. You may want to count that raise in your figuring.

Building an emergency fund

As one of your major long-term goals, you should have between 6 and 12 months of living expenses in an unallocated emergency account for unforeseen financial emergencies. A number that big can seem impossible to achieve. But remember: You only need to cover *expenses*. You don't have to replace your entire annual salary, just the expenses you'd have during, say, a lengthy period when you may not be working. Thanks to your spending plan, you know what your expenses are, so the number is a real one.

Some people used to say that a home equity line of credit was as good as an emergency savings fund. They've learned otherwise. Using credit to cover an emergency can leave you much worse off if the emergency (such as a layoff) lasts longer than your credit does. Use up your savings and you're back to square one. Use up your savings and all your credit, and you're at the bottom of a deep hole.

To start, shoot for something — even one month or one *week* of expenses. All you need to do is start building today. Having one week of expenses saved can be a world of difference from having none. Two weeks is divine. And a month — you're ahead of most people. So relax, start small, and keep at it.

Put aside money for emergencies while you're saving for other things. But if you're saving for three things at once, won't it take three times as long? No! Because you'll be more likely to stick with a savings plan if you're saving for three things at once and at least two of them are things that have a personal payoff to you — like a vacation. When you have emergency cash socked away, turn the money that would have gone into savings toward achieving one of your other planned goals.

I mention this strategy earlier, but it bears repeating: Automate your savings plan. Arrange to automatically deposit part of your pay into different savings, checking, or investment accounts. If you never see the money in your paycheck, you won't miss it. As you get raises or bonuses, put at least half into your savings account. Tax refunds get the same treatment. Make it easy and automatic, and your savings will grow faster than you can imagine.

Step 4: Managing your credit to improve your spending plan

Credit and the loans made possible by credit have a place in your plan. Credit is a tool to be used — as long as the tool fits the job. In fact, credit can make things easier. It can enable you to defer a payment to a more convenient time or to make a payment in such a way that it benefits you more than paying cash does. However, you should use credit cards only for spending money you already have or know you'll have soon.

I'm talking about consumer credit here. A number of different incarnations of consumer credit exist, and you can use each type to your advantage:

- **Noninstallment credit:** This is the type of credit I grew up with. My dad had a charge account at the local gas station. I gassed up the family car, and he stopped by the station and paid the bill in full at the end of the month. With noninstallment credit, you pay the entire balance each month. This type of credit is used by some retail stores, membership clubs, and the like. It is credit in its simplest form, available as a convenience to you — and a benefit to the merchant. You're not deterred from spending simply because you don't have the cash in your pocket. You get what you want, the merchant makes a sale, and everybody's happy — which is the essence of using credit properly.

You can use this type of credit to handle expenses for local services like trash removal, gardening, or lawn care. An extra benefit is that you get the service first, so if it's faulty, the provider is more likely to fix it.

✔ **Installment, closed-end credit:** Frequently used by department and furniture stores, this type of credit involves loaning an amount equal to the amount of a specific purchase to you for repayment in installments.

Here's an example of how you can use this type of credit: You buy a new bedroom set at a local furniture store, and the store offers you installment credit, giving you 12 months to pay in full. Normally, interest is associated with this type of loan, but the McKay boys were having a special sale — no payments for six months, and no interest for the next six. A sweet deal from your perspective, and a sweet sale from theirs.

If you use this type of credit, make sure that you pay off the entire amount before the end date, or you may be charged a high rate of interest starting from the original date of purchase.

✔ **Revolving, open-end credit:** This is how most credit cards work. You're granted an amount of credit — with a limit, say, of $5,000 — to use any way you want. You choose how much of the limit to use at any point in time. As you use the card, you must make payments on time and for the amount agreed. As you make payments, the amount that goes to principal recharges the line. You can pay off the entire amount, which restores the credit line to its original and full amount, or you can just pay what your spending plan will allow — or even make only the minimum payment. You get to decide.

An example of using this type of credit is to spread the cost of airline tickets. You need to have a set time frame for paying off the purchase (preferably 90 days or fewer) and make sure that the needed monthly amount is available in your spending plan before making the purchase. Don't forget to include the interest charged for carrying a balance when you come up with your monthly payment amount.

You're supposed to *benefit* from the use of credit, not get taken advantage of. Use credit cards as tools when they fit short-term needs and you can pay them off quickly and with certainty. Remember that bedroom set? You could have used a credit card to finance it, but you would have paid 18 percent interest, and you'd have had to make payments right away. The installment, closed-end type of credit clearly fits the job better.

Step 5: Looking at your insurance options

Insurance is dull — until you need it! It is, however, an essential part of planning for your future. A catastrophic illness, an accident, or a loss of property can crush the best-conceived plans. I don't advocate insurance for every little thing that comes up. The amount of insurance you buy is a personal decision. To a degree, it depends on your resources and willingness to absorb the cost of lower-level exposures in your life, such as car insurance deductibles.

But you should be concerned about the major life events that can dramatically affect your finances at all stages of your life — from the death of a spouse, to a major medical disability that prevents a wage-earner from working, to being responsible for a serious car accident.

Here are a few critical coverage areas to consider as you pull together your plan:

- ✔ **Life insurance:** If someone will miss your income if you die, you need life insurance. *Term life insurance* covers you for a specified time frame, but you can usually renew it at an increasing cost as you age. It has no cash or investment value — your beneficiary gets paid only if you die. Make sure that you have enough coverage to bridge the shortfall that your death would cause to the household budget. And, of course, you want to have appropriate coverage on your partner as well. ***Note:*** A good credit rating can reduce your life insurance costs (see Chapter 14).

- ✔ **Disability insurance:** If you're unable to work for a period of time, disability insurance helps cover your expenses. It's available to cover both long-term and short-term problems. Be good to yourself and your loved ones, and be sure that you get this insurance.

- ✔ **Homeowners insurance:** Your home is one of your biggest assets and one of your biggest liabilities. As an asset, you'd have a tough time replacing it if an uninsured event took away part or all of your home. Keep up with building-code changes that affect your replacement costs, and add insurance to cover the unlikely stuff. If it happens, you'll be glad you did. Examples of the types of insurance you should have include flood insurance, earthquake insurance, and umbrella coverage on top of your limits (to insure you for personal and medical liability if someone falls down your front steps and you become the long-term disability insurer by default). Be sure to deduct the value of your lot from the insured value.

I favor high limits and as high a deductible as you are comfortable with. The best use of insurance is not to reimburse you for everything that may go wrong — just the big things that you can't handle on your own. So if you can handle a $1,500 or even a $3,000 surprise using your emergency fund, you'll eventually save enough in lower premiums to cover the deductible. After that, you get to keep it all.

✔ **Car insurance:** Insuring yourself against being sued for running into or over someone, medical payments, and uninsured motorists is actually more important than having coverage to replace or repair your damaged vehicle. Many states require certain levels of insurance to drive. Your insurance agent can help you choose a policy that meets your needs. *Note:* In a number of states, bad credit can increase your auto premiums.

For much more information on insurance policies, check out *Insurance For Dummies* by Jack Hungelmann (Wiley).

Step 6: Planning for the IRS

Okay, I understand that planning for the IRS may be like planning for the dentist, but pretax flossing and brushing make this unpleasant subject a lot easier to swallow. Without getting into Novocain-like numbing details, you're better off if you look at this issue as an important component of your spending plan. Why? Because if you owe tax money, if you're counting on your tax refund to fill out your budget, or if you're considering bankruptcy, then drilling down into this subject can save you from a financial toothache.

Typically, you pick a number of deductions and your employer withholds money from your paycheck and sends it to the IRS. The deductions reflect an *estimate* of what you'll owe, but most people end up either owing too much to the government on April 15 or getting too large a tax refund.

Not all income is subject to withholding. Among the exceptions are dividends, interest, income from side businesses or hobbies, tips, investment gains, gambling winnings, money paid to you as an independent contractor, small-business income, forgiven debts, rents, and gifts above a certain dollar amount. But that doesn't mean you don't have to pay taxes on that income! Know what you owe, and prepare yourself for that inevitability.

As you do your planning, you can choose one of three approaches to what I very generally call Goldilocks tax planning:

- ✔ Overpay

- ✔ Underpay

- ✔ Strive to pay just the right amount

You can probably guess which strategy is the right one, but just in case, I cover them all in the following sections.

Overpaying your withholdings

Many people tell me, "I don't want to owe any money," or, "I use my refund to pay down my credit cards after holiday shopping," so they deliberately overpay their taxes as a budget-balancing/forced-saving strategy. But overpaying is too hard on your budget. At a minimum, you're giving the IRS an interest-free loan that you could be using to pay down your debt, build up savings, or achieve any of a zillion other good purposes. If you've overpaid all year and an emergency comes along in November, you can't ask the government for an advance of your refund to cover it. But you could use that money if you had it in a savings account, or even under your mattress.

If you're consistently getting a refund check, go over your situation with a qualified tax preparer. You can likely find a better way not to owe on April 15 without overpaying every pay period.

Underpaying your withholdings

A too-soft approach to taxes ends with a nasty surprise. If you under-withhold and owe a big tax bill in April, you may find your credit cards absorbing even more unplanned expenses, including tax penalties, interest, and a fat convenience fee. Ouch! Plus, your cards may well be full already.

Most local, state, and federal taxes usually can't be discharged in a bankruptcy, nor can credit card debt incurred from paying your taxes.

Paying just what you owe

Oh, this feels just right! Adjusting your withholdings so you either give a little or get a little is not as difficult as it may seem.

You may be surprised to discover that you can have more deductions than you have people in your household. It's true. I don't recommend adding the cat as a dependent, but a deductible mortgage payment can count as one or two additional deductions. I suggest that you consult with a tax preparer to get a good forecast of your tax commitments for the year. You may get an early budget bonus if you find that you're over-withholding and can decrease your deductions, which may enable you to fund some of those short-term goals you've been saving for.

On the other hand, if some nasty bears are in your future, you're much better off knowing about them in advance so that you can be prepared and not be caught asleep when they come in the front door.

The right amount isn't a precise number. Until all the figures are in, there's no way to know exactly what you'll owe. I suggest that you pad your estimates of what you'll owe in April by $600 to $1,000. An amount of $50 to $80 a month won't make a big difference to your monthly budget, and as long as your income is relatively stable and your deductions from last year haven't changed a lot, tax time may be a walk in the woods.

Step 7: Planning for retirement

Unless you're one of those people who can't imagine not working, planning for retirement is important stuff. In fact, even if you can't imagine it, pay attention, because the choice of staying or leaving may not be up to you. Health issues, economic contractions, and more can influence when you leave your job. If you're like me, you can't wait!

I suggest that you find either a Certified Financial Planner (CFP), a Chartered Financial Consultant (ChFC), or, if you're in the heavy-duty-investment end of things, a Chartered Financial Analyst (CFA) to help you develop a plan that meets your retirement goals. The spending plan and goals you have developed will make you look like a star when you walk into a planner's office. If you tend to be more of a do-it-yourselfer, you can find good resources to get you started on this topic at both Charles Schwab (www.schwab.com) and Fidelity (www.fidelity.com).

Whether you're doing your planning face to face or over the Internet, you're better off if you have an idea of what you need to save to fund your retirement plans. Here are some simple tips as you look into the near or distant future:

✔ **Estimate your life expectancy.** Chances are it's longer than that of your parents. Just don't guess too conservatively. The Centers for Disease Control (CDC) estimates between ages 78 and 80. You can also find some fun web calculators that can help you with an estimate. I tried www.livingto100.com as an example. If you, like me, weren't born yesterday and are still in reasonably good health, you are looking at more than that. Check out the good news at www.cdc.gov/nchs/fastats/lifexpec.htm.

✔ **Pick the right retirement date.** The difference between the age at which you want to retire and your last birthday is the time period you need to budget for.

✔ **Consider inflation.** After you have a number that you think you'll be comfortable living on in retirement, be sure to increase that number for future inflation — the further out your retirement, the happier you'll be if you increase it. A number of good websites and financial planning programs adjust for inflation and investment experience (how much your investments will earn).

✔ **Don't underestimate medical expenses.** The good news is that you've got years to go. The not-so-good news is that medical expenses can be a big part of your future. No one knows for sure how the government's actions to reduce medical costs will work out, so it pays to do some preparing on your own by budgeting for medical expenses and insurance coverage in your retirement planning.

✔ **Remember that time is still money.** If you end up with too little money and too much retirement, I recommend three courses of action: Save more for the same amount of time, save the same for longer, or spend less in your retirement budget. You can increase your current savings by earning more or spending less today. You can just keep pushing out the retirement date until the surplus you've accumulated or an increased retirement benefit makes your numbers work. Or you can do with less later. The choice is up to you.

Compounding interest: Investing for the future

One of the key components of successfully budgeting for your future is having your savings earn as much as possible for your future needs. You've seen the charts loudly proclaiming that if you had only saved XX dollars a year from the time you were 10 years old, you'd have a zillion dollars when you retired.

Well, behind all the smoke and mirrors is a grain of truth. Prudent investing is an important tool. However, you have the right to feel comfortable with the process. If you haven't started, it's never too late. Check out some of the resources in this chapter and start at your own speed and with your own goals in mind.

Whether you do it yourself or use a paid professional doesn't matter. The compounding of interest and tax advantages available today from some types of investments makes investing too great an opportunity to miss.

Using Cool Tools to Help You Build and Stick to a Spending Plan

With computers and smart phones, tools to help you develop — and stick to — a spending plan fill the shelves of most office-supply stores.

Not all budgeting tools have to be electronic to be cool or even useful. If you want a less technologically based approach to budgeting, here are some suggested tools to add to your budgeting kit:

- **Pencil:** Lead, not ink, is the tool to use when developing a plan that you'll be adjusting throughout the process.

- **Sticky notes:** An easy way to supplement your planning ideas, sticky notes can be moved to different places on a planning board or document as you make changes.

- **Envelopes:** They're handy for keeping money to be spent or receipts for what was spent, by category. Consider using one envelope for tax-deductible receipts, for example. Filing by expense categories or pay periods can be helpful.

- **Accordion files:** They work similarly to envelopes, but they're more portable — and you're less likely to misplace them.

This section takes a closer look at different tools you can use when keeping good records.

Web-based financial calculators

Web-based financial calculators are cool tools to help you figure out where you stand and what it will take to get you where you want to be. They're great at helping you manage your money because they give you the information you need to make informed choices about what a course of action or purchase will actually cost you and for how long.

You can find calculators to figure out your mortgage payments at different interest rates, calculators to tell you the true cost of a loan and its impact on your budget, and even calculators that tell you how much you need to budget for how long to pay off those credit cards.

If you need a web-based calculator, check out the following:

- ✔ `www.choosetosave.org`: A nonprofit clearinghouse, this site has a large number of calculators from many different sources, such as the investment regulators at the Financial Industry Regulatory Authority and the American Institute of CPAs.

- ✔ `www.myfico.com`: Fair Isaac, or FICO, developed the original (FICO) credit score. This website has excellent tools for determining the effects that different credit scores have on loan interest rates and the total costs to you.

- ✔ `www.bankrate.com`: Bankrate.com is a trusted financial resource and megasite that has general calculators for many financial functions. Plus, it's the home of yours truly, the Debt Adviser, at `www.bankrate.com/brm/archive_debtadviser.asp`.

Budgeting websites

You can find easy-to-use, basic budgeting and spending advice and tools online. The following are a few of my favorites:

- ✔ `www.sharpentoday.com`: A three-step approach from the National Foundation for Credit Counseling. You can get live help if you like.

- ✔ `www.daveramsey.com/tools/budget-forms/`: Not only does Dave look like me when I had a beard, but his site offers both online and paper budgeting help.

- ✔ `www.moaa.org/calculators/`: This is a good site for all military personnel, officers or not. The Military Officers Association of America (MOAA) is the United States' largest veterans organization for active-duty, National Guard, Reserve, former, and retired military officers and their surviving spouses. It even has an office in the Pentagon! Although the MOAA focuses a fair amount of its efforts on lobbying, its financial calculators impress me.

Smart-phone apps

Every smart phone has a zillion different apps that you can download (some for a price) that can jazz up your spending planning. Apps are so numerous and new ones are coming on the scene so quickly that I suggest you do a search for your phone's financial apps when you're ready to go. User reviews are readily available.

Spending plan assistance

There's no shortage of places you can go to get free help building a spending plan that works for you. But beware of scammers who promise help and just help themselves. Here are two great nonprofit associations whose members can help for free:

- ✔ **The National Foundation for Credit Counseling (www.debtadvice. org)** has good advice and referrals along with a high-level budgeting calculator that plots your spending, based on income, against national averages to let you know whether you're in the ballpark of your peers. Its member-agency network offers budgeting assistance as well as debt management solutions.

- ✔ **The Association of Independent Consumer Credit Counseling Agencies (www.aiccca.org)** has a listing of member agencies, many of which can help you with budgeting issues, but all of which have debt management products.

Adjusting Your Priorities and Your Plan

Depending on your stage of life, your primary budget needs vary. The basic tools of planning your spending remain the same, but the emphasis of your plan shifts as you move to each new stage:

- ✔ **In your first job:** Chances are you have big ideas and little money. At this stage, just establishing good habits, such as developing a spending plan and beginning a small savings program, is most important. Be sure to keep current on student loan payments, or get deferrals if needed.

- ✔ **As a couple:** Your focus may be paying off old debts, finding out how to communicate about money, agreeing on financial goals and a spending plan, establishing joint and separate credit and savings accounts, setting up a household account, and preparing for a family.

- ✔ **With a growing family:** Adjusting to a stay-at-home spouse or childcare expenses, paying for your kids' sports programs and braces, expanding living expenses, and saving for education and weddings are just some of the issues a family with children faces.

- ✔ **Going solo:** Whether you never marry or you go through a split, you're likely to confront situations such as adjusting to living and saving on one income, taking care of children solo, and perhaps paying off divorce expenses and dealing with alimony and child support.

✔ **In an empty nest:** As the kids fly the coop, it's time to confirm your vision for the future and recast your budget for a new lifestyle. This may include enjoying retirement, exploring estate planning, considering Social Security and Medicare issues, and having some fun with your savings.

Credit and financial challenges await you at different times and under differing circumstances. You'll be so much better prepared to weather any turmoil the future may bring and to take advantage of opportunities if you have a plan that enables you to know where your money is going and how to maximize your savings. As your priorities change, a dust-off of your goals, income, and expenses offers all you need to make successful adjustments. A good rule is to revisit your plan whenever one of life's big events occurs.

Chapter 19

Knowing Your Rights to Protect Your Credit

*Y*ou've heard it more than once: "I'm never going to use credit again." Whether this statement comes from a perception that credit grantors, bankers, or Wall Street tycoons have fixed the game in their favor or you've been burned with loans that never should have been made, the truth is that you'll continue to have to deal with credit in one form or another for the rest of your life.

Because credit is used for so much more than lending and fine print matters, you need to understand what protections you have to help level the playing field. You need to be prepared when dealing with multibillion-dollar organizations that have proven difficult to deal with after a transaction is closed or even less than fully reliable as a long-term partner. Maybe the financial services industry has changed. But until you know how it may have changed, speak softly and carry a big stick. Where do you find that big stick? Right here in this chapter. I explain your protections and what you have a right to expect from lenders, credit reporters, and collectors just in case they forget.

Why You Have the Right to Credit Protections

Americans value fair play. Many were told growing up that good guys never start a fight, that the hero shoots only in self-defense and only after the bad guy shoots first, and that lenders don't lend money to just anyone or lend more than you can possibly afford to repay. Whether you agree that the first two are still part of our culture, most people who've lived through the last recession agree that no one fully trusts a lender to be conservative, to offer only loans that people can afford, or to fully disclose all the terms of a deal.

What caused this big change in lending? I could tell you that it was greed, pure and simple, but the situation was more complex than that. In a few words, these lending changes resulted from the decoupling of the ability to make money from being held responsible for results. Lenders were able to originate (make) a loan, earn a commission on it, and then turn around and package and resell the loan (and the risks of default) to someone thousands of miles away. So if your bank can give you a mortgage, package it with others in a security, and sell it on Wall Street to a hedge fund, and that fund sells your mortgage to investors in China, I think you'll agree that you need more protections than you might if your local credit union owned the mortgage on your home! Millions of Americans have been frustrated by credit decisions made in the 2001-to-2007 boom that preceded the recession that began at the end of 2007. That frustration filtered down to Washington and resulted in new regulations and an extension of consumer protections.

The Credit Card Accountability, Responsibility, and Disclosure (CARD) Act of 2009 was designed to curb lending practices that many people perceived as unfair and unfriendly to consumers. If that wasn't enough, and it wasn't, the CARD Act was followed by the Dodd-Frank Wall Street Reform and Consumer Protection Act, which established the Consumer Financial Protection Bureau (CFPB). This bureau regulates a wide range of financial products and services, including credit counseling, payday loans, mortgages, credit cards, and other bank products. The Fair Access to Credit Scores Act piggybacked on Dodd-Frank and allows you free access to your credit score in the case of an *adverse action* (denial of insurance or utilities, for example). These new pieces of legislation join older consumer protection laws such as the Fair Credit Reporting Act (FCRA).

Table 19-1 gives you an at-a-glance look at the best and most important consumer protection laws and what they cover. I provide details on most of them in this chapter.

Table 19-1	Consumer Protection Laws
Law	*Main Areas Covered*
CARD Act	Credit cards
Dodd-Frank Act	Wall Street regulation, consumer protection
FACT Act	Identity theft
Fair Access to Credit Scores Act	Adverse actions, credit scores
Fair Credit Reporting Act	Credit reporting
Fair Debt Collection Practices Act	Debt collection

The CARD Act: Shielding You from Credit Card Abuse

The Credit Card Accountability, Responsibility, and Disclosure (CARD) Act of 2009 focuses on your protections from credit card industry practices that have been deemed to be either unfair or just plain tricky. Among the key protections are easier-to-understand terms, fewer retroactive interest rate increases on existing card balances, more time to pay your monthly bills, more notice of changes to your credit card terms, and the right to opt out of many changes in terms on your accounts.

Here's a list of the top protections that consumers are due:

- **No more bait and switch:** Card issuers can't hike interest rates on existing balances except under certain conditions. Consequently, interest rates on new card charges can't change in the first year, major terms of the agreement can't change overnight, and you get 45 days' advance notice of any big changes.

- **No more universal default gotcha:** You may have heard of people having their rates raised on one card when they have a problem with another one (known as *universal default*). This practice has been severely curtailed. (See Chapter 21 for details.) Card issuers may use universal default only on future credit card balances that exist at the time of the default, and they must give you at least 45 days' notice of the change. You now have time to change cards, get other financing, or pay off the balance.

✔ **Limits on interest rate increases:** Card issuers may raise your interest rate on existing balances only if

  • The rate was part of a promotional period that ended.

  • The index used to set your variable interest rate rises.

  • You're at the end of a hardship or special payment agreement.

  • You have late payments of 60 days or more.

✔ **Credit-granting restrictions for young adults:** Creditors can't give credit cards to kids with no income. People under 21 must show that they have enough income to repay the card debt or have a cosigner who does. What a concept! Additionally, credit card companies must stay at least 1,000 feet away from colleges if they offer free pizza or other gifts to entice students to apply for credit cards.

Avoid cosigning like the plague. In addition to high rates of default, missing a payment for any reason hurts your credit as well as your relationship. Rather than cosigning, make the kid(s) an authorized user on your account or get the student a debit card.

✔ **Graceful grace periods:** Card issuers must give you "a reasonable amount of time" (at least 21 days after the bill is mailed) to pay monthly bills. More time to get your payment in should result in fewer late fees.

✔ **No tricky due dates or times:** Card issuers can no longer set early-morning deadlines (before the mail is delivered) for payments. Cutoff times must be 5 p.m. or later on the date due, and due dates can't be on a weekend, a holiday, or a day when the card issuer is closed for business.

✔ **Payments must be applied fairly:** If you owe money at different rates on the same card (many cards have different rates for regular purchases versus cash advances and balance transfers), payments over the minimum due must go to the balance with the highest interest rate first. Consequently, your payment will reduce more of your balance faster.

✔ **Easy on the over-limit fees:** Card issuers can't charge you over-limit fees without your permission. If you opt out, or say no, transactions exceeding your credit limit are rejected. This is good news for controlling over-limit fees. Plus, if you opt in, no fees can be larger than the amount of the overage. For example, going $10 over your limit can't incur a fee of $39; the limit is $10.

✔ **No double-dealing double-cycle billing:** Interest on outstanding balances must end in the billing month in which you pay off the balance. For example, your statement runs from June 1 to June 30, but the payment is due on July 20. The interest from June 30 to the payment due date of July 20 can no longer be charged if you pay off the balance in full, even though the card issuer didn't get your payment until July 20.

✔ **Disclosing minimum payment impact:** Card issuers must indicate how long paying off the entire balance will take if you make only the minimum monthly payment. They must also indicate how much you need to pay each month to pay off a balance in 36 months, including interest. Seeing the high cost of minimum payments enables you to make better-informed decisions about how you pay for the use of credit.

✔ **Restricted late fees:** Late fees are limited to $25 unless you're late more than once in a six-month period. Your late payment is not reported to the credit bureau until your account is a full 30 days past due. This restriction results in fewer and lower fees charged to your account and less credit report damage.

✔ **Right to opt out of changes:** Card issuers must give you advance notice of changes to the terms of use for your credit cards. Therefore, you now have the right to reject many significant changes in terms to your credit card accounts.

If you opt out of some changes, you may be required to close your account and pay off any balance under the old conditions.

Although the CARD Act provides a lot of consumer protections, it's not all-encompassing. It doesn't cover business and corporate accounts or interest rates on future purchases. Cards with variable or floating interest rates (which includes most cards) are subject to interest rate increases as the prime rate goes up. And a card issuer can still close your account or lower your limit without warning.

If you believe that a card issuer has violated any of the provisions of the CARD Act, contact customer service and ask for an explanation or a rebate. If you disagree with the answer, you can contact the Federal Trade Commission (www.ftc.gov), your state's attorney general or consumer protection department, or the Consumer Financial Protection Bureau's Consumer Response Center (www.consumerfinance.gov/complaint/).

For the full text of the CARD Act, go to www.dummies.com/extras/creditrepair.

The Consumer Financial Protection Bureau: Your BFF (Best Financial Friend)

The Consumer Financial Protection Bureau (CFPB) was created by the Dodd-Frank Wall Street Reform and Consumer Protection Act. It's a new and powerful executive agency that has a substantial budget and broad consumer protection powers. The CFPB has the power to regulate a wide range of financial products and services, from smaller players like credit counseling agencies and payday lenders to big guys like mortgage originators, underwriters, and servicers; credit card issuers; and various bank products. The CFPB is vested with exclusive rulemaking authority over all federal consumer financial law. This authority extends to new rules to prohibit unfair, deceptive, or abusive acts, practices, and disclosures for financial products and services.

So who's protected by the CFPB? You, that's who! The CFPB is dedicated to making sure that consumers are treated fairly and are protected when dealing with the U.S. financial system. Through the use of strict regulations, the CFPB seeks to protect you from any person or organization that offers or provides a consumer financial product or service for personal, family, or household purposes. It also has specific authority to crack down on a person or company identified as being unlawful, unfair, deceptive, or abusive to any consumer financial product or service transaction.

Think of the CFPB as a tough but consumer-friendly cop on the financial product and services beat that aims to level the playing field so that you know what you're buying. See Chapter 21 for details on the work the CFPB is doing that may affect you in today's financial marketplace.

Safeguarding Your Credit Data through the FACT Act

The Fair Credit Reporting Act (FCRA) and its update, the Fair and Accurate Credit Transactions Act (the FACT Act or FACTA), were put in place to ensure that anytime your record of credit use is reported to a credit bureau, the record is accurate, timely, fair, and private. The FACT Act applies not just the three big bureaus (Equifax, Experian, and TransUnion), but also to a large number of specialty consumer-reporting agencies (see Chapter 14). Some agencies accumulate and sell information about your check-writing history, medical records, and rental history.

So what are your rights and protections? Here's a summary of the biggies. For the full story, check out the FACT Act at www.dummies.com/extras/creditrepair.

> ✔ **You must be notified if anyone takes a negative action based on your credit report.** Anyone using a credit report or specialty-bureau consumer report to deny your application for credit, insurance, or employment — or to take any adverse action against you — must tell you so and give you access to the information by telling you how you can get a free copy of the report used to make the decision.

✔ **You have the right to know what's in your file.** You can get a copy of all the information about you in the files of a consumer-reporting agency.

✔ **You can get a free copy of each of your reports annually at www. annualcreditreport.com.** Reviewing your credit reports every 12 months is just what the doctor ordered for good credit health.

Beware of imposter websites! When you order your free annual credit reports online, be sure to type in www.annualcreditreport.com to avoid being misdirected to other websites that offer supposedly free reports but only with the purchase of other products and services, such as credit monitoring. Also, be aware that while you're on the authorized free site, you'll be offered additional products or services for a price. You're not required to make a purchase to receive your free annual credit reports.

✔ **You can get an extra free copy of your credit report if an adverse action has been taken against you because of information it contains.** For example, if you're the victim of identity theft or if your file contains inaccurate information as a result of fraud, you're entitled to a free report. You can also get a free copy if you're on public assistance or if you're unemployed but expect to apply for employment within 60 days. See Chapter 14 for details.

✔ **You have the right to know your credit score.** Believe it or not, this didn't used to be the case. Your score was kept secret from you, but not from your creditors! Well, that's changed, and now you have the right to get your score from consumer-reporting agencies, but chances are you'll have to pay for it. (See Chapter 14 for more info.)

✔ **You have the right to dispute incomplete, out-of-date, or inaccurate credit information and have it removed from your reports.** After you report an issue to the consumer-reporting agency, the agency has to investigate (they say *reinvestigate*). Unless your dispute is frivolous, the agency must correct or delete the erroneous information, usually within 30 days.

✔ **You have the right to limit access to your file to only those who have a legitimate business purpose for requesting it.** A consumer-reporting agency may sell information in your file only to people with a valid use, called a *permissible purpose* — usually to consider an application with a creditor, insurer, employer, landlord, or other business purpose. You must give your approval for anyone to access your information, and you can limit access to your information for unsolicited prescreened offers for credit and insurance.

You can opt out of such preapproved credit offers with the nationwide credit bureaus at 888-5-OPTOUT (888-567-8688).

✔ **You have the right to collect damages for violations of your rights under the FACT Act.** If a credit-reporting agency or user or furnisher of information violates the FACT Act, you can sue the party in state or federal court.

✔ **You have additional rights if you're an identity theft victim or an active-duty military service person.** For example, you can appoint a personal representative to handle your affairs while you're deployed outside the U.S. Additionally, you may place an active-duty alert on your file, which requires creditors to exercise greater caution and verify your identity before making credit decisions. For more info, see Chapter 20.

Although the FACT Act is a federal law and is enforced by the FTC and the CFPB, states may also enforce the law, and some states have their own consumer-reporting laws. You may have additional rights under your state's laws. To find out what applies in your state, contact your state or local consumer protection agency or your state attorney general. Explain your concerns and ask what your rights are and how you can get help. Be sure to record names, dates, and actions in case you need to follow up.

The FDCPA: Providing Protection Against Debt Collectors

What do you do when a debt collector sends you a letter or calls to say how much he or she misses your payment? Whether you're feeling helpless or angry, knowing the rules that apply is important — specifically, what collectors really can and can't do. The Fair Debt Collection Practices Act (FDCPA) is the key piece of legislation that regulates debt collectors. It prohibits debt collectors — meaning collection agencies, lawyers who collect debts, and companies that buy delinquent debts and try to collect them — from using abusive, unfair, or deceptive practices to attempt to collect from you. This section gets you better acquainted with the FDCPA.

The FDCPA covers most personal, family, and household debts, such as personal credit card accounts, car loans, medical bills, and mortgages. Notably, it doesn't cover debts incurred in running a business.

Controlling the contacts

A collector may contact you at a reasonable time, such as after 8 a.m. or before 9 at night. If these times don't work, you get to define what a reasonable time is. But you must allow collectors to do their job, so you can't be too restrictive. A collector also may not contact you at work if you tell the collector (orally or in writing) that you're not allowed to get calls there.

Be sure to follow up any conversations or agreements in writing as soon as possible. Doing so documents what you and the collector have agreed to and helps eliminate miscommunications in a stressful environment.

Got an attorney? Let the collector know. After you do, the collector must contact the attorney and only the attorney, rather than you or anyone else. If you don't have an attorney, a collector has the right to contact others to get your address, home phone number, and place of employment. However, collectors can't tell anyone else why they're calling or that they're debt collectors.

Finding out about the debt

You have the right to receive a validation notice from the collector within five days of contact that tells you how much money you owe. The notice must include the name of the creditor to whom the collector claims you owe the money and procedures to follow if you don't think you owe the money.

If you don't owe the money or an error has been made, send the debt collector a letter (certified mail with a return receipt) within 30 days of receiving the validation notice and state that you're disputing the debt. If you're not 100 percent sure whether you owe the money, ask for verification of the debt. The good news is that, until the debt is verified, the law prohibits further collector contacts.

Collectors can begin contacting you again after they send you written verification of the debt, like a copy of a bill for the amount you owe.

Stopping a collector from contacting you

When a collector first contacts you about a debt, it usually comes as a surprise. If you decide after being contacted by the collector that you don't want to hear from the collector again, you have the right to tell the collector (in writing) to stop contacting you. Here's how.

Send an original copy of your demand by certified mail, and pay for a return receipt so you can document that the collection company received it. Keep copies of everything you send or receive. After the collector receives your letter, the collector may not contact you again. Well, there are two exceptions: The collector may contact you to tell you that no further contact will occur. I know, it sounds silly, but that's the law. Second, the collector may let you know that the collector or the creditor intends to take a specific action as a result of your ending the conversation, such as filing a lawsuit, but only if it actually intends to do so. No idle threats are allowed. For example, if you owe a debt to a hospital, it may hire a collection agency to collect the debt. If the collector knows that the hospital's policy is not to sue a former patient, then the collector can't threaten to sue.

Sending a letter to a debt collector stopping all contact doesn't get rid of the debt, but it should stop the collector from contacting you. The creditor or the debt collector still can, and often will, sue you to collect the debt.

Spotting prohibited behavior

Debt collectors aren't allowed to get away with certain behaviors. Here are some highlights, or lowlights, of what a collector may not do:

- ✔ **Harass or threaten you:** Debt collectors may not harass, oppress, or abuse you or any third parties they contact. They may not threaten violence or harm, publish your name as someone who refuses to pay your debts (but they can report you to a credit bureau), use obscene or profane language, or repeatedly call to annoy you.

- ✔ **Lie to you:** Like Pinocchio, debt collectors who lie get in trouble. Their noses may not grow, but they can be sued if they pretend to be attorneys, government representatives, or employees of a credit bureau. They also get in trouble if they claim that you've committed a crime or lie about the amount you owe. They also can't pretend that the papers they send you are legal forms if they aren't or indicate that the papers they send you aren't legal forms if they are.

- ✔ **Be unfair:** Collectors may not engage in unfair practices. So what's not fair play? Trying to collect more than what's due unless the contract that created your debt — or your state law — allows an additional charge; depositing a post-dated check early; or contacting you by postcard to embarrass you with the mail carrier or your family. That's really not fair!

If a collector violates any of the provisions of the FDCPA, contact your local consumer protection agency, your state's attorney general, or your lawyer. The first two public resources should be able to stop the abusive or unfair behavior with a phone call or letter. Your attorney may also file suit for damages against the collector/collection agency.

Suing a collector

You (hopefully your attorney and not actually you) can sue a collector in a state or federal court within one year if the collector violates the law. If you win, you can win big. You can be awarded any damages you can prove resulted from the illegal collection practices, like lost wages and medical bills. You also can be reimbursed for your attorney's fees and court costs.

If a debt collector violates the FDCPA in trying to collect a debt and you win a lawsuit against that collector, the debt doesn't go away if you owe it. Also, if you lose your suit, you may owe more in fees and costs.

Exploring Other Protections

People turn to payday lending and debt settlement when they find traditional financing difficult or even impossible to obtain. These industries weren't tightly regulated before the 2007 recession, but nowadays, protections are available if you know where to look. In this section, I take you on a quick tour of these businesses and the protections you can take advantage of if you decide to use them. I also introduce you to an age-old protection called the statute of limitations that's worth knowing about.

The ins and outs of payday loans

If you think payday loans are small time, think again. There are more than 20,000 payday lending storefronts in the U.S. (In comparison, there are about 14,000 McDonald's restaurants in the U.S.)

Astronomical interest rates, predatory lenders, and unsuspecting people forever in debt: That's generally what comes to mind when people think of payday loans. Well, the reality isn't so simple. A *payday loan* is a short-term cash loan secured by a personal check. Say you need a short-term loan to cover some unexpected expense. You may not have access to credit lines or cards. Your bank won't give you a short-term loan. So you go to your local payday lender. You write a personal check for the amount you want to borrow, plus a fee, and you receive cash. Your check is held for future deposit or electronic access to your bank account, usually on the date of your next payday, hence the term *payday loan* and the short period of the loan (usually one or two weeks). Payday loans charge extremely high fees: Using a not-atypical $17.50 for every $100 borrowed up to a maximum of $300, the interest rates run 911 percent for a one-week loan, 456 percent for a two-week loan, and 212 percent for a one-month loan.

These loans are small in dollars and high in transaction costs. Many banks find them unprofitable and won't make them. The result is the payday loan industry. As expensive as these loans are, they can be less expensive than overdraft charges on your bank account, which are now limited by law but used to be so steep and unfairly applied that payday loans were cheap by comparison.

Payday lenders claim that their loans aren't high-cost if they're used properly. Here's an example of their thinking: You take a taxi for short distances and a plane for long ones. You wouldn't take a taxi from coast to coast, nor would you take a plane to the local grocery store. Just because the taxi's rate per mile is higher than the plane's cost per mile doesn't necessarily mean that the taxi is overcharging for its service. Unless, of course, the taxi takes you from Times Square to Lincoln Center via Los Angeles.

Looking at the rules of payday loans

Lenders are required to quote the cost of a payday loan as both the dollar finance charge and the annual percentage rate (APR). In addition, many states have rules and limits for payday lenders. Find out your state's rules at www.ncsl.org/issues-research/banking/payday-lending-state-statutes.aspx.

Here are the rules for the five largest states:

- **California** allows loans of 31 days of up to $300. Fees allowed are up to 15 percent of the amount loaned. The APR for a $100 loan for 14 days is 459 percent.

- **Florida** allows loans of not less than 7 or more than 31 days of up to $500, exclusive of fees. Fees allowed are up to 10 percent of the loan plus a verification fee. The APR for a 14-day, $100 loan is 419 percent.

- **Illinois** allows loans of 13 to 120 days of up to the lesser of $1,000 or 25 percent of the borrower's gross monthly income. Fees allowed are $15.50 per $100 loaned. The APR for a 14-day, $100 loan is 403 percent.

- **New York** prohibits foreign banking corporations from issuing payday loans. It also has a 25 percent interest rate cap on loans. Payday loans are effectively illegal in New York: It is a violation of state law to make payday loans in person, by telephone, or over the Internet. It is also illegal for a debt collector to collect, or attempt to collect, on a payday loan in New York.

- **Texas** allows loans of 7 to 31 days without limitation. Fees allowed vary according to a chart contained in state legislation. The effective APR for a 14-day, $100 loan is 309 percent.

On the federal level, the Department of Defense provides protections for men and women in the armed forces and their families. Specifically, lenders may not charge more than 36 percent annual interest, including most fees and charges. Instead of payday loans, military personnel may get financial assistance from military aid societies, such as the Army Emergency Relief, Navy and Marine Corps Relief Society, Air Force Aid Society, or Coast Guard Mutual Aid.

If you're in the Navy or the Marine Corps, the Navy and Marine Corps Relief Society will pay off your payday loan if you're having trouble repaying it, and then you can pay back the relief organization on better terms.

Getting help if a lender violates the rules

If you think that a payday loan lender has taken advantage of you, you have a couple places to turn:

✔ **Your state's lender regulation agency:** Regulators may be able to help you work out a payment arrangement with a lender. And if you live in a state that doesn't allow payday lending, the state regulator can take action against a lender. Go to `www.consumerfinance.gov/askcfpb/1637/how-do-i-find-my-states-bank-regulator.html` to find a link that helps you find the right agency.

✔ **The Community Financial Services Association of America (CFSA):** More than half of payday lenders are members of the CFSA, an organization that requires its members to subscribe to a code of conduct that goes beyond state laws. You may complain to the CFSA (`www.cfsa.com`) if you feel you've been treated unfairly or abused. Under its code of conduct, you can request and receive an extended payment plan that allows you to extend your loan for four payday cycles without any additional fees or charges.

Many nonmember payday lenders don't offer payment plans. Their idea of a payment plan is a loan rollover until you collapse under the weight of the fees and cumulative interest charges.

The details of debt settlement

Wouldn't it be nice if you could put your bills under your pillow at night when you go to sleep and the debt fairy would take them away, just like the tooth fairy? That's the premise behind the debt settlement industry. Don't get me wrong: Debt settlers expect you to pay them all that you owe them, but they don't expect you to pay the others to whom you owe money! In a nutshell, debt settlers try to get lenders to settle or accept a lower payment than is due to satisfy a debt. Why would a lender accept less? Because less is better than nothing!

A debt settler generally collects a monthly amount from you, but instead of paying your creditors, it holds onto the payments for at least three to six months, depending on your circumstances and your creditors. Next, it tries to negotiate with your creditors on your behalf to settle the accounts for less than the full balance. Some creditors will negotiate, and others will not. During this lengthy process, nothing is being paid to your creditors, and all the while they use all the remedies they have to collect the debt from you, including judgments and garnishments.

Unless the debt settlement company is able to settle all or most of your debts, the penalties and fees you may incur on the unsettled debts can cost you more than you save. And the settlement process seriously damages your credit whether it's successful or not.

The CFPB and the FTC regulate debt settlement. Debt settlers can't charge fees before actually settling a debt. The FTC's debt settlement rules apply to for-profit debt settlement and credit counseling, debt negotiation companies, and companies that falsely claim to have nonprofit status.

The new rules don't apply to in-person or Internet-only debt settlers, nor do they limit how much you can be charged for a debt settlement service.

Credit counseling agencies may be a viable alternative to debt settlement, plus they are free. See the section "Considering credit counseling" in Chapter 4 for details.

Beware of any company promising to settle your debt if it

- ✓ Charges a fee before settling your debts.
- ✓ Claims that there is a "new government program" to eliminate debts.
- ✓ Guarantees to make your debt go away.
- ✓ Tells you to stop communicating with your creditors.
- ✓ Claims to be able to stop collection calls and legal actions.

Debt settlers must

- ✓ Represent their services accurately.
- ✓ Tell you how long paying off your debt will take, inform you of the conditions under which the settlers will negotiate settlements with creditors, and tell you how much money you must pay before a settlement offer is made.
- ✓ Disclose that debt settlements will trash your credit rating and potentially expose you to lawsuits from creditors.
- ✓ Successfully settle or negotiate at least one of your debts, with at least one payment going to a creditor before you're charged any fees.
- ✓ Provide you with a written contract, debt settlement plan, or oral agreement outlining the payback strategy, as well as details of the potential pitfalls of debt relief services.

A debt settled is a debt forgiven. You may owe taxes on any forgiven portion of debts settled.

If you think that a debt settler has taken advantage of you, you have a couple places to turn. Your state agency that regulates debt settlers may be able to help. Look for the agency in the consumer protection department or the attorney general's office. Also, the CFPB may be able to help. Here's how the CFPB works: Go to its website (www.consumerfinance.gov/complaint/) and enter your complaint. It forwards your complaint to the company and works to get a response, or it forwards your complaint to another government agency if it thinks that agency can better assist you. The company reviews your complaint, communicates with you as needed, and reports back to the CFPB about the steps that have been taken or that will be taken on the issue you identified in your complaint. Then the CFPB lets you know that response and gives feedback. As a bonus, it shares this data with state and federal law enforcement agencies.

You can also contact the Better Business Bureau, but doing so may not be an effective alternative because it relies on cooperation from the debt settler to help you.

The scoop on the statute of limitations

The *statute of limitations (SOL)* provides that you can't be held accountable for past mistakes forever. When I was in third grade, Sister Mary Assunta told me that this exemption didn't apply in her class. But elsewhere, each state has a law restricting the time that legal proceedings may be brought against you to collect a debt. Each state sets a maximum period for a creditor to file a lawsuit, depending on the type of loan or claim. The period varies by state. Federal statutes set the limitations for suits filed in federal courts. If you're not sued before the statutory deadline, the lender loses its right to sue you.

For a list of SOL laws for different states, check out www.nolo.com/legal-encyclopedia/statute-of-limitations-state-laws-chart-29941.html.

Statutes of limitations go way back to early Roman law and were designed to prevent fraudulent and stale (really old) claims from arising after all evidence was lost or after the facts became obscured through the passage of time, defective memory, death, or the disappearance of witnesses.

To use this protection, you must show up before the court and answer the lender's complaint. If you don't, you waive the use of this defense and aren't permitted to use it in any subsequent proceedings.

Here's what you need to keep in mind about the SOL:

✔ If your debt is older than allowed under your state's SOL, you can't be sued in court to collect it.

✔ The SOL has nothing to do with the time a debt stays on your credit report. A debt can be on your credit report for seven years but be uncollectible after a much shorter period.

✔ The SOL begins to run from the day the debt — or payment on an open-ended account — was due and not paid.

✔ The SOL doesn't eliminate your debt after it expires. It keeps you from being sued in court. A collector can still ask you to repay the debt.

✔ Depending on your state's law, making a partial payment may restart the SOL clock and extend the time you may be sued. States that specify that a partial payment doesn't restart the clock, unless there's a new written promise to pay, include Arizona, California, Florida, Iowa, Kansas, Maine, Massachusetts, Michigan, Minnesota, Mississippi, Missouri, Nevada, New York, Texas, Virginia, West Virginia, and Wisconsin.

Chapter 20

Protecting Your Identity

. . . .

In This Chapter

▶ Using technology safely

▶ Keeping your financial documents secure

▶ Watching for signs of identity theft

. . . .

*I*dentity theft doesn't involve someone dressing like you and copying your hairstyle. It's much simpler than that. The thief simply acquires and uses the myriad numbers associated with your name to become you, electronically and financially. But how does an identity thief get this valuable data about you? Often by stealing your mail, hacking into your computer, breaking into your home, or sifting through receipts and personal information found in your trash can.

The most recent Bureau of Justice statistics say that 7 percent of U.S. households — that's 1 in 14, or about 8.6 million households — had at least one member who experienced identity theft. The cost for this theft came in at about $13.3 billion in direct financial losses! Not exactly chump change, and certainly worthy of your attention.

Depending on what information the thief steals from you, he can use your favorite credit card or open new credit card accounts in your name. He can buy a car in your name, rent an apartment and leave you to pay the damages, order furniture, and stay a week at the Ritz in Buenos Aires — all while posing as *you*. And, of course, the thief makes no payments on any of the debts. The negative credit activity is reported on your credit report, and if the thief is lucky — and you aren't — you may not discover him living it up and wrecking your credit rating for months (or longer!). You may discover that your identity has been stolen only when you apply for a line of credit and are rejected, or when you receive a flurry of aggressive calls from collection agencies for not paying bills of which you aren't even aware.

After you discover the ID theft, you do get to defend yourself and prove that the fraudulent accounts aren't yours, but the process can be expensive and may take a long time to resolve. Worse yet, while you're dealing with the mess the thief has made of your finances, you may suffer harassing phone calls and be denied credit or a job because your credit report includes negative information. In this chapter, I tell you the important steps you need to take to protect yourself, your identity, and your credit from identity theft. See Chapter 9 for guidance on repairing the damage if it does occur.

Keeping Thieves at Bay

Your identity may be stolen by a stranger. Then again, as often happens, it may be stolen by someone you know and willingly let into your life, such as a friend, relative, or coworker. To reduce your chances of falling victim to identity theft, make sure that you protect your personal information at home and at work. In short, don't leave financial or confidential documents out in the open where others have easy access to them.

In the following sections, I walk you through some simple steps you can take to reduce the chances of your identity being stolen.

Getting on the technology train

One of the easiest ways to protect yourself is to simplify bill-paying, information transfers, and financial transactions by performing them all securely and electronically. Having bills and statements delivered to your password-protected computer is much safer than having them delivered to your mailbox outside your home. Statistics say that the more information you send and receive electronically, the lower your chances of identity theft.

Using a computer has other benefits as well: When you receive your information online, as in the case of your bank statement, you can check it anytime you want — no need to wait until the end of the month for a statement to arrive. I recommend that you do a quick once-over of your checking account activity weekly or have preset dollar-level alerts e-mailed or texted to you. For example, you can arrange for transactions that exceed $1,000 to generate an e-mail or text automatically. Set your alert level so that it doesn't result in dozens of notices but does catch the transactions you're most concerned about. That way, you can spot a problem early.

Take precautions when conducting business via the web. As long as you use only secure websites and ensure that you're protected by a firewall, you're much better protected than you are with snail mail. (See the next section for info on determining whether a website is secure, and see the section "Safeguarding your computer data" for a few words on firewalls.)

Looking out for phishing scams

Phishing occurs when a stranger pretending to be someone you trust (for example, a Facebook friend, a credit card company, or a representative of your bank) e-mails you and asks you to confirm critical information about your account — for example, by replying with your password or Social Security number. Phishing can also be perpetrated via a spyware program that you unwittingly download to your computer by clicking a link or opening a file; the program then records your personal information and sends it to the thief.

Phishing scams are increasing and becoming more sophisticated. Bottom line: Think twice before replying to unsolicited requests or giving out your personal information over the Internet. As with phone solicitations, don't give out your personal information unless *you* initiate the transaction. You can find out more about preventing Internet fraud, securing your computer, and protecting your personal information by visiting www.onguardonline.gov.

Here are some do's and don'ts that can help keep you and your personal info safe:

- ✔ **Do be suspicious of any e-mail with urgent, exciting, or upsetting requests for personal financial info or money.** The sender is using your emotions to stimulate an immediate, illogical response to the request.

- ✔ **Don't give out personal or financial info unless you're certain of the source and you can confirm that the link is secure.** You can tell that you're on a secure website if the site's address begins with https:// rather than http://.

    E-mail is almost *never* secure, which means that you should never e-mail your credit card number, Social Security number, or other personal info to anyone, even someone you're sure you can trust.

- ✔ **Don't respond to e-mails that aren't personalized or that have your name misspelled.** If the message has your name wrong or doesn't include your name at all, chances are high that it's a fraud.

- ✔ **Don't click links in e-mail messages to find out what the great offer is unless you know you signed up for that service.** If you click the link, you may end up downloading spyware onto your computer, and your security may be compromised.

✔ **Don't unsubscribe to e-mails unless you know that you subscribed in the first place.** Some phishers send you e-mails hoping that you'll respond or unsubscribe, thereby confirming that your e-mail address is valid.

✔ **Do be careful of e-mails pretending to be from companies you do business with.** I periodically get e-mails that look like they're from banks I use, but the e-mails lack the detailed logo or look and feel of the real companies, or they ask me to update information that I know the banks already have.

✔ **If you suspect that you're being phished, do forward the e-mail to the Federal Trade Commission at** spam@uce.gov **and file a complaint with the Internet Crime Complaint Center (IC3) by going to** www.ic3.gov. The IC3 is a partnership among the FBI, the National White Collar Crime Center (NW3C), and the Bureau of Justice Assistance (BJA). The IC3 website not only lets you report suspected Internet fraud but also provides disturbing statistics about this growing crime.

Safeguarding your computer data

You need to safeguard your computer so that it doesn't give up its secrets without a fight. Here are some computer-safety rules to consider:

✔ **Don't leave your laptop, smart phone, or tablet out where it can be picked up.** Whether at home, in a hotel, or at work, when you're not in the same room as your device, put it away out of sight. Would you leave a $100 bill lying around? The same consideration applies here.

✔ **Don't walk away from your computer and leave files with personal information open, particularly if you're online.** If you're offline, anyone in the room can see your information. If you're online, especially with a broadband connection, your computer can be hacked and your data stolen, or you can be observed for sensitive information like passwords.

✔ **Come up with a username and personal identification number (PIN) or password that isn't obvious, and set your computer so that this information is required in order to log on.** You can also use a screensaver that has a password so that if you walk away from your desk for a certain period and the screensaver comes on, you need to enter a password to get back to your desktop.

✔ **Include at least one number, capital letter, or special character in your password as a minimum precaution.** A good example is Steve@1. Don't use birthdates or Social Security numbers; they're too easy for hackers to guess.

✔ **Don't use your kid's or pet's name or birthday as your password.** These things are easy for someone who knows you to guess.

✔ **Don't keep a list of your passwords under your keyboard or near the computer.** That's the equivalent of leaving your house key under the mat.

✔ **Install a firewall.** A *firewall* is a program or device that filters information before it gets to your computer. If you use a wireless network, make sure that the network and firewall are encrypted. (You can get firewalls for your home computer at most office-supply stores.)

✔ **Use antivirus and spyware protection programs to keep key loggers off your computer.** *Key loggers* are programs that send to a crook any information you type while on your computer, including your credit card numbers, usernames, passwords, Social Security number, and so on.

✔ **Make sure to delete all personal information on your computer if you decide to get rid of it.** Your best bet is to reformat your hard drive, which wipes it clean and gets rid of everything. You may want to reformat your drive more than once to do a thorough job of permanently erasing data. (Check with your computer manufacturer to find out how to scrub your hard drive.)

Keeping passwords secret

A testament to the trusting nature of Americans is that if you want to know something personal or secret about them, all you have to do is ask. But you'd be wise to keep your computer password secret because it protects you from others — even trusted coworkers — accessing your personal information. To make sure that you don't get taken advantage of, follow these suggestions:

✔ **Don't give anyone your password.** If the guy in the next cubicle wants to be helpful, you can enter your password for him.

✔ **If you have to give out your password, be sure that you trust the source, and then change your password immediately.** And by immediately, I mean right after you give out your password. Don't wait until the next day or the next week.

Avoid giving confidential information to friends, acquaintances, or even your kids. They may not be identity thieves, but they sure are great, naive sources of information.

Protecting your mail

The fact that tampering with the U.S. mail is a federal crime doesn't seem to deter identity thieves from helping themselves to the contents of people's mailboxes. And your mail often contains sensitive information. For example, although some credit card issuers don't include your full account number on your monthly statement, others still do. And you don't want a thief to have access to your bank account numbers. Unless you write with a Uni-ball Gel Pen, which uses the only type of ink that thieves can't acid-wash, an enterprising identity thief can also easily convert that check you sent off for the heating bill into ready cash by acid-washing the original recipient off the check and replacing the name.

Following are some easy ways to reduce your exposure to mail fraud:

- ✔ **Move as much of your financial business online as you can.** Doing so helps you avoid delivering information to the waiting hands of the criminal scouting your unattended mailbox.

- ✔ **Explore alternatives to your unlocked, end-of-the-driveway mailbox.** Consider using a post office box or a locked mailbox that accepts mail (not unlike the old slot in the door).

- ✔ **Don't mail checks or financial information from your home mailbox.** Use a post office mailbox or bring your mail to work with you. (Don't forget the stamps, or the boss may cancel your work identity.)

- ✔ **Ask your bank to hold new check orders and pick them up at the bank.** Check reorder boxes are easy to spot with a trained eye. You wouldn't send cash through the mail; don't send checks, either.

- ✔ **If you're away for a day or more, have someone pick up your mail or, better yet, have the post office hold it until you return.** Don't let it sit in your mailbox overnight.

Storing financial data in your home

You may believe that your financial information is safe inside the sanctuary of your home, no matter where it's located. Unfortunately, even in your home, securing your documents and personal information by keeping them out of sight is best. Your information is still accessible to anyone who may gain access to your inner sanctum, friend or foe. The following sections describe ways to protect your information and yourself in your home.

Securing confidential documents and information

Keep all confidential, financial, and legal documents and information in a secure place — a strong box, a locked desk drawer, or a locked file cabinet. Doing so ensures that your valuable data is safe from prying eyes and sticky fingers, and you benefit from having all critical information in one place in case you need to access it quickly.

Sometimes, a simple thing can save the day. Making and securely storing a photocopy of your account numbers and your wallet's contents is one of them. If you haven't already done so, empty the contents of your wallet and photocopy everything, front and back. Write the contact phone numbers next to each item and file the paper in a locked cabinet. Voilà! You're now better prepared to deal with an identity-theft crisis.

Destroying information

Your mailbox isn't the only place that identity thieves look for useful information. Your garbage can is also ripe with potential. A determined thief doesn't mind sifting through your detritus if it means snagging a credit card number from those coffee grounds–covered statements. A fishing expedition in the backyards and trash cans of suburbia can yield a good return.

Purchase a good crosscut shredder and shred all financial documents that contain account numbers (including savings, checking, and credit card statements) before you discard them. Don't overlook all those preapproved offers for credit you receive, either; a thief can send them in with a change of address and get new credit that you won't know about until it's too late. Look for a shredder that takes multiple sheets of paper, is easy to use, and can be emptied without making a mess. Why? Because you're more likely to use it if it meets these criteria.

Putting your credit information on ice

Frozen margaritas, frozen yogurt, frozen credit? The option to freeze your credit to keep it from identity thieves is available to everyone. The concept is simple: You can freeze, or lock up, your credit information at the major credit bureaus (meaning that your credit report won't be available for new creditors to view) so that anyone who's looking to extend credit has to ask you to thaw (unlock) your file. Freezing your credit information seriously hampers an identity thief from opening credit in your name without your knowledge because few lenders extend credit without a credit report in hand.

When deciding whether to freeze your credit information, the main consideration is whether you value access to instant credit more than you fear your personal information being compromised. Only you know the answer to that question.

Of course, the freeze-your-credit-info strategy isn't foolproof. Thieves can still pirate and abuse existing accounts by using such tactics as swiping your mail, changing your address from Peoria to Las Vegas, and getting replacement cards issued. So a freeze may help protect your *information,* but it may not protect your *money,* although hopefully you'd notice a problem before it got too far out of hand. Given the low personal level of liability on credit cards, your monetary losses shouldn't be significant.

The bottom line of a freeze is as follows:

- All the bureaus allow you to freeze your credit files regardless of the laws in your state.

- Freezing doesn't prevent abuse of existing accounts.

- Thawing an account takes a few days and may keep impulse or sale purchases from happening — which can be a good thing or a bad thing, depending on how you look at it.

If a freeze seems extreme to you, consider a fraud alert. It's like an account "chill" rather than a hard freeze in that it requires only enhanced verification of identity. To place an alert, contact any of the three credit bureaus using the information in Chapter 14. The bureau you contact will automatically forward your request to the other two bureaus for action. For details, see the section "Sending out a fraud alert" in Chapter 9.

Shielding your credit card number

One of the easiest ways to safeguard your identity is to ensure that thieves don't have access to your credit card numbers. Luckily, the Fair and Accurate Credit Transactions Act (the FACT Act or FACTA) has made this task a tad easier. Electronically generated receipts for credit card and debit card transactions may not include the card's expiration date or more than the last five digits of the card number. If you receive a receipt that has your full account number on it, bring it to the attention of the business and insist that it get with the program — now! Some credit card issuers print only partial account numbers on statements as well.

You can find out more about the FACT Act in Chapter 19 and at the Federal Trade Commission website (www.ftc.gov/os/statutes/fcrajump. shtm). A copy of the act is available at www.dummies.com/extras/ creditrepair.

Safeguarding active-duty military personnel

While on duty outside the United States, military personnel — as well as their families at home — may lack the time or means to monitor their credit. After all, calling TransUnion about an error isn't exactly a high priority when someone is trying to blow you up, and families back home can understandably get distracted and let their guard down when a loved one is serving overseas. So it seems only fair that while soldiers are protecting their country, their country should protect them from credit problems. Thanks to the FACT Act, active-duty military personnel can place an *active-duty alert* on their credit reports as a way to notify potential creditors of possible fraud.

If you're in the military and away from your usual base or deployed, place an active-duty alert on your credit report by contacting any of the three major credit-reporting bureaus (don't bother calling all three bureaus, because the one you contact will notify the other two; see Chapter 14 for contact info). You'll be required to provide proof of identity, which may include your Social Security number, name, address, and other personal information.

The active-duty alert stays on your credit report for at least one year. It helps minimize the risk of identity theft by requiring that a business take reasonable care to verify your identity before issuing you credit. However, if you're in a distant land trying to keep the peace, verifying your identity may not be feasible. So before you leave your base or home for active duty, be sure to appoint a personal representative and provide that person's contact information to the credit bureau. If you don't, a creditor only has to "utilize reasonable policies and procedures to form a reasonable belief" before granting credit to someone claiming to be you. This is way too *reasonable* for my comfort level. Be sure to appoint someone you trust!

With an alert in place, lenders have to take further steps before issuing additional credit cards or changing your limits. When you place the alert, you can get an additional free credit report in addition to the annual report you're already entitled to (see Chapters 13 and 14 for more on this). Plus, your name is removed from preapproved offer lists for credit cards, insurance, and loans. To lessen the chances of an identity theft, you can place additional alerts if your deployment is to last longer than a year. (To delete an alert, just contact one of the bureaus; it will notify the others of your desire to deactivate the alert.)

Remember: If your contact information changes before your alert expires, update it or have your representative do so.

Catching Identity Thieves in the Act

If your identity is stolen, you may not notice it for days, weeks, or even months. If a thief sets up a phony identity at another address and you don't get the bills, you may not know about the crime until the debts go bad and a collector finds you. Called *skip tracers,* these collectors look for people who don't pay their bills and then move — which is what they'll consider you until you straighten matters out.

The IRS may contact you if your identity is stolen. The IRS uses your Social Security number (SSN) to make sure that your tax filing is copacetic, and that if you are due a refund you get it. A notice or letter from the IRS could alert you that someone else is using your SSN. *Note:* The IRS doesn't initiate contact with taxpayers via e-mail, text, or social media message. If you get an e-mail that claims to be from the IRS, do not reply or click any links it may contain. Instead, forward it to phishing@irs.gov.

By being vigilant, you can spot signs of identity theft. Vigilance can make all the difference between a minor and a major crime. The following sections introduce you to some key indications of identity theft so that you can be on the lookout for them.

Predicting identity theft

The FACT Act demands that financial institutions establish procedures to attempt to spot identity theft *before* it occurs. Predicting identity theft may seem as farfetched as calling in a psychic on a missing person's case. But like our trusty weather forecasters who look to the skies for clues to tomorrow's weather, financial prognosticators are writing programs to look for specific activity in your financial records that may indicate a problem. In fact, several credit card companies now tout their own programs to fight identity theft. Chapter 15 talks about the efforts American Express is making to spot fraud and theft as quickly as possible. A change in pattern or type of spending can trigger an alert to your phone or e-mail if you have an alert in place. Alerts are free and easy to set up; see Chapter 15 for more information.

Certain events — such as a change of address, a request for a replacement credit card, or efforts to reactivate a dormant credit card account — may trigger a fraud alert. That said, you can do only so much to protect yourself from identity theft. Even with prevention programs in place, in many cases you won't know about a problem until after the fact.

Watching for early-warning notices

To help spot identity theft early on, the FACT Act requires creditors to give you what may be called an *early-warning notice* (and it may be the first sign of a problem). When credit is used within 30 days of a missed, late, or partial payment or other type of default, you must be sent a one-time notice letting you know that this information is being sent to the credit bureau(s) to which the creditor reports data. This notice has to be sent by collection agencies, too, as long as they report to a credit bureau.

The FACT Act doesn't dictate how *big* of a notice you get. You may have to look closely even to see it, so do your part by closely monitoring your credit reports, bank account statements, and credit card statements.

An early-warning notice means that something bad is in your account history, and if it's reported to a credit bureau, it has a negative effect on your credit and score. Whether or not it's reported, it's lurking out there. Before negative information is reported, the early-warning notice may look something like this:

> *We may report information about your account to credit bureaus. Late payments, missed payments, or other defaults on your account may be reflected in your credit report.*

After negative information has been reported, the notice may look like this:

> *We have told a credit bureau about a late payment, missed payment, or other default on your account. This information may be reflected in your credit report.*

The wording makes it sound as though the bad information may not show up. It will, and probably already has.

So what do you do if you get a notice? Immediately contact the issuer and find out what's going on. The issuer will be as interested as you are in shutting down a thief, so you can expect cooperation and maybe even a thank-you for acting quickly.

Early warnings from the IRS

What's worse than having your identity stolen? Having it stolen and used to cheat the IRS. If someone uses your Social Security number (SSN) to get a job, her employer will use the stolen identity to report any earned income to the IRS using your SSN. Because you don't know about it, you won't report those earnings, thereby failing to report all your income from the IRS's point of view. You'll receive a notice or letter saying that you failed to report income.

Also, if someone uses your SSN to file for your tax refund before you file, that person may get your refund instead of you.

If you think that someone used your SSN to get a job or a tax refund — or the IRS sends you a notice or letter indicating a problem — contact the IRS immediately. Specially trained agents will work with you to file your tax return, get you any refund you are due, and protect your IRS account from identity thieves in the future. The IRS will want a copy of your police report or an IRS ID Theft Affidavit Form 14039 (available at www.dummies.com/extras/creditrepair) and proof of your identity, such as a copy of your Social Security card, driver's license, or passport.

Contact the IRS Identity Protection Specialized Unit at 800-908-4490.

Handling a collections call

If you're the victim of identity theft, you may receive a collections call, likely a demanding and unpleasant one, from a collector insisting on payment for an overdue account — an account that the collector is certain you owe but that you've never heard of. What should you do? The FACT Act, designed to address identity-theft issues, states that you need to tell the collector very clearly that you didn't make the purchase and that you believe your identity may have been stolen.

After you tell the collector that you believe your identity may have been stolen, the collection agency is required by law to inform the creditor. You're also entitled to a copy of all the information the collection agency or creditor has about this debt, including applications, statements, and the like, as though this really were your account or bill. I suggest that you request your copy before the collector gets off the phone or in your written response if the collection activity is in the form of a letter.

The best part is that, under the FACT Act, as soon as you notify the creditor or collector that the debt is the work of an identity thief, the debt can't be placed for collection or sold to another collector.

Detecting unauthorized charges

Are you among the many people who just look at the amount due on your monthly statement and pay it? Or is your credit card bill automatically paid from your bank account and you check the details later? In either case, you may be paying for purchases you didn't make, and more important, you may be missing an opportunity to stop a thief!

Take the time to review your statements to ensure that all the charges are legitimate. Set a reminder to alert you to check your statement in detail on a regular basis. Remember, you have a limited time to dispute an error. Plus, an identity thief is faster than the proverbial speeding bullet! I recently had a card stolen while on vacation. In a matter of hours, the thief racked up over $9,000 in bogus charges — even a lunch at McDonald's! So don't delay checking your statements, or you may be in for quite a surprise.

Don't rely on your memory as you review your statement. My memory isn't the greatest (or so my wife says, although I can't remember why). So I keep all my credit card receipts in a file and pull them out when reviewing my monthly statement. Keep all credit card receipts in a convenient place, at least until you receive, verify, and pay your bills.

If you see any unauthorized charges on your statement, call the card issuer's customer service number and get the details. You may have to dispute the charge, but that's no big deal. Also, the representative may see some indication of identity theft. That happened to me — I saw a stray charge and called the credit card company, and the customer service rep recognized it as fraud right away. Make the call.

Being denied credit or account access

Rejection is always a painful thing, but it's especially painful when you're rejected because of something you didn't do. If you are rejected for credit, you may want to ask why, but your best bet is to order a copy of your credit report and look for evidence of identity theft (accounts you never opened and/or activity you don't recognize). You can get a free copy of the credit report used to deny your application in addition to the free annual reports you get normally. (I tell you how to order those in Chapter 14.)

Another sign of identity theft is receiving a notice that you've been rejected for credit that you never asked for. Take this notice seriously. Someone may be applying for credit in your name.

You may try to access an ATM and get a denial message. If this happens, contact your bank immediately to determine whether it's the result of identity theft.

Noticing missing account statements

Your monthly bank statement is really late. Hmm . . . now that you think of it, you didn't receive a statement last month, either. Yes, I know this was one of your birthday wishes, but the real reason you're not hearing from your creditors may be more sinister. It could mean that an identity thief has changed your address in order to use your bank account, hoping that you won't notice for a few months.

Create a system to remind yourself when statements are due and bills must be paid. This way, you're more likely to stay on top of your payment schedule and be alerted when something is amiss. Paying bills and getting statements online instead of by snail mail makes it harder on thieves (and easier on you).

Part VI
The Part of Tens

In this part . . .

- ✔ Be aware of the consumer protections in place to shield you from shady practices.

- ✔ Understand your options for repaying your student loans.

- ✔ Avoid defaulting on your student loans, or minimize credit damage in the wake of a default.

- ✔ Lower your student loan bill even before you graduate.

- ✔ Know when your mortgage is in trouble.

- ✔ Decide whether to stay in your home or leave, and reduce credit damage in the event of a foreclosure.

Chapter 21

Ten Consumer Protections Everyone Needs to Know

*I*t has been said that a person can't be too good-looking or have too many friends. This has never been truer than in the world of credit — at least the part about friends. The world of credit can be complex, unforgiving, and very expensive! The credit-granting, credit-reporting, and credit-scoring industries have become increasingly complex and powerful to the point where they are used for everything from issuing credit cards to getting jobs. Consumer advocates recognized that we need effective ways to keep errors, both yours and theirs, from seriously complicating your life. The result is a series of laws, protections, and agencies whose purpose is to keep the credit game honest and give consumers a fair opportunity to access the American financial system. These protections may not always work as you'd like, but if they didn't exist, you'd be at the mercy of big business, and that's no place you want to be.

In this chapter, I cover my top ten legal protection resources you have to guide you in dealing with the world of consumer credit.

The Fair Debt Collection Practices Act

Being protected is especially important when a debt collector comes a-calling. The Fair Debt Collection Practices Act (FDCPA) limits debt collectors' activities and spells out your rights. Highlights include

✔ Prohibiting collectors from abusing you, being unfair, and trying to trick you into paying.

✔ Applying the law to most personal debts, including credit cards, auto loans, medical debts, and debts secured by your home.

✔ Defining when and where a debt can be collected — for example, between 8 a.m. and 9 p.m., or not at work.

✔ Requiring a validation notice that specifies how much you owe and what you should do if the debt isn't yours or has been paid already.

✔ Allowing you to just say no. If you don't want to hear from a collector, you can write to the collection agency and demand that it not contact you again. Doing so doesn't satisfy a legitimate debt, but it ends collector contact. It may, however, begin legal contact to sue you for the debt.

✔ Giving you the right to sue for breach of the rules. You have a year to bring action for violations.

The Bankruptcy Abuse Prevention and Consumer Protection Act

The Bankruptcy Abuse Prevention and Consumer Protection Act (BAPCPA) revised the process of getting a fresh start when you are overwhelmed by debt. The major provisions in this law include

✔ Mandatory credit counseling before filing

✔ Stricter eligibility for Chapter 7 filing to encourage Chapter 13

✔ Fewer debts discharged and fewer state exemptions

✔ Tax returns and proof of income required for means test

✔ Mandatory five-year Chapter 13 plan if over your state's median income

✔ Mandatory financial management education after filing

✔ Time between Chapter 7 filings increased to eight years

Bankruptcy was designed to give you the ultimate protection of the courts from your creditors. The process can be as effective as it is damaging to your credit, and you should use it with great care, and only if you've already considered less damaging courses of action.

In some states, you can file your own bankruptcy petition (called *pro se*); in others, you need an attorney. Regardless, I recommend that you use an attorney who does this for a living. A poorly thought out or executed bankruptcy can leave you with unresolved debts and deprive you of the opportunity to use this protection again for several years. A good bankruptcy attorney will spend a significant amount of time with you to compare bankruptcy with other possible ways of handling financial problems.

See Chapter 8 for advice on how to determine whether bankruptcy is for you.

Your Lawyer

Lawyers often get a bad rap, but if you want an effective weapon in providing consumer protection, you need look no further. Whether your issue is a debt collector, a retailer who won't step up to resolve a problem, or a contract with unsuspected gotcha clauses, a knowledgeable and persistent attorney is hard to beat. Yes, I know, lawyers are expensive, but there are times when only the best will do. Using a second-rate attorney is like showing up at a gunfight with the second-fastest gunslinger. Better not to show up at all!

Here are some points to consider when looking for a consumer attorney:

- Nothing is better than a referral from a satisfied friend, colleague, or relative. Ask someone in whom you have confidence. You may get a great referral or a solution you hadn't thought of.
- Look for someone who does a lot of what you need. Like picking a heart surgeon, you want lots of experience here.
- If you already have a lawyer, ask her for a specialist recommendation.
- Check your local American Bar Association affiliate or attorney association. They often maintain lawyer referral services.
- Look for someone your gut says you can work with. Is the lawyer concerned about you and your problem? Always interview more than one attorney. This situation is important.
- Don't be deterred by hourly rates. A good attorney who charges more can be a bargain if you get resolution quickly and permanently.
- Get all agreements in writing to avoid miscommunication. Be sure to read the agreement before you sign it, and ask about anything that's not clear to you.

Consumer Credit Counseling

Sometimes, protection comes in the form of helping you reach agreements with your creditors rather than going through an exhausting collection and legal process. Nonprofit consumer credit counseling agencies act as intermediaries on your behalf with creditors who won't listen to you. They've been helping consumers come to mutually satisfactory debt repayment arrangements for more than 50 years, and they offer their services for free or for a nominal cost.

You can find a good agency online at www.debtadvice.org or www.aiccca. org or by calling 800-388-2227 or 866-703-8787. Look for third-party accreditation and HUD certification. For more information about credit counseling, see Chapter 4.

Statute of Limitations Laws

This protection is worthy of Perry Mason: "I object, Your Honor, for this charge is too old." Well, maybe Perry didn't say exactly that, but he'd be happy to see that each state has a law called a *statute of limitations (SOL)* that sets a limit on how long a debt collector can sue you in court, depending on the type of loan you allegedly owe. This is only fair, because after several years, who keeps all those receipts and slips of paper? Either hurry up and sue or forget about it!

This protection isn't automatic; you have to ask for it. What do you need to know and do? Read on.

- ✔ If a debt is past the SOL, the creditor can't successfully sue you in court to collect it. But you must show up and prove that the debt is too old.

- ✔ Credit reports show a delinquency for seven years. This has nothing to do with the time a debt is collectible.

- ✔ The period used to figure how old your debt is starts when you miss a payment and never make another one. A payment may restart the SOL clock, depending on the state in which you live.

Your State Attorney General

Every state has an attorney general. All attorneys general have at least one thing in common: One of their primary responsibilities is to enforce their states' consumer protection laws. Every state has a consumer protection statute prohibiting deceptive acts and practices. These statutes include laws that address specific industries or practices. For example, many FACT Act protections, especially for credit reporting, have stricter state regulations, giving you more rights and a local resource for help.

State attorneys general love to go after abuses and illegalities in the market-place, including deceptive trade practices, telemarketing and Internet fraud, fake charities, ID theft, and false or misleading advertising. It's good press for them and good protection for you. Generally, these public officials have a low tolerance for financial shenanigans. So if you think you're being abused, taken advantage of, or scammed in a credit or personal finance transaction, this is the office to call.

I've had good luck working with the consumer protection sections of several state attorneys general. If you decide to ask them for help, I suggest that you be organized and to the point, and have the pertinent information at hand. Attorneys general are no-nonsense law enforcement officials who appreciate you calling for their help but not wasting their time.

The Consumer Financial Protection Bureau

Reforming our financial system isn't easy, and the Feds know it, so they formed a new agency — the Consumer Financial Protection Bureau, or CFPB — to carry on the fight of protecting you long after the ink dried on the Dodd-Frank Wall Street Reform and Consumer Protection Act (the legislation that created the CFPB). Not since J. Edgar Hoover headed up the FBI has a federal agency had such far-reaching powers. The CFPB sets rules for payday lenders, credit card issuers, and all the players in between. Here are the major protections this agency delivers:

✔ Need information? Use the question-and-answer service at `www.consumerfinance.gov/askcfpb/` for inquiries about mortgages, student loans, debt collections, credit reports, and more.

✔ Have a complaint? Go to `www.consumerfinance.gov/complaint/` and let 'em have it. Bank accounts, credit cards, credit reporting, debt collections, money transfers, mortgages, student loans, and consumer loans are among the topics you can get help with. You complain, and the CFPB forwards your beef to the company and works to get an answer. It reviews the response and shares it with other agencies to identify patterns of abuse and write better regulations. It also sends you e-mail updates and has a secure consumer portal that you can use to track your complaint and give feedback about company responses to help the CFPB prioritize complaints. Just like the *Dragnet* guys: dum-ta-dum dum!

✔ It requires anyone who issues credit or prepaid cards to give you better, more easily understandable terms-and-cost disclosures.

✔ If you have to sign it, you should be able to understand it. The CPFB assures that paperwork is understandable.

✔ It helps set rules on transaction fees for interchange activity, like on your Visa or MasterCard.

✔ It closely regulates consumer credit counseling, debt settlement, and debt collectors to keep you from being victimized.

The Credit Card Accountability, Responsibility, and Disclosure Act

Fed up with tricky terms, excessive penalties, fees, and unfair banking practices, Congress enacted the Credit Card Accountability, Responsibility, and Disclosure Act (CARD Act) to give you a fair playing field in the area of credit cards. Here are your major protections:

✔ Credit card companies can't raise card interest rates except under specific circumstances, such as at the end of a promotional rate, or when a variable interest rate index to which your card is tied rises, or if you're 60 days late on a payment. Also, double cycle interest billing, which used your average daily balance for the current and previous billing cycles to charge you more, is no longer allowed.

✔ If your rate or terms change, you get 45 days' notice to plan what to do.

✔ You can opt out of changes you don't like. Doing so may cause your account to be closed, but you can pay off the debt under the old terms.

✔ Card companies can't issue cards to people under 21 who have no income. This sounds like a no-brainer, but for years creditors had been giving students credit despite their having no income to repay their charges.

✔ Creditors must give you at least 21 days after a bill is mailed to make your payment. The due date can't be before the mail is delivered or on a weekend, a holiday, or a day when the creditor is closed for business. If you're late, fees are limited to a maximum of $25.

✔ All payment amounts above the minimum payment due must be applied to the balance with the highest interest rate, not the lowest.

✔ If you exceed your credit limit, the card company must ask you whether you want that transaction to be processed and incur an over-limit fee. Saying "no thank you" results in the purchase being denied but also saves you the over-limit fee. Even if you say yes, the fee can't exceed the amount by which you exceed the credit limit. So if you exceed your limit by $10, the fee can't be more than $10.

The Fair and Accurate Credit Transactions Act

Fairness is something you can hope for in your dealings with the credit bureaus and those other consumer-reporting bureaus that are increasingly in the news. But before the protections afforded in the Fair and Accurate Credit Transactions Act (FACT Act or FACTA) became effective, fairness was strictly in the eye of the beholder. And the beholder wasn't you! Congress acted to end a number of perceived and real abuses.

Congress understood that the nation's banking system was becoming increasingly dependent on credit reporting, that inaccurate reports resulted in unfair and inefficient banking, and that you have a right to privacy. The result is that you now have more control over what's said about you in credit bureau files and who can access your information. You also have the right to dispute errors or out-of-date information and to get a free copy of your credit report from each bureau every year. Not bad for the crowd from Washington, D.C.! Here are your main protections:

✔ You must be told about any negative action taken as a result of information contained in your credit report, and you must be given free access to the same information. If the interest rate on your favorite credit card goes up, for example, you get to see a copy of the report that contains the data that led to that increase.

✔ You can find out what information is in your personal file. No more secrets! It's your information and your file, so you can look at it.

✔ You can get a free copy of your credit report at least every 12 months if you ask for one. You can also get a free report whenever you're the object of identity theft or fraud, you're on public assistance, or you're unemployed but expect to apply for employment within 60 days.

✔ You have the right to know your credit score. This score used to be as big a secret as what was in your bureau files. Score watching has become a favorite pastime for many and a profitable business for others.

✔ The data in your file must be accurate, verifiable, and current. If data is incorrect or too old, you need only to ask, and it will be verified or removed pronto.

✔ Only those who have a legitimate business purpose can see your file, and you can stop everyone from accessing your file without your express permission if you like. Usually only creditors, insurers, employers, landlords, and others with whom you do business get to see what's in your file. You can slam the door on everyone with a credit freeze.

The Federal Trade Commission

The Federal Trade Commission (FTC) is the alter ego of the Bureau of Consumer Protection (BCP). Although it doesn't deal with individual consumer complaints, it does protect consumers by accumulating and analyzing complaints and then taking industry-wide action to address issues that you bring to it. Some examples of BCP protections are your ability to get a free annual credit report, the National Do Not Call Registry to block unwanted telemarketing calls, and appliance disclosure stickers that show the energy costs of home appliances, to name just a few.

The BCP looks out for unfair, deceptive, or fraudulent practices in the marketplace. It investigates and sues companies and people who violate the law. It also develops rules to protect you and requires businesses to give you better disclosure of your costs, rights, and dispute-resolution options. It also collects complaints about consumer fraud and identity theft and makes them available to law enforcement agencies across the country.

Of the bureau's seven divisions, here are the five that you may find useful:

- **Advertising practices:** Enforces truth-in-advertising laws. If an offer seems too good to be true and it is, complain to the FTC.

- **Financial practices:** Protects you from deceptive and unfair practices in the financial services industry, including predatory or discriminatory lending practices, deceptive or unfair loan servicing and debt collection, and fraudulent credit counseling and debt settlement companies.

- **Marketing practices:** Responds to Internet, telecommunications, and direct-mail fraud; spam; fraudulent work-at-home schemes; and violations of the Do Not Call provisions of the Telemarketing Sales Rule.

- **Privacy and identity protection:** Protects your financial privacy, investigates data breaches, helps consumers whose identities have been stolen, and implements laws and regulations for the credit reporting industry, including the FACT Act.

- **Enforcement:** Sues to address issues on these practices.

Your complaint, comment, or inquiry may help identify a pattern of violations requiring law enforcement action, but the FTC doesn't resolve individual consumer disputes.

Chapter 22

Ten Strategies for Dealing with Student Loans

....

In This Chapter

▶ Understanding how student loans are different

▶ Knowing your options

▶ Finding special help for military personnel

....

S tudent loans are hard to live with and, for many, hard to live without! Few question the value of a post-secondary education, whether it be in a technical field, for a skilled trade, or for a four-year (or more) degree. More education frequently yields a better, fuller life as well as more income. But with the cost of education rising fast and the job market expanding slowly, there is a growing disconnect between the cost and the benefit. This is demonstrated by the default rate of student loans, which has been on an upward trend, with a recent two-year default rate of 10 percent and a three-year default rate of 14.7 percent. So how do you get the benefits you want and need without the risk of owing more than you can pay? This chapter is just what you're looking for, with my favorite heads-up advice to keep you moving in the right direction.

Knowing How Student Loans Are Reported Differently Than Other Loans

Most of the loans that are reported on your credit bureau files get reported just once. Student loans are an exception. Depending on how your education is funded, you may have a new loan every semester. That equates to two loans per year, or a total of eight loans hitting your credit report while you are preparing to make some money to pay them back. All this activity can build your credit score, but because there are so many of the little darlings, they can sink you big-time if you end up defaulting.

Another unique feature of student loans is that they are not normally dischargeable in a Chapter 7 bankruptcy. A student loan is a commitment that follows you until you honor it, regardless of how long it takes.

If you are not yet convinced that student loans are different from garden-variety credit card and auto loans, don't forget that in a Chapter 13 bankruptcy, they can grow even bigger! See the section on bankruptcy later in this chapter.

Dealing with the Collection Process

Now that you know the stakes are high, you'll want to handle any collection process quickly. The key to minimizing damage from a defaulted student loan is to address it right away. Don't procrastinate or ignore the letters and calls. Private student loans may charge off in as few as 120 days rather than the traditional 180 days for normal loans. Early action can enable you to handle loan issues quickly with the servicer rather than a collection agency. Servicers are more likely to work with you to come up with a solution that works for both you and the lender. For more information on charge-offs, see the section "Getting a Handle on Charge-Offs" in Chapter 6.

Before you call or write to the loan servicer (I suggest that you begin with a call and follow up in writing), organize your thoughts. Treat this as a very important job interview. Explain coherently why you weren't able to pay: medical issues, job loss, pay reductions, armed-service call-up, or family emergency. If you're calling to propose a payment alternative, have a number prepared and be able to justify it based on your budget. Call your servicer or the U.S. Department of Education information line at 800-872-5327, but be sure to do it before you miss a payment.

Collectors are not obligated to offer you the best repayment terms you can get. They just want to get as much money from you as fast as they can. A loan servicer is much more likely to steer you to programs that will keep you out of collections, but you have to act fast.

Quick action also means that any delinquencies will be early, which typically gives you more options to get on top of the situation. The later you are, the fewer options are available to you.

Identifying the Best Repayment Option for Your Situation

A huge number of repayment programs are available, and they change all the time. I suggest that you check out the big sites that deal with them, such as Federal Student Aid (studentaid.ed.gov/repay-loans/ understand/plans) and FinAid (www.finaid.org).

Here is a synopsis of what's currently available and how each plan works:

- **Standard Repayment Plan:** Payments are fixed and made for up to ten years. This plan may save you money over time. Although your monthly payments may be slightly higher than payments made under other plans, you'll pay off your loan in the shortest time.

- **Graduated Repayment Plan:** Payments are made for up to ten years. They begin at a very low rate and increase every two years. If your current income is low and you expect that it will go up and continue to rise over an extended period, the GRP may be a good bet.

- **Extended Repayment Plan:** Payments are made for up to 25 years. The good news: lower payments. The bad news: You pay more interest and pay more overall for longer. You must extend a minimum of $30,000 in outstanding Federal Family Education Loans (FFEL) or Direct Loans.

  Some important options for student loan borrowers are based on your earnings. Forgiveness may be available after 10 to 25 years of these payments, depending on the plan you choose.

- **Income-Based Repayment Plan (IBR)** caps your monthly payment amount at an amount that the government thinks is affordable based on your income and family size. Your monthly payment is less than the monthly amount calculated under a 10-year Standard Repayment Plan. Some good news is that if you repay under the IBR plan for 25 years, any remaining balance of your loan(s) may be cancelled. Plus, if you work in public service and repay through IBR, the remaining balance could be canceled after 10 years in a public service job. See studentaid.ed.gov/sites/default/files/ income-based-repayment.pdf or www.ibrinfo.org/index.php for more info.

- **Pay as You Earn Repayment Plan** is an income-sensitive plan for those with a partial financial hardship. It helps keep your monthly student loan payments affordable and usually has the lowest monthly payment amount of the repayment plans that are based on income.

- **Income-Contingent Repayment Plan** is for Direct Loans only. This plan is based on your adjusted gross income, family size, and the total amount of your Direct Loans.

- **Income-Sensitive Repayment Plan** is for FFEL loans only. The payments under this plan increase or decrease based on your annual income.

Taking Your Loans to Bankruptcy

Because the value of your education can't be repossessed, a student loan generally can't be wiped out in a bankruptcy. And if you're not careful, you could end up increasing the amount you owe if you choose a Chapter 13 bankruptcy filing. Trying to get rid of student loan debt through a bankruptcy is difficult and perilous, but in some cases it can be done.

Most debtors do not qualify to discharge (eliminate) student loan debt in a Chapter 7. The exception comes when you can prove to the court that repaying your student loans would cause you undue hardship. This provision is known as the *hardship exemption*. One size doesn't fit all, and the criteria can vary by court. Your best chance is if your income is very low or your loans are from a for-profit trade school.

Here are some factors the court may look for:

- **Poverty:** Based on your current income and expenses, you can't maintain a minimal standard of living for yourself and your dependents if you are forced to repay your loans.

- **Persistence:** Your current financial situation is likely to continue for a significant part of the repayment period.

- **Good faith:** You have made a good-faith effort to repay your student loans.

If you have a Health Education Assistance Loan (HEAL), your loan is more than seven years past due, and repayment would impose an "unconscionable" burden on your life, you may be able to get a discharge. A qualified attorney can advise you on your chances for a discharge.

Dealing with the Prospect of Default

Before you can be late on your loan, you have to have used up your grace period (the length of time you have after leaving school before you have to make your first payment). Determining when you have used up your grace period can be complex. Each type of loan may have a different grace period. For example, if you have a federal Stafford loan, your grace period is six months, while it is nine months for a federal Perkins loan. Federal PLUS loans can be based on when they were issued (see `studentaid.ed.gov/types/loans/plus` for more info). Check your loan documents or contact your lender to find out when your grace period runs out.

Here are some simple steps that may help keep you out of trouble:

✔ Keep in communication with your lender or servicer. If you move, tell them. Being hard to find isn't a plus. If they send you a letter or an e-mail, read it. Ignoring a potential problem only allows it to grow more serious.

✔ Find out which plans are available to you. (See the earlier section "Identifying the Best Repayment Option for Your Situation.") Federal loans are usually based on a ten-year repayment plan. If you can't or don't want to have that big a bite taken out of your earnings, change your repayment plan. Extending your payments costs you less each month but more over time. You get to decide what's best for you.

✔ Private loans are different from federal loans and are not eligible for income-based repayment or other federal plans, deferments, or forgiveness. Your private lender may offer other types of forbearance plans, but expect to pay for them. They include interest-only payments for a set period.

✔ Community banks and credit unions are good places to look for refinancing options of private student loans. An example is the cuGrad Private Student Loan Consolidation program (www.custudentloans.org). Available from many not-for-profit credit unions, it can be used to refinance and consolidate existing private student loan debt into one payment at a lower monthly rate.

 Interest accrues on all types of loans during forbearances and on some types of loans during deferment, increasing your total debt.

Gaining Student Loan Forgiveness

In most cases, your loans are yours to have and to hold until you pay them back or expire trying. However, on some occasions student loans may be forgiven, canceled, or discharged. Following is a summary of the types of loan absolution that are available.

Different rules govern Direct Loans, Perkins Loans, and Federal Family Education Loans (FFEL). Be sure to know which rules apply to your loans.

✔ **Total and Permanent Disability Discharge:** Like the name says, this discharge is for those who have been permanently disabled by military service or those receiving Social Security Disability. You also qualify if your physician certifies that you couldn't work for the last five years, your impairment can be expected to last for at least five years, or you are expected to die.

✔ **Death Discharge:** This one comes into play if you die. No life, no loan.

- **Discharge in Bankruptcy:** See the section "Taking Your Loans to Bankruptcy" earlier in this chapter.

- **Closed School Discharge:** Direct Loans and FFEL are forgiven only if your school folds.

- **False Certification of Student Eligibility, Unauthorized Payment Discharge, Unpaid Refund Discharge:** To qualify for this discharge, your school has to have messed up in a major way, like approving your loan for a degree in law enforcement when you have a felony record disqualifying you as a law enforcement officer or giving money to an identity thief in your name.

- **Teacher Loan Forgiveness:** This discharge may be yours if you have taught full-time in a low-income elementary or secondary school or educational service agency for five consecutive years. Only $17,500 of your subsidized or unsubsidized loans are forgiven. PLUS loans cannot be included.

- **Public Service Loan Forgiveness (includes Teacher Loan Forgiveness):** If you work in a specified public service job and make 120 payments on your Direct Loans (beginning after October 1, 2007), the remaining balance that you owe may be forgiven.

- **Perkins Loan Cancellation and Discharge:** Federal Perkins Loans may be cancelled if you perform certain types of public service or are employed in certain occupations. Generally, each complete year of service gets a percentage of your loan canceled. Occupational categories include volunteers in the Peace Corps or ACTION program (including VISTA), teachers, members of the U.S. armed forces (serving in areas of hostility), nurses and medical technicians, law enforcement and corrections officers, Head Start workers, child and family services workers, and professional providers of early intervention services.

You can find more info at studentaid.ed.gov/repay-loans/forgiveness-cancellation.

Lowering Your Bill While You're in School

There is no need to let the bill for your student loans grow while you're in school. Unless you have a subsidized loan, interest accrues and accumulates during the term of your education. Consider these strategies to reduce or eliminate your interest buildup.

Pay your interest as it accrues. For students trying to save money on student loan debt, one solution is to make payments of at least the new interest that accrues during the in-school and grace periods. There are no prepayment penalties on federal and private student loans, so you can make interest-only payments. When making a payment, include a note asking for the payment to be applied to interest.

If you have both subsidized and unsubsidized student loans, specify that the extra payment should be applied to the unsubsidized loans.

Paying off interest early not only saves you money, but also enables you to get used to working with your student loan servicer and helps you establish a relationship for successful repayment. It also gets you in the habit of making payments. Plus, you may get some tax benefits! As much as $2,500 in interest paid on student loans may be deductible on your federal income tax return. This may result in a refund that you could use to prepay a portion of your loan to lower the cost of your loan even further. Sweet! See IRS Publication 970 (www.irs.gov/publications/p970) for details.

Pay both interest and principal. Doing so gives you all the benefits listed in the preceding section, plus it reduces your principal, which seriously lowers your future payments. A $5,500 loan might accrue $31 a month in interest. Paying the interest as you go could result in a savings of about $1,500. Paying on the principal will lower the debt even more.

Work a little to save a lot. You don't need a full-time job to make a big difference in future loan payments. If you can earn only $57 per month (or $13.25 a week, or $1.89 a day), you can pay all the interest that will accrue on a typical $10,000 unsubsidized Stafford loan throughout four years of college and your six-month grace period. This means you can get your diploma owing only $10,000 instead of $13,060 (your principal plus interest). And don't forget, you may get a fat tax deduction as a bonus for deducting the interest you pay on your loans each year.

Keeping Up with Your Loans After You're Out

Remember, federal student loans are real loans, just like car loans or mortgages. You must repay your student loans even if your financial circumstances become difficult. Your student loans cannot be canceled because you didn't get the job you expected or you didn't complete your education (unless you couldn't complete your education because your school closed, as explained in the earlier section "Gaining Student Loan Forgiveness").

You need to make payments to your loan servicer. Each servicer has its own process, so check with your servicer if you aren't sure how or when to make a payment. You are responsible for staying in touch with your servicer and making your payments, even if you do not receive a bill. It's your job to know who services your loan(s).

A lot of repayment plan options are available; see my summary earlier in this chapter. How much you have to pay and for how long depends on the plan you choose, so it's critical that you understand and act on your options. I strongly suggest that you figure your real repayment amount under each plan before you pick one.

You may be able to consolidate your loans. Understand what consolidating means for you and how it may affect your future payments. You may also want to consider loan forbearance or deferment to temporarily reduce or postpone payments if you go back to school, join the military, or experience a hardship.

You may qualify for discharge, cancellation, or forgiveness in certain circumstances that I cover earlier in this chapter.

Although student loans do offer generous terms, the danger here is that many young people just out of school don't have much experience budgeting and living on their own. You may find yourself in a real-live "grown-up" job with a salary that makes you feel like a millionaire, and you may start spending like a millionaire, too. Without tools such as a spending plan, you may quickly lose control of credit and debt responsibility and find negative items being added to your credit report. See Chapter 18 for tips on creating a spending plan so you're sure to have the money to pay your loan installments.

Setting Limits During the Planning and Application Process

Beware of passion and peer pressure. Deciding your financial limits early in the game saves you from the emotions that are sure to surface as you narrow down your choices. Begin by setting a value for the education you're pursuing get in the field you plan to enter. Don't know your career choice yet? Then I strongly suggest that you minimize loans until you do. Consider community colleges. Like buying a house before you know where you'll be working or what you can afford, buying an expensive education without knowing what type of job or salary you're likely to get is a mistake.

Shop around with different types of lenders, including the government, private nonprofit sources like your state student loan authority, private lenders, banks, and credit unions. Give extra points to those lenders that keep and service the loans they originate. Keep Parent PLUS Loans and cosigning to a minimum.

Getting Help if You're in the Military

The GI Bill (gibill.va.gov) offers substantial benefits to service personnel who have at least 30 days of active duty. More than one program is available, and programs typically offer tuition, books, and housing allowances. Be sure to check your eligibility before you take on any student loan debt. Here are three simple steps to consider:

- **Reduce your interest rates.** Currently serving active-duty personnel are eligible to have interest rates lowered to 6 percent on *all* student loans taken out prior to active-duty military service under the Servicemembers Civil Relief Act (SCRA or Soldiers and Sailors Act) (50 U.S. Code App. §527(a)(1)(A)). Ask your loan servicer how to apply.

- **Opt for Income-Based Repayment (IBR) and Public Service Loan Forgiveness (PSLF).** These are two great options to repay federal student loans. IBR ties the amount of your monthly payment to your income and family size. PSLF can forgive any remaining balance on federal student loans after you make ten years of on-time qualified payments while working full-time in public service, like active-duty military service or service with the government or certain nonprofit organizations.

    Begin IBR as soon as possible so that every payment you make is a qualifying monthly payment. Make 120 qualified monthly payments, and the balance of your loan can be forgiven.

- **Manage your private loans.** After you've chosen options for your federal loans, remember that private loans don't qualify for IBR or PSLF. Postponing payments on private loans through deferment or forbearance may give you short-term relief if you're having trouble making ends meet. The terms and conditions of these payment plans vary, but for most private student loans interest continues to accrue after you suspend your payments. This means that your debt grows while you wait. You may be better off paying back your private loans if you can afford it. If you can't afford to repay your loans while you're on active duty, ask your servicer about interest-only payments instead of deferment or forbearance. This stops your loan balance from growing while providing you with some relief.

If you run into trouble keeping up with your payments, contact your Judge Advocate General for assistance.

Chapter 23

Ten Ways to Deal with a Mortgage Meltdown

In This Chapter

▶ Understanding when you are in trouble

▶ Getting the best help

▶ Preparing your credit and minimizing the damage

*B*etween misinformation, stress, and plain old denial, reading the writing on the wall can be difficult when you are or are soon to be in trouble with your mortgage. Lenders don't make it any easier with a soft approach to early mortgage delinquencies followed by a hard line on foreclosures. If you owe a past-due balance on a credit card, you'll get phone calls and letters that may border on harassment. Mortgage holders don't usually get excited when you're late on your payments. After all, they have security for their loan: your home.

This chapter outlines ten things you need to know and do before you leave or are asked to leave your home.

Knowing When You're in Trouble

You are not in trouble if you owe more than the value of your home. You are not in trouble if your roof leaks and you can't fix it. You may be in trouble if you can't pay your real estate taxes, but chances are that trouble from taxes is pretty far off. But you are *definitely in trouble* if you are late on your mortgage payments and don't know on which specific day you and your mortgage will fall off a cliff and enter the foreclosure process. I mean knowing for sure and marking the date with a big red circle on a calendar.

If you are late on a single payment, you can just make it up. Sometimes there is fee, a hike in interest rate, or a penalty. But who says no to a payment for an overdue loan? Your mortgage lender might! Here's how it works: Because most mortgages are packaged into securities and sold in bulk, their default terms must be spelled out in great detail and generally be the same. The result is a set of rules that were made up in advance and have very little flexibility when applied.

If you are more than 90 days late and attempt to make a payment or even two, there is an excellent chance that your money will be refused and returned to you. You may need to make up *all your payments at once* to get any payment applied to your mortgage. A day late is indeed a dollar short when it comes to home mortgages. To further complicate matters as only bankers and lawyers can, the 90-day payment cliff does not include your grace period (typically 15 days). See Chapter 7 for more information about crossing the 90-days-late line, and check out `portal.hud.gov/hudportal/HUD?src=/topics/avoiding_foreclosure/foreclosureprocess` for more details on the foreclosure process.

If you are late on your mortgage, it is important that you open and answer your mail. The notices you receive generally offer good information about your options. The sooner you seek help, the more options you will have.

Knowing How Your State's Laws Treat Foreclosures

Every state has its own foreclosure laws. It is important to know how your state's laws work so that you don't inadvertently cross a line or miss an important date. You can find summaries of the laws in all states at `www.foreclosurelaw.org`. The following sections outline are a few critical differences.

Nonrecourse or recourse

If your lender is foreclosing on your mortgage, whether you live in a recourse state or a nonrecourse state makes a big difference. In general, if you live in a nonrecourse state, you can't be held liable for any deficiency between the amount you owe and the amount your home sells for in the foreclosure. If you live in a recourse state, the lender may get a deficiency judgment against you in court. For example, if you owe $200,000 on your mortgage but your home nets only $150,000 at the foreclosure sale, the deficiency is $50,000.

But the issue may not be as simple as listing the nonrecourse states, because some states define some loans as nonrecourse if, for example, they were used to purchase a home but not if part of the proceeds of the loan were used for some other purpose, like paying off credit card debt. Other states limit the amount of the deficiency to the fair value of the property versus the sale price. Still other states have a one-action limit. For example, New York makes lenders choose between the acts of foreclosing on the property and suing to collect the debt.

Consult a HUD-certified housing counselor or an attorney to find the rules for your state.

State nonrecourse rules don't apply to the IRS. If you lived in your home for less than two years, you may not qualify for the $250,000 individual home sale exclusion, so you may have a capital gain or phantom income from a foreclosure. See your tax professional for definitive advice.

Judicial or nonjudicial

It is important to know whether your state handles foreclosures on a judicial or nonjudicial basis. If you live in a nonjudicial foreclosure state, your lender does not have to go to court in order to foreclose on your home. This means that the foreclosure can proceed more quickly. In judicial states, foreclosures go through a court. These are called *judicial foreclosures* and may take longer to finalize.

The nonjudicial states include Alabama, Alaska, Arizona, Arkansas, California, Colorado, District of Columbia, Georgia, Idaho, Maryland, Massachusetts, Michigan, Minnesota, Mississippi, Missouri, Montana, Nebraska, Nevada, New Hampshire, New Mexico (sometimes), North Carolina, Oklahoma (unless the homeowner requests a judicial foreclosure), Oregon, Rhode Island, South Dakota (unless the homeowner requests a judicial foreclosure), Tennessee, Texas, Utah, Vermont (sometimes), Virginia, Washington, West Virginia, and Wyoming.

Time is your enemy in a nonjudicial state. Lenders give very little notice of foreclosure sales, and once the foreclosure process begins, you may have no further options.

Deciding Whether to Stay or Go

This decision used to be a no-brainer; almost everyone wanted to stay in their homes if they could, as the stigma of losing the roof over one's head was a big one. This is less the case today. Faced with seemingly unrecoverable deficits, some homeowners crunch the numbers and decide to save time, money, and stress by letting the foreclosure process run its course. Some move out, and others stay until the home sells to a new owner or the bank forces them to leave. The following sections describe your options.

Walking away

Strategic default is a new term in the language of mortgages. Because of the housing bubble bust, some properties have become so far *underwater* (more is owed than the home is worth) that it may take years or even decades for the home to regain the value of its mortgage — or it never will. Some borrowers choose to stop making payments, even if they can afford to make them, because they see their home as just another investment, and a bad one at that. Walking away is known as a strategic default.

Potential drawbacks to strategic default include deficiency judgments, significant credit score damage, problems buying or renting in the future, the personal impact of a major life failure, and stigma in the eyes of others.

Working with the lender to exit

A more lender-friendly version of a strategic default is the deed-in-lieu of foreclosure option. Rather than go through a long and expensive foreclosure process in order to obtain title, the lender agrees to accept the deed to the property. This option may also incur a deficiency judgment for the difference between the fair market value of the property and the total debt owed.

Another option in this category is a *short sale,* which involves selling your home for less than what you owe. If you choose this option, you may be subject to a deficiency judgment, depending on the terms you work out with your lender and the laws in your state.

In March 2013, Fannie Mae and Freddie Mac began letting some borrowers who are current on their payments give up their underwater properties and cancel the debt under their Mortgage Release and Standard Deed-in-Lieu of Foreclosure programs. If this option is of interest to you and you have a Freddie Mac mortgage, go to www.freddiemac.com/corporate/housingpros/pdf/deed_in_lieu_fact_sheet.pdf for more information. If you have a Fannie Mae mortgage, go to www.fanniemae.com/singlefamily/mortgage-release.

Staying the course

If you decide to do all you can to stay in your home, several courses of action are open to you. The major ones include the following:

- ✔ **FHA Short Refinance:** If you owe more than your home is worth and you want to refinance, the lender can reduce the amount you owe on your first mortgage to no more than 97.75 percent of your home's current market value.

- ✔ **Home Affordable Refinance Program (HARP):** HARP is part of the government's Making Home Affordable initiative. For eligible mortgages from Fannie Mae and Freddie Mac, this program allows borrowers who have a good (but not perfect) payment history, have little or no equity, and are currently on time with their payments to refinance and take advantage of lower interest rates. Your loan's principal stays the same, but your payment may be reduced, making the loan more affordable.

- ✔ **Loan modification/refinancing:** The two main types are the Home Affordable Modification Program (HAMP) for Freddie Mac and Fannie Mae mortgages and conventional refinancing for others. A conventional mortgage servicer or lender may modify your loan to make it more affordable, but each one has its own programs and guidelines. Speak to your servicer about HAMP. If your loan is owned or guaranteed by Freddie or Fannie and you are ineligible for conventional refinancing, HAMP can change the type of your loan from adjustable to fixed, to a longer fixed term, or to a lower interest rate and can add past-due payments to the principal balance to be repaid over the full mortgage term.

Tightening Your Spending to Stay in Your Home

Whether your financial life has a ding or two or is upside-down, tightening your budget can help you free up sorely needed cash and get back in control of your situation. If you don't have a budget, now is the perfect time to make one. (See Chapter 18 for details on budgeting.)

Making a budget is basic but effective. Begin by listing all your expenses and then list your income. Look carefully at both sides of the equation, make some cuts to expenses, and look for ways to add to your take-home pay (like reducing your tax withholding or stopping 401(k) contributions temporarily) or increase your income. For example, if the bank forecloses, you'll lose your cable TV anyway. Cutting cable now may give you the extra cash that helps keep you in your home.

Technically it's not a spending cut, but you can also try to sell some stuff to raise cash for a mortgage payment. We've all seen the "Cash for gold!" signs. Selling old and unused gold or jewelry is something you may want to consider. Having a yard or garage sale, downsizing to one car, and selling your violin should also be on your list. You get the idea. Lightening your load of stuff may buy you the time you need to catch up.

Prioritizing Your Spending to Build Cash

No matter what you choose to do in the event of a mortgage crisis, you're going to need some cash. It may be to pay an arrearage. It may be to come up with first and last month's rent and a damage deposit on a new apartment. Either way, I want you to tighten your budget (or create one; see the preceding section). Yes, this step is basic, but I suggest that you start here. As described in the preceding section, list all your expenses and then list your income. Take a look at both sides of the equation and determine where you can make changes — by cutting expenses and/or increasing income. (See Chapter 18 for details on budgeting.)

Car repossessions can happen within weeks — not months — of missing a payment. So if you need your car to get to work, keeping up on your car payment is critically important.

If you can't make your mortgage payment, it's important to save as much of the money you're not sending to your lender as possible. If your payment is $1,000 and you can only scrape together $800, don't spend it on something else. Put the money aside to help ease your transition into a new place.

Want some help with creating a spending plan? Try a nonprofit consumer credit counseling agency member of the National Foundation for Credit Counseling (www.debtadvice.org) or the Association of Independent Consumer Credit Counseling Agencies (www.aiccca.org).

Lessening the Damage to Your Credit

In a nutshell, if you stiff your mortgage lender with a loss in the form of a short sale or foreclosure, your credit will take a much bigger hit than if you come to an agreement to repay or forgive any deficiency. See the section "Assessing the Damage from a Mortgage Meltdown" in Chapter 7 for more on what you'll need to negotiate.

For a person with decent credit and a FICO score in the 720 range, the difference in credit score deduction between a short sale with a deficiency and one without can be more than 50 points. See Chapter 7 for details on the damage to your credit and credit score that various mortgage problems can cause.

Knowing Who to Call

You may be the strong, silent type, believing that silence is golden and that suffering in silence is a virtue, but this is the wrong approach in a mortgage crisis. If you're behind on your payments, your lender will communicate with you by mail. The worst thing you can do is to remain silent, which could leave the bank no other option than to take legal action. See the section "Working with your mortgage servicer" in Chapter 7 for details.

The best thing you can do is to open your mail and speak to your mortgage servicer at once. I also strongly recommend that you contact an independent HUD-approved mortgage counselor at Hope Now (www.hopenow.com or 888-995-HOPE) or your state housing agency. Avoid foreclosure-prevention companies like the plague they are. The best help is easy to find and available for free.

Beware of Scams

It's easy to forget a lifetime of wisdom when the pressure is on and you are desperate for a solution. Knowing that you are not entirely in your right mind during a mortgage crisis, scammers will try to charge you money or even trick you into signing your deed over to them. Keep in mind that not everyone out there wants to help you; many just want to help themselves.

Here are some quick scam signs to watch out for:

- ✔ Never pay a fee in advance. The best help is free.
- ✔ Never believe someone who guarantees that they can stop your foreclosure.
- ✔ Be wary of anyone who contacts you and offers to help. Always get a second opinion from a person or an organization you trust.
- ✔ Never hand your mortgage money over to anyone other than your mortgage servicer.

Beefing Up Your Credit with Lines of Credit

As soon as you know that a default is likely in your future, begin to prepare your credit for what I call a "credit winter." Before your credit suffers a drop from the fallout of missed payments, open some new accounts to establish new lines of credit and make any big purchases you are going to need to finance (like a major appliance, furniture, or a car) in the next few months. I'm talking about *essentials,* not stuff you don't absolutely need.

Once you default on your mortgage, you won't have access to new credit for a long time. Stocking up on credit now makes sense if you can use it wisely. Having four credit cards reporting on-time payments rather than just one also means that more positive information is being reported in your credit report faster and helps your score recover faster as well.

Consulting an Attorney

You have rights and you have legal options. Only an attorney can give you sound legal advice, so before your mortgage crisis gets too far along, spend the money to get a competent assessment of where you stand and what the law can do to help.

For example, a bankruptcy filing can stop a foreclosure in its tracks — not forever, but maybe long enough. A Chapter 7 or 13 bankruptcy may be a way to reduce other debt or the amount of your mortgage that exceeds the value of your home. It may be enough to get you back on track with your mortgage payments. Also, not all mortgage documents are properly drawn and executed. Have a lawyer review your files to see if they are unenforceable or flawed in any way.

A good lawyer who does a lot of foreclosure-prevention work can sometimes work minor miracles, maybe even delaying foreclosure for years, which can help you begin to build your savings account to pay for your next move.

Index

• H •

harassment, 80
hard inquiry, 224
hardship program, 204, 362
HARP (Home Affordable Refinance
    Program), 373
Healthcare Advocates, Inc., 207
Hill-Burton Act, 212
hobby expense, 301, 303
home
  in-home data storage, 340–341
  selling, 120
Home Affordable Refinance Program
    (HARP), 373
home maintenance expense, 301
home-equity lines of credit, 31–32
home-equity loan, 31–32
homeownership, 286, 310–311. *See also*
    mortgages
homestead exemption, 130
Hope Hotline, 119
HOPE NOW website, 117, 119
hospitals, 30
Household Budget Plan form, 93–94
household income, 37
housing authority, 62
HUD website, 12, 116, 119
HUD-certified mortgage counselor, 61

• I •

IBR (Income-Based Repayment), 106, 367
ICR (Income Contingent Repayment)
    plan, 106
identity, specialty credit report, 242
identity theft
  accounts, closing and opening, 152
  canceling credit card, 146–147
  collection call, 346
  computer safety, 338–339
  confidential document, 341
  contacting credit bureau, 147
  credit after, 151–154
  credit card, 342–343
  credit freeze, 147
  credit lines, blocking, 151
  denial of credit or account access, 347

driver's license protection, 153–154
early-warning notice, 345
fast action, taking, 145
fraud alert, 47, 147, 150–151
freezing credit, 341–342
FTC, contacting, 147–148
in-home data storage, 340–341
identifying, 17
insurance, 264
mail protection, 149, 340
military member, 343
missing account statements, 347–348
monitoring, 263
password protection, 152–153, 339
personal identification number
    protection, 152
phishing scam, 337–338
police, notifying, 148–149
predicting, 344
protecting through FACT Act, 149–151
radio transmission protection, 152–153
safety, 170
Social Security number protection, 153–154
statistics, 335
technology awareness, 336–337
unauthorized charge detection, 346–347
victim statement, 147
income
  counting on, 284
  counting up, 298–300
  credit ecosystem, 284
  spending plan to add up, 38
Income Contingent Repayment (ICR) plan,
    106
income worksheet, 299
Income-Based Repayment (IBR) plan,
    106, 367
indirect disclosure, 251
inflation, 314
inquires, credit report, 224
installment loan, 207
insurance
  car, 311
  claim errors, 210
  claim report, 187–188
  cost, 133
  credit and insurance premium
    relationship, 186–188
  credit history, 188

About the Author

Steve Bucci has been helping people decode and master personal credit and debt issues for the last 20 years. For over a decade he has authored a popular twice-weekly personal finance column as the Debt Advisor for the financial mega-site Bankrate.com. His column is frequently featured on AOL, Yahoo! Personal Finance, and other websites. The Scripps-Howard News Service syndicate distributes his column to newspapers nationally. Steve is also a personal credit coach, speaker, and expert witness.

Steve was formerly president of the Consumer Credit Counseling Service of Southern New England, and he founded the Consumer Credit Counseling Service of Rhode Island and the University of Rhode Island Center for Personal Financial Education.

He began his career in counseling at the Yale Psychiatric Institute before switching to business careers in management consulting and then finance developing and bringing to market both publicly and privately traded investment products. Steve returned to his first love, helping individuals, in 1991, this time using his financial and management experience to launch Rhode Island's first private, nonprofit financial counseling agency.

Steve has served as director of the CDNE Education Foundation, the URI Center for Personal Financial Education, the National Foundation for Credit Counseling, the Better Business Bureau of Rhode Island, and National Network Non-Profit Services and is currently the treasurer at Saint Peter's by-the-Sea Episcopal Church. He was named Visiting Executive in Residence at the University of Rhode Island in 2005. Steve received his BA and MA degrees from the University of Rhode Island at Kingston. He and his wife, Barbara, live with their two cats, Peanut Butter and Sadie, at Sand Hill Cove in the seaside community of Narragansett, Rhode Island.

Dedication

This book is dedicated to my wife, Barbara, without whom my life would be so much less fun and interesting.

Author's Acknowledgments

I want to thank John Wiley and Sons for asking me to update this book — not only because so much has changed in the world of credit, but also because it represents a vindication of the holistic approach to credit that I have been espousing for the last two decades. Credit can only be repaired from the bottom up, not the top down. That is to say, you can only build and maintain excellent credit by beginning with a strong foundation and then adding on more layers in stages. This method relies on addressing the root causes of your credit problems as a way of building a sound financial base, improved credit, and a better life for you and your family. The two are inseparable!

No successful person I know of works alone. Certainly, in my case, I received support, help, encouragement, and at times great tolerance from many of those in my life and a number of understanding colleagues. My thanks to them all, in particular to credit reporting and scoring gurus Anthony Spauve at Fair Isaac and Jeff Richardson and Mike Dunn at VantageScore; Rod Griffin at Experian; Noel Simpson at Rhode Island Student Loan Authority; Mark Leone at Webster Bank; Michelle Person at the Consumer Financial Protection Bureau; Amelia Woltering at American Express; Clifton O'Neal at TransUnion; David Aronson at the Medical Information Bureau; Helen Iasimone at the RI Housing Network; Jessica Faust, my agent; and my editors at Wiley, especially Pam Mourouzis and Tracy Boggier.

Publisher's Acknowledgments

Acquisitions Editor: Tracy Boggier

Project Editor: Pam Mourouzis

Technical Editor: Michael Staten

Project Coordinator: Sheree Montgomery

Media Project Manager: Laura Moss-Hollister

Media Supervising Producer: Rich Graves

Cover Photo: ©iStockphoto.com/YinYang

Apple & Mac

iPad For Dummies,
5th Edition
978-1-118-49823-1

iPhone 5 For Dummies,
6th Edition
978-1-118-35201-4

MacBook For Dummies,
4th Edition
978-1-118-20920-2

OS X Mountain Lion
For Dummies
978-1-118-39418-2

Blogging & Social Media

Facebook For Dummies,
4th Edition
978-1-118-09562-1

Mom Blogging
For Dummies
978-1-118-03843-7

Pinterest For Dummies
978-1-118-32800-2

WordPress For Dummies,
5th Edition
978-1-118-38318-6

Business

Commodities For Dummies,
2nd Edition
978-1-118-01687-9

Investing For Dummies,
6th Edition
978-0-470-90545-6

Personal Finance
For Dummies,
7th Edition
978-1-118-11785-9

QuickBooks 2013
For Dummies
978-1-118-35641-8

Small Business Marketing Kit
For Dummies,
3rd Edition
978-1-118-31183-7

Careers

Job Interviews
For Dummies,
4th Edition
978-1-118-11290-8

Job Searching with
Social Media
For Dummies
978-0-470-93072-4

Personal Branding
For Dummies
978-1-118-11792-7

Resumes For Dummies,
6th Edition
978-0-470-87361-8

Success as a Mediator
For Dummies
978-1-118-07862-4

Diet & Nutrition

Belly Fat Diet For Dummies
978-1-118-34585-6

Eating Clean For Dummies
978-1-118-00013-7

Nutrition For Dummies,
5th Edition
978-0-470-93231-5

Digital Photography

Digital Photography
For Dummies,
7th Edition
978-1-118-09203-3

Digital SLR Cameras &
Photography For Dummies,
4th Edition
978-1-118-14489-3

Photoshop Elements 11
For Dummies
978-1-118-40821-6

Gardening

Herb Gardening
For Dummies,
2nd Edition
978-0-470-61778-6

Vegetable Gardening
For Dummies,
2nd Edition
978-0-470-49870-5

Health

Anti-Inflammation Diet
For Dummies
978-1-118-02381-5

Diabetes For Dummies,
3rd Edition
978-0-470-27086-8

Living Paleo For Dummies
978-1-118-29405-5

Hobbies

Beekeeping
For Dummies
978-0-470-43065-1

eBay For Dummies,
7th Edition
978-1-118-09806-6

Raising Chickens
For Dummies
978-0-470-46544-8

Wine For Dummies,
5th Edition
978-1-118-28872-6

Writing Young Adult Fiction
For Dummies
978-0-470-94954-2

Language &
Foreign Language

500 Spanish Verbs
For Dummies
978-1-118-02382-2

English Grammar
For Dummies,
2nd Edition
978-0-470-54664-2

French All-in One
For Dummies
978-1-118-22815-9

German Essentials
For Dummies
978-1-118-18422-6

Italian For Dummies
2nd Edition
978-1-118-00465-4

Available in print and e-book formats.

Math & Science

Algebra I For Dummies,
2nd Edition
978-0-470-55964-2

Anatomy and Physiology
For Dummies,
2nd Edition
978-0-470-92326-9

Astronomy For Dummies,
3rd Edition
978-1-118-37697-3

Biology For Dummies,
2nd Edition
978-0-470-59875-7

Chemistry For Dummies,
2nd Edition
978-1-1180-0730-3

Pre-Algebra Essentials
For Dummies
978-0-470-61838-7

Microsoft Office

Excel 2013 For Dummies
978-1-118-51012-4

Office 2013 All-in-One
For Dummies
978-1-118-51636-2

PowerPoint 2013
For Dummies
978-1-118-50253-2

Word 2013 For Dummies
978-1-118-49123-2

Music

Blues Harmonica
For Dummies
978-1-118-25269-7

Guitar For Dummies,
3rd Edition
978-1-118-11554-1

iPod & iTunes
For Dummies,
10th Edition
978-1-118-50864-0

Programming

Android Application
Development For
Dummies, 2nd Edition
978-1-118-38710-8

iOS 6 Application
Development For Dummies
978-1-118-50880-0

Java For Dummies,
5th Edition
978-0-470-37173-2

Religion & Inspiration

The Bible For Dummies
978-0-7645-5296-0

Buddhism For Dummies,
2nd Edition
978-1-118-02379-2

Catholicism For Dummies,
2nd Edition
978-1-118-07778-8

Self-Help & Relationships

Bipolar Disorder
For Dummies,
2nd Edition
978-1-118-33882-7

Meditation For Dummies,
3rd Edition
978-1-118-29144-3

Seniors

Computers For Seniors
For Dummies,
3rd Edition
978-1-118-11553-4

iPad For Seniors
For Dummies,
5th Edition
978-1-118-49708-1

Social Security
For Dummies
978-1-118-20573-0

Smartphones & Tablets

Android Phones
For Dummies
978-1-118-16952-0

Kindle Fire HD
For Dummies
978-1-118-42223-6

NOOK HD For Dummies,
Portable Edition
978-1-118-39498-4

Surface For Dummies
978-1-118-49634-3

Test Prep

ACT For Dummies,
5th Edition
978-1-118-01259-8

ASVAB For Dummies,
3rd Edition
978-0-470-63760-9

GRE For Dummies,
7th Edition
978-0-470-88921-3

Officer Candidate Tests,
For Dummies
978-0-470-59876-4

Physician's Assistant Exam
For Dummies
978-1-118-11556-5

Series 7 Exam
For Dummies
978-0-470-09932-2

Windows 8

Windows 8 For Dummies
978-1-118-13461-0

Windows 8 For Dummies,
Book + DVD Bundle
978-1-118-27167-4

Windows 8 All-in-One
For Dummies
978-1-118-11920-4

e **Available in print and e-book formats.**